Karl Polanyi and twenty-first-century capitalism

Manchester University Press

Geopolitical Economy

Series Editors
Radhika Desai and Alan Freeman

Geopolitical Economy promotes fresh inter- and multi-disciplinary perspectives on the most pressing new realities of the twenty-first century: the multipolar world and the renewed economic centrality of states in it. From a range of disciplines, works in the series account for these new realities historically. They explore the problems and contradictions, domestic and international, of capitalism. They reconstruct the struggles of classes and nations, and state actions in response to them, which have shaped capitalism, and track the growth of the public and de-commodified spheres these dialectical interactions have given rise to. Finally, they map the new terrain on which political forces must now act to orient national and the international economies in equitable and ecological, cultural and creative directions.

Previously published

The US vs China: Asia's new Cold War? *Jude Woodward*
Flight MH17, Ukraine and the new Cold War: Prism of disaster *Kees van der Pijl*

Karl Polanyi and twenty-first-century capitalism

Edited by Radhika Desai and Kari Polanyi Levitt

Manchester University Press

Published by Manchester University Press
Oxford Road, Manchester M13 9PL
www.manchesteruniversitypress.co.uk

British Library Cataloguing-in-Publication Data
A catalogue record for this book is available from the British Library

ISBN 978 1 5261 2788 4 hardback
ISBN 978 1 5261 9567 8 paperback

First published 2020
Paperback published 2026

EU authorised representative for GPSR:
Easy Access System Europe – Mustamäe tee 50, 10621 Tallinn, Estonia
gpsr.requests@easproject.com

Typeset by Servis Filmsetting Ltd, Stockport, Cheshire

Contents

Contents

List of figures

List of tables

Acknowledgements

Most of the contributions in this volume were presented to the conference organised by the Karl Polanyi Institute of Political Economy in Montreal on 'The Enduring Legacy of Karl Polanyi' held on 6–8 November 2014. The year marked the fiftieth anniversary of Karl Polanyi's death and the seventieth anniversary of the publication of *The Great Transformation*. These anniversaries also coincided with the centenary of the start of the First World War and Thirty Years' Crisis (1914–45) whose transformative effect was the focus of that work.

While unexpected problems have delayed publication, we are pleased to present this critical volume just after the seventy-fifth anniversary of the publication of *The Great Transformation*.

We would like to thank our contributors for their cooperation and patience in the unfortunately drawn-out process of preparing this volume. We would also like to thank Brendan Devlin for his speedy and careful work on the references and Bibliography and Ajit Singh for helping with the proofs. Finally, we would like to thank Bryan Khan for his invaluable help in the final stages of preparation.

Introduction: Karl Polanyi in the twenty-first century[1]

Radhika Desai

Karl Polanyi's intellectual influence has arrived at its current growth phase in a curious and unconventional manner. Charles Kindleberger noted it already in the 1970s. Commenting on *The Great Transformation* as one of the classics of the twentieth century, he said,

> Some books refuse to go away. They get shot out of the water by critics but surface again and remain afloat. *The Great Transformation* by Karl Polanyi doesn't exactly refuse to go away, but it was slow in arriving and it has kept on coming. Robert MacIver wrote a glowing preface for it when it was published in 1944, but few scholars took notice. Then it was discovered by economic historians. In the last decade, radical youth has adopted it as gospel. (Kindleberger, 1974: 45)

Polanyi's thinking long remained confined to relatively marginal heterodox institutionalist economists and economic historians. He could secure a minor appointment at Columbia University in 1947 only because the institutionalist tradition had persisted there. Even so, Polanyi's course on General Economic History did not address the recent historical developments discussed in *The Great Transformation* and it was not on the reading list. The course focused instead on economic institutions in primitive and archaic civilizations. No wonder the United States came to know Polanyi as an economic anthropologist, rather than as an economic historian.

Even in these decades of relative neglect, however, those Polanyi's thought did reach felt its unmistakable pull. Abe Rotstein recalls (in this volume) how his substantivist approach was his 'exit from the maze' of neoclassical economics at the University of Chicago. Polanyi's early following may have been small, but it was loyal. After Polanyi passed away in 1964, George Dalton published an influential collection of Polanyi's essays (Polanyi, 1968) while Harry Pearson produced *The Livelihood of Man* from lecture notes and other unpublished writings in 1977.

If Polanyi was relatively unknown in the post-war 'Keynesian' decades, neoliberalism would surely have made matters worse. After all, its free market thinking rolled back the intellectual influence of the much more eminent John Maynard Keynes. Instead, however, the neoliberal decades witnessed a big rediscovery of Polanyi. Against neoliberal advocacy of free markets and rolling back the state, against its claim that globalization was an unstoppable juggernaut, Polanyi's ideas proved natural intellectual weapons. A widening circle of critics of neoliberalism and globalization – activists, scholars and even politicians – began to wield them. In the wake of the 1997 East Asian financial crisis, Harvard economist, Dani Rodrik, for instance, relied on Polanyi to point to dangers the world economy had not faced since the 1930s (Rodrik, 1998). By the late 1990s, his thinking was entering the broad left of British political life (Marquand, 1997), while influential scholars such as Fred Block and Margaret Somers were extending his influence in US left-wing and progressive scholarship. Following the 1999 Seattle anti-globalization demonstrations, the New Right dubbed Polanyi 'a kind of patron saint of globalization's critics' (Lindsey, 2001). In the new millennium, but most strikingly since the financial crisis of 2008, scholars across disciplines and political persuasions have cited Karl Polanyi in analyses of the wrongs of financial markets. Polanyi's ghost even came to haunt the 2012 Davos World Economic Forum, where world leaders could not have been more aware of the problems neoliberalism had created and less capable of handling them (Elliot, 2012). In answer to the question of who will 'guide us through the problems of the twenty-first century', the liberal economist, J. Bradford DeLong (2016), identified Polanyi, alongside Tocqueville and Keynes.

The rediscovery of Polanyi is also leading many to unearth the full extent of his past influence. Daniel Immerwahr brought to light the link between Polanyi's thinking and that of his lifelong friend, the post-war management guru, Peter Drucker (Immerwahr, 2009) who shaped so much of the US's post-war intellectual life. A recent British study, which calls for reviving a moral critique of capitalism alongside the material critique of its inequality so prominent since 2008, puts Polanyi at the centre of the British socialist tradition. When Polanyi fled Hitler and fascism and arrived in Britain, he was naturally attracted to Christian socialism and the 'moral economics' of figures like R. H. Tawney and G. D. H. Cole (Rogan, 2017: 53–55). Polanyi linked their criticism of the morally corrupting effects of capitalism to continental political and intellectual traditions, including the Marxist. This very British socialism became influential in Corbyn's Labour Party which aimed at 'giving workers more bargaining power and influence over economic decisions[,] … constraining the power of finance, [a]nd … removing certain aspects of society from market exchange altogether' (*The Economist*, 2018).

Why does Polanyi's thinking resonate so widely and deeply today? While clear economic, social and political parallels between his time and ours lay down the necessary condition, the sufficient condition is provided only by the insight and prescience of his analysis. It was the product of the singular course of his life and intellectual evolution. Polanyi's life (1886–1964) spanned the most tumultuous decades of human history and was tossed about by its defining events (Catanzariti, 2014: 221), giving Polanyi's intellectual agenda its ambition as well as its personal and experiential depth (as Polanyi Levitt and Brie discuss in this volume). Add to this a mind formed in the fecund intellectual environment of *belle époque* Central Europe and you have an analysis to stand the test of time (on Polanyi's biography and intellectual biography see, *inter alia*, Dale, 2010a, 2016a, 2016b, and Polanyi Levitt 1990b and in this volume).

Polanyi's encompassing historical explanation of the 'great transformation' that Europe underwent in his time is so original in its components and their configuration that even those versed in history and interdisciplinary studies approach its full meaning only gradually. And it is so suggestive that it has kept generations trying. This collection contains many contributions, by established and new Polanyi scholars, that push back the bounds of our understanding on many fronts, whether the ideas of fictitious commodities, particularly money, and the double movement, of socialism or of the different historical evolution of continental, British and American societies. The following brief outline of Polanyi's ambitiously original historical argument as it emerges from our collective efforts in this volume will help readers fit individual contributions in their proper places within it.

Polanyi's historical diagnosis

Polanyi's diagnosis of the most profound crisis of European civilization traces its genesis back not just decades, as so many did and still do, but centuries, implicating capitalism itself. The crisis persisted through the inter-war period, Polanyi argued, because major governments did not yet realize that the world of 1914 was the Humpty Dumpty that could no longer be put back together. The outlines of a civilization beyond it were only beginning to be glimpsed when war erupted again in 1939. They included an international economy beyond the gold standard, the movement of political opinion to the left (Marwick, 1964) with the realization that a liberal order could no longer be recreated, the New Deal and Soviet industrialization. In many ways, the Second World War sharpened the view of possibilities on the horizon and, by writing *The Great Transformation*, the condensation of his historical explanation, Polanyi was making his own contribution to their post-war realization and contesting the competing neoliberal vision that had already emerged (Desai, 2019).

Polanyi traced the crisis of nineteenth-century civilization to what he dubbed its *utopian project* of founding society on a self-regulating market. The words 'utopian' and 'project' are significant. Seeing it as a project rather than accomplished reality constituted a momentous correction. What made it utopian, in the worst sense of the word, was that it extended the market far beyond real commodities, that is, goods produced for sale. Three elements of society's productive organization, its substance and very conditions of possibility – land, labour and money – were also commodified. They were, Polanyi argued, fictitious commodities. Unlike real commodities, they were either not produced at all, or not produced for sale. The crisis of societies that embarked on this project was as inevitable as the project was utopian.

Two implications were important. First, contrary to liberal ideology, market society was neither natural nor spontaneous. It had to be constructed through radically, indeed violently, transformative state legislation. In England, which was both paradigmatic of the process and its origin, the Poor Law Amendment Act of 1834, the Bank Act of 1844 and the Anti-Corn Law Bill of 1946 commodified labour, money and land respectively. Secondly, the need to maintain society against their onslaught induced a set of reactions, movements for social protection which, together with the spread of market society, formed the famous 'double movement'. This reaction of social protection, essentially what the jurist, A. V. Dicey (1905) meant by the move from individualism to collectivism in English society, was spontaneous.

These implications were critical to Polanyi's argument. With them, he overturned liberal views that treated market societies as spontaneous and natural and all effort to control them as artificial, violent and unnatural. On the contrary, Polanyi insisted that it was the creation of the market for these fictitious commodities by the state that was planned and violent. The social reaction, now involving the state in the protection of society from the dangers it had itself created, for its part, was spontaneous and natural.

The dialectic of this double movement, rather than the establishment of market society which remained both utopian and a project, framed nineteenth-century European developments and defined Europe's liberal civilization. It culminated in the crisis that destroyed that civilization and, along with it, the quartet of institutions – the self-regulating market, the liberal state, the gold standard and the balance of power; two economic, two political; two domestic and two international – that sought to realize the project. Now liberal society – both the project of creating a market society and managing its impact in an ad hoc and spontaneous manner – was no longer viable. Illiberal alternatives, alternatives involving the state centrally, this time in consciously organizing other, non-market, forms of social integration, were bound to emerge. Would they be fascist and National Socialist or Socialist? Would they point towards reconstructing human, democratic and just societies or towards barbarity and the physical as well as moral destruction of humanity? Since refusing this choice in favour of trying to reconstruct the nineteenth-century liberal civilization of 'universal capitalism' would only once again prepare the soil for fascism, a new socialist civilization of national and regional planning was imperative (Polanyi, 1945). This was the great transformation to which the eponymous book referred.

Polanyi's understanding of socialism is worth pausing over. He clearly distinguished it from the nineteenth-century spontaneous movement for social protection. Socialism, by contrast, had to be a consciously chosen and pursued goal. This understanding also draws a clear line between limited social reforms and socialism. The latter must re-make society, and our conceptions of it, root and branch. Secondly, socialism was not, he had concluded quite early in his life when he intervened in the socialist calculation debate, about a centrally planned economy in which money and markets played no role. Precisely because he understood both money and markets so well (as Desai argues in this volume), he assigned them clear roles in socialism. Money as purchasing power was a useful social institution and could serve an egalitarian and morally desirable form of society, unlike money as a store of value and capital, which could dominate and destroy society. Well-regulated markets limited to real commodities could serve society while those for the fictitious commodities undermined it.

Polanyi's intervention in the socialist calculation debate also made clear to Polanyi that the alternative was not between unrestricted markets and central planning, as Ludwig von Mises's opening salvo in that debate contended. Polanyi rejected that choice, as Brie (in this volume) so well explains. Polanyi agreed with Mises that the problem with central planning in 'complex society' was that it assumed a level of overveiew (*übersicht*) of one's actions and their social consequences that was impossible. Taking inspiration from Guild socialism, he re-conceived of socialism as creatively designing social and productive arrangements such that they permitted ever-greater levels of overview in a society rendered complex by the machine age. As Brie discusses, this was why Polanyi thought of socialism as the realization of freedom in a complex society, the title of the closing chapter of *The Great Transformation*. This was not, however, the liberal 'freedom that kills' but a new freedom that was truer for being responsible.

Already a year after the publication of *The Great Transformation*, however, Polanyi knew that his vision of socialism would not be realized. The problem was that the Great Transformation had not advanced uniformly in different parts of the world. And the Second World War had dealt them very different hands. The United States had not undergone the great transformation and had, therefore, remained committed to realizing the liberal utopia. At the same time, it had emerged from the Second World War with its productive capacity massively boosted, while that elsewhere was destroyed. This placed it in a position to attempt to realize the liberal utopia on a world scale. And it was now zealously attempting to do so.

Even so, its power was not unlimited. As Polanyi Levitt and Somers and Block discuss in their different ways, the Keynesian welfare state of the West, the actually existing socialisms of the communist bloc, the developmental arrangements that emerged in the Third World and the international arrangements that permitted all three after the end of the Second World War were at least partial realizations of Polanyi's vision. The US was forced to accept them. They furnished the world its 'golden age' but were brought to an end by their own incompleteness, making way for neoliberalism which, for four decades now, has been engaged in a renewed attempt to realize the liberal market utopia.

The neoliberal New Right was never without socially authoritarian politics (Desai, 1994, 2006), though the world remained mesmerized by its economic liberalism for decades. This ever-present authoritarianism has swelled after decades of zealous neoliberal ministrations, as Polanyi would have predicted. Today this is widely acknowledged. Our politics are taking ominous forms as virulent fascist foam appears on the crest of waves of right-wing ascendency, just as in the 1930s (Hobsbawm, 1994). Moreover, there are reasons to believe that the dangers this time are much greater. On the one hand, as Polanyi detected long ago and as Thomasberger (in this volume) shows, neoliberalism no longer relies on arguments about the naturalness or spontaneity of markets, making it harder to refute even as it becomes more urgent to do so (see also Crouch, 2011; Slobodian, 2018). On the other, neoliberalism's discontents are being organized almost exclusively by the far and farther right. In the 1930s, socialist formations were, by contrast, much more prominent on the political landscape, fighting and limiting the appeal of fascism. Today, by contrast, just when socialist forces are needed to counter the appeals of the entire menagerie of the rough beasts of the right, we find most parties of the left bereft of the requisite political capacity.

They squandered it by following neoliberal economic policy nostrums, offering only a limited social liberalism without any economic socialist accompaniment. No wonder it failed to acquire broad appeal among populations suffering from unemployment or precarious employment, debt, social service erosion, degradation of urban and other environments, and, increasingly, physical insecurity and political marginalization. The manner in which the entirely salutary increase in productivity and the transformation of labour into higher and more productive forms plays out under neoliberalism only exacerbates these problems. Instead of liberating humankind from the less pleasant forms of labour, leaving it free to raise its levels of culture and knowledge as never before, these trends have contributed to deprivation, precarity and wearying uncertainty. This state of affairs recalls Polanyi's profound analyses of 'machine civilization' and the conundrums they pose for humanity which Polanyi Levitt discusses (in this volume).

Unable to address these problems, most centre left parties are today part of the discredited establishment. From Trump's United States to Brexit Britain to Macron's France, Orban's Hungary and lately even Merkel's Germany, the ascendance of the forces of the far right has underlined Polanyi's prescience. As Ann Pettifor points out in trying to make sense of the Brexit vote,

> Karl Polanyi predicted in *The Great Transformation* that no sooner will today's utopians have institutionalized their ideal of a global economy, apparently detached from political, social, and cultural relations, than powerful counter-movements—from the right no less than the left— would be mobilized (Polanyi, 2001). The Brexit vote was, to my mind, just one manifestation of the expected resistance to market fundamentalism. The Brexit slogans 'Take Back Control', 'Take Back Our Country', and 'Britannia waives the rules' represented an inchoate and incoherent attempt to subordinate unfettered, globalized markets in money, trade, and labour to the interests of British society. (Pettifor, 2017: 131)

However, as Polanyi also points out, unless we go beyond inchoate responses towards socialism, the dangers of fascist solutions to the inevitable breakdown of efforts to erect market societies will only grow.

As the relevance of Polanyi's analysis becomes clear to a widening circle of scholars, obstacles to its full comprehension remain. The articles in this volume, each in their own way, either take up the challenge of addressing some of the most critical of these problems, or explore and develop his ideas in hitherto unanticipated ways. In the rest of this introduction, we discuss the contributions that follow and how they aid in overcoming obstacles to understanding Polanyi and constructing a saner politics and political and geopolitical economy for socialism in the twenty-first century.

The Great Transformation and since

The overarching narrative of Kari Polanyi Levitt's opening essay on 'The Return of Karl Polanyi' reconstructs how Keynes's and Hayek's ideas have shaped recent history, and contemplates how Polanyi's prescient ideas might yet shape developments.

Introduction

Polanyi Levitt stresses how quintessentially Central European Polanyi's outlook was. The worlds that structured Polanyi's formative experiences, the worlds of the German Kaisers, the Ottoman Sultans, the Romanov Czars and the Hapsburg King-Emperors, collapsed in revolutions amid and after the First World War. The contrast between their vulnerability and the relative social stability of the Western imperial powers concentrated Polanyi's mind. The result was Polanyi's treatment of the Anglo-American historical trajectory as the exception and today it permits us to understand why the Anglo-American world has led the neoliberal counter-revolution and thus shaped the contemporary re-emergence of authoritarian and far right forces.

The bulk of Polanyi Levitt's contribution is taken up with reflections on the recently unearthed Bennington Lectures, 'The Present Age of Transformation', delivered in 1941. While they anticipated *The Great Transformation*, they also contained lectures on the US and Soviet Russia and the progress of the great transformation there, themes not fully covered in the book. Arising equally from her own personal knowledge of her father, her profound and original understanding of his work and from her own distinguished scholarship on the economy of the post-war world, these reflections deepen our understanding of Polanyi's signature arguments.

The first lecture, anticipating the conceptual framework of *The Great Transformation*, also emphasizes just how slowly the great transformation unfolded. In the 1920s vain efforts at restoration of the pre-war order were made and only their failure finally drove governments' new departures: the New Deal in the United States, Soviet Five-Year Plans in Russia, the 'National Socialist revolution' in Germany and various autarchic regimes in Europe. For Polanyi, these diverse processes had a single and external cause: the gold standard.

In the second lecture, 'The Trend Towards an Integrated Society', the originality of Polanyi's thinking on social integration comes through. Never in human history was the economy disembedded from the social matrix and when it was 'an unheard-of thing [was] brought into existence – an economic society, i.e., a human community based on the assumption that society depends for its existence on material goods alone'. Eventually, such a society exhausts the ability of democratic politics to achieve social integration, opening the door for authoritarian politics to impose a 'false integration'.

More than any passage in *The Great Transformation*, the Third Bennington Lecture on 'The Breakdown of the International System' speaks to us today. Polanyi observes that 'the more close the interdependence of the various parts of the world grew, the more essential became the only effective organizational unit of an industrial society on the present level of technique: – the nation'. As in our day, nationalism became 'a protective reaction against the dangers inherent in an inter-dependent world' as is clear in the rise of far right and illiberal politics in countries as diverse as the US and Britain, Brazil and India, and Turkey and Hungary or Poland.

Polanyi Levitt argues that the first post-war decades in Britain and Western Europe can be seen as a partial realization of Polanyi's vision as capital was sub-ordinated to the reconstruction of society on the basis of full employment and social security financed by progressive taxation. By the mid-1970s, three decades of full employment had strengthened labour and diminished the power of capital, as Kalecki predicted. However, then came the neoliberal counter-revolution, which restored the discipline of unemployment in the labour market, and other free market policies gained favour. While the conventional account of the birth of neoliberalism is focused on the Chicago School, Polanyi Levitt suggests, relying on Quinn Slobodian's excellent recent research (2018), that it should perhaps be complemented by the more global approach of the Geneva School.

For Polanyi Levitt, the demise of the Soviet Union in 1991 was a watershed event equal in importance to the First World War. It led to triumphant globalization and unprecedented financialization, culminating in the 2008 financial crisis. The tri-umphalism was short-lived, however, and Polanyi Levitt notes how China proved the bigger winner of 'globalization'. Indeed, the fast-growing emerging economies recovered from the financial crisis faster and more completely than did the heart-lands of capitalism. The baleful influence of the International Monetary Fund and the World Bank over the developing world declined, expanding their policy-space. The resulting acceleration of the trend towards multi-polarity is reminiscent of Polanyi's 1945 vision in 'Universal capitalism or regional planning'.

Money as a fictitious commodity

A unique section on what Polanyi meant when he designated money as a ficti-tious commodity follows. Market-driven economics assumes that everything that is bought and sold is a commodity. Those immersed in it cannot understand what Polanyi meant by 'fictitious commodities'. Polanyi developed this concept out of intellectual traditions of long standing (Desai in this volume) that questioned the naturalness of markets. He understood money as a social institution emerging from state and credit relations, one that far pre-dated capitalism, took specific, and dangerous, forms under it, and could survive in socialism in suitable forms.

The pervasiveness of neoclassical market-driven thinking confines even those sympathetic to Polanyi's idea that land, labour and money are fictitious commodities to a sort of moral position that they should not be. While such a moral position is not wrong, those who do not venture beyond it will be ill-equipped to understand that Polanyi's argument about fictitious commodities was historical (Desai in this volume). Polanyi drew on classical political economy, Marx, and later adherents of Marx such as Ferdinand Tönnies, to argue that these elements of industry *are not* commodities. They are not produced, not produced for sale and, because of that, unlike other commodities, their supply and thus their prices are subject to vagaries that those of real commodities are not. The supply of real commodities can be increased or decreased in response to rises and falls in price and demand. The supply of fictitious commodities cannot, in the short run. That is why their prices are subject to wild swings which so often prove devastating to entire societies. The treatment of land, labour and money as commodities led, *inevitably*, to movements for social protection.

While land and labour as fictitious commodities are at least discussed, if in moral terms, the topic of money as a fictitious commodity is generally avoided. At best, scholars enlist Polanyi's authority in demands for financial regulation amid the numerous financial crises of our time. One of the distinctive features of this volume is that three contributions explore Polanyi's idea of money as a fictitious commodity, and thus of the peculiarities of money under capitalism, in hitherto unprecedented detail.

Hudson uncovers the historical origin of the commodification of money, tying Polanyi's work on contemporary capitalist society with that on older social formations. Desai explores the meaning of money as a commodity in modern times, and uncovers its close alliance with what Polanyi dubbed the 'crustacean' nation state. Finally, Ugarteche Galarza casts light on the continuing relevance of the impossibility of financial market self-regulation by investigating how, alongside financial deregulation, at least a partial re-embedding of the financial sector has been unavoidable, yielding not so much a financial system but a complex of at least two major parts, one largely embedded, the other mostly disembedded.

Michael Hudson's historical essay tracks the first step in the commodification of money. It was taken when the debt relation was transformed from the social and political relation it was, into one of exchange. In the ancient Near East, the management of the debt relation originally included jubilees – celebrations that extinguished all debts so that all could make new beginnings with 'Clean Slates' – at regular intervals. Jubilees served to maintain social cohesion and economic stability by releasing debtors from unpayable debt. When debt came to be considered a relation of pure exchange in Roman times, it led to the one-sided emphasis on debtor responsibility for discharging debt, forgetting creditor responsibility.

Without periodic stabilizing jubilees, and with interest rates unhinged from real growth rates and thus the ability to pay, debts inevitably mounted to unsustainable levels and racked Rome with recurrent and politically destabilizing debt crises.

However, commodification in general having been still limited in Roman society, this problem appeared full blown only in capitalist society. It took particularly destructive forms in ages of financialization that followed slowing growth, investment and profits unable to keep up with the alchemy expected by compound interest. The gilded age of the early twentieth century and the financialization of our neoliberal age are the two most recent. Hudson's historical investigation is the result of a much larger research project on the origins of money in the Near East.

Desai tackles why money is a fictitious commodity, exposing the limitations of market-driven understandings that simply consider money a commodity, or a symbol of a commodity. She first investigates what fictitious commodities are and reveals the proximity of the idea that land, labour and money were not real commodities to classical political economy, Marx and other thinkers inspired by Marx, chiefly Ferdinand Tönnies. Commodifying money required artificially restricting its supply, as the 1844 Bank Act did (while, interestingly, commodifying labour involved artificially increasing its supply by severing its link to land and society). Though systemically necessary for capitalism, this commodification of money posed equally systemic dangers for it: 'the resulting monetary system could "periodically liquidate business enterprise for shortages and surfeits of money would prove as disastrous to business as floods and droughts in primitive society"', as Polanyi noted (Polanyi, [1944] 1957: 73).

Removing misunderstandings of money as a fictitious commodity is especially important. It is true that Polanyi identified three fictitious commodities, and labour had a certain priority since it was human life itself. However, it is the treatment of money as a commodity and the movement of social protection against it – as central banks linked national currencies to the international gold standard and protected their societies against its harsh vagaries at the same time – that structures the narrative of *The Great Transformation*. The collapse of the gold standard was the 'proximate cause' of the collapse of nineteenth-century civilization.

Desai's contribution also sheds light on a normally obscured theme in Polanyi's thinking: the emergence of what Polanyi called 'crustacean nations'. While the movement for social protection principally implicates the nation state generally, that relating to money implicates the nation state most directly. Central banks, in commodifying money as well as protecting society against its consequences, constitute the outer layer of the system of social protection that nation states became with the development of capitalism. Capitalism requires the development of 'crustacean nations'– nation states with hard protective shells. This gave the crisis of nineteenth-century civilization the form it took, one of violent confrontation between imperialist nations and eventually war. The same form laid the foundation, however, of the world of planned national or regional economies that Polanyi anticipated at war's end and which, he argued, made the world more amenable to socialism.

This understanding of the historical role of nation states in capitalism is nascent and developing in the work of Marx (Desai 2013, 2012, 2018b) and Polanyi developed our understanding of the umbilical link between capitalism and the nation state, including their centrality both as agents of imperialism and those of resistance to it, most fully. However, no aspect of his work has been less commented on in our world – dominated as it has been by market-driven 'globalist' thinking or what Friedrich List labelled 'cosmopolitan' thinking, disdaining the national realities of the capitalist world.

Ugarteche Galarza, who cautions against the common confusion of Marx's concept of fictitious capital and Polanyi's concept of money as a fictitious commodity, harnesses Polanyi's concepts of embeddedness and disembeddedness in a novel argument about the organization of money and finance in contemporary capitalism. Precisely because money is not a commodity, the neoliberal deregulation of the financial sector could only be incomplete. No sooner had it got into its stride early in the neoliberal era than it caused crises and these, in turn required forms of re-embedding. It turned out to be, Ugarteche Galarza's original argument goes, partial in a most interesting way. The re-embedding process gave a special status to the most powerful financial institutions, that of being 'Too Big to Fail' (TBTF), effectively creating a two-tier system, or rather, not a system at all, but a complex.

In this complex, privileged firms enjoy greater freedoms to speculate as they please as well as more or less blanket state protection when speculation inevitably lands them in trouble. The TBTF concept emerged in the first major financial crisis of the neoliberal age to hit US financial institutions, the Third World debt crisis of the early 1980s, which threatened major US banks such as Continental Illinois. While the large financial institutions enjoy these privileged freedoms as well as protection, other banks and financial institutions, including worker pension funds and other savings institutions, face greater regulation and are only partially protected, and their clients, working people and the lower middle classes, have lost their savings in every financial crisis. The former are fully embedded in financialized capitalism while the latter are more disembedded: after all, as they say, 'competition is for losers'. Ugarteche Galarza's analysis demonstrates that the rhetoric of competition is, and can only be, used conveniently: it cannot describe the real world of money in capitalism. He also provides powerful justification for the socialization of private financial institutions if economies are to be prosperous, productive and equal.

The double movement: from social protection to socialism

Apart from a few 'greats', like the Weber–Durkheim–Pareto and the Menger–Walras–Jevons triumvirates of Sociology and Economics respectively, few writers of the late nineteenth and early twentieth century are studied and, if they are, they are studied in the disciplinary silos in which we have become accustomed to live and think. This has led to two problems. First, because Polanyi is isolated from his intellectual milieu, many attribute to Polanyi an originality he did not have while not appreciating his true originality. For instance, Polanyi is widely believed to have originated the ideas of the fictitious commodities and the double movement. However, Dale (2010a: 71) traces the origin of the idea of fictitious commodities to Tönnies and Desai (in this volume) argues that the idea was likely common in the intellectual culture of the time. Similarly, we have already indicated the relationship between the idea of the double movement and the account of the transition from individualism to collectivism in England by Dicey (and here we do well to remember that Polanyi's formal training was in Law). Moreover, Thomasberger's contribution in this volume points out that Polanyi himself attributed the idea of the double movement to 'Liberal writers like Spencer, and Sumner, Mises and Lippman' who, however, put 'an entirely different interpretation on it' (Polanyi, [1944] 1957: 141). Understanding Polanyi's intellectual setting permits a better appreciation of his true originality, his deft deployment of carefully chosen ideas to diagnose the crisis and the stakes in it.

The second problem is that while the inviting suggestiveness of Polanyi's ideas has contributed greatly to their currency, it has led to their all-too-easy employment. More serious scholarly engagement and debate have uncovered their often more complex and even opposite meanings, leading Michael Brie (in this volume) to call Polanyi 'the best-known unknown intellectual'. We have already discussed the problems in the appropriation of the idea of fictitious commodities. The contributions in this part deal with our understanding of the double movement and the ideas – of society, social protection and socialism –, deeply connected with it. Rotstein ruminates on Polanyi's understanding of the Reality of Society. Thomasberger reveals how Polanyi really understood the 'double movement'. Lacher illuminates Polanyi's understanding of the incompleteness of the great transformation in the US. Finally, Brie not only rejects the portrayal of Polanyi as a social democrat seeking only to re-embed markets but also provides a deeply insightful account of what socialism meant to Polanyi and how he delinked socialism from liberal 'freedom that kills' and founded it on the type of freedom compatible with human sociality, what he called 'freedom in a complex society'.

In his posthumous contribution, Polanyi's student and colleague, Abe Rotstein, provides us with a document of living history, based on conversations with Polanyi in which he spoke of 'a topic he called "the reality of society"', the fundament of his thinking. Early on in these conversations, spanning some twenty-eight visits to Polanyi in Pickering, Rotstein began taking extensive notes. These notes were read, approved and corrected by Polanyi and he suggested Rotstein help him write the sequel to *The Great Transformation*. The title eventually settled on was 'Freedom and technology'. In contrast to *The Great Transformation*, which 'was built on a social sciences approach using institutional analysis', the sequel would be based on the confluence of religious and philosophical thinking. Like Hegel, who wished to transform religious representations into philosophical ideas, Polanyi asked 'Were there important truths that lay behind and beneath these beliefs and practices?'

For Polanyi they consisted of three 'revelations': the knowledge of death and finitude; that of the inner life, whether dubbed 'soul' or 'conscience', which was higher than physical existence and involved an awareness of the rest of society; and that of freedom, the way to a clear conscience, which became the foundation of our civil liberties. Polanyi believed that industrial society increases both interdependence and reliance on technological systems. 'As we realize the full extent of that dependence, our own vulnerability hits home: we realize that we must protect these arteries of our life at any price. We offer our tacit consent to hand over to our government the virtually unlimited power to do whatever is "necessary".' Bearing in mind that these conversations took place amid the Cold War and McCarthyism provides a clue to their contemporary relevance in 'the new world that Edward Snowden and Julian Assange have uncovered for us', the world of 'Homeland Security', 'cyber attacks', 'global epidemics' 'drones' and 'Big Data'. It is against this world that our freedom needs to be built.

Thomasberger, like Brie (see below), argues against the view that markets are 'always already embedded', which erases the distinction between market and non-market societies. He also challenges the widespread notion that the double movement is the eternal repetition of embedding followed by disembedding. In place of this 'theorem of the double movement', Thomasberger emphasizes the necessity of taking *The Great Transformation*'s opening sentence more seriously: that nineteenth-century civilization, in which the double movement had operated, had collapsed. This argument denies that the double movement that characterized nineteenth-century civilization is relevant today and implies that the nineteenth-century movement to re-embed society was not socialism. By the twentieth century, the double movement no longer operated: as long as the countermovement of social protection was necessary, 'as a protective movement, it depended on economic liberalism. … the countermovement was a reaction to the liberal utopia, which made it an integral part of this civilization.'

After the collapse of that civilization, the left needs to discuss socialism rather than 're-embedding' markets. Even on the right, the argument has long shifted away from laissez-faire towards 'developing new justifications for the market system'. For Lionel Robbins, 'The issue is not between a plan and no plan, it is between different kinds of plan' and for Hayek, 'Laisser-faire has been replaced by "planning for the market" or "planning for competition"'. The new position, as it emerged in the work of Austrian economists such as Ludwig von Mises and Friedrich Hayek in the socialist accountancy debate, was that 'complex societies' were necessarily opaque to their members. Only the market could provide humankind with a way of dealing with this problem, only it could synthesize the necessarily partial knowledges of individuals into complex social decisions. Opposing such arguments requires us to move forward from simple state–market or society–market dualisms and towards a socialism that challenges the power and property relations that underlie capitalism.

Polanyi accepted the terms of this challenge, in the process also accepting that this problem faced all modern 'complex' societies, not just capitalist societies, and sought to make a case for socialism on this far more difficult terrain. In the twentieth and twenty-first centuries, rather than any spontaneous movement for social protection, the politically organized and ideological imposition of market disciplines can only be combatted by equally political, organized and conscious movements for democratic socialism. Only such a well-organized ideology could counter the dangers of the other alternative to the unbearable burdens of market society, fascism. This was also the root, Thomasberger argues, of Polanyi's interest in institutions and of his enduring relevance as an institutionalist economist.

Based on extensive archival work into Polanyi's writings, including many unpublished manuscripts, Hannes Lacher contests views that the international order originating in Bretton Woods was a realization of Polanyi's vision of (re)-embedded markets, and that the New Deal anticipated Polanyi's vision of socialism. On the contrary, like Polanyi Levitt, Lacher argues that Polanyi sharply distinguished the European from the American experience. He emphasizes how Polanyi believed that, owing to the deep roots of capitalist ideology among the working class, and the relative weakness of both class and state structures there, the US would prove a capitalist outlier in a post-war world dominated by a European socialism. Agreeing with Sombart (and disagreeing with Stalin and International Workers of the World leader Daniel De Leon's judgements at various points), Polanyi insisted on American exceptionalism.

Though *The Great Transformation* was written in Vermont, Polanyi does not discuss the New Deal in it. So the argument that he considered it a model for the rest of the world does not seem credible. The New Deal remained too committed to private property. While it could have played a progressive role in the US context, it was nowhere near the socialism Europe needed. And, while in writing *The Great Transformation*, Polanyi might have entertained the hope that the New Deal might develop into a socialism, he was never in doubt about how far it had to travel to do so.

Lacher's careful reconstruction of Polanyi's views as they evolved and even fluctuated, at least in their estimation of the centrality of the US post-war world, impresses upon us just how much Polanyi's analysis depended on understanding history and the course it was taking in very contemporary events. Realizing that the Bretton Woods agreements represented not the triumph of his hopes for Europe and the world, but their frustration by the post-war might of the US, Polanyi also re-evaluated the New Deal. Where he had once 'considered the New Deal one of the modalities through which liberal capitalism and market-economy had been overcome', Polanyi's writings in the mid- and late 1940s saw 'the US, once more, as a market-economy... [one] hell-bent on stopping the disappearance of market-economy elsewhere in its tracks, including – and especially, in Britain'.

Finally, in the ultimate chapter of this part, Michael Brie also challenges the notion that Polanyi believed that 'the unleashing of market forces would always be answered with the "protection of society"'. This 'pendulum' view of history and the relative obscurity of Polanyi's understanding of socialism make him the 'best known unknown intellectual'. Brie seeks to rectify this. He traces the intellectual journey Polanyi took as he developed his understanding of socialism, beginning by identifying the guiding question of his work. It arose out of his understanding of his generation's responsibility for the First World War and concerned two opposed conceptions of freedom: the liberal conception and his own. There was, he felt, a 'contradiction between the freedom of the individual to make clear decisions and the senselessness and absurdity of the complex relationships that lead to civiliza-tional catastrophes'. What was the concept of freedom that might deal with it? In answering this question, Polanyi was also aware that, after that war, socialism faced new intellectual challenges from the extreme free market Austrian economists such as Ludwig von Mises and new political ones from the emerging fascism. From the first challenge, whose axiom of capitalism as a 'complex society' he accepted, he asked: 'How is freedom possible in a complex society?' From the experience of fascism, he drew the conclusion that fascism and socialism were two stark alternatives: while fascism was capitalism's Plan B, socialism had to be made democracy's Plan A, the foundation of its existence without which it risked slipping back into the conditions that made fascism possible.

Polanyi's responses to the two challenges were combined by putting individualism and freedom at the centre of his socialist vision but also by framing them in the 'reality of society' that Rotstein discusses. In this socialism, 'everyone can and must take responsibility for the impact of her or his free actions on the lives of others. This is not a comfortable socialism of passive well-being, but a challenge for the transformation of both society and the individuals.' This was a socialism of freedom as solidarity, one that was constantly striving to expand real freedom.

Polanyi's wide-ranging influence on social and political thought

Somers and Block's contribution shows that Polanyi's approach is still productive of new concepts and can throw into relief the limitations of some of the best-known analyses of arguably the gravest economic malaise of our time: inequality. Somers and Block demonstrate that the chief argument of Thomas Piketty's best-selling *Capital in the Twenty-first Century*, that the rate of return on capital tends to exceed the economy's growth rate, leading to constantly rising inequality, is too economistic. It assumes that capitalism has certain inexorable economic laws when, in fact, the distribution of incomes, a Polanyian perspective shows, is the result of key political decisions which create a structure of 'predistribution' of incomes. It comes before the better-known 'redistribution' effected through fiscal – taxation and spending – methods and is equally political. Somers and Block also demonstrate that explaining, as Piketty does, the reversal of that trend of rising inequality between 1914 and 1970 by the two world wars ignores the centrality of developments on which Polanyi focused. It is the deep and wide mass mobilizations of the period, which determined predistribution, that provide a more convincing explanation of the fall in inequality of that time, as well as indicating what needs to be done to achieve such a reversal again, hopefully permanently. Finally, Somers and Block show that while for Piketty capitalism remains the same throughout, a substantivist Polanyian perspective, which was attuned to the concern about the transition to a 'post-industrial society' from its beginnings in the 1950s, helps us take into account changes in the economy that emerge from changes in the productive structure.

Chikako Nakayama's contribution draws our attention to the structural similarities as well as links between many of Polanyi's arguments – such as that about the relation between Lancashire and India or the role of haute finance in *The Great Transformation* – and the distinctive World Systems analysis of Giovanni Arrighi. Polanyi's influence, Nakayama shows, particularly that of his historically grounded understanding of the foundations of British imperialism in India, enabled Arrighi to arrive at a richer understanding of imperialism and hegemony in the world system, including an appreciation that the transition from British to American 'hegemony' was also a weakening of imperialism. In particular, Nakayama stresses the extent to which, far more than most Western understandings of imperialism, Polanyi was aware of the benefits that the imperial countries derived from their colonies, benefits that could not be had without direct colonial control. This understanding permitted Arrighi to see clearly how 'American hegemony could not enjoy such advantages as Britain' and how 'America fell into crisis owing to its quagmire of the Vietnam War'.

Finally, Jamie Peck explores the affinities of Polanyi with a whole range of thinkers in geography, economic history and political economy, such as the French Regulation School, who 'share the same object of inquiry – the culturally inflected, institutionally mediated, politically governed, socially embedded and heterogeneous economy, one subject neither to self-governing equilibrium nor to incipient convergence, but to restive restructuring and divergent development'. Building on this element in Polanyi's oeuvre, Peck proposes a substantivist project of comparative political economies that seeks to comprehend their similarities and differences as they have come to be historically constituted. Peck also explores the origin of Polanyi's perspective in his peripatetic personal and intellectual biography, in which his personal experience of the variations among major capitalist economies founded his substantivist conception of the economy, and the potential of the intellectually ambitious if also incomplete, suggestive if also at times ambiguous, 'moving system of thought' that was the result.

Note

1   I would like to thank Kari Polanyi Levitt for her valuable input into this introduction and regret that, due to other demands on her time, she could not co-author it, as originally planned. While Kari's input has greatly enhanced it, all responsibility for remaining errors of fact or judgement remain, of course, mine.

Part I

The great transformation and since

2

The return of Karl Polanyi: from the Bennington Lectures to our present age of transformation

Kari Polanyi Levitt

Introduction: the return of Karl Polanyi to critical discourse

European intellectuals of the generation of Keynes (b. 1883), Polanyi (b. 1886) and Hayek (b. 1899) were socially conditioned to assume responsibility for the welfare of society. They shared the experience of the collapse of the nineteenth-century liberal order. They understood the power of ideas. If full employment, rising real wages and social security financed by progressive income taxation in the early decades of the post-war era can be attributed to Keynes, and if Hayek played a foundational role in the neoliberal counter-revolution which reinstituted the dominance of capital on a world scale, what does the return of Karl Polanyi signify in terms of civilizational challenges facing humanity in the twenty-first century (Polanyi Levitt, 2012: 5–15)?

The return of *The Great Transformation* (*TGT*) to economic discourse can be traced to the 1990s, beginning with the implosion of the Soviet Union and the celebration of globalization. The financialized prosperity of the Clinton years invited comparison with the Roaring Twenties, which culminated in the Wall Street Crash of 1929 and the World Economic Crisis (Polanyi Levitt, 2006a: 152–177). As the increasing frequency and severity of economic crises in the developing world culminated in the Asian financial crisis of 1997, Dani Rodrik recalled Polanyi's warning that unregulated markets could put the world economy in danger of a collapse resembling that of the 1930s (Rodrik, 1998: 17).

Interest in Polanyi has continued to grow. There are now twenty translations of *TGT*. The financial crisis of 2008 moved questions regarding the future of capitalism into the public arena. Karl Polanyi joined Karl Marx in a return to public discourse (Elliot, 2012). Major critical works on Polanyi were published and reviewed in prestigious literary publications (Block and Somers, 2014; Dale, 2016a; Kuttner, 2017, 2018; Rogan, 2017; Brie and Thomasberger, 2018; Crain, 2018; Polanyi, 2018a). When asked to rank the ten most important books written by economists in the past hundred years, a 2016 survey of over three thousand heterodox economists placed *The Great Transformation* second only to Keynes's *General Theory of Employment, Interest and Money* (1936), with Schumpeter's *Capitalism, Socialism and Democracy* (1942) in third and John Kenneth Galbraith's *The Affluent Society* (1958) in fourth place (*Real World Economics Review*, 2016).

Unlike Keynes or Hayek, Polanyi did not acquire his knowledge of economics by formal academic accreditation but by independent study of the classics of the Austrian School of Economics, founded by Carl Menger (b. 1840) in the nineteenth century and represented by Ludwig von Mises (b. 1881) and Friedrich von Hayek in the twentieth century. Described variously as an economic anthropologist, sociologist or historian, Polanyi's ultimate vocation was that of a social philosopher and socialist educator. His critique was directed at the capitalist market society which reduces the worth of all human activity to exchange value; what has no price appears to have no value. His abiding concern was with freedom in an increasingly commercialized society characterized by an ever more artificial relationship with nature since the advent of the machine age some two hundred years ago.

Wherever he lived, in Budapest, Vienna, London, New York or Canada, Polanyi was an engaged observer of national and international affairs. He wrote to communicate ideas clearly and directly. With some exceptions, he rarely published in academic journals but in periodicals addressed to the general public. It was not until Polanyi was past the age of retirement that he was invited to join the Department of Economics at Columbia University as a visiting professor in 1947.

His course on General Economic History investigated economic livelihoods in primitive and archaic societies with the aid of his now well-known paradigm of reciprocity, redistribution and exchange as general patterns of integration of economic activity (Polanyi, 1957b: 243). His research suggests that never in human historical experience has the economy been uprooted or disembedded from its societal matrix as by the English industrial revolution, which opened the Pandora's Box of exponential economic growth accompanied by social dispossession on a global scale.

As Gareth Dale notes, few other thinkers have been 'subject to such varying interpretations' (Dale, 2008: 495–496). In part, this is because few critics have read more than his masterwork, *The Great Transformation*, or select chapters from *Trade and Markets* and the posthumously published *Dahomey and the Slave Trade* or *The Livelihood of Man*. Most readers in English are unaware of the vast body of Polanyi's work during the quarter-century preceding the writing of *TGT* in Vermont. Not surprisingly, they do not appreciate how much Polanyi's Central European perspective shaped his thinking. The recently published collection of selected translations, *Economy and Society* (2018a), presents Polanyi's early work in historical and thematic form.

In this chapter, we provide a brief summary of Polanyi's Central European experience, as well as reflections and writings from Budapest, Vienna, England and brief visits to the United States. It accords special importance to the recently discovered five lectures on 'The Present Age of Transformation' delivered at Bennington College late in 1940. The first three lectures summarize the basic insights of the book while the fourth and fifth outline original approaches to planned works on America and Russia which remained unwritten.

This chapter continues earlier work on the 'Power of ideas: Keynes, Hayek, and Polanyi' (Polanyi Levitt, 2012: 5–18), tracking how Keynes's and Hayek's ideas have shaped our world centrally since the Second World War, and traces a historical path to account for the relevance of Polanyi today. Finally, it concludes with hypothetical reflections of Karl Polanyi on our present age of transformation and the future of humankind. We roll back the canvas of history to assess Polanyi's relevance in the context of the two hundred years since the industrial revolution. We contemplate what Polanyi would have to say on the current state of world affairs. We tell him of the successes of his intellectual adversary Mises and ask him how he might conceive of a socialist response to the challenges facing humanity in our present age of transformation.

From Budapest, Vienna and London to Vermont and back

Karl Polanyi was the third child born in Vienna to a Jewish bourgeois family. His mother's language was Russian and his father's Hungarian, but the common family language was German. In the mid-1890s, his father moved his business to Budapest. In pre-1914 Hungary, Polanyi was known as the founder and first president of a Hungarian student society named for Galileo. Its journal was called *Szabad Gondolat* (*Free Thought*). It was modelled on early Russian student movements engaged in popular education, including classes for young workers and peasants. His admiration for the Russian revolutionary socialists of the late nineteenth century originated from a close family relationship with the Klaschkos in Vienna.

For Polanyi, the Great War was a traumatic experience, which shattered all the certainties of the *belle époque* that preceded it. He served as a cavalry officer on the Russian Front. When his horse tripped and fell on him, he expected to die but woke in a Budapest hospital. He was consumed by a sense of the responsibility of his generation for the meaningless suffering in the war, which was ultimately about nothing of importance. The revolutions which ended the war and the Habsburg

Empire in 1918 had massive popular support. In Hungary, Polanyi supported the 1919 Béla Kun Regime of the Councils. When asked by his friend and former schoolmate Georg Lukacs to defend Budapest from invasion by Romanian forces, he expressed his solidarity with the fight to save the city but was physically unable to engage in combat. He left for Vienna for medical treatment, followed by a large exodus of all sections of the Hungarian left seeking refuge from Admiral Horthy's White Terror.

By the end of the war, the former Habsburg Empire was in ruins. With a population of two million, Vienna was now the capital of the Republic of Austria of only six million. Vienna, with the status of a state, had continuous social democratic administrations from 1918–33 but socialists were a minority in the federal government.

For celebrated Austrian economist, Ludwig von Mises, socialism presented a threat to Western civilization. His 1922 book opens with the observation that 'Socialism is the watchword and the catchword of our day. The socialist idea dominates the modern spirit. The masses approve of it. It expresses the thoughts and feelings of all' (Mises, [1922] 1951: 25). Mises employed a sweeping conception of socialism, defined in terms of 'state interference in all forms of economic life' (ibid.: 25). He considered the English Liberals of his day 'more or less moderate socialists' (ibid.: 27).

In the intellectual milieu of 1920s Red Vienna, Mises and his associates were the misfits grieving the passing of the old Habsburg order (Polanyi Levitt, 2013b: 24). For Mises, 'private property in the means of production' was the critical factor in the success of the capitalist market economy: 'All efforts to realize Socialism lead only to the destruction of society. Factories, mines, and railways will come to a standstill, towns will be deserted. ... The farmer will return to the self-sufficiency of the closed, domestic economy' ([1922] 1951: 511). We note that at that time no country in the world had yet constructed a socialist economy. The early Soviet Union was engaged in a civil war of survival. Mises believed that without individual responsibility associated with the ownership of property, there would be chaos. He argued that traditionally 'property was sacred' but liberalism had debased property into a utilitarian matter (ibid.: 513). The role of the state is the maintenance and enforcement of the legal order securing private property.

Mises's book initiated the Socialist Accounting Debate in the pages of *Archiv für Sozialwissenschaft und Sozialpolitik*, the premier academic social science journal of the German-speaking world (Polanyi Levitt, 2018: 24–26). Some contributors, like Otto Neurath, believed in a moneyless or natural economy of barter. In Polanyi's contribution, prices were determined by negotiation between associations representing enterprises, workers, consumers and communities at the local, regional and national levels (Polanyi, 2016: 385–427). Mises responded and Polanyi replied (Polanyi, 2018e: 51–60). Polanyi's socialism was neither that of traditional European social democracy, nor of centralized communist planning. It was more akin to the third stream of the socialist tradition – the syndicalist, popu-list, associational and communalist (Polanyi Levitt, 2018: 24–26). Polanyi admired the achievements of socialist Red Vienna, including the eradication of tenement slums and the construction of social housing that was designed by Austria's leading architects and financed by progressive taxation. More than that, he considered the achievements of Red Vienna to be 'one of the high points of western civilization' (Zeisel, 1968: 172).

In 1922, Polanyi married the legendary communist and polymath intellectual, Ilona Duczyńska, forming what György Dalós called the 'fidelity of equals' (Dalós, 1990). From 1924, he was an editor of Austria's leading economic and financial weekly, *Der Österreichische Volkswirt*, specializing in international affairs. In his weekly column, he followed the international political and financial negotiations in the daily newspapers from Paris, London and Frankfurt. Polanyi's column was reproduced in three German-language volumes, *Chronik der großen Transformation* (Polanyi, 2002, 2003, 2005a).

The accession of Hitler to office and the rise of Austro-fascism caused Polanyi to leave Vienna for England in 1933, but he continued to write for the journal until it ceased publication in 1938. Like Marx a hundred years earlier, Polanyi's encounter with the physical and human ravages of industrial capitalism in England was a profound shock. According to Ilona, it was in England that Karl acquired a sacred hatred of capitalism. In London, Christian Socialist colleagues provided a supportive intellectual and social environment. Polanyi co-edited *Christianity and the Social Revolution* (1935), to which he contributed 'The essence of fascism'. In the course of two lecture tours under the auspices of the International Educational Institute, he visited almost every state of the United States (Polanyi, 2014a).

In 1937 Polanyi found employment with the Workers' Education Association (WEA) as a lecturer in small provincial towns in Kent and Sussex. In England, the richest country of Europe, he found that the quality of life of the working class was inferior to that of workers in impoverished post-war Vienna. He compared British class distinction by speech to the role of caste in India or race in the United States. The WEA curriculum included courses on contemporary international affairs and on English economic and social history, a subject entirely new to him.

Thanks to a family connection, Karl, Ilona and Kari were granted British natu-ralization early in 1940. This saved Polanyi, then in his mid-fifties, from internment as an enemy alien and enabled him to undertake a lecture tour in the US while maintaining the right to return to England. While in New York, Polanyi accepted an invitation from Bennington College to deliver 'Five Lectures on the Present Age of Transformation' in the autumn of 1940. When President Leigh of Bennington College obtained a two-year grant from the Rockefeller Foundation, Polanyi was able to write his most important work (Rockefeller Foundation Records, 1942). In 1941 Ilona joined him in Bennington, where she taught physics and mathematics at the college. I did not wish to leave England.

In a letter written to me in 1941, my father indicated that *The Great Transformation* would have some five hundred pages including a treatment of 'America, Russia, the history of economic theory and the history of the liberal state' but these chapters were never written. Initially he wished to call the book *The Liberal Utopia: Origins of the Cataclysm*. This title was rejected because it would be misunderstood in the United States, where the term 'liberal' was associated with the New Deal and not with the laissez-faire free market. The final version of the book was less than three hundred pages in length.

Although written in Vermont and first published in the United States, the essential insights of *The Great Transformation* were grounded in European history and experience. More specifically, Polanyi sought to uncover the ultimate roots of the triumph of fascism over democracy in 1930s Europe. When Polanyi delivered the Bennington Lectures in late 1940, the outcome of the war could not be known. Germany had occupied France, the Battle of Britain was raging in the skies of England and Hitler's armies were poised to conquer Russia. The declared ambition of the Third Reich was to dominate Europe for a thousand years.

When Stalingrad turned the tide of the war towards an Allied victory, Karl and Ilona hastened to return to England in 1943, to participate in discussions on the post-war future of Europe. The two penultimate chapters (19 and 20) were left unfinished. Before leaving the United States, Polanyi obtained a contract for a popular version of *The Great Transformation* called *The Common Man's Masterplan*, to be sent from England in 1943. A draft of this document indicates a programmatic approach to a democratic socialist post-war Britain. It was his hope that socialist policies in Britain would receive the support of a United States characterized by the New Deal. Following the dismissal of Winston Churchill and the election of the Labour Party in 1945, Polanyi envisioned a socialist British commonwealth in a world of coexistence of the United States with the Soviet Union, Europe, China, India and other regional blocs, or 'tame empires' as he called them (1945: 86–91).

In the absence of opportunities for academic appointment in England, Polanyi accepted the offer of a visiting professorship from Columbia University in 1947.

Without the invitation from Bennington College, *TGT* might never have been written. Without the accreditation Columbia University provided, it is unlikely the book could have survived to be hailed a twentieth-century classic (Polanyi Levitt, 2018: 28).

Ilona was barred from entry to the United States on account of former communist affiliations in Hungary and Austria. She created a home on the outskirts of Toronto so Karl could commute to New York. The stream of visitors to the small house on the banks of the River Rouge included his graduate students, Marshall McLuhan and other close friends, as well as Kari, her husband Joe Levitt and the two grandchildren. In the last years of his life, Karl founded the journal *Coexistence* and with Ilona published *The Plough and the Pen*, an anthology of English translations of the work of Hungarian poets as tribute to intellectuals who remained to struggle for a socialist Hungary. Shortly before his death, they travelled to Europe and Karl visited Hungary for the first time since leaving in 1919. He wrote that all he had achieved in life was owed to Hungary. Karl and Ilona rest together in a Budapest cemetery (ibid.: 28–30).

The Bennington Lectures on our age of transformation

The 2017 rediscovery of the Bennington Lectures was timely. Their focus on the World Economic Crisis and related rise of fascism in Europe in the 1930s sheds light on the 2008 financial collapse, the most serious since the Great Depression, and help us understand its connection to the rising tide of nationalist populist political currents. It also underlines another theme that is demanding better understanding today: the necessary role of the nation in the protection of society from the dangers inherent in an interdependent, now globalized world.

It is remarkable that in the twelve pages of the first three lectures Polanyi summarizes the principal argument of *TGT*. The fourth and fifth lectures treat America and Russia. We present comments on each of these lectures, with particular emphasis on texts which most speak to us today.

The passing of nineteenth-century civilization[1]

The first lecture outlines the two chapters of *TGT* constituting Part One on 'The International System'.

Drawing on Polanyi's Central European perspective, the first lecture argues that the long nineteenth century did not end in 1914 but crashed in the World Economic Crisis of 1929–33. After the war, the victorious Western European imperial powers, although impoverished, experienced no substantial transformative change. Instead, in the 'Conservative Twenties', they were determined to restore the pre-1914 economic order, giving priority to re-floating the international gold standard. The pound sterling was restored to its pre-war gold value, favouring overseas investors of the leisure classes. By contrast, the defeated central powers of Germany and the fragile succession states of the former Habsburg Empire lacked the resources to meet the conflicting demands of workers for living wages, farmers for remunerative prices and middle-class rentiers for security for their savings from inflation (Polanyi, 2018d: 66–80). These troubles were only exacerbated as the League of Nations, acting on behalf of Western creditors, imposed on them austerity measures akin to the IMF's Structural Adjustment Programs of the 1980s and 1990s. In 1932 Germany, with eight million unemployed, Chancellor Brüning proudly announced that the government had balanced the budget, precipitating the political crisis that brought Hitler to office in March 1933.

Polanyi contrasted the Conservative Twenties with the Revolutionary Thirties when suddenly, 'with an awe-inspiring vehemence, change set in'. Its landmarks were the abandonment of the gold standard by Great Britain and the United States; the Five-Year Plans, especially the collectivization of the farms in Russia; the launching of the New Deal; the National Socialist Revolution in Germany; and the collapse of the balance of power in favour of autarchic empires. By 1940, 'every vestige of the international system had disappeared'. New Deal America and socialist Soviet five-year planning are presented as embodying the future and countering the threat to humanity posed by the National Socialist revolution.

The sudden and world-wide change encompassing such diverse countries and regions in the 1930s 'must be attributed', Polanyi concluded, 'to a single external cause'. The common source of this crisis was traced to the international gold standard. Polanyi observed that all political crises in Europe had a monetary origin: 'An unbroken sequence of currency crises linked the indigent Balkans to the affluent U.S.A. through the elastic band of an international credit system.'

The only substantial addition in the book compared with the lecture is the importance accorded to England as the origin of liberal capitalism and market society. In the closing passage of *TGT*'s Part One, Polanyi writes 'the nineteenth century … was England's century. The Industrial Revolution was an English event. Market economy, free trade, and the gold standard were English inventions', and so the market economy should be studied in England (Polanyi, [1944] 2001: 32). Indeed, Part Two of the book, fifteen chapters on the Rise and Fall of Market Economy, treats English social and economic history. The statement that 'Market society was born in England – yet it was on the Continent that its weaknesses engendered the most tragic complications. In order to comprehend German fascism, we must revert to Ricardian England' (ibid.: 32) could only have been made by a continental European or, more exactly, a Central European.

The trend towards an integrated society

The second lecture outlines the fundamental ideas underlying *TGT*: the separation of the political and economic spheres in nineteenth-century market society and the historically unprecedented disembedding or uprooting of the latter from the former.

People must have both food and safety, but capitalist market society is unique in providing for these needs by separate sets of institutions with separate sets of actors. As Polanyi writes:

> Nineteenth century society was based upon the two pillars of liberal capitalism and representative democracy. The economic and the political spheres were separate. This is the clue to its rapid downfall. For the expectation that such a state of affairs could be anything but transitory was an illusion. A society containing within its orbit a separate, self-regulating and autonomous economic sphere is a utopia.

A laissez-faire competitive price-making market economy requires free markets for the factors of production. That is where the problems begin. 'Amongst the factors of production there are land and labour, both of which can be treated as commodities only on a more or less fictitious basis. For labour means the human beings of whom society consists, and land is only another word for the mother earth on whom they subsist.' As a result, 'Almost unwittingly an unheard of thing is brought into existence: – an economic society, i.e., a human community based on the assumption that society depends for its existence on material goods alone.'

Polanyi maintains that the profit-maximizing decisions of the free market cannot produce a stable society because material goods, however plentiful, cannot provide the sole basis for our existence as social beings. We require personal security, law and order, and a 'reasonably stable relationship to our environment, to nature, our neighbours [and] a sufficiently stable outlook on the future such as would allow the laying of the foundations of human character and the raising of a new generation'. Polanyi states that 'for the sake of society the market mechanism must be restricted'. This, however, may incur significant economic costs. He concludes that 'We are caught up on the horns of a dilemma: – either to continue on the path of a utopia bound for destruction, or to halt on this path and risk the throwing out of gear of this marvellous but extremely artificial system.'

In reality, Polanyi recognized that the utopian project of a self-regulating market could never be fully implemented. It was essentially an ideology rather than a realistic political project. From its beginnings, nineteenth-century liberal capitalism encountered opposition in the form of factory legislation and protectionism, trade unions and the Church. These were part of 'the violent reaction against the assumptions of an unrestricted market for land and labour'.

Where the conflict between capital accumulation by market expansion and protection of society by legislation and social movements could not be mediated by democratic process, Polanyi introduced the concept of the 'false integration' of economics and politics. The late nineteenth century was replete with examples of false integration, such as the concentration of industrial production in trusts, monopolies and cartels; protection of agriculture and industry by tariffs and subsidies; and national competition for resources and markets by colonial expansion and conflict. The latter, as noted by Polanyi, paved the way for the First World War between the rival European imperialist powers.

In post-war Europe, Polanyi attributed the rise of fascism to a deadlock resulting from irreconcilable conflict between economics and politics: 'the captains of industry undermined the authority of democratic institutions, while democratic parliaments continuously interfered with the working of the market mechanism'. The alternative solutions to this deadlock appeared to be 'an integration of society through political power on a democratic basis, or, if democracy proved too weak, integration on an authoritarian basis in a totalitarian society, at the price of the sacrifice of democracy'. Polanyi concluded the second lecture by stating that the American social system was not (had not yet been) faced with the same predicament. In the fourth lecture, Polanyi compares the enactment of New Deal legislation, which did not compromise American democratic institutions, with the obstacles to essential reforms in Europe. The vulnerability of European governments to financial panic resulted in deadlock resolved by false integration achieved by authoritarian regimes.

The breakdown of the international system

The third lecture is perhaps the most relevant to our present-day political landscape. It opens by stating that the breakdown of the nineteenth-century international system resulted from the same failings that plagued national market economies. The term 'world market'

> [s]eems to suggest the existence of some market external and additional to the national markets. Such a separate international market, however, does not exist. In respect to each national market the other national markets form together the international

market, every part of which, therefore, is under a definite jurisdiction and carries on its dealings in one currency.

The nineteenth-century world market was created by assigning each national currency a value in terms of a fixed quantity of gold. The pound sterling maintained its value in gold until 1931 and was considered 'as good as gold'. Stability of the value of the pound sterling in world markets depended on the ability of nations to maintain the external value of their currencies; this implies flexibility of domestic prices and wages. An international market for commodities and capital was thus created.

This gave national boundaries a new role as 'shock absorbers'. While Polanyi recognized the beneficial effects of the international division of labour and international trade, they frequently induced external shocks which compounded the existing problems of domestic markets and introduced a new protective role for the state:

> [T]he more intense international cooperation was and the more close the interdependence of the various parts of the world grew, the more essential became the only effective organizational unit of an industrial society on the present level of technique: – the nation. Modern nationalism is a protective reaction against the dangers inherent in an interdependent world.

The concluding passages contrast the regulation of every aspect of economic life during the mercantilist era with the construction of laissez-faire capitalism in early nineteenth-century England. The free market economy is a social construct enacted by the political authority of parliamentary legislation. It rested on the three pillars of free labour, free trade and the gold standard. The Poor Law Amendment Act of 1834 created a free labour market, which liberated the ruling classes from traditional obligations to care for the working population. Free trade was implemented by England by the unilateral repeal of the Corn Laws in 1846, at the sacrifice of domestic agriculture. As an island with a growing population and manufacturing industry, Britain benefited from the unlimited import of food and raw materials to lower the real cost of the subsistence wage. The Bank Charter Act of 1844 empowered the Bank of England as the sole issuer of pound sterling, at a parity with gold which remained unchanged until 1931. As Polanyi famously wrote, 'While laissez-faire economy was the product of deliberate State action, subsequent restrictions on laissez-faire started in a spontaneous way. Laissez-faire was planned; planning was not' (Polanyi, [1944] 2001: 147).

In a brief historical passage, Polanyi noted that initially free trade was a great success, and Britain benefited greatly as the workshop of the world. As the nineteenth-century commercial revolution unfolded, and trans-Atlantic steamships flooded European markets with cheap grain, the livelihood of millions of peasants was threatened with destruction. Polanyi reminds us that the 'European peasant is not a small businessman engaged in agriculture, but a member of a traditional social group bound to the land'. Protective tariffs on imported food were complemented by bounties and other subsidies to industrialists, to offset the increase in the costs of subsistence wages. We remember Bismarck's marriage of rye and iron.

On American exceptionalism

The first three lectures were based on Polanyi's intimate observations of the political and economic events of the inter-war period in Europe. The fourth lecture, titled 'Is America An Exception?', asks whether Europe holds up a mirror to America's future. How did American democracy survive the Great Depression and the unprecedented interventions of the New Deal?

Polanyi rejected the prevailing belief that America would follow the European path. 'The response of a people to the stimulus of change is mainly the result of its internal organisation' and America's was very different from Europe's. Their similarities were limited to the advent of industrial capitalism in the nineteenth century. Some two centuries prior to the industrial revolution, however, Americans had settled a borderless continent with a moving frontier. They were farmers and artisanal manufacturers, and their government was essentially local. The American constitution was designed to favour its states and limit any expansion of the powers of central government. The country was not unified until the mid-nineteenth century, and America existed without a modern national state until the 1930s. This contrasts with Europe, which 'at least since the 16th century possessed a state power on which the actual social system rested'.

If the Roosevelt administration was able to pass the comprehensive New Deal legislation in the 1930s despite Republican opposition and without straining the democratic process, this was, Polanyi pointed out in one of his most acute insights, due to 'the absence of the control of the financial market over the credit of the state itself'. The conflict of White House and Wall Street in the first years of the New Deal, in conjunction with the dropping of the gold standard, may have had greater importance than it is usually credited with. This comment is indeed prophetic of the control of finance to which the American political system would later succumb.

In contrast, the three reforms Europe needed – countercyclical fiscal policy, social security and redistribution of incomes – appeared to threaten property rights. 'Reform was met by panic', financial markets signalled loss of confidence, and 'the reforming government was thrown out of office and the body politic had been forced to give up at any attempt at reform in order to restore confidence'.

It is in concluding this discussion that Polanyi presents his most concise explanation of the triumph of fascism in 1930s Europe:

> The rise of fascism on the European continent was due to the fact that the vitally necessary reform of liberal capitalism could not be carried through under our democratic institutions. Such a reform was inevitable owing to the devastating effects of a separate, self-regulating economic system on the tissue of society.

On the Russian socialist revolution

In the fifth lecture, 'Marxism and the Inner History of the Russian Revolution', Polanyi maintained that the Bolsheviks never intended to implement socialism in 1917. The revolution 'regarded itself as, and actually was, a continuation of the Western revolutions of the 17th, 18th, and 19th Centuries'. The lecture outlines a proposed study on the Russian Revolution from 1917 to the collectivization of agriculture and industrialization through Five-Year Plans. Using original documentation to contest unsatisfactory existing accounts, the study would address the following questions: 'If the October Revolution of 1917 did not aim at introducing socialism into Russia, why did this revolution take on a socialist character, at least for a time? And what connection was there, if any, between the first period of the Russian revolution, 1917–1923, and the Five-Year Plan period dating from 1928, which deliberately aimed at making Russia a socialist country?' Regrettably, this study was never undertaken.

The Russian experience is unique. Occurring in an underdeveloped agrarian economy with a peasantry only recently freed from serfdom, it was informed by Marxist doctrines which accorded a leading role to the working class. Socialism, in all its varieties including Marxism, was historically associated with advanced capitalist economies. According to Marxist doctrine, 'Socialism presupposes an abundant supply of capital in the form of plant and machinery, which cannot be present in a backward agrarian feudal society. No society can pass from feudalism to socialism without having first passed through capitalism', to which Polanyi emphasized that 'There can be no skipping.' The reference here is to the populist Narodniki peasant movement, which believed in the implementation of Communalist institutions and 'denounced the endeavour to introduce capitalism into Russia as a piece of fantastic and immoral pedantry'.

In Polanyi's account, initially the Soviet Union was engaged in a struggle for survival in the face of hostile foreign intervention. War communism was 'a genuine attempt to abolish money and the market and to institute an economy of state-barter' and resulted in the tragedy of famine. Polanyi noted that Lenin declared war communism to be a departure from the teachings of the revolution, and the transition to socialism.

In 1921, the New Economic Policy restored capitalism and the free market system for peasant production. At this stage, with Tsarism gone and the peasants owning the land, Polanyi felt 'Nothing remained to be done but to settle down to some advanced form of agrarian democracy.' However, what followed was constant conflict between the state acting on behalf of the urban working class, and the peasantry. 'Unless this breathing space could be used to bring about a world revolution, the political victory of the peasants could not be prevented, and the power of the industrial workers would have to go. This was the view of Lenin.' The choice seemed to be between the acceptance of a free market economy, or a return to war communism as advocated by Trotsky.

By 1928, the Russian economy had recovered its 1913 pre-war levels, and might have found resolution to its internal conflicts by rejoining the international system. By this time however, the world market was in a process of collapse. Polanyi thus concludes that 'Five Year Plan Russia was thus ultimately the result not of forces operating in Russia alone, but of a general trend at work both inside and outside Russia at the critical period'. Polanyi thereby incorporates the example of Russia into his description of the global transformations that occurred in the 1930s and concludes that '[t]he deliberate establishment of a socialist economy was apparently much more closely related to the Age of Transformation outside Russia than to the overthrow of Tsarism in 1917'.

To add to these external forces, Russia's industrialization was also motivated by the increasing urgency of responding to the threat of invasion by Hitler's armies in the 1930s, and the failure of Soviet diplomacy to enlist support of Britain and France for collective security. In concluding the lecture, Polanyi comments that 'It was the tragedy of Russia, and not of Russia alone, that in spite of the socialist forms of integration the democratic tendency succumbed in the long run to the totalitarian trend.'

The writing of *The Great Transformation*

The first three Bennington Lectures summarize the basic insights and leading concepts of *TGT*. They are the evidence that Polanyi came to the writing of *TGT* with a clear plan in mind. As noted, the first lecture is a detailed preview of the first two chapters of *TGT*. Central to *TGT* was the thesis that never in human history had the economy been disembedded from the social and political matrix as it was in nineteenth-century laissez-faire capitalism. The result was the creation of an 'economic society'. The second lecture refers to the disembedded economy as the separation of the economic from the political sphere. The creation of a market for labour power and the exploitation of nature for profit were countered by societal reactions in what Polanyi called the 'double movement'.

Gareth Dale reminds us that Polanyi owes a debt to the German sociologist, Ferdinand Tönnies for the concept of fictitious commodities and the double movement (Dale, 2008: 497). The expansion of the market and the benefits of the social division of labour are social constructs in the space of *Gesellschaft* (society). They engender counter-movements of resistance to the inhumanity of wage slavery and the abuse of nature in the space of *Gemeinschaft* (community) (ibid.: 496–524). In the Bennington Lectures the separation of the economic and political spheres in market society is discussed in terms of trends towards social integration. This is perhaps preferable to the potentially confusing language of the 'disembedding' and 'embedding' of the economy, which has acquired multiple meanings in contemporary discourse (Polanyi Levitt, 2018: 32–36).

Understanding the relationship between the Bennington Lectures and *TGT* allows for assessing problematic claims on Polanyi's work. Block and Somers claimed that *TGT* was 'written across a period of time when [Polanyi's] thinking was changing', leaving the manuscript with 'contradictions and conflicts' (Block and Somers, 2014: 73). They suggest that Polanyi came to the work with a Marxist approach but then shifted away from it in the course of writing *TGT*. As a result, Polanyi 'glimpsed the idea of the always embedded market economy, but he was not able to give that idea a name or develop it theoretically' (ibid.: 73).

In earlier comments on this issue, I reproduced a letter from my father dated 23 February 1941 (Polanyi Levitt, 2006b: 387). He explains his decision to refrain from further research and expressed that the book was virtually writing itself. Now, the Bennington Lectures show, even more decisively, that Polanyi was clear that nineteenth-century laissez-faire capitalism was historically unprecedented, and that he approached the writing of *TGT* with ideas honed over the previous decades, contrary to the argument of Block and Somers.

However, the occasion presents an opportunity to clarify Polanyi's relationship to Marx. Polanyi shared Marx's insight into the universalization of the market principle, including private ownership of the means of production. Polanyi's account of the consequences of the commodification of money, land and labour recalls Marx's early writing. However, Polanyi rejected Marx's 'too close adherence to Ricardo and the traditions of liberal economics' (Polanyi, [1944] 2001: 131). He did not believe in the Marxian stagiest theories of growth and did not ascribe necessarily to the eventual breakdown of the capitalist order on account of inherent *economic* contradictions. Polanyi instead emphasized the contradictions of the market economy and limitless expansion with its requirement for humans to be sustained by mutually supportive social relations. In this existential contradiction the outcome is not determinate. Polanyi rejected a grand design of progress.

Keynes and the Bretton Woods financial order

Polanyi identified the New Deal in the United States, socialist Five-Year Plans in the Soviet Union, the National Socialist revolution in Germany and a variety of nationalist autarkic regimes across continental Europe as constituting his great transformation. By contrast, pre-war Britain, with never fewer than two million unemployed from the end of the First to the start of the Second World War, did not undergo transformative change in the 1930s.

Unemployment due to the loss of export markets as a result of the First World War was further aggravated by the return of pound sterling to gold at its traditional pre-war value. The resulting overvalued pound sterling favoured the overseas investments of the British rentier leisure classes. In contrast, coal miners were required to work longer and accept wage cuts to maintain pre-war levels of export earnings. The class nature of the exchange rate caused Keynes to comment that the gold standard was 'an essential emblem and idol of those who sit in the top tier of the machine' (Keynes, 1925: 23).

At that time, the British academic establishment did not consider unemployment to be a matter of importance. According to the president of the Royal Economics Society, unemployment was due to the refusal by workers to accept a wage cut.

In the 1920s, Keynes unsuccessfully advocated public works to offset Britain's chronic structural unemployment. His seminal *General Theory of Employment, Interest and Money* (1936) was neither understood nor welcomed by the majority of the UK economics profession. In the early 1930s, Lionel Robbins was instrumental in importing Hayek from Vienna to the London School of Economics, to engage Keynes and his Cambridge friends in intellectual combat. The City was hostile to the inflationary implications of Keynesianism and was believed to have had influence with the administration of the LSE. When I graduated in 1947, Keynes was not on the curriculum.

It was not until Britain was faced with the threat of invasion and Churchill replaced Chamberlain in 1940 that Keynes was called to London to assist in the planning of the war economy and found reluctant acceptance. This was when Britain's own great transformation occurred: the economy was planned, millions of women 'manned' war factories, seventy-two-hour work weeks became common, wages were frozen, and rationing and price-control resulted in substantial improvements in the physical health of the working population.

The social contract implicit in the national engagement in the war effort, together with the equitable management of the war economy, created the determination that the unemployment and insecurity of the pre-war years would never again be tolerated. Churchill asked William Beveridge to draw up a plan for social security 'from cradle to grave' (Beveridge, 1942). On his own initiative, and based on Keynesian principles, Beveridge published proposals for *Full Employment in a Free Society* (1944). The labour market, he stated, should at all times be a sellers' market because involuntary unemployment is an affront to human dignity. The right of employers to own the means of production and employ labour is not an 'essential citizen liberty' because 'it is not and never has been enjoyed by more than a very small proportion of the British people' (ibid.: 21). Full employment and social security became the official national policy objectives of post-war Britain and Western Europe.

Already in 1941, Keynes was designing an international central bank which would permit nations to pursue full employment through capital controls. Keynes was appointed by Churchill to represent Britain at the 1944 Bretton Woods conference, and his innovative proposal for an International Clearing Union became Britain's official negotiating position. As a country with external payment deficits, it did not wish to be forced to undertake structural adjustment by deflationary compression of demand. However, Keynes was at a disadvantage on account of Britain's unresolved war debt to the US. High on the American agenda for the post-war order was the elimination of the Sterling Bloc and the preferential British Commonwealth system. The American Bankers' Association and the US Congress were hostile to Bretton Woods, and Keynes conceded on almost all points in order to conclude an agreement. When he considered that further concessions would violate the purpose of the reforms, Keynes offered his resignation, which was accepted by Churchill. The British government supported his position and refused to sign the agreement.

In late 1945, the newly elected Labour government sent Keynes to Washington to negotiate the conditions of the American Loan to cover Britain's war debt. It was believed that the American ally would write down some of the debt in light of the circumstances that gave rise to it. Contrary to such expectations, the terms of the loan were unfavourable, and the Americans required full convertibility of the pound sterling, including the Sterling Bloc balances of India and other wartime sources of supply. A good half of the loan vanished in a few days of convertibility as unblocked creditors withdrew funds (which the blocked creditors, India, Egypt and some Latin American countries could not do) and exchange controls were reinstituted. The conditions of the loan agreement, including Britain's signature of the Bretton Woods agreement, were met with disapproval from the right and the left, and Keynes's defence of the American loan may have contributed to his untimely death in 1946. Though the US succeeded, Britain's great transformation ensured the post-war Keynesian welfare state.

Ultimately, Keynes believed that capitalism, if well managed, was the best social and economic system available. He believed that 'the great problem of the age is to free modern industrialism from the fetters of financial capitalism' (Dillard, 1948: 117). He looked forward to the euthanasia of the rentier because he believed there would soon be no need for net national savings for economic growth. Indeed, he expected that the generation of his grandchildren would have to work only fifteen hours per week to enjoy a lifestyle permitting more leisure and freedom to pursue a variety of interests. Though most post-Keynesian theorists assume that economic growth is a necessary goal for society, Keynes himself did not share this view.

America's rise to world power

Younger American economists, many employed in the New Deal apparatus, including John Kenneth Galbraith, greeted the Keynesian revolution with excitement, invited Keynes to visit US universities and sought his advice. The New Deal, however, was not influenced by Keynes: it was Roosevelt's pragmatic response to a disastrous 50 per cent decline of industrial output, mass unemployment, heavy loss of agricultural markets and failures of thousands of banks. This response, which included labour rights and collective bargaining; a minimum wage; unemployment insurance and old age security; deposit insurance for retail banking; and mortgage finance for social housing, defended the interests of main street, not Wall Street. Soon after he assumed office, Roosevelt declared a one-week bank holiday. No bail-out assistance was offered to failing banks.

As Polanyi noted in the fourth lecture, the massive public works and other public expenditures, together with the comprehensive nature of the legislative and administrative infrastructure of the New Deal, transformed Washington from its original minimalist role to an effective modern state. It set America on a new social and economic course of partnership with industrial capital and organized labour.

When Roosevelt was re-elected in 1936, the economy had recovered but unemployment was still high. It was not until the Japanese attack on Pearl Harbour brought the United States into the war that the labour demand exceeded supply. The post-New Deal American state was, however, remarkably effective in mobilizing resources for America's massive war production, though special relationships between the state and the private sector created what President Eisenhower would call the military-industrial complex.

With Allied victory in sight, widely held fears of a return to pre-war mass unemployment cast a long shadow over a return to peacetime. In his State of the Union address of 1944, Roosevelt affirmed his vision for post-war America, in the form of a second bill of social and economic rights to complement the American constitution. He expressed his conviction that 'true individual freedom' was not possible without 'economic security and independence'. Roosevelt's initiative in convening the 1944 Bretton Woods conference, followed by the San Francisco conference which founded the United Nations in April 1945, established America's leading role in shaping the post-war international order.

The emergence of the United States as leader of the Western world was due more to circumstance than to a predestined role. While other major powers suffered devastating losses of material and human resources, the United States gained significantly in economic strength from the Second World War. As victory in Europe was celebrated in 1945, the United States identified the Soviet Union as the dominant military and ideological threat to the West. In this contest, America was at an advantage as the primary source of economic resources to assist reconstruction and revive international trade. The defeated countries were folded into the US security system in Europe and Asia.

In Western Europe laissez-faire capitalism was generally discredited as the cause of mass unemployment and war. Important industries were nationalized. Most Western countries adopted some form of national economic planning. There was considerable support for communist parties, most notably in France and Italy. While the reconstruction of war-damaged Europe was achieved by the mobilization of domestic resources, a chronic dollar shortage was alleviated by economic assistance extended by the United States on highly favourable terms. The Marshall Plan was designed to offset Soviet influence and secure markets for American industry, and from 1948 to 1952 assistance averaged 2 per cent of US GDP, approximately equalling the capital flight from Europe during and after the war.

In Asia, American concerns of Soviet influence took the form of direct military engagement in Korea and subsequently in Vietnam. Following the victory over Japan, the United States initially attempted to dismantle Japan's industrial and war capacity, but later suspended it to transform Japan into a logistical supply base for American military operations.

The US may have succeeded in tying Europe and Japan to itself, but Asia and Africa were a different matter. There, beginning with the 1955 Bandung Conference and progressing to the Non-Aligned Movement (NAM), the newly independent world set out 'to complete the reconquest of their sovereignty by moving into a process of authentic and accelerated inward-looking development, which is the condition for their participating in the shaping of the world system on equal footing with the States of the historic imperialist centres' (Amin, 2017: 609–619). This peaked in the early 1970s when the NAM supported OPEC price hikes and initiated the call by the UN General Assembly for a New International Economic Order. Following extensive international negotiations, the Western powers definitively rejected this initiative.

In retrospect, the rejection of laissez-faire capitalism in the 1930s, which Polanyi named the great transformation, can be extended to embrace the Bretton Woods order of the first three post-war decades. In this era of historic compromise of capital and labour, also known as the Keynesian consensus, the gains of productivity growth were shared. In the United States, this was rooted in the social contract of the New Deal, which recognized organized labour together with business as partners of the government. In Western Europe, where trade unions were historically well established, wage bargaining frequently took place at the national industry level in the context of social partnership. Both developed and developing countries witnessed a remarkable increase in the material standard of living. In the late 1960s in the United States, the earnings of a blue-collar worker could equal or exceed those of a manager in the late 1940s (Levy and Kochan, 2012: 739–764).

From the 1960s onward, the United States was the driver of the technological innovation that created what came to be known as the American way of life. The motor vehicle played a central role in this Fordist era of mass production for mass consumption. It required the construction of highways and encouraged suburban home ownership, the acquisition of labour-saving domestic appliances, shopping malls, supermarkets and bulk retail. At the same time, advertising, product differentiation, constant novelty and planned obsolescence contributed to the increasing commercialization of daily life. All of this created a consumer society and a new middle class. The aspiration to this lifestyle in the developing world constituted the soft power of American imperialism.

Strong economic growth peaked in the 1960s in the United States. Slowing growth and reduced competitiveness combined with war expenditures, foreign investment by US multinational companies and strong domestic demand for imports demand resulted in ever-larger external payment deficits and outflow of gold reserves. Unwilling to implement structural adjustment, President Nixon suspended gold convertibility of the dollar in 1971 and major currencies floated against each other from 1973. From this time onward, the United States enjoyed the unique privilege of seigniorage in making external payments with its national currency, and the US dollar became the principal international reserve currency. To protect the value of money, the Federal Reserve raised the interest rate to 20 per cent in 1979 to dampen inflationary expectations in the so-called Volker shock.

The Bretton Woods era was over, and the decade was marked by unprecedented inflation. Keynesian policies appeared ineffective in these conditions, contributing to the increasing appeal of market-oriented solutions, paving the way for the neoliberal counter-revolution.

The neoliberal counter-revolution

Polanyi's *The Great Transformation* and Hayek's *The Road to Serfdom* were both published in 1944, in the United States and Great Britain respectively. *The Road to Serfdom* was motivated by fears that post-war economic planning was the road to Socialism (Hayek, [1944] 2001). It argued that any form of economic planning is a step towards collectivist totalitarianism. The association of freedom of choice with optimal market outcomes is Hayek's seminal contribution to the ideology of the neoliberal counter-revolution.

Upon publication, Hayek's book was largely ignored in Britain, but with its reproduction in *Reader's Digest* it found favour among American Republicans and businessmen. In 1947, Hayek convened the Mount Pelerin Society, a transnational thought collective of like-minded intellectuals who opposed planning (Mirowski and Plehwe, 2009). Initial members were principally European, but Hayek's 1950 appointment at the University of Chicago, together with the installation of his mentor Ludwig von Mises at the Foundation for Economic Education, served to extend participation to American academics and businessmen (Polanyi Levitt, 2013b: 23–38).

The Mount Pelerin Society launched a systematic campaign to win influence by engaging journalists to popularize its views beyond the academy. As neoliberal ideology gained influence in the business community, think-tanks in the United States were established to design market-friendly policies. Hayek was awarded the Nobel Prize (shared with Gunnar Myrdal) in 1974, followed by a Nobel for Milton Friedman in 1976.

By the end of the 1970s, business-financed think-tanks and university research institutes had furnished the political and economic directorates of the West with theoretical justification for neoliberal policies of monetarism, liberalization, deregulation, privatization, balanced budgets and 'independent' central banks.

As anticipated by the Polish Marxist economist Michal Kalecki, three decades of full employment had strengthened the position of labour and diminished the power of capital (Kalecki, 1943). The oil price shocks of 1973 and 1979, persistent inflation and the associated price–wage spiral diminished business profitability in the 1970s. The Volcker shock of 1979 and the consequent recession served to restore the discipline of unemployment in the labour market.

With the election of Prime Minister Thatcher in 1979 and President Reagan in 1980, Hayek had achieved his objective of turning the ideological clock back to the pre-Keynesian era. In Britain, where strong unions often won wage increases above productivity growth in the 1970s, Thatcher launched an attack on organized labour, and privatized industries, utilities and Britain's large stock of council houses. Hayek personally advised Thatcher, who praised his *Constitution of Liberty* as the type of constitution necessary to protect the market economy from democratic legislation (Hayek, 1960).

The Reagan administration cut taxes on the rich. Though the neoliberal Laffer Curve purported to show that lower taxes on high incomes would create investment and growth sufficient to offset lost revenue, in reality Reagan offset lost revenues through borrowing and regressive sales taxes. Individuals and corporations that previously had to pay taxes were now owners of bonds that yielded interest.

In the mid-1980s at the World Bank, the departure of eminent development economists and their replacement by international trade theorists signalled a policy shift from support for Basic Human Needs and domestic industrialization to export-oriented development. Development economics was dismissed as structuralist, a heresy bordering on socialism. Mainstream economic theory was held to be universally applicable to all countries, rich and poor.

By the end of the 1980s, the neoliberal counter-revolution had succeeded in re-establishing the discipline of capital over labour by undermining the social contract that sustained the Keynesian consensus of the thirty golden years.

The victory of the West in the Cold War and the implosion of the Soviet Union in 1991 marked a political watershed. The Western powers had illusions of the end of history. Thatcher declared that there is no alternative to capitalism ('TINA'). In 1994, there appeared a word we had never heard before: 'globalization'. The word could not be found in the shorter Oxford dictionary, nor in computer spell-checks of that time. The World Development Report of 1995, *Workers in an Integrating World*, greeted globalization as inevitable and beneficial to workers in advanced and developing countries alike, provided they conform to the neoliberal Washington

Consensus. Language matters. When the word 'global' is used to replace 'international', what disappears from view is the nation. When globalization replaces international interdependence what disappears is internationalism, or cooperation between nations. This is not accidental. As noted by James Galbraith, the term 'globalization' 'emerged from nowhere at that time and for a reason: to cast a light of benign inevitability over the project of Western hegemony offered up as the future following the collapse of the USSR' (Galbraith, 2019: 30).

Economic globalization is best understood in terms of the ability of large transnational corporations to construct international supply chains and other economic linkages within corporate structure. Through globalization, these international structures of private economic power have escaped national regulation by circumventing what Wolfgang Streeck has called the 'national cage' (Streeck, 2017: 5).

Globalization has delivered on its promise of creating winners and losers. The biggest winner has been China, which has achieved a revolutionary economic transformation, drawing millions into industrial employment for export markets, resulting in massive poverty reduction. As described by Dani Rodrik, China and other East Asian countries 'played the globalization game by different rules. They opened their markets only partially, governing the pace and impact of economic integration with interventions ranging from subsidies for favored industries to controls over cross-border capital flows' (Rodrik, 2017: 1).

As Richard Kozul-Wright, the principal author of the 2017 UNCTAD Trade and Development Report, concluded, the dominant force shaping the trajectory of the global economy since the 1990s has been neither trade nor technology but finance.

In his 1979 Nobel Lecture on 'The Slowing Down of the Engine of Growth', Sir Arthur Lewis drew attention to a trend that has continued to the present. In the OECD countries economic growth has slowed decade by decade since 1970, and slow growth has become 'the new normal' (Galbraith, 2014). From 1980, median wages stagnated and increasing gains from productivity accrued predominantly to capital. With slowing economic growth and diminished purchasing power of the masses, opportunities in the real economy declined, channelling investment increasingly into financial claims.

Large complex financial institutions – ranging from banks, bond investors and pension funds to big insurers and speculative hedge funds – together with the insurance and real estate industries now account for some 20 per cent of GDP in the advanced countries.

The iconic American corporation of the early post-war era was known for the products it produced. It sought to increase long-term profits by expanding sales, retaining earnings and reinvesting in real capital formation. The difference in remuneration between management and common labour was in the order of 40 to 1, and there was low turnover of staff (Lazonick, 2014). The profitability problems of the 1970s resulted in the progressive financialization of the corporation. Maximizing shareholder value replaced long-term profitability as the metric for successful management, and this was achieved by the downsizing of labour, the buyback of stock and the acquisition of companies with liquid assets. Instead of 'retain and reinvest', companies distribute earnings to shareholders who are increasingly not individuals but complex financial institutions. Real investment has diminished and the difference in remuneration between management and labour is now in the order of 400 to 1 (ibid.).

Banks too have become financialized. Whereas they once acted as intermediaries in channelling household savings to finance investment in the real economy, today they lend to households to sustain effective demand. As borrowing supplements incomes, financialization is transforming household budgets. Family incomes are more dependent on financial transactions. Pensions, traditionally designated in terms of previous income, have become ever more dependent on stock market earnings. Personal savings take the form of contributions to pension, investment or mutual funds. Additionally, there is a massive growth in credit card and student debt. Financial capital is directly exploiting the population in the sphere of circulation. Financialization 'has allowed the ethics, morality and mindset of finance to penetrate into the deepest recesses of social and individual life', reflected in the pervasiveness of short-term and consumerist thinking (Lapavitsas, 2009: 116). Today, World Bank economists lend their support to extending financialization to the poorest 40 per cent of households in the belief that 'financial inclusion allows people to make many everyday financial transactions more efficiently' (Storm, 2018: 308).

While the 2008 financial crisis was not unexpected by some observers, the mainstream economics profession erroneously believed in the ability of financial markets to accurately judge the risks associated with financial interests, as admitted by Alan Greenspan (Financial Crisis Inquiry Commission, 2010). The crisis is described by Palma as the outcome of 'an attempt to use neo-liberalism as a new technology of power to help transform capitalism into a rentiers' delight' (Palma, 2009: 833). It was seen as the most serious crisis since the Great Depression of the 1930s, and the meltdown of the world financial system was averted by massive government support. Very little has changed. The liberalization of capital flows has continued.

According to Giovanni Arrighi, successive great hegemons in decline – from Genoa and the Dutch Republic to Britain and the United States – consolidated territorial gains by financialization (Arrighi, 2010). This made Amsterdam the financial capital of Europe, the city of London the financial capital of the world and Wall Street the financial centre of American empire. The Great Financialization and the proliferation of financial centres may therefore be symbolic in indicating the decline of American political hegemony and its rise to a global financial empire.

Neoliberalism has regressed to a predatory rentier capitalism. The acquisition of existing assets, both financial and real, for the purpose of receiving a stream of rentier income, has displaced investment in productive activity in the real economy. In the current recovery from the global crisis, declining unemployment has not resulted in increasing wages (Chandrasekhar, 2018). Such 'wageless growth' also reflects the increase in involuntary temporary and precarious work and a decline in regular full-time employment. Moreover, unregulated markets have aggravated ecological damage resulting in a deteriorating environment and runaway climate change while restricting public revenues required to fulfil climate commitments. Financialization has corrupted the political process of representative government resulting in a loss of legitimacy of the democratic system. The Neoliberal Utopia has created the Illiberal Democracies.

Our present age of transformation

Some five years after Polanyi delivered the Bennington Lectures in the peaceful surroundings of Vermont, Europe had undergone a geopolitical transformation. At the sacrifice of over twenty million casualties, principally civilian, Soviet armies defeated and rolled back Hitler's divisions while British and Commonwealth forces engaged the Germans in Italy, North Africa and ultimately on the Western Front. The post-war division of Europe into spheres of influence was negotiated by Churchill, Stalin and Roosevelt in conferences held in Tehran (November 1943), Yalta (February 1945) and Potsdam (July 1945). The terms of Allied occupation effectively divided Europe between East and West, with Austria declared neutral by the peace terms imposed on the country.

On 8 May 1945, we celebrated victory over fascism in Europe on VE Day in London. We did not imagine that the wartime alliance would unravel so quickly, nor did we know that hostilities had begun even before the war was over. On 6 August the Americans dropped the atomic bomb on Hiroshima, followed by a second on 9 August on Nagasaki. Polanyi called this 'scientific barbarism' (Polanyi, 1947: 117). At that time, negotiations with Japan of the terms of surrender were well advanced. The major issue to be resolved was the retention of the emperor. The evidence suggests that the demonstration of the power of the A-bomb was intended to send a message to Russia that the Americans were not reluctant to use it on civilian populations.

Our present age in historical perspective

To gain a perspective on possible futures we roll the canvas of history back to 1820, the year for which the economic historian Angus Maddison has provided us with data representing the birth of the machine age (Maddison Project, 2018). Prior to the Renaissance and the Iberian Voyages, there were no significant differences in the average living standards of the common people on the Eurasian continent. In the mercantilist era (1500–1800), Western economic progress owed more to overseas trade and conquest than to domestic technological advances. In the age of Adam Smith, China was respected as the oldest and most advanced civilization, but stationary and lacking dynamism. Its production was believed to equal that of Western and Eastern Europe combined, including Russia (33 per cent), while all of Asia accounted for some 60 per cent of world output.

Given the importance Polanyi ascribed to the advent of the machine age, he would surely have agreed with the Brazilian historian Celso Furtado that the industrial revolution was a 'genuine mutation', or a 'historical accident', as Paul Bairoch described it, of significance equalling the Neolithic Revolution which transformed hunter-gatherers to cultivators of the soil (Furtado, 1978; Bairoch, 1995). Industry was transformed from its traditional artisanal mode to the application of alienated labour power to machinery. The resulting system of industrial capitalism produced historically unprecedented increases in material wealth. In the 130 years from 1820 to 1950, world production increased six-fold and world population more than doubled. Over the same period, Western technological and imperial dominance raised the Western share of world output from 25 per cent to 57 per cent; these benefits accrued to less than 20 per cent of the world population. By 1950, Asia's share of world production was less than 20 per cent and China's was reduced to less than 5 per cent. In the second half of the twentieth century and continuing to the present, Asia is returning to the importance it occupied before the advent of industrial capitalism. Today, in purchasing power parity terms, China's economy is second only to the United States, and in 2018 Asia's estimated 45 per cent share exceeded the 39 per cent share of the West.

As we approach the year 2020, we undertake a review of 200 years since the birth of industrial capitalism. We compare nineteenth-century liberal capitalism, which collapsed in the Great Depression, with its briefer neoliberal reincarnation from 1980 to the present.

In the long nineteenth century, from 1815 to the 1930s, Britain was the undisputed hegemonic power of the world until forced to abandon gold convertibility in 1931. During the last three decades of the nineteenth century, British supremacy was challenged by late industrializers and rival imperialist powers, paving the way to the Great War. Efforts by Western powers to re-establish the pre-1914 order failed, resulting in the World Economic Crisis (1929–33) and Polanyi's great transformation. From this time until the emergence of the United States as leader of the West in a post-war bipolar world order, there was no world hegemon.

In the first Bennington Lecture on the collapse of nineteenth-century civilization, Polanyi suggested that the transformative changes of the 'revolutionary 1930s' could shape the post-war world. Polanyi stated that 'by the end of the Twenties, change surged forth in a vast transformation'.

Polanyi's great transformation, followed by three decades of the Keynesian consensus, can collectively be seen as an epoch of resistance to the unregulated market. It can also be perceived as a half century interlude (1930–80) in the expansion of market capitalism from the industrial revolution to the present age of globalization. The era of neoliberalism (1980 to the present) appears as a counter-revolution to the historic compromise when gains from productivity and growth were shared by capital and labour.

Some scholars argue that economic change is a pendulum which swings between surges of expansion and counter-movements of resistance to market forces. This implies the capacity of effective political intervention by the state. However, we remind the reader that the three post-war decades of the Keynesian consensus were a response to the Great Depression and a war that consumed an estimated 30 million lives. A more likely outcome of neoliberal globalization is an ecological and financial crash on a scale exceeding the crisis of 2007–8.

Polanyi insisted that nineteenth-century laissez-faire was established by state legislation and accompanied by the liberal creed of the self-regulating market. Prior to the First World War, franchise was limited to propertied classes. In Britain, classical Liberals like Keynes and Beveridge were social reformers, and American Liberals supported anti-trust legislation to break up monopolies. For neoliberals, the role of the state is to deconstruct the social security system in order to create new spaces for market expansion. The most important instrument to moderate the concentration of private economic power, and to provide universally available public services, is the power to tax. The intended effect of neoliberalism is precisely the dismantling of progressive tax systems and the privatization of public services and infrastructure.

Karl Polanyi has returned to public discourse due in part to comparisons of the

2008 financial crisis with the Great Depression of the 1930s. International finance played an important role in both cases but the parallels that are drawn are simplistic, and the outcomes are very different. Since 1980, increased productivity combined with stagnant wages has led to increasing inequality. In the heartlands of capitalism, effective demand, even when enhanced by borrowing, is insufficient to sustain profitable investment in the real economy. Investment in financial assets is more attractive to capital than investment in the real economy, and real capital formation is in decline. Neoliberalized capitalism has more in common with the crisis of overproduction and declining profitability of the late nineteenth century known as the Long Depression (1873–96) than with the World Economic Crisis of the 1930s.

The Geneva School: a conversation with Karl Polanyi

We promised the reader a conversation with Karl Polanyi. Regrettably, there is no telephone number where he can be reached. We inform him of the success of his intellectual rival and contemporary, Mises. In an important book, Quinn Slobodian (2018) describes a Central European account of the birth and rise of neoliberalism which is less well known than the Atlanticist version associated with the Chicago School previously discussed.

From Mises's seminar room located at the Austrian Chamber of Commerce on the Ringstrasse, he gathered modest support for what appeared to be a hopeless challenge to socialist Red Vienna. He found comfort in the failure of the Socialists to respond to the events of 1927 when the police opened fire on a crowd of protesting workers, killing eighty-nine people (ibid.: 30).

In Geneva, the presence of the League of Nations, the Graduate Institute of International Studies and a variety of other international organizations created a forum for debate on the post-Empire reconstruction of Europe. Mises moved to Geneva in 1934, and collaborated with fellow Austrians – Hayek, Fritz Machlup and Gottfried Haberler – and other Mont Pelerin associates including Lionel Robbins, Wilhelm Röpke and Michael Heilperin. This 'Geneva Group' was concerned with recreating the freedom of trade and capital movement of the pre-1914 order, driven by fears that the economic aspirations of self-reliance of the new nation states constituted a threat to private property. They advocated for 'encasing' private property and markets in law 'to inoculate capitalism against democracy' (ibid.: 2). For global capital, national borders fulfil a necessary function but 'the task is to weaken the nation state as an agent of economic redistribution' (Streeck, 2019: 837).

The new small nation states of Central Europe had neither the advantage of a large domestic market like that of the United States, nor overseas empire like that of

England or France. The concern was thus with securing the advantages of division of labour on a world scale.

While the Atlantic version of neoliberalism was a retaliation against Keynesian economics, Geneva School neoliberalism was driven by fears of socialism and disposition of property. Fundamentally, Geneva School neoliberalism was less a discipline of economics than a discipline of statecraft and law (Slobodian, 2018: 11). They did not believe in *homo economicus*, a borderless world, nor any form of world government. They did believe that there is a positive role for national governments in matters including culture and language, but sovereignty should not extend to economic affairs. International law should secure the recognition of property rights. They appropriated the language of human rights to claim the right of capital to exit a country with full compensation.

At the core of the Geneva School ideology is the idea that 'Globalism trumps nationalism. Only capitalism is internationalist; socialism is always nationalist' (ibid.: 271). The emergence of financialized rentier capitalism, where finance – the most abstract form of capital – drives the globalized economy is a testament to the fact that some one century after the Social Accounting Debates, the globalists have won … this round.

The security of private property and the mobility of capital are now firmly recognized, implemented and enforced through international legal frameworks. In the era of globalization, the General Agreement on Tariffs and Trade was transformed into the World Trade Organization (WTO), which enforces competition in world markets with no concessions favouring weaker countries of the Global South.

The neoliberal state is a very active state in constructing this international framework which has pried open national economies, increasing dependence on international trade. Neoliberal states have created a complex network of agreements: from 1990 to 2018, the number of Regional Trade Agreements grew from a mere 25 to 465 (WTO). Additionally, states have negotiated some 4,000 Bilateral Investment Treaties which serve to protect foreign investors from labour, environmental and other protective legislation in the host countries. All of this requires the employment of a small army of professional lawyers, economists, statisticians, accountants and other technocrats by the participating states.

The Geneva Group ideologically opposed the United Nations system because it granted every member country one vote. In collaboration with the International Chamber of Commerce, it aborted the International Trade Organization, opposed the New International Economic Order and destroyed United Nations efforts to regulate transnational corporations. Wolfgang Streeck suggested that the long view of the Geneva School can only be compared to 'the Bolsheviks under Lenin … who were in many ways the only serious competitors of Hayek and his combatants until their final defeat in 1989' (Streeck, 2019: 839).

The double movement in the neoliberal era

Like many other admirers of the work of Karl Polanyi, I often wonder what his unique way of thinking can tell us about possible futures for humanity in the twenty-first century. Perhaps the Bennington Lectures can initiate such an inquiry.

Though the Bennington Lectures do not refer to the 'double movement', they do refer to a 'protective counter-move of society against laissez-faire' exemplified by the Ten-Hour Bill, the Consumer Cooperatives and the birth of the trade union movement. Contrary to Thatcher's statement that there is no such thing as society, Polanyi ascribes agency to society in the form of social counter-movements to protect social cohesion and the natural environment from the impact of market expansion. Streeck observed that capitalism requires counter-movements to market expansion to prevent the destruction of its non-capitalist foundations (Streeck, 2014b: 50). Schumpeter (1942) made a similar observation regarding capitalism's dependence on the pillars of traditional social values. According to Streeck, the role of social democracy is to prevent capitalism from destroying itself, after which it becomes redundant (Streeck, 2019: 838).

Where is the double movement today? The failure of social democratic parties to offer effective opposition to neoliberal policies is a tribute to the success of the neoliberal ideology in appropriating the socialist tradition of internationalism. The appeal of identity politics across the class divide and the prioritization of electoral success have supplanted the traditional role of socialist parties in defending the working class. Tony Blair and Bill Clinton acted as cheerleaders for globalization while French socialist Delors initiated the European liberalization of cross-border capital movements (Rodrik, 2018).

Whereas Polanyi had argued that Washington was able to implement the New Deal legislation because it was free from 'the control of the financial market over the credit of the state itself', today, as Simon Johnson (2009) has noted, the great majority of states are captive of the undue influence of financial capital. There is a constraint on what is politically feasible, and opposition parties tend towards the political centre. This has stopped the double movement from manifesting itself at the legislative level.

Forty years of neoliberal consumerism have conditioned populations into possessive individualist thinking, in what Bauman called 'Liquid Modernity'. This has eroded social solidarity. The failure of social democratic political parties has increased the importance of social movements in offering local solutions. Local food systems aim to reduce dependence on industrial agriculture, through community and rooftop gardens, land banks, Via Campesina and the advocacy of food sovereignty. New forms of urban living, including comprehensive systems of public transport and restrictions on the use of private automobiles, aim to reduce carbon emissions. Cooperative social housing counters gentrification, which prioritizes real estate value and disembeds social relations within long-established communities. The objective of these and other social movements is the re-embedding of economic activity in societal relations of solidarity and cooperation. They are examples of counter-movements in a Polanyian context.

The most challenging problem facing social and solidarity economy projects is the increasingly precarious nature of work.

A new class divide and the false integration of illiberal democracy

In the second Bennington Lecture, Polanyi addresses social integration, or the embedding of economic activity in social life. The financialized globalization of the 1990s generated winners and losers. Accelerated de-industrialization by digital information technology has created the new phenomenon of a de-industrialized working class. Job losses are not confined to manufacturing but also affect transportation, distribution and all other service industries.

My wake-up call came in 2016 when the reactionary nationalist candidate almost won the Austrian presidential election, with the support of working-class areas of Vienna that had traditionally voted Social Democrat. After this, the Brexit vote and the election of Trump were not surprising. Support for Brexit came from the industrial towns of the Midlands and Northern England where factories had closed, good employment disappeared, communities were impoverished and the working class felt a genuine sense of loss. The predominantly middle-class London and the Home Counties overwhelmingly voted to remain in the EU. In the United States, a similar class divide of winners and losers created the political base for the rise of Trump. Both in England and the US, the educated professional elites in urban centres dismissed the former industrial workers with scorn and contempt and characterized them as ignorant and racist 'deplorables'. The new economic divide is also an educational and cultural divide. Today, as automation is displacing labour in all industries, digital literacy and a high level of education are becoming essential to earning a living wage.

Many have invoked Karl Polanyi in comparing the populist politics of our time with 1930s fascism. While the comparison is valid, we must be cautious about using the term 'populism'. In North America, the populists of the nineteenth century were the militant miners, loggers, the IWW Wobblies and also farmers of the Western Regions who opposed exploitation by the financiers and robber barons of the Eastern seaboard. Today's populists are the de-industrial workers and losers from technological advance and globalization, who look to the past and provide the base for nationalist politics. Regrettably, the left has abandoned its traditional role of defending the working class. It has enabled populist right-wing leaders to appear as champions of the now de-industrialized working class and as defenders of the nation.

We remind the reader that Polanyi wished to title his masterwork *The Liberal Utopia*, suggesting that the liberal creed of the self-regulating market was unachievable. Today, the global neoliberal utopia is equally unachievable and has given us the Illiberal Democracies. The false integration of illiberal democracy signals a deficit of societal integration. Only integrated societies can successfully sustain genuine democratic governance.

The nation state in the global economy

In the third Bennington Lecture, Polanyi drew attention to the increasing importance of the nation state in the nineteenth-century capitalist order. He explained that there is no such thing as a world market distinct and separate from the national economies which together constitute an international market. In reflections on the Asian crisis of 1997, Dani Rodrik recalled Karl Polanyi's important insight 'that markets could not exist outside the web of social relations for long without tragic consequences' (Rodrik, 1998: 17). Contrary to general belief, Rodrik stated that 'we have never had a global capitalist system … Capitalism is, and will remain, a national phenomenon' (ibid.: 17). Rodrik insists that nation states are absolutely essential to globalization because they provide public goods, ranging from law enforcement to macroeconomic stabilization, needed for open markets to thrive, and for the construction of international supply chains (Rodrik, 2017: 1).

In 1860, historical rivals France and Britain concluded a free trade agreement. The following decade saw the consolidation and unification of the nation state in Germany, Italy, Russia, the United States and Canada. These late industrializers emerged to challenge British free trade hegemony and created the nineteenth-century world market. In the closing decades of the nineteenth century, protectionism became the common way to expand national industries, and world growth exceeded that of the earlier free trade era dominated by Britain (Bairoch, 1995).

Japan's defeat of the Russian navy in 1905 was the first victory of an Asian nation over a Western power. It reverberated from Persia (Iranian Revolution of 1905) to

China (Revolution of 1911). From the ruins of the Ottoman Empire, aspirations to national sovereignty culminated in revolutions of independence in Turkey and in Egypt in 1919. The decolonization of British and other Western empires, following the Second World War, resulted in the accession of Asian and African states to political independence. They were all built on the conviction that an effective modern nation state is essential for inclusive and sustainable economic and social development.

Dani Rodrick framed the well-known 'trilemma': among hyper-globalization, national sovereignty and effective democracy, only two can be attained at once (Rodrik, 2007). In reality, the political process operates exclusively at the national level. People can influence the outcome of national elections; they have no say or control over corporate or financial global giants, nor over supranational organizations. There cannot be meaningful democracy, liberal or illiberal, in the absence of sufficient policy space to determine and achieve national objectives. Keynes insisted on capital controls over all external payments to protect national sovereignty. Neoliberal policy favours freedom of international capital flows at the expense of national sovereignty and meaningful democracy. As Polanyi explained in the third lecture, as globalization intensifies, the nation state behaves as a 'shock absorber' protecting society from the disruptive impact of trade and capital flows. He concluded that 'Modern nationalism is a protective reaction against the dangers inherent in an interdependent world' (Polanyi, [1940] 2017: 24).

Geopolitical shift towards a multi-polar world?

At the time of the Bennington Lectures, Polanyi considered the American New Deal and Soviet Five-Year Plans as transformative responses to the menace of fascism in Europe. In the twenty-first century, the Soviet Union is history and the US is in decline, with the President of the Council on Foreign Relations proclaiming that the US era of dominance is over and 'the principal characteristic of twenty-first century international relations is turning out to be non-polarity' (Haass, 2008: 44).

We are now living in a dangerously disordered world. The West continues to act with imperial arrogance in its military and other international interventions. In this new age, no single state has a political hegemony, and the world is dominated by multiple actors exercising economic and political power. The contest between a multiplicity of powers is eerily reminiscent of the atmosphere that preceded the First World War (Escobar, 2018). There is a proliferation of weapons of mass destruction and former hegemonic powers are exhibiting symptoms of failed states. In our disordered world, the stakes are much higher than those before 1914.

Contrary to general belief, it is not the proliferation of weapons of mass destruction by 'terrorists' and 'rogue states' that constitute the gravest danger to peace and the future of humanity, but rather the vast nuclear arsenals of the former Cold War adversaries, the United States and Russia. The 2019 decision by President Trump to withdraw from the Intermediate-Range Nuclear Forces Treaty followed by Russia is a reminder that the dangers of a nuclear exchange, possibly by accident, would result in a devastating death toll and a nuclear winter which could block the Sun from sustaining life on Earth. To alert the world, the Bulletin of Atomic Scientists moved the Doomsday Clock closer to midnight than at any time since the Cuban Missile Crisis of the 1960s. We would be wise to remember that in 1913 nobody believed that an incident in Sarajevo could result in a major European war.

The trend towards economic multi-polarity is reminiscent of Polanyi's 1945 vision of regional blocs corresponding to historic and cultural commonalities. In his day, his vision for the post-war world was the coexistence of the United States, the Soviet Union, the British Commonwealth, China and India in arrangements of negotiated and managed international trade (Polanyi, 1945: 86–91).

Late in life, in a letter addressed to an old friend of his youth, Karl Polanyi wrote that his work was for the 'New Nations of Asia and Africa'. He hoped that these countries would not follow Rostow's stages of capitalist development which rested on the assumption of the 'economizing' behaviour of *homo economicus* and would instead take a substantivist approach to economic institutions with reciprocity and redistribution as well as exchange as patterns of economic integration.

In the new millennium, but especially since the 2008 financial crisis, world growth is shifting from West to East. China's historic industrial revolution of the past decades was accompanied by a major and ongoing transformation in international economic and financial governance with new institutions emerging. They include the Belt and Road Initiative, the Asian Infrastructure Investment Bank, the BRICS Development Bank and other examples of South–South cooperation that reflect the growing importance of the developing world. China's development has both benefited from and contributed to the economic development of other developing countries.

With the exception of the southern periphery of the United States (Mexico, Central America and the Caribbean), the recovery of the developing world from the financial crisis of 2007–8 was more rapid and complete than in the heartlands of capitalism; very few developing countries requested IMF assistance. The financial crisis expanded the policy space for innovative development, including 'a growing diversity of financial architectures across the global South' (Chang and Grabel, 2014: 31). In this shifting landscape, we share the hopes of Samir Amin for a renewal of the Bandung spirit, where the states of Latin America and the Caribbean can join Africa and Asia in a united front to resist neo-colonialism and neoliberal globalization (Amin, 2017).

Although Polanyi envisaged a world order shaped by regional economic planning, regional integration in many cases has not turned out to be the unifying force once anticipated. The European Union project shows that free trade and capital flows without social security and fiscal integration can restrict the sovereignty of member countries and give rise to nationalist resentment. Perhaps the European Union today resembles the schemes of the Geneva Group to recreate the Habsburg Empire in the form of a Federation of European States, which would secure freedom of capital from the jurisdiction of member countries.

Existential civilizational challenges

Polanyi often expressed his fears that humankind may not survive the machine age and what he called our progressively artificial relationship with nature. For economists, 'land, labour, and capital' are factors of production to be represented by the appropriate letter in a production function. For Polanyi, land, labour and money were fictitious commodities.

Land represents the entire ecological environment; labour represents all of humankind. However, what is money and what is capital? Capital can be a stock, merchant wares, a tool, a machine, or even the stock of knowledge acquired by education, now called human capital. However, capital can also be simply a pile of money, the most abstract form of capital. It can be in the real economy where it has led to a historic increase in production by social labour by turning artisanal workers into alienated labour power operating machinery. This logic leads to humankind's progressively artificial relationship with nature and has turned artisans into appendages of machines. On the other hand, money can also be 'invested' in speculation, effectively making money out of money. Indeed, financialization has driven the world economy since the 1980s.

Of the fictitious commodities, money capital has come to dominate and rule. The neoliberal financialization described earlier has transformed capitalism from producing goods and services into money-making. The result is outrageous inequality. Trillion-dollar fortunes are sheltered in tax havens while private investment in the real economy is in decline. In the next financial crisis, government support for failing financial institutions must be accompanied by the acquisition of public equity (Hudson, 2015). Global finance has acquired power far in excess of the requirements of gross fixed capital formation, including infrastructure. This raises the question of whether financial institutions should be treated like public utilities in order to serve the real economy.

In utilitarian economic calculus, land is a factor of production which has no value if it does not contribute to increasing material wealth. Nature's revenge in the form of fires, floods, hurricanes, tornadoes and other natural disasters is a reminder of the urgency of action on climate change. The accelerated depletion of plant and animal life on Earth, with a 60 per cent reduction in diversity since 1970, signals the dangers of ecological collapse (World Wildlife Fund, 2018: 7). Attaining a zero-carbon economy requires a revolutionary transformation to renewable sources of energy. However, the priority accorded to the economy and the domination of public decision-making by private economic interests have disempowered even the societies of rich countries to take effective action.

And what of labour? Humanity is now faced with the existential challenge of a revolution in information technology. Nouriel Roubini celebrated the micro-chip as the most disruptive invention of the twentieth century (Roubini, 2014). Conventional economic wisdom is that workers displaced by technological revolutions have always found employment in new manufacturing or service industries. While this has historically been the case, information technology is qualitatively different. Unlike previous technological revolutions that created new processes for producing new products, the information technology revolution has affected every sector by offering means to reduce costs by reducing employment. This displaced labour can no longer be absorbed or redeployed in voluntary full-time employment producing new products. The leading enterprises of the present time are companies producing information technology which exponentially increases the capacity of the industry to digitalize the economy and reduce employment.

Implicit in the digital revolution is an inevitable concentration of power. The fear is that society will tend towards the dystopian vision of Roubini and Leontief, where a well-educated, highly skilled and highly paid 20 per cent of the population produce all essential output, inviting authoritarian rule over the 80 per cent that have been rendered redundant (Roubini, 2014; Polanyi Levitt, 2018: 18–50). Leontief predicted that it would require a cultural revolution of the magnitude of the industrial revolution for humankind to benefit from this digital revolution (Leontief, 1983: 3–8). To rise to the challenge, we must liberate ourselves from the legacy of the 'obsolete market mentality' and create a new consciousness of the society in which we would like to live. We must reject the wasteful and noxious patterns of production and consumption of rich societies, which are not sustainable. Polanyi used to say that we are rich enough to be inefficient.

The digital revolution results in increasing alienation in everyday life by the progressive elimination of human interaction in the provision of services. The addiction of individuals to personal electronic devices and social media is a substitution of virtual for personal interaction. Artificial intelligence is depriving humans of independence, judgement and individual responsibility. While Polanyi asked whether mankind could survive the machine age, in our time he would have joined the increasing number of voices of those who question the wisdom of the abrogation of responsibility implicit in artificial intelligence.

As technology relieves us of the constraints of scarcity, and an increasing number of goods become available at minimal marginal cost, people have become redundant. What is the relevance of full employment as a social objective in a world that requires ever less labour? Perhaps work could be shared between all those wishing to participate, in order to arrive at Keynes's fifteen-hour workweek and liberate our lives from work. How do we create a society that assigns equal intrinsic value to all human beings? These are the challenges of a socialist society.

Polanyi self-reflectively identified key polarities governing his thought: society and community; science and religion; technological and social progress; efficiency and humanity; and institutional and personal needs. Western modernity has elevated science, technology and efficiency to governing principles. He firmly rejected technological determinism, and in his anthropological work he found that, at the same level of technology, there were a great number of ways in which different societies organized economic life.

What makes Polanyi relevant today as we face this daunting set of civilizational and existential challenges? It is a fact that he, unlike any other notable economic thinker since his time, has questioned putting the economy at the centre of civilization and insisted that the economy is a social construct – an instituted process providing the basic material requirements of life. There is no one common model for social organization, as implied by globalized capitalism. Solutions for these civilizational challenges must embrace and conserve diversity – ecologically, culturally and with respect to historical differences. Polanyi said that

> what we all need is a broader contact with nature, art and poetry; the enjoyment of language and history, the perspectives of science and exploration, security against the avoidable accidents of life and above all a self-respecting person's assurance that he can lead his life without a humiliating dependence upon an employer. ... Not another car, a more expensive suit of clothes. (Polanyi, 37–11: 2)

It is up to us to value our life on Earth. We should stop thinking about the kind of economy we want to have and start thinking of the kind of society in which we want to live.

Note

1 All quotations in this section are from the Bennington Lectures unless otherwise stated.

Part II

Money as a fictitious commodity

3

Debt, land and money: from Polanyi to the new economic archaeology

Michael Hudson

Inspiration for *The Great Transformation* in the post-war monetary breakdown

Karl Polanyi's formative years in the aftermath of the First World War were a period of monetary turmoil. The United States became a creditor nation for the first time, and demanded payment of the war debts that Keynes warned were unpayable without wrecking Europe's financial systems. (Hudson, [1972] 2003 summarizes this era.) France and Britain subjected Germany to unsustainably high reparation debts, while imposing austerity on their own economies by adhering to the gold standard. Jacques Rueff in France and Bertil Ohlin in the United States argued that Germany could pay any level of reparations in gold – and the Allies could pay their foreign-currency arms debts – by imposing unemployment high enough to make wages low enough to make its products cheap enough to run a trade surplus large enough to pay its debt service (Rueff, 1929, 1967; Ohlin, 1929).

Most countries followed the 'hard money' idea that money was (or could be made to act as a proxy for) a commodity by making it convertible into gold. Advocated most notoriously by the Austrians Ludwig von Mises and Friedrich von Hayek, the result was monetary deflation. It was a replay of what had occurred after 1815 when the banker David Ricardo insisted that returning to the gold standard would restore balance in the face of any given foreign debt payment or military subsidy. He claimed that any such payments deficit would automatically be recycled in the form of the recipient country's demand for imports from the 'capital-paying' economy.[1] No such balance resulted.

When the gold standard was re-imposed after the First World War, economies were starved of money in order to reduce prices and wages in a futile attempt to pay their debts. Rueff, Ohlin and Hayek claimed that imposing this deflation and poverty on debtor economies would (and should) represent a stable equilibrium.

Everything – including money, land and labor – was viewed as a commodity whose price would be set fairly by supply and demand, subject to 'demand' being eroded by debt service paid to creditors without limit. Money creation was to be kept out of the hands of government, because, as Margaret Thatcher paraphrased Hayek's ideology: 'There is no such thing as society.' There is (and should be) only a market – one that inevitably is dominated by financial fortunes, banks and property owners.

Polanyi blamed the post-war breakdown and Great Depression on the imposition of free market ideology. Writing that 'The 1920s saw the prestige of economic liberalism at its height', he forecast that 'Undoubtedly, our age will be seen as the end of the self-regulating market' (Polanyi, 1944: 148). He expected the chaos resulting from implementing this manic ideology to demonstrate the fallacy of claims that markets are self-regulating and can be 'disembedded' from their social regulatory context without causing economic destruction, unemployment and poverty.

To demonstrate the need for public regulation, Polanyi undertook a review of what modes of organizing money, credit and land use had sustained prosperity and which ones failed. Rejecting what he took to be Marx's sequence of modes of production, he emphasized modes of exchange.[2] He accused Marx's set of 'historically untenable stages' as flowing 'from the conviction that the character of the economy was set by the status of labor' (Polanyi, 1957a: 256) from ancient slavery and usury, to serfdom under feudalism and wage labor under capitalism. Focusing on the transition from feudalism to industrial capitalism, driving labor off the land to become wage labor working for employers, Marx's aim was not to review the history of land tenure. Polanyi urged that 'the integration of the soil into the economy should be regarded as hardly less vital'. 'Under feudalism and the gild system', Polanyi wrote, 'land and labor formed part of the social organization itself (money had yet hardly developed into a major element of industry)'. Land was allocated as the basis of maintaining 'the military, judicial, administrative, and political system; its status and function were determined by legal and customary rules' (Polanyi, 1944: 69). The proper task of government is to socialize rules for what its rent is to be used for – taxes, or payments to rentiers?

In Volumes II and III of *Capital*, Marx traced land rent and usury as survivals from feudal times, '*faux frais* of production', that he expected industrial capitalism to do away with by freeing economies from landlords extracting ground rent, and from usurious banking. Instead, these rentier interests have regained control of economies, opposing public regulation by waving the flag of free market individualism. Idealizing monetary gains without concern for how this affects the public good, bankers and other rentiers define 'natural' or 'pure' economies as meaning no regulation of prices or markets with social welfare in mind. The economy is seen as a market free-for-all, not as a social system regulating property, credit and debt to prioritize social stability and rising living standards.

By depicting public regulatory power as 'unnatural', free market policy assumes that relinquishing the rules of property ownership, credit and debt to private wealth is natural and desirable. The reality is that there never has been a 'natural' market existing without social regulations. What passes for a free market amounts to little more than a jockeying for position, with the advantage lying with the wealthiest individuals. Their interest lies in minimizing public oversight and taxation of their rent-seeking, credit and foreclosure, and other business activities.

Polanyi set out to demonstrate the folly of subjecting labor, land and monetary policy to unregulated 'free markets'. What really is at issue is what *kind* of markets economies will have, and who will be their major beneficiaries – or victims. *The Great Transformation* credited feudalism and England's early industrial capitalism with its still-operating Poor Laws for preserving broad social objectives and regulations instead of throwing labor and land to the wolves (the wealthy) by treating them as commodities. Even in the earliest days of the development of capitalism, mercantilist nations 'were all equally averse to the idea of commercializing labor and land – the precondition of market economy. … Mercantilism, with all its tendency towards commercialization, never attacked the safeguards which protected these two basic elements of production – labor and land – from becoming objects of commerce' (ibid.: 70).

From antiquity down through feudal Europe, land formed the universal tax base. In contrast to normal commodities that have a cost of production, land is provided freely by nature. 'Land, labor and money are obviously not commodities,' Polanyi explained. Labor is life, and 'land is only another name for nature', not having been produced by labor and hence not having a cost of production (classical value), and its rent is a legal property claim. But markets give it a price so as to transfer ownership rights, enabling landlords to extract rental income without work (ibid.: 72). Although land's site value is created mainly by public infrastructure investment, landholders fight to keep the land's rent for themselves. That prevents governments from keeping land rent in the public domain as the tax base. And in antiquity, foreclosing creditors and large investors displaced smallholders, depriving governments of taxes as well as corvée labor and a free citizen-army.[3]

When Polanyi called money a fictitious commodity, he was rejecting the idea of making it scarce by limiting its supply to that of gold, mimicking commodities as if money were part of a barter system. Doing so also gave creditors overwhelming power over the rest of the economy, especially over its labor and land by pushing wage levels and crop prices below basic break-even needs when governments were deprived of the ability to create credit to employ labor. He criticized Ricardo for having 'indoctrinated nineteenth-century England with the conviction that the term "money" meant a medium of exchange', with bank notes readily convertible into gold (ibid.: 196). That policy led to deflation, given gold's limited supply. Falling prices and wages penalized debtors when countries returned to gold convertibility after wartime inflations. That occurred in Britain after 1815, and in the United States after the 1870s when it sought to roll back prices so that the price of gold – and hence, wages and commodity prices – would be driven back down to their pre-Civil War level. The result was prolonged economic depression, causing land and other property to be transferred from debtors to creditors.

Polanyi's preferred alternative was to make money serve social aims by making it a public creation of law. Such token money has no inherent cost of production, 'but comes into being through the mechanism of banking or state finance', and thus is not a commodity with an ultimate labor cost of production: 'actual money, finally, is merely a token of purchasing power which, as a rule, is not produced at all but comes into being through the mechanism of banking or state finance' (ibid.: 72).

Polanyi's Austrian adversaries argued that public money creation, social spending programs, regulations and subsidies distorted the supposedly efficient 'natural' economy of price-setting markets. In practice this meant low wages and a transfer of land to the wealthy. Unregulated market forces and gain-seeking led the social system to be run for the purely financial aim of 'maximum money gains', subjecting land, labor and money to pro-creditor bias instead of favoring the population's indebted majority. It was to prevent this economic polarization and austerity, Polanyi claimed, that 'Regulation and markets ... grew up together'. Trade and incomes were regulated for most of history, thanks to the fact that 'As a rule, the economic system was absorbed in the social system' (ibid.: 68).

But by the mid-1920s money-seeking drives were destabilizing agriculture and industry. France imposed austerity by adhering to the gold standard, and Britain's similar policy led to a nationwide General Strike in 1926. The moral, Polanyi said, was that:

> To allow the market mechanism to be the sole director of the fate of human beings and their natural environment, indeed, even of the amount and use of purchasing power, would result in the demolition of society. ... the market administration of purchasing power would periodically liquidate business enterprise, for shortages and surfeits of money would prove as disastrous to business as floods and droughts in primitive society. (Ibid.: 73)

Polanyi's interdisciplinary project at Columbia

The Great Transformation's publication in 1944 led to Polanyi's appointment at Columbia University (1947–53), where he organized a group of anthropologists and ancient historians to review how non-market societies shaped their labor, land and monetary relations. This provided an empirical alternative to the assumption that price-setting 'free' markets had always existed without government 'interference'.

The group's first research into alternatives to the free market version of history was *Trade and Markets in the Early Empires* (Polanyi, Arensberg and Pearson, 1957), an outgrowth of the early twentieth-century debate between the so-called primitivists and modernists. The modernist reading of history insists that self-seeking individuals innovated money and enterprise spontaneously, without chieftains, palaces or temples playing a role. Against this idea, Karl Bücher (1847–1930) countered that ancient economies were not organized along modern individualistic lines. He 'objected to both classical and neoclassical economics on the grounds that these theories had a narrow-time-bound concept of economy, a concept which they assumed was applicable to all historical periods' (Polanyi, 1962: 164).

Like Bücher, Polanyi rejected reconstructions that read as if a free market economist got into a time machine and went back to the Neolithic to organize credit and markets along modern lines. If any archaic economy had followed that idealized textbook model, his follower Johannes Renger (1972) observed, debtors would have fled, or defected to rivals promising to cancel their debts. Mutual aid and its associated constraints on profiteering were preconditions for survival. Chiefs were expected to be openhanded, protecting the weak and needy.

Elaborating on the ideas developed in *The Great Transformation*, Polanyi drew on anthropology and ancient history to show that monetary 'obligations do not here commonly spring from transactions' to exchange goods in markets. They had more to do with the payment of taxes, debts and other obligations: 'The equating of such staples as barley, oil and wool in which taxes or rent have to be paid or alternative rations or wages may be claimed is vital' (Polanyi, 1957a: 264f).

Polanyi characterized market exchange as one of three distinct exchange systems: reciprocity (gift exchange), redistribution and 'market' exchange. 'Reciprocity behavior between individuals integrates the economy only if symmetrically organized structures, such as a symmetrical system of kinship groups, are given.'[4] Such symmetries can be disturbed by 'the rise of the market to a ruling force in the economy', above all as 'land and food were mobilized through exchange, and labor was turned into a commodity free to be purchased in the market' (ibid.: 225). He did not see this as having developed already c. 1800 BC in the Old Babylonian period, or that debt was the major lever enabling wealthy individuals to obtain land from smallholders. Creditors often got themselves adopted as 'sons' of the indebted landholder, so that they could inherit the land in due course under existing rules to keep land in the hands of hereditary families.

Polanyi summarized his hope that society would cure itself from having disembedded markets from their social context by restoring 'shapes reminiscent of the economic organization of earlier times' (Polanyi, Arensberg and Pearson, 1957: xviii). Society needed to re-embed market structures for goods and services by administering key prices and incomes in a new redistributive economy. Such redistribution 'presupposes the presence of an allocative center in the community', a palace or temple in earlier times, democratic government offices in today's world (ibid.: esp. 251).

Polanyi's influence on Assyriology

Two of Polanyi's followers, Leo Oppenheim and Johannes Renger, described Sumer and Babylonia as redistributive temple and palatial economies (see most notably Oppenheim, 1957: 27–37; Renger, 1979: 249; 1984: 31–115).[5] Renger's 1984 article on the palatial context for trade and enterprise showed the role of these large institutions in allocating and pricing resources. To undertake forward planning for their own operations and for transactions with the economy at large, palaces and temples needed to value payment of grain rents and fees in a consolidated overall balance sheet along with trade, herding and other activities. Their solution to this problem was to create what we know today as money.

Polanyi's characterization of redistribution as an economy-wide mode of exchange – as if Mesopotamia could not be both redistributive *and* a market economy – implied that Mesopotamia did not also have a thriving profit-seeking trade in a sector where prices varied, especially among cities. This lay him open to criticism, most notably by Morris Silver, who cited examples of private profit-seeking trade such as that of the Assyrians in Cappadocia, as well as evidence that prices often exceeded those prescribed in royal proclamations (Silver, 1983, 1995).

Renger has described how many of the palace needs of the neo-Sumerian Third Dynasty of Ur III (late third millennium BC) 'were handled by entrepreneurs for the [royal] household for which they acted ("*Palastgeschäft*")' (Renger, 1994: 197). Merchants conducted entrepreneurial trade on their own account, often on consignment from the palace but also selling at a markup to the rest of the economy. They also lent on their own account, and collected taxes and fees for the palace. The intermixing between the redistributive palatial economy and the less formal parts of the economy where prices were more flexible makes it often difficult to distinguish between 'public' and 'private', and thus between redistributive and 'market' exchange, lending and interest, and rents or other obligations (Yoffee, 1977: 6, see also Hudson, 2002).

Entrepreneurial trade for the market and credit in Mesopotamia coexisted with palace redistribution with administered pricing *and* gift exchange, each in its own sphere. And Mesopotamia was not alone as a 'mixed economy'. Almost every society for the past five thousand years has been multi-layered, featuring all three of Polanyi's modes of exchange simultaneously. Even today, gift exchange among family and friends and administered prices for public goods and services coexist with market exchange.

However, monetary gain-seeking usually was 'embedded' in an overall social context. Royal Clean Slate proclamations of 'justice and equity' annulled the backlog of grain taxes and other agrarian debts, liberated bondservants and restored land forfeited by smallholders. (I provide a history of such acts in '... *and forgive them their debts*' (Hudson, 2018).) This preserved a free citizenry to serve in the army and provide corvée labor instead of falling into permanent debt bondage to non-official creditors.

The past few decades of Assyriological research have shown that Mesopotamia was neither primitive nor modern as such. As Dominique Charpin has summarized, Polanyi's idea of Hammurabi's Babylonia as a non-market economy was formulated theoretically without the benefit of the documentation that is now available. Many of the texts published in recent years show very clearly that fluctuating prices characterized the market. It is all too easy to use these terms anachronistically and to allow misunderstandings to arise (Charpin, 2003: 196).

Such misunderstanding had far-reaching consequences half a century ago. One of Polanyi's most influential followers, Moses Finley, excluded the ancient Near East from the narrative of Western civilization. Driven out of teaching in America during the McCarthy Red Scare of the 1950s for having been a Communist, Finley insisted that Western civilization developed out of primitive communities whose chieftainship practices evolved directly into the classical Greek and Roman city-states. In his view:

The Near Eastern economies were dominated by large palace- or temple-complexes, who owned the greater part of the arable, virtually monopolized anything that can be called 'industrial production' as well as foreign trade (which includes inter-city trade, not merely trade with foreign parts), and organized the economic, military, political and religious life of the society through a single complicated, bureaucratic, record-keeping operation for which the word 'rationing', taken very broadly, is as good a one-word description as I can think of. …The exclusion of the Near East is therefore not arbitrary. (Finley, 1985: 28)

This exclusion of Near Eastern economies on the wrong-headed ground that they had no entrepreneurial mentality missed their 'mixed' character. Its dualistic attitude epitomizes the tendency of some of Polanyi's followers to think of societies as being either 'social' or 'free market', as if commercial enterprise and interest-bearing debt were incompatible with public regulations and administered pricing. Finley treated it as a primitivist blind alley, like Karl Wittfogel's (1957) interpretation of 'Oriental despotism' imagining that irrigated economies had a totalitarian Stalinist-type authoritarianism. In reality, palaces were sponsors of enterprise and a resilient mixed economy that later provided classical Greece and Rome with their basic techniques of commercial enterprise and interest-bearing debt.

Commenting on how Finlay's dualistic view has been controverted by the mass of documentation from merchants and investors, Steven Garfinkle notes:

> The use of the term 'primitive', therefore, becomes particularly objectionable when applied to the Mesopotamian economy. … To Finley, the ancient Near East was not just primitive, it was strange and, therefore, not part of 'our' history. By placing the ancient Near East outside of the western experience, Finley was able to justify its exclusion from ancient history; but only if we understand the term 'ancient history' to apply exclusively to the carefully screened origins of the 'West'. (Garfinkle, 2012: 6–7)

Assyriologists have shown the role of monetary gain-seeking entrepreneurs emerging above all in conjunction with the palatial economy, managing royal enterprises and trading with other cities and regions. Indeed, how else could trade and privatization have taken place (Garfinkle, 2004a, 2004b)?[6]

The new economic archaeology as an outgrowth of Polanyi's approach

The New Economic Archaeology is in many ways an outgrowth of Polanyi's Columbia University group, emphasizing that markets almost always have been regulated to avoid chronic imbalance and insolvency. This school goes beyond Polanyi in emphasizing the role of debt and also the role of enterprise that emerged out of a symbiosis between Mesopotamia's palatial economy and individual merchants. The International Scholars Conference on Ancient Near Eastern Economies (ISCANEE) has sought to fill the gap in the history of civilization by surveying Bronze Age palace and temple enterprise, land tenure, debt and the early development of money, as well as the primordial distinction between commercial credit and agrarian usury.

Debt, land and money

Our group began in 1994 when I worked with Karl Lamberg-Karlovsky at Harvard's anthropology department – the Peabody Museum – to organize a series of colloquia to which we invited leading Assyriologists, Egyptologists and archaeologists to find the origins of civilization's commercial and monetary practices and how early society managed to prevent personal debt from destabilizing and polarizing economies, as became the case in Greece and Rome. Our group has produced five colloquium volumes on land tenure and urbanization, money and interest, the organization of labor, commerce and enterprise. Together, they show how the basic techniques of commercial enterprise were innovated in the Bronze Age Near Eastern mixed economies.

The first conference was held in November 1994 at New York University, on *Privatization in the Ancient Near East and Classical World* (Hudson and Levine, 1996). It focused on the relationship between the large institutions and the rest of the economy in an era when land was held by clan units and mercantile activities were dominated by the palace, while temples acted as what today would be called public utilities, supplying handicraft exports to merchants engaging in the import and export trade.

That colloquium was followed by a combination of two meetings, hosted first by New York University in 1996 and the next year by Russia's Oriental Institute in Saint Petersburg, on *Urbanization and Land Ownership in the Ancient Near East* (Hudson and Levine, 1999). Its contributors pointed to the role of usury in undermining clan-based land tenure. Debt historically has been a lever to concentrate land in the hands of foreclosing creditors.

These two volumes laid the groundwork for what we intended to be the capstone in our series, dealing with the logic that led Bronze Age rulers to annul rural usury debts and arrears so as to preserve economic stability. The third colloquium was held in 1998 at Columbia University: *Debt and Economic Renewal in the Ancient Near East* (Hudson and Van de Mieroop, 2002). In contrast to the then-widespread modernist belief dismissing Clean Slates as a utopian ideal of the past, our group documented legal records showing that these royal amnesties were indeed enforced in practice.

The reason was clear enough: societies would have succumbed to bondage and monopolization of the land millennia ago had they viewed 'free markets' to mean the sanctity of personal debts being paid. Rome was the first major society *not* to cancel agrarian and personal debts. For its oligarchy, the 'sanctity of property' meant a license to foreclose on the self-support land and other property of debtors.

Our group was recognized as extending the work of Polanyi's generation, and the colloquium included a visit to the archive of his papers at Columbia.

We received such positive responses that we held a fourth colloquium in 2000 at the British Museum on the origins of money, *Creating Economic Order: Record-Keeping, Standardization and the Development of Accounting in the Ancient Near East* (Hudson and Wunsch, 2004). The next colloquium was held in Germany in 2005: *Labor in the Ancient World* (Steinkeller and Hudson, 2015). Together, these five volumes have drawn a new picture of the Neolithic and Bronze Age Near East that extends the fundamental insights of Karl Polanyi.

The role of temples and palaces in the origins of money

Money originated in the accounting practices developed by Mesopotamia's large institutions in the third millennium BC to denominate transactions between them and the rest of the economy, headed by payment of taxes and fees and payment for goods and services. Silver served to denominate the debts run up by merchants for consignments to trade for raw materials and luxury goods (with the palace usually being the major customer), while land rent, fees for services and advances to cultivators during the crop year were measured in grain. Most exchange occurred on credit, to be settled at the end of the crop season on the threshing floor, or at the end of a stipulated trade-venturing period. Acceptance of silver and grain by the palace made them acceptable as general means of payment for the economy at large.

Polanyi emphasized money's legal creation by government. Aristotle long ago noted that the Greek term for coinage, *nomisma*, is based on the root *nomos* (the root of our term 'numismatics'), meaning 'law'. What gave monetized commodities currency above all was being accepted as payment of taxes or fees for palace and temple goods and services.[7] Modern governments can pay for social spending and provide the economy with money to grow as long as they levy taxes to create a use value for this money.

Taxes, debt service and public creation of money are ignored by those who follow the Austrian economist, Carl Menger and the fable of money he drew up in 1871. He depicted money as emerging among individuals bartering commodities and preferring small portable objects as their vehicle for exchange and eventually also for saving and wealth accumulation (Menger, [1871] 1892). Subsequent Austrians denounced *Trade and Markets* as a threat to this individualistic and outright anti-government line of theorizing. Fritz Heichelheim called the academic effort 'amateurish' and 'a most regrettable book', and said that it should not have been published. 'Systematic economic theoreticians will either have to reject or to remodel the ideas about economic history which are expressed in this book' (Heichelheim, 1960: 108).

Debt, land and money

Heichelheim earlier created a 'private enterprise' fable that had no role for archaic temples and palaces. He theorized that interest originated when Neolithic creditors 'advanced' animals and seed crops in exchange for a share in the surplus. His 'modernist' assumption that early interest rates reflect productivity, profit rates and risk is not even valid today, yet is applied back in time as if it explains the origin of interest (Heichelheim, 1958: 54).[8]

The individualistic creation myth of money and interest depicts cultivators and craftsmen bartering their products with each other, and asking for interest for loans of cattle and grain to produce a surplus, out of which the debtor pays interest to creditors. More affluent creditors are said to have preferred pieces of metal for compact and non-perishable means of saving. Left out of account is where this metal is supposed to have come from. Throughout all antiquity it was refined in the temples, which guaranteed its degree of purity, while the palace sponsored the trade to obtain silver and gold. Imported silver was the most prestigious item, with royal donations to temples establishing their social and ceremonial status.[9] The palace made it the main medium for trade and mercantile contracts, and for management of palatial-sector enterprises.

Private individuals bartering cannot be a realistic explanation. A long thread of denunciation of merchants and creditors using false weights and measures runs from Babylonian 'wisdom literature' through the Bible – a light weight for lending or selling, and a heavy weight for debtors repaying and for buying. This literary record makes it clear that even commodity money could never be left to private individuals, because doing so would have opened the gates for creditors and tradesmen to act crookedly. Effective public authority always has been necessary to rein in fraud and guarantee fair dealing in market exchange. That is why fraudsters seek to dismantle government's regulatory ability whenever possible, using the hypocritical slogan of free markets.

Who else but temples and palaces could have provided honest standards? Monetary exchange could not have been workable without their oversight of standardized weights and measures – attesting to the purity of the monetary metals – and sanctions against fraud. That is why silver was minted in temples from Mesopotamia through Rome. Our word for 'money' comes from Rome's Temple of Juno Moneta – the 'warner', whose honking geese warned Rome of the threat of invasion. (The word *moneta* originally referred to an omen.)

It is not possible to explain the origins and early development of money without recognizing the catalytic role of the temples and palaces in the third millennium BC. In addition to denominating debts owed to the palatial economy, money provided a basis for palace and temple cost accounting and resource allocation. Employment and production in these large institutions was on a scale far beyond that of interpersonal barter. As part of the redistributive economy, Sumerian temples provisioned labor employed in their workshops to weave textiles and make other handicrafts, which the palace exported for silver and other raw materials.

Temples created and regulated weights and measures for silver shekels and minas, and *ku* 'bushels' of grain in their sexagesimal (sixty-based) calendrical allocation system based on standardized thirty-day months for ease of distributing salaries. Silver (minted at a specified purity) and grain were designated as the major means of paying taxes, fees and other debts at harvest time. The value of a silver shekel was set as equal to a *gur* 'quart' of grain for payment of fees and taxes to the palace or other rural creditors. (To be sure, grain was traded among cities at prices that might rise steeply in times of crop failure, such as occurred at the end of the neo-Sumerian Ur III Empire.)

As Lamberg-Karlovsky (2009: 8) points out, 'In the patrimonial state there is little functional division between private and official spheres. Official offices originate in the ruler's household.' In this relationship, profit is not the aim, but stable continuity. Ease of account-keeping and stable price relations were a logic for *not* letting prices vary. And silver is the prime luxury, exempt from supply-and-demand or cost–profit calculations. In addition, reciprocity and redistribution are organized along lines just as rational as a market economy, but the logic is different. It is based on establishing a system of regularity and order, not flexible price-making markets.

Third millennium Mesopotamia's imports did not affect prices either by varying supply and demand or by being substantially more or less expensive. Market prices either were administered or, once set, continued by inertia with little response to shifts in supply and demand except for seasonal variations in crop prices or responses to crop failure. Moreover, rather than relying on trade for everyday essentials, as advocated by today's trade enthusiasts, the main imports to Mesopotamia (where prices, weights and measures, and hence monetary equivalency, are first documented) included producers' goods such as ores, tin or copper, and luxuries such as gold, silver and luxurious gemstones. The main exports were prestige textiles woven in the temple and palace workshops (mainly by dependent war widows and their children), as well as functional items such as knives and chisels. 'Trade in luxuries (a significant percentage of Mesopotamia's long-distance trade – as evidenced by their archaeological recovery) involved a very small part of the population' (ibid.: 12).

These findings are consistent with the findings of Polanyi's early collaborator, Leo Oppenheim, who described Mesopotamia's economy as based neither on price-setting 'free' markets nor as primitive, but as a mixed economy with administered prices within the large institutions for their own account-keeping and to denominate payments owed to them.[10]

The dominant role of debt

In view of the problems that debt has caused through the ages, the analysis of how societies have regulated credit and debt should be at the very center of our understanding of money. And in view of the fact that the paradigmatic Mesopotamian debts were owed to the palaces, temples and collectors in their bureaucracy – for fees and taxes, tribute from conquered peoples and by merchants acting on consignments or orders from the palace – the analysis of early money, debt and fiscal policy must logically go together.

Mainstream economists treat credit (and implicitly, arrears as well as loans) as always being productive and helpful, not as extractive and socially destabilizing. They depict government intervention to annul debts as leading to economic crisis, not as saving populations from impoverishment and disorder. This doctrinaire approach ignores the fact that, in practice, the 'security of debt' meant making ancient debtors falling into arrears liable to lose their land and personal liberty. This meant insecurity of *their* property rights. That is the real crisis.

Much as Ricardo argued that all foreign debts could be paid by automatic reciprocal demand, modern business cycle theorists describe equilibrium as occurring as a result of wage and price flexibility. To deem widespread foreclosure on debtors' property a viable policy requires an assumption that economies self-adjust in a stable, fair and efficient way. The reality is that deregulating debt and land tenure relationships imposes debt-ridden austerity.

Depicting credit and the financial business plan as having only positive economic effects produces a travesty of history. Viewing debt and its interest charges simply as a bargain between individuals fails to recognize how the economy-wide debt burden tends to grow beyond the ability to be paid. It casts a blind eye towards the behavior of financial oligarchies in the absence of public checks. Money-greed is applauded as if securing creditor claims is the most rational way to organize an economy. The implication is that there is no need for government action from 'outside' the market, for example by Clean Slates, to reverse the effects of the rural usury that eroded traditional land tenure in the Old Babylonian period (2000–1600 BC).

Throughout history debt has been the major lever privatizing land and reducing populations to bondage. Mesopotamia managed to delay this polarizing dynamic by subordinating creditor rights to the aim of dynastic survival. But classical Greece and Rome lacked the tradition of royal Clean Slates. That was the great turning point. Livy, Plutarch and Diodorus described how debt disenfranchised the Roman population, yet a modern survey citing a seemingly comprehensive list of 210 causes on which posterity has blamed Rome's decline and fall at one time or another does not even include debt (Demandt, 1984).

Western civilization as a disembedding of economics from its social context

Records disappear in the Aegean after 1200 BC. By the time they reappear six centuries later, Greek and Italian chieftains and warlords had adopted the practice of interest-bearing debt brought by Syrian and 'Phoenician' traders around the eighth century BC. Crucially, however, they adopted it selectively, without the Clean Slates that liberated debtors from bondage and restored land rights that had been lost to foreclosing creditors.[11] Greek and Roman oligarchies privatized credit and freed themselves from royal overrides.

'Free market' advocates pick up the thread of Western civilization 'in the middle', only *after* credit, debt and property relations became disembedded and decontextualized from the checks and balances that sustained the Near Eastern takeoff. It is as if the Bronze Age agrarian debt cancellations were a blind alley (or even 'Oriental despotism'). Their exclusion fosters the idea that from classical Greece and Rome to today's wave of pro-creditor austerity and deregulation, the 'sanctity of debt' and foreclosure are a primordial result of Darwinian natural selection and survival of the fittest (namely, the richest), not as leading to social dissolution.

The inherent conflict between rulers seeking to keep their citizens free of debt bondage on the one hand, and creditors seeking their own gains at the palace's expense on the other, has been a thread running down the history of civilization. The distinctive feature of Western economies is privatization of credit, land and public infrastructure. That is the real detour from earlier millennia. Archaic societies treated land required for subsistence as a basic right for their citizenry. Instead of commodifying labor and land ownership to make debt bondage and foreclosure irreversible, Mesopotamian rulers proclaimed Clean Slates so as to avoid the financial polarization between creditors and debtors that later brought on a Dark Age. Today the debt dynamic is imposing austerity on the Western world, transferring property to creditors who have gained enough control over government to block protection of debtors.

Polanyi's optimistic theory of the 'double movement' asserts that when society becomes too exploitative and polarized, there is a reaction to re-socialize it. That is done by re-establishing public regulation of money, exchange and land, with a view to long-term growth instead of short-run financial gain-seeking. He expected socialism to provide basic services as a human right, on the premise that people should not have to lose their liberty and rights as the price of paying for basic needs:

> Socialism is, essentially, the tendency inherent in an industrial civilization to transcend the self-regulating market by consciously subordinating it to a democratic society. It is the solution natural to industrial workers who see no reason why production should not be regulated directly and why markets should be more than a useful but subordinate trait in a free society. From the point of view of the community as a whole, socialism is merely the continuation of that endeavor to make society a distinctively human relationship of persons. (Polanyi [1944] 1957: 234)

In his view, 'free market' policies lead to so much poverty and strain that they create a reaction towards greater social regulation. This is a political version of Newton's Third Law of Motion: Every action creates an equal and opposite reaction. That was the essence of classical political economy's nineteenth-century reforms moving towards socialism: 'Society protected itself against the perils inherent in a self-regulating market system' (Polanyi, 1944: 76). Polanyi expected the devastation wrought by the Second World War to create political pressure to renew the path along which Western economies seemed to be moving before the Great War.

We can now see that there is no assurance that societies automatically evolve onward and upward. Such determinism focuses on potential – what economies *could* achieve if they use all knowledge to best advantage. Warlords, creditors, landlords and monopolists have deprived populations of the fruits of technological potential throughout history. Neither Polanyi nor any other economic futurist of his day focused on the exponential growth of debt as the main dynamic polarizing economies and serving as the lever to force privatization and reverse Progressive Era reforms.

Polanyi's 'double movement' may take the form of a reaction sponsored by the vested interests against reforms as well as for them. Despite the flowering of British and European democratic socialism after the Second World War, the 1980s saw such a reaction, in the neoliberalism of Thatcherism and Reaganomics ushering in a post-1980 wave of privatizations and deregulation of property markets. Today's financial lobbyists and their pet academics are advocating government intervention not to stabilize economies but to prevent a social reaction such as Polanyi's double movement.

All forms of society have managed markets. The key is who manages them, above all in the sphere of credit relations and the balance between government authority and private wealth. Freeing monetary gain-seeking from regulation is economically polarizing, as when antiquity's long collapse into serfdom sidetracked many societies for many centuries. Polanyi's contribution to social history demonstrates the need to regulate finance, land and labor markets in an overall social context in order to maintain prosperity instead of impoverishment.

Polanyi's focus on modes of exchange emphasized that land and its tenure should be treated as a social institution, not as a commodity. This was not at odds with Marx's view. Each of his economic stages had its own mode of land tenure as well as labor's role in production. Self-support land was the basis for antiquity's citizens and military (until they lost their land and liberty through usury). Under feudalism, conquerors appropriated the land's rent as lords of the land. Under industrial capitalism, Marx expected, land and its rent would be socialized (as it would be for Polanyi). Instead, real estate ownership under finance capitalism has been democratized on credit, with most land rent being paid to bankers as mortgage interest.

Modes of money and credit also evolved from antiquity via feudalism to the modern era. Reflecting the Bronze Age origin of general-purpose money in payments to the palace (or in classical antiquity to civic authorities), prices and interest rates for debt and fiscal payments were administered. That was an initial precondition for stability. Before markets for wage labor, usury was the easiest way to obtain dependent labor and the land of smallholders. However, Mesopotamian rulers proclaimed Clean Slates to avert debt bondage and loss of land tenure on more than a temporary basis.

Roman emperors engaged in fiat currency issue, leading to price inflation as a result of their inability to tax the wealthy families – the only ones able to pay in the shrinking imperial economy. Medieval kings likewise 'cried down' the coinage in an attempt to pay for their wars. The alternative was a 'financial innovation': royal debt to bankers and foreign bondholders.

When royal war debts could not be paid, creditors demanded mineral rights, public infrastructure and the creation of royal monopolies (such as the East and West Indies trading companies of the Netherlands, France and England). Finance thus became the main lever to privatize the public domain, much as it pried away land rights in antiquity by making the land 'marketable' to the wealthy and subject to foreclosure by predatory creditors – irreversibly.

Interest rates are 'redistributive', set by government. So are prices for bonds and stocks under the post-2008 Quantitative Easing pursued by US and European central banks. Pentagon capitalism is not a market minimizing costs as is depicted in textbook free market competition. It operates on cost-plus contracts, in which military-industrial companies increase their profits by maximizing costs of production.

Debt, land and money

Behind today's 'free market' advocacy is the power of financial wealth to appropriate the political, fiscal and central planning role that Polanyi, Marx and other socialists hoped to see expanded in the hands of democratic government. The resulting financialized market in property and debt instruments is the opposite of what reformers hoped to create a century ago. The financial takeover of government policy reflects a business plan of asset-stripping and economy-wide austerity.

This is not what either Marx or Polanyi expected. If it is where Western civilization's financialized market dynamics are leading, we shall witness a replay of the collapse of antiquity collapse into feudalism.

Notes

1 I review this line of theorizing in *Trade, Development and Foreign Debt* (Hudson, 2010).
2 I contrast Polanyi's approach with that of Marx in my review of surveys of Polanyi's work by Chancier, Joannès, Rouillard and Tenu, and Manning and Morris (Hudson, 2005/6).
3 My *'... and forgive them their debts'* (Hudson, 2018) discusses this conflict of interest over land tenure from Sumer and Babylonia down through the Byzantine Empire.
4 Bondage to creditors is found in archaic tribal communities, for instance in cases where lawbreakers could not pay wergild-type reparations to their victims. But such personal compensation was managed in a way that maintained social harmony, being kept in line with the means to pay. It often was subject to amnesties.
5 Renger became a member of the ISCANEE group described below.
6 For the Assyrian trade, see Larsen (2015).
7 Economists call this the State Theory of Money, the term coined by George F. Knapp in the *State Theory of Money* ([1905] 1924). Another term is 'chartalism'. I review this discussion in Hudson (2003, 2004a and 2004b).
8 I discuss his anachronistic theory in Hudson and Van De Mieroop (2002: 19f.).
9 See for instance Oppenheim (1949).
10 Oppenheim (1957, 1964).
11 I trace this diffusion in Hudson (1992).

4

Commodified money and crustacean nations[1]

Radhika Desai

Polanyi's 'great transformation' refers to the 'collapse' of 'nineteenth century civilization' and the emergence from it of a vastly different one. The story revolved around the unfolding consequences of the commodification of three fictitious commodities: land, labour and money. However, the consequences of the commodification of the last structured the dramatic plot of *The Great Transformation* (*TGT*). Though the gold standard, the apex structure commodifying money, was only one of four institutions whose collapse brought down nineteenth-century civilization (the others being the self-regulating market, the liberal state and the balance of power), its collapse was 'the proximate cause of the catastrophe' (3).[2] By the time it failed, most of the other institutions 'had been sacrificed in a vain effort to save it' (3).

So, money's commodification structured the book's master narrative. Commodified money's rigours being intolerable for societies, central banks created and controlled national token or fiat moneys for domestic circulation. However, central banks also commodified money, tying token moneys to the gold standard. They transmitted as well as moderated commodified money's pressures on national money. As such, central banks both enabled the (only partial) commodification of money and then provided (only partial) protection against it. As the cataclysmic dialectic between the effort to maintain this fiction of fictions, commodified money, and the need for social protection against its consequences unfolded, the latter prevailed. It took the form of 'crustacean nations' (202) with hard economic borders. Forged in the heat and pressure of this violent dialectic, crustacean nations transformed the 'universal capitalism' of the nineteenth century (Polanyi, 1945: 86) into a 'new permanent pattern of world affairs', which, Polanyi argued, 'greatly improved' the 'chances of democratic socialism' (ibid.: 87).

If *TGT*'s chief referent was the fracturing of 'universal' capitalism through the solidification of national economies and the formation of the inter*national* world economy they composed, if this transformation also moved the world closer to socialism, it was a great transformation in the political, and what I have recently dubbed the geopolitical, economy (Desai, 2013) of world capitalism. It was also the result of one of capitalism's formative contradictions, its need to commodify money and the impossibility of doing so. While there are many accounts of the momentously turbulent history of the decades before 1914, Polanyi's is arguably unique in linking the unravelling of the gold standard to the emergence of 'crustacean nations' and, through them, to the prospects of socialism.

This centrality of money in *TGT*'s account of capitalism and socialism could not contrast more with the deafening silence among Polanyi and *TGT* scholars on money as a fictitious commodity. This chapter ends it. Doing so requires, first and foremost, appreciating just how much Polanyi shared with classical political economy, Marx and Marxists, and others such as the social liberal, John Hobson, notwithstanding Polanyi's ambivalence about them. If this is not widely appreciated, it is not only because Polanyi's relation with these traditions and, above all, with Marx is so ill-understood. It is also because most discussion of Marx focuses on classes, class exploitation and class struggle. Certainly this was the focus of *Capital I*, and most of his other writings. However, Marx also believed that, among the historical agents making, re-making and eventually unmaking the capitalist world, nations were as important as classes (Desai, 2012, 2013). It is only because Marx completed only a small part of the larger work he planned that he could not develop his account of nation states. Had he done so, it should become clear below, it would have been broadly along the lines traced by *TGT*. Though Polanyi overtly dismissed them, his account of the great transformation also shares a great deal with the accounts of imperialism given by Hobson and the Marxists, Hilferding, Luxemburg, Bukharin and Lenin, while complementing them in an important way. While they focused mainly on relations between imperial states, Polanyi also shed light on the dynamics of national resistance against imperialism. As such *TGT* is close to Marx and the ideas of Uneven and Combined Development in their original form (as outlined in Desai, 2013).

If this chapter restores to Polanyi his rightful place in the understanding of world affairs, it will not be a moment too soon. I have argued for some time (see, for example, Desai, 2009a, 2009c, 2013) that the hitherto dominant 'universalist' (as Polanyi would have called them) or 'cosmopolitan' (as Friedrich List called them) accounts of world affairs, such as US hegemony, globalization and empire, in which either no nations mattered or only one did, were always questionable. Today their credibility is eroding further and faster as the outlines of a 'deglobalizing' multi-polar world of competing national economies directed by states emerges ever more distinctly.

We need new approaches – I recently proposed geopolitical economy (Desai, 2013) – which take the 'materiality of nations' seriously. Polanyi was an important source for it (ibid.: 58–63) and this chapter, by elucidating *TGT*'s principal argument, the argument linking money and 'crustacean nations', will also extend the theoretical basis of geopolitical economy.

We begin below with appreciating how and why this theme is ignored in Polanyi scholarship. We then clear some interpretational difficulties before going on to discuss fictitious commodities, money as a fictitious commodity and the role of central banks in its double movement. This culminates in showing how this double movement gave rise to crustacean nations and how this development became the 'proximate cause' of the 'catastrophe'. The conclusion stresses the originality of *TGT*'s account of the geopolitical economy of capitalism and urgency of recognizing the political possibilities of socialism (still) contained in the end of 'universal capitalism'.

The lacuna in Polanyi scholarship

Most scholars of Polanyi's idea that land, labour and money are fictitious commodities assume he was staking out a moral position that they ought not to be commodities. This is not wrong; it only fails to recognize that Polanyi was making a historical argument that they *are not* commodities and that when they were treated as such, there were historical consequences. Scholars who deal with Polanyi's ideas about money usually confine themselves to his post-war anthropological works on pre-capitalist societies while those who discuss *TGT* and its organizing concepts focus on land and labour and their respective double movements. Even here, they focus on the domestic plane, usually overlooking their critical international dimensions. For instance, few appreciate that, for Polanyi, the repeal of the Corn Laws commodified land by mobilizing the products of the land elsewhere to feed the English working class. Most neglect the linked themes of money, the national and the international in *TGT*.

Fred Block and Margaret Somers's valuable recent (2014) volume, for instance, synthesizes their decades-long engagement with Polanyi and *TGT*, making a Polanyian case against neoliberalism. Crucially, it rescues Polanyi's critique of Speenhamland from appropriation by the neoliberal right to dismiss the welfare state. However, beyond some discussion of the gold standard and central banking, which does not rely on Polanyi's distinctive insights in any case, they entirely ignore the theme in question: the index has no entry for money. Gareth Dale's extensive work on Polanyi (2010a, 2016a, 2016b) takes up the theme of money. However, the resulting discussion is coloured by Dale's liberal inclinations – Polanyi, for instance, is said to oppose trade protection and national economies recede into the background (2010a: 64–68). Specifically on money, moreover, Dale relies on dubious critiques of Polanyi which appear to believe (rather incredibly) that gold or specie, rather than money, is the fictitious commodity (Knafo, 2013: 31, compare Dale, 2016b: 121). No wonder Polanyi is more frequently cited than understood in international political economy. His views are generally folded into Keynes's, while the opposition of both to economic liberalism – as in *TGT* and Keynes's 'National Self-Sufficiency' (1933) – is largely ignored (Hellenier and Pickel, 2005; Eichengreen, 2008 are two examples). They miss the more fine-grained picture, detailed below, that Polanyi paints of the political and geopolitical vicissitudes of commodified money and the gold standard.

Why this neglect of money, nations and the inter*national* in *TGT* scholarship? Ultimately it is because neoclassical economics, with its famous incomprehension of money, has dominated the twentieth century, particularly in recent neoliberal decades, severing our connection with the tradition of classical political economy. The two traditions are antithetical. Nineteenth-century classical political economy focused on social relations not on markets (Desai, 2018b). Neoclassical economics, which emerged with the marginalist revolution in the 1870s, rested on the twin Ricardian Fictions, Say's Law and Comparative Advantage (Desai, 2013: 34–36), thereby erasing the contradictions of capitalism on the domestic and international planes respectively, leaving a harmonious system, natural as well as eternal. Neoclassical economics does not dwell on the specificity of relations arising from the commodity form, it simply assumes that everything that is bought and sold is a commodity. It also treats money as just another commodity, which happens to facilitate exchange and cannot have an independent effect on the economy, something Keynes directly criticized.

While neoclassical economics has all but erased classical political economy, it was a live legacy well into the twentieth century. Historical and institutionalist thinkers (though not all Marxists, see Desai, 2016) contested the market-driven theoretical and methodological thrust of neoclassical economics. Such contestation threw both traditions and their differences into sharp relief and constituted the fertile ground on which Polanyi's thinking grew (Cangiani, 2010). Indeed, as we shall see below, he did not invent the fundamental building blocks of his thinking, including the signature concepts of fictitious commodities and the double movement, but found them ready to hand among thinkers who retained a connection with classical political economy.

This is, however, precisely why they have proved hardest for scholars of our time, inured as they are to neoclassical economics, to grasp. Take the following entirely serious pronouncement of one of today's better-known economists:

> Polanyi notoriously [sic] insisted that land, labour, and money were fictitious commodities, hinting that because they were 'unnatural', they were in some sense artificial or illegitimate … insisting labour and land are not actual commodities because they were not 'produced for sale' and, more curiously [sic], he insisted money was not 'produced' at all … Apparently, the market can only legitimately deal in the artifactual: things produced through human intentionally to be sold on the market. This weird [sic] insistence upon intentionality at the heart of his definitions constitutes Polanyi's own strangulated appeal to Nature. (Mirowski 2018: 8)

The fact that this rather prominent economist finds the concept of fictitious commodities 'notorious', 'curious' and 'weird', and does not appear to know that intentionality was precisely at the heart of how classical political economy understood the commodity, indicates the depth of the problem. There is a further irony here. Mirowski does not understand that Polanyi, with his powerful critique of how Malthus and Ricardo 'made the fertility of man and soil constitutive elements of the new realm … [e]conomic society … as distinct from political state' (115), is an aid to his larger critique of naturalism in economics. Instead, Mirowski makes him a target of this critique, all on the basis of neoclassical misunderstanding. In this situation, even those sympathetic to Polanyi but disconnected from classical political economy would find it difficult to do more than take a moral position on the question.

Such incomprehension also plagues contemporary understanding of nations and the international, and this problem has worsened in the neoliberal decades. Left critique of neoliberalism tended to be confined to domestic questions and to those of inequality and distribution. The international and productive realms, deeply interconnected, as Polanyi knew them to be, because the international system is fundamentally a hierarchical ordering of more and less productive, and more and less powerful, economies, were neglected as was the idea of imperialism. This neglect left progressive thought prey to the universalist or cosmopolitan theories – of US hegemony, globalization or empire – which extend neoliberalism to the international (and inevitably the) productive sphere by considering the world economy a seamless whole, united by markets or a single state (Desai, 2013). Against this the left remains unable to offer viable alternative understandings of either the productive organization of the economy or international affairs. Without them, large swathes also ended up supporting Western aggression in the name of 'democracy' and 'human rights' against necessarily national resistance to the punishing pressures of an international system dominated by the West, whether in Iraq, Libya or Venezuela.

Polanyi's arguments about money and its double movement would have formed a critical part of such alternative accounts, consubstantial as they were with the constitution of the world order of capitalism as a plurality of modern national economies and interventionist 'crustacean' states in competition and struggle. With some exceptions who at least approached the theme, though independent of Polanyi (Amin, 1990; Block, 1977 and the developmental state tradition including Alice Amsden, Robert H. Wade and Ha-Joon Chang), this understanding and its connection to Polanyi were missing from discussions of the world economy until the publication of my *Geopolitical Economy*. So even when Polanyi was invoked in discussions of the post-war world economy of 'embedded liberalism' (Ruggie, 1982), most emphasized liberalism over embeddedness.

Ironically, all this happened for reasons Polanyi foresaw: even as he hailed the new pattern of international life that improved the chances of socialism in 1945, he noted warily that the United States remained vested in the old universalist pattern (Polanyi, 1945: 86–87). This would prove fateful. After 1945, the US resumed its decades-long efforts at a diluted emulation of pre-1914 British dominance over an open world economy. Accepting the impossibility of acquiring a comparable empire, focusing instead on making the dollar the world's currency, the US was armed with the tremendous relative productive and political power the Second World War bequeathed to it. It allowed the US to abort proposals – Keynes's proposals for 'bancor' and an International Clearing Union and White's very similar proposals for international economic governance (see Desai, 2009c) – that would have realized the new pattern of politically managed multilateral relations between nations and international institutions based on mutual agreement and benefit between state-managed national economies. However, this power was limited and temporary. The US could not wish away the world of crustacean nations. With historical momentum behind them, two tumultuous decades later, US efforts had patently failed: it had to close the gold window, faced defeat in Vietnam and could only look on as the world economy fractured further in the 1970s (Hudson, [1977] 2005). Thereafter, the US reacted to these failures by seeking to achieve dominance in even more volatile financial ways. Probably because barks get louder when bites weaken, these efforts, now bound up with a series of dollar-denominated financializations, came to be dressed up in the ideological garb, successively, of the new cosmopolitan ideologies of 'US Hegemony' (1970s), 'Globalization' (1990s) and 'Empire' (2000s) (this paragraph relies on Desai, 2013).

Much of the left accepted these accounts as descriptions of the world, rather than as US ambitions, importing their liberal free market, free trade biases into its own thinking. However, these views cannot be long for a world being rapidly changed by interventionist states, led by China, that have advanced multi-polarity and it is high time that we recover *TGT*'s overarching argument as a cornerstone of a fresh approach to world affairs. To do this, we must first clear certain interpretational difficulties.

Some questions of interpretation

In *TGT*, Polanyi's scholarship, journalism and personal experience are compressed into an argument of diamond-like structure and clarity. It is satisfyingly, intriguingly and sometimes infuriatingly suggestive, casting refreshing new light from unfamiliar angles on taken-for-granted realities and problems, producing startling new realizations. It often makes bold claims while offering scant evidence, either because, as we know, Polanyi wrote it hurriedly or because he just assumed knowledge.

Gareth Dale identifies three problems with interpreting Polanyi: English-speaking scholars focus exclusively on works available in English; they are unfamiliar with his Central European origins and mind-set and the vast corpus of his still-untranslated work in German and Hungarian; and Polanyi was not systematic but innovative, eclectic and inconsistent, his concepts prone to 'semantic slippage' (2016b: 10). To these problems, we might add at least three more.

The fourth and the weightiest is Polanyi's close but tangled relationship with Marx. Untangling it begins with noting that Polanyi's generation received the positivistic and economistic 'Marxism of the Second International' (Colletti, 1974). Undoubtedly, it led Polanyi to consider Marx 'dogmatic' (x), economic determinist (151) and 'state socialist' (108). The contemporaneous emergence of neoclassical economics made matters worse. It aimed to displace Marx's analysis of capitalism as inherently contradictory and volatile value production rooted in labour, and socialist currents generally (Bukharin, [1914] 1972; Clarke, 1991). Rather than contesting it, moreover, Marxists founded a 'Marxist economics' which sought to fit Marx's analysis, which stood squarely within, even if it was critical of, the tradition of classical political economy (Desai, 2018b), into the alien and antithetical neoclassical theoretical and methodological frame (Desai 2010, 2013, 2016). The resulting blurred boundaries account for Polanyi considering Marx, classical political economy and the neoclassicals as equally positivist and economistic.

Like Eduard Bernstein and the Fabians to whom he was close for a time (Dale, 2010a: 7), Polanyi rejected Marx's analysis of capitalism as the production of value rooted in labour, referring to 'Locke's false start on the labor origins of value' (124). He expressed a preference for neoclassical subjective utility because it was grounded in human volition and so preferable to Marx's apparently deterministic and positivistic 'laws of motion' of capitalism. In reality, however, Polanyi was rejecting the 'Marxism of the Second International' in much the way Marx would have.

When Marx sought to discover capitalism's laws of motion, he did not hold that human actions were always governed by opaque laws, only that they were in *capitalist* societies. Both thinkers pointed to powerful ideological barriers that stood in the way of understanding capitalist society. Marx discussed them as the fetish character of commodities to which vulgar economists were prey, focusing only on apparently 'voluntary' commodity exchange and taking no account of value production, the unchosen *social* relations on which it is based, little appreciating how historically unprecedented they were. This misdirection of attention, which also afflicts neoclassical economics, means that capitalism's laws of motion remain undetected, leaving them to govern human behaviour all the more relentlessly. Polanyi's idea of the invisibility of *society* was remarkably similar: it was 'the radical illusion that … there is nothing in human society that is not derived from the volition of individuals and that could not, therefore, be removed again by their volition' (258). Polanyi seems unaware of this similarity, clarifying only that 'Marx's assertion of the fetish character of the value of commodities refers to the exchange value of genuine commodities and has nothing in common with … fictitious commodities' (72).

Moreover, Marx hardly overlooked human agency. For him, people 'make their own history' even if it is not in 'the circumstances of their own choosing' (Marx, 1973: 146). As a method, historical materialism is centrally concerned with the relation between structure and agency, between historically inherited circumstances and the competing and cooperating, colluding and colliding vectors of human actions, which they both constrain and support. Indeed, Marx makes a practically Polanyian point when he remarks, in discussing struggles over the length of the working day, that 'Capital takes no account of the health and length of life of the worker *unless society forces it to do so*' (Marx, [1867] 1977: 381, emphasis added). For his part, moreover, Polanyi also retained a strong sense of structural necessity: while market society was the result of conscious social engineering, it was bound to call forth the spontaneous reaction of social protection (see Thomasberger in this volume). Nor, finally, did Marx confine political agency to classes. He was aware that nation states managed economic breakdown and political class struggle, and necessarily national revolutions would beat the path out of capitalist society (Marx and Engels, [1848] 1967).

Polanyi's analysis of capitalism also had links to Marx's. While Marx concentrated on the exploitative and contradictory dynamics of value production, as we see below, he assumed the non-commodity reality of land, labour and money. And Polanyi, though he accepted the neoclassical account of utility and prices if only to construct models of socialism (Desai, 2019), remained a lifelong critic of the liberal market economy embodied in neoclassical – free market, free trade – economics. Moreover, he could not have constructed his account of imperialism and national resistance to it if he did not reject, perhaps in Austrian fashion (Polanyi does not explain why), Say's Law and the associated doctrine of comparative advantage. Polanyi's account of the functioning of the capitalist economy is remarkably similar to Marx's even though he eschewed talk of exploitation, surplus extraction and the contradictions of value production. Like Marx, Polanyi also considered capitalism a historically specific form of social production.

By now it should be clear why contrasting Marx, the revolutionary, and Polanyi, the reformer, is mistaken. Decades of neoliberalism and anti-Marxism may make this impulse understandable and it has certainly given Polanyi wider currency. However, Dale, whose careful historical contextualization of Polanyi's thinking insists on its debt to Marx and Engels, is right to point out that this 'soft' interpretation has 'a greater following but less textual support' (Dale, 2016b: 6).

The fifth major difficulty with interpreting Polanyi is that he tended to fight many battles at once: *inter alia* against 'economistic' thinking, against marginalism and the Austrian School, against liberalism and against fascism. The accurate interpretation of any point required placing it in the intersection of the relevant battles.

Finally, Polanyi had his way with references: considering the wealth of influences that flow into *TGT*, thanks to Polanyi's voracious intellectual appetite, it is remarkably ill-referenced. Let us take just two examples. First, the concept of fictitious commodities. It is not referenced at all. Daniel Immerwahr discussed its appearance two years before *TGT* in a book by Peter Drucker, Polanyi's friend from their Vienna days and a major American management guru (Immerwahr, 2009). Gareth Dale pushes the origin of the concept further back to Ferdinand Tönnies (Dale, 2010a: 71). Secondly, the similarity between Keynes's and Polanyi's thinking on the gold standard leaps out at sufficiently informed readers and, according to Abraham Rotstein, Polanyi's ideas about the gold standard were derived from Keynes (cited in Dale, 2016b: 101). However, Keynes rates only one mention in *TGT* on a quite unrelated matter (185).

Bearing these difficulties in mind, we can now begin the substantial task of appreciating *TGT*'s principal argument.

Fictitious commodities

The idea that land, labour and money were fictitious commodities served Polanyi as the principal lever for his critique of capitalism or market society. Though *prima facie* dramatically different from Marx's, Polanyi's approach could only arise in that liminal moment between the apex of classical political economy that was Marx's oeuvre and the growing influence of marginalist neoclassical economics.

In that moment, while 'Marxist economists' distorted Marx's ideas, many others, like Tönnies, looked askance at the endeavour. Marx was his intellectual lodestar. *Community and Society* is about nothing if not the historically unprecedented social form that was capitalism, the society or *Gesellschaft* contrasted with previously existing forms of community or *Gemeinschaft*. Moreover, Tönnies accepts that labour is the source of value and that, under capitalism, value is an objective measure based on socially necessary labour embodied in commodities. Tönnies's knowing (rather than blind) faithfulness to Marx is clear in his defence of Marx against the spurious accusation that neoclassical and Marxist economists hurled at him – that his work could not reconcile average profits with value and thus suffered from the infamous 'transformation problem'. It demonstrates a remarkably lucid understanding of Marx's value analysis (Tönnies, [1887] 1957a: 101).

Community and Society rests on the idea that money, land and labour are fictitious commodities. However, Tönnies deploys the concept so casually as to suggest that it was fairly current in his time. Certainly thinkers of any substance would have been aware that classical political economy did not regard the three, though they were bought and sold in capitalism, as ordinary commodities. They were not produced for sale (in the case of land, not produced at all). That was why they did not have 'natural prices', prices based on production costs, or values. The reason was simple. Unlike real commodities, their supply could not be increased or decreased in the short term with a 'supply response' to higher or lower prices. In the case of real commodities, such a supply response increases or decreases their prices back down to their natural, production-based value after temporary scarcity or glut bumps them up or down. Classical political economy was also deeply aware that the prices of the fictitious commodities, which determined the distribution of incomes in society, were determined through social not market relations (Dobb, 1973: 34). When neoclassical economics came along to insist that they were commodities like all the others, it was only a matter of time before those who retained the essentials of the classical approach labelled them special or fictitious commodities.

Tönnies's famous distinction between capitalist 'civil society' or *Gesellschaft*, 'the artificial construction of an aggregate of human beings' (Tönnies, [1887] 1957a:

64) and the older kinship-based forms of community, or *Gemeinschaft*, reflects Marx's own conception of the historical specificity of capitalism. Capitalism's origins lay, he famously argued in Part VIII of *Capital I*, not in Adam Smith's 'original accumulation' – essentially a heap of saved money – but in the historic, world-changing sundering of the natural bond of human societies and individuals to land, their natural source of subsistence (Marx, [1858] 1973: 497). This original separation, itself the product of a long and complex history (Hobsbawm, 1964; Desai, 2018b), lays the basis of the unnatural commodification of labour and land. Without it, no hoard of money, however great, could become capital, value capable of being valorized further. This, in turn, required that the social institution of money, which capitalism found pre-existing, have commodity dynamics imposed on it so money could become capitalism's lifeblood.

Money as a fictitious commodity

Polanyi shared the widespread misconception that Marx had a commodity theory of money: '*Das Kapital* implied the commodity theory of money in its Ricardian form' (25). Though Marx never completed the planned volume of *Capital* on money, and though *Capital I* is concerned to demonstrate how money behaves in the system of generalized commodity production that was capitalism, Marx is clear that money originates in state issue and commercial credit (Marx, [1867] 1977: 224). Indeed, Marx's dialectical method led him to demonstrate money's social and symbolic character, and the inevitability of politically managed fiat money. Not only is money national – 'The business of coining, like the establishing of a standard measure of prices, is an attribute proper to the state' – not only does it wear 'different national uniforms', but there is also a strict separation between the national and international spheres of circulation (ibid.: 221–222). If token money circulates in the former, it is because the social reality of money asserts itself in that most resolute of attempts to commodify money, the minting of precious metals. Coins suffer wear in circulation and the divergence of the face and bullion values of coin was a problem that, Marx notes, defined the history of coinage down to the eighteenth century: 'The fact that the circulation of money itself splits the nominal content of coins away from their real content, dividing their metallic existence from their functional existence, … implies the latent possibility of replacing metallic money with tokens made of some other material' (ibid.: 222–223). Finally, Marx notes in *Capital III*, money is not a commodity in another sense: it has no 'natural' price, no cost of production (Marx, [1894] 1981: 478).

Inheritors of the classical, necessarily historical, understanding of money as

Tönnies and Polanyi were, they saw through Ricardo's attempt to force the commodity form on fiat money by making it artificially scarce and through the neoclassical attempt to erase the social nature of money. Such attempts could only create, Tönnies pointed out, reflecting Marx's opposition of money and commodities, a most odd sort of commodity, a 'commodity without intrinsic value', wanted merely for what it could purchase, its social value. Money exchanges for commodities precisely because of its 'absence of worth' which arises from its social character (Tönnies [1887] 1957a: 70–71). Tönnies even spelled out a key implication of Marx's critique of Say's Law, that money turns the formally equal relationship of exchange into one between those with a petition and others with command (ibid.: 71). The seller is, in capitalism, usually the supplicant. The seller must sell but the buyer is not compelled to buy. Herein lay the 'antithesis, immanent in the commodity', which implied 'the possibility of crises' (Marx, [1867] 1977: 209).

Secondly, Tönnies pointed out, selling money as credit ended up, ironically, creating the only social bond (rather than market relation) ever to be created by capitalism:

> The obligation [debt] … is absolutely legal power. … The exchange of money for a good is a real process even if it can be explained only through Gesellschaft. But to receive money payments because of the possession of a commodity (for this is the nature of obligation) without delivering it, is a transcendental condition in the Gesellschaft. For, in contradistinction to the concept of Gesellschaft, a bond has been created, uniting not objects but persons. … In the act of exchange the reaction [sic: this must be 'relation'] was of mutual balance; here it appears as a one-sided dependence. (Tönnies [1887] 1957a: 74)

Taking this understanding further, Polanyi considers commodity money not just a fiction but an oxymoron: in a 'closed system', commodity money 'is simply a commodity which happens to function as money' whose amount can increase only by 'diminishing the amount of commodities not functioning as money' (193). In line with Keynes, he also remarked that the amount of commodity money, rather than reflecting the needs or the state of the economy, would be 'controlled by the supply and demand of the goods which happen to function as money'. The value of the money commodities would be determined as if they 'were sought only for their usefulness' even though they function as money, that is, without intrinsic value (131).

So, the idea of fictitious commodities, latent in classical political economy and Marx, was developed by Tönnies and further by Polanyi. For the former, labour was a 'fictitious, unnatural commodity' (Tönnies, 1957a: 101) which, like land, was not a product of labour; their supply could not be increased at will (ibid.: 93). Labour is 'human activity which goes with life itself' (72). Compare Marx on the 'separation of free labour from the objective conditions of its realization ... of the worker from the soil as his natural workshop' (Marx, [1858] 1973: 471) which is the historical basis of capitalism. Land is 'nature, which is not produced by man' (72). Money, for its part, is merely 'purchasing power' (72). It is not produced but emerges from 'credit or state finance' (72). None of these is 'produced for sale' (72), none of them has a 'natural' price deriving from its established costs of production and thus they are not commodities.

Polanyi's innovation was to take the idea of fictitious commodities and develop a fresh new line of fundamental critique of capitalism: that the drive, as strenuous as it was vain, to create a 'self-regulating market system' in which all land, labour and money were commodified defined nineteenth-century capitalism. A fresh critique was necessary because the emergence of neoclassical economics had dispatched the problematic of value so central to classical political economy and naturalized the idea that anything that is bought and sold is a commodity. Polanyi provided it. One may note, as an aside, that this move has an analogy in Keynes. He considered Marx's critique of Say's Law, which distinguished a barter from a money economy and the circuit of commodities, C–M–C from the circuit of capital, M–C–M', to be the essential starting point of a critique of capitalism and a stroke of genius on Marx's part. He even started a draft of the *General Theory* on its basis, only to re-formulate it because Say's Law had acquired a new form with neoclassical economics so its critique had to as well (see Sardoni, 1997).

Two things must be appreciated about Polanyi's innovation. First, it was a fundamental critique of neoclassical economics. The idea of the self-regulating market naturalized the commodification of the three elements of production. It assumed

> markets for all elements of industry ... their prices being called respectively commodity prices, wages, rent and interest ... [with] the income called profit being actually the difference between two sets of prices, the price of the goods and their costs. ... If these conditions are fulfilled, all incomes will derive from sales on the market, and incomes will be just sufficient to buy all the goods produced. (69)

Polanyi, however, problematized this view. The self-regulating market did not emerge either naturally or spontaneously. It was the result of a concerted effort to erect a historically unprecedented form of society (72). In previous social forms, such as feudalism for example, 'land and labour formed part of the social organization itself (money had yet hardly developed into a major element of industry)' (69).

Since the self-regulating market was based on fictions, it had to be enforced by the state. Whereas neoclassical economics considered the self-regulating market natural and planning an artificial, statist interference in it, Polanyi demonstrated that laissez-faire was the product of deliberate state action. The Poor Law Amendment Act of 1834, the Bank Act of 1844 and Anti-Corn Law Bill of 1946 comprised the trio of measures legislating the three commodity fictions into being (138). By contrast, subsequent restrictions on laissez-faire started in a spontaneous way quite simply because these fictions, once instituted, 'implied a latent threat to society in some vital aspect of its existence' (162).

> The competitive labor market hit the bearer of labor power, namely man. International free trade was primarily a threat to the largest industry dependent on nature, namely agriculture. The gold standard imperilled productive organization depending on their functioning on the relative movement of prices. (162)

Laissez-faire was planned; planning was not (141).

Secondly, it is important to note that this argument was fundamentally historical and in making it Polanyi was relying on the conservative jurist, A. V. Dicey. His inquiry into the

> 'anti-*laissez-faire*' or, as he called it, 'collectivist' trend in English public opinion since the 1960s … [found] no evidence of the existence of such a trend … *save the acts of legislation themselves.* … The upshot of his penetrating inquiry was that there had been complete absence of any deliberate intention to extend the functions of the state, or to restrict the freedom of the individual, on the part of those who were directly responsible for the restrictive enactments of the 1870s and 1880s. The legislative spearhead of the countermovement against the self-regulating market as it developed in the half century following 1860 turned out to be spontaneous, undirected by opinion and actuated by a purely pragmatic spirit. (141)

How money was commodified

Money was the core of Marx's critique of capitalism, as it was of Keynes's. Precisely because commodities exchange for money, not other commodities, contrary to Say's Law, in which markets therefore always clear, hoarding and gluts inhere in the fundamental building block of capitalism: the commodity. Not only did Keynes consider Marx's distinction between the circuit of commodities (C–M–C) and the circuit of capital (M–C–M') a brilliant insight, as mentioned already, but both thinkers also explored how the commodification of money under capitalism gave rise to specifically monetary and financial crises.

Polanyi took the innovative step of problematizing the political requirements and consequences commodifying money nationally and internationally for society and for capitalism itself. When capitalist nations forced money to behave like a commodity, artificially restricting its supply by linking its value to gold, the resulting monetary system could 'periodically liquidate business enterprise for shortages and surfeits of money would prove as disastrous to business as floods and droughts in primitive society' (73).

Since commodity money was an oxymoron and, as Marx noted, fiat money was a necessity that asserted itself in the very coining of precious metals, it was inevitable that 'Token money was developed at an early date to shelter trade from the enforced deflations that accompanied the use of specie when the volume of business swelled' (193). Equally inevitably, when token money was created, 'whether by banks or by the government', it 'constitut[ed] an interference with the self-regulation of the market' (131). Capitalists were reduced to forcing states to operate under a self-limiting ordinance when issuing money. The Bank Act of 1844, the (apparent) victory of the Ricardian currency school over the Banking school, sought to make money mimic gold by placing strict limits on the issue of bank-notes: 'no other method was conceivable which would keep the monetary system from being interfered with by the state, and thus safeguard the self-regulation of the market' (131–132).

Like scholars of his time, Polanyi 'could see that the gold standard ... meant danger of deadly deflation and, maybe, of fatal monetary stringency in a panic' (138). Historically, commodity money had been deflationary (Vilar, 1976) and had led to the mercantilist penchant for trade surpluses and bullion inflows to increase money supply (Keynes, 1936; Wiles, 1987). Only when imperialism furnished precious metals in vast quantities at the earliest beginnings of capitalism and in the late nineteenth century, Keynes remarked, did the gold standard function tolerably (Keynes, 1980: 30) and even then would have proved unnecessarily restrictive in the later period of vigorous capitalist expansion had not the cheque-writing practice spread (Keynes, 1913).

Polanyi's advance here was to expose the delicious irony at the heart of the commodification of money: that capitalist enterprise itself required saving from the capitalist organization of money. Polanyi was not without his pleasure in it: he privileged the commodity treatment of money over that of land or labour in part to 'dispose of the suspicion which the very terms "man" and "nature" ... awaken in sophisticated minds who regarded their protection as outmoded if not a downright capitulation to vested interests' (192). Even they could be brought up short by the realization that 'a system of commodity money, such as the market mechanism tends to produce without outside interference, is incompatible with industrial production' (193). When money's value was tied to that of precious metal irrespective of the economic situation, it fluctuated dangerously:

The danger was to the single enterprise – industrial, agricultural, or commercial – in so far as it was affected by changes in the price-level. For under a market system, if prices fell, business was impaired; unless all elements of cost fell proportionately, 'going concerns' were forced to liquidate, while the fall in prices might have been due not to a general fall in costs, but merely to the manner in which the monetary system was organized. (131)

By the 1870s, when Britain's gold standard became international as other countries linked their own currencies to sterling or directly to gold, these domestic dangers were compounded by international ones.

The domestic commodification of money may be a half-way house between fiat and commodity money but in foreign trade 'nothing else but commodity money could serve … for the obvious reason that token money, whether bank or fiat, cannot circulate on foreign soil. Hence the gold standard, the accepted name for a system of international commodity money – came to the fore' (193). That, however, constrained how much token money supply could expand. If it expanded too much or too little, it could lead to equally disastrous declines or rises in the gold exchange rate of the currency.

'In its simplest form the problem was this: commodity money was vital to the existence of foreign trade; token money, to the existence of domestic trade. How far did they agree with each other?' (193). That disagreement between the two typically required the latter to adjust, leading, particularly in weaker economies, to bouts of deflation to maintain the gold value of the currency. The gold standard was thereby widely appreciated, and here Polanyi's (see Desai, 2018a) and (the mature) Keynes's analysis of the ills and wrongs of the gold standard were not materially different.

The distinction of *TGT* lay in its explication of how central banks organized social protection and consolidated national economies in the process. It amounted to a veritable theory of the relationship between capitalism and nation states, including an understanding of the tendency of the most powerful among them towards imperialism, and the impulse of those that could, to resist it. A veritable geopolitical economy.

The central banking protection racket

Central banks linked national token money to international commodity money, opening the way for international pressure on currencies. The deflation that then became necessary was imposed through credit restrictions which central banks could organize because they also centralized credit supply. So, 'the working of commodity money [also] interfered with the credit system' (194).

If, uniquely among the three fictitious commodities, the institution commodifying money and that providing protection against its consequences by interfering in the market mechanism were one and the same, 'interference', in this case, was a radical understatement.

> Central banking reduced the automatism of the gold standard to a mere pretence. It meant a centrally managed currency; manipulation was substituted for the self-regulating mechanism of supplying credit, *even though the device was not always deliberate and conscious.* (195)

This made the resulting entity 'a construction entirely different from market economy' (196).

Domestically, politicized monetary policy became embroiled in 'clashes of economic classes' over monetary, fiscal and exchange rate policies (198). Internationally, while ample lip service was paid to the allegedly automatic gold standard, central banks embodied an increasingly hard sovereignty and acted as 'buffer[s] between the internal and the external economy' (198–199). They became the unconsciously erected impregnable bastions of a new nationalism (198) and levels of activity and employment competed with concerns of international investors over the gold or international value of a currency.

This negation of the market economy in 'crustacean nations' was practically required by the gold standard. The rise of such nations accounted for the failure of attempts, which continued to be made as late as the 1930s, to resurrect the gold standard. Only in the early 1930s was their 'final failure' (200) pronounced.

Crustacean nations against imperialism

The new 'crustacean type of nation [that] expressed its identity through national token currencies safeguarded by a type of sovereignty more jealous and absolute than anything known before' contrasted with the 'easy going nations of the past' (202). If 'social protection was the accompaniment of a supposedly self-regulating market' (202), and if that 'protectionism everywhere was producing the hard shell of the emerging unit of social life … cast in the *national* mold' (202, emphasis added), modern national states and the states system they comprised had been called into being by the self-regulating market or capitalism itself. Central banking, as the institution that commodified money and provided social protection against it, played a privileged role in this process. It signified the inevitable union of money and nationality: money was national and it organized the national social and productive formation.

The liberal creed, which sought so vainly to create and maintain a self-regulating market, could only be oblivious to these truths: for it nations were at best as quaint cultural vestiges of the past or annoying interference with its project at worst. Not so for Polanyi.

> The constitutive importance of the currency in establishing the nation as the decisive economic and political unit of the time was … thoroughly overlooked by the writers of the liberal Enlightenment. … Actually, the new national unit and the new national currency were inseparable. … The monetary system on which credit was based had become the lifeline of both national and international economy. (203)

While social protections against all three fictitious commodities were increasingly intertwined – for instance if tariffs governed the price of food and hence the wage level, they could not be easily disentangled from labour legislation – the import of monetary protection was far greater.

> [I]f customs tariffs and social laws produced an artificial climate, monetary policy created what amounted to veritable artificial weather conditions varying day by day and affecting every member of the community in its immediate interests. … What the businessman, the organized worker, the housewife pondered, what the farmer who was planning his crop, the parents who were weighing their children's chances, the lovers who were waiting to get married, resolved in their minds when considering the favor of the times, was more directly determined by the monetary policy of the central bank than by any other single factor. (205)

Crustacean nations also lay at the heart of Polanyi's understanding of imperialism. He dismissed the well-known works on the subject by the social liberal, John Hobson and the Marxists, Rudolf Hilferding, Rosa Luxemburg, Nikolai Bukharin and Vladimir Lenin:

> We have become too accustomed to think of the spread of capitalism as a process which is anything but peaceful, and of finance capital as the chief instigator of innumerable colonial crimes and expansionist aggressions. Its intimate affiliation with heavy industries made Lenin assert that finance capital was responsible for imperialism, notably for the struggle for spheres of influence, concessions, extra-territorial rights, and the innumerable forms in which the Western Powers got a stranglehold on backward regions, in order to invest in railways, public utilities, ports and other permanent establishments on which their heavy industries made profits. (16)

Such views amounted to 'popular political theology' in which 'imperialism stands for the old Adam' and 'states and empires are congenitally imperialist' (212). However, *TGT*'s account shares so much with these understandings that Polanyi repeats a mistake made by some of them. He agreed with Lenin, Bukharin and Hilferding that 1870 opened the imperialist phase (as opposed to Hobson and

Luxemburg, who regarded imperialism as an enduring feature of capitalism which entered a new, dangerously competitive phase in the late nineteenth century; see Desai 2013). Polanyi insisted that 'modern capitalism started with a long period of [territorial] contractionism; only late in its career did the turn toward imperialism happen' (212). The conclusion of the Seven Years' War unleashed an expansion of markets so rapid as to send empires 'out of fashion', separating politics from economics as firmly on the international stage as on the domestic. 'Gladstone', he said, 'would have branded it a calumny that British foreign policy was being put at the service of foreign investors' (213). 'Not only at home but also abroad, the principle of non-intervention of the state in the affairs of private business was maintained' (213) until late in the century. This thesis was conclusively refuted long ago by Gallagher and Robinson (1953), who demonstrated the reality of British imperial expansion throughout the nineteenth century.

Nevertheless, like Lenin, Bukharin and Hilferding's works, *TGT* had the merit of exploring the novelty of the new phase of capitalism characterized by the second industrial revolution with its high capital requirements and greater role of finance (Hilferding), industrial concentration or monopoly (Lenin) and their national organization (Bukharin) (Desai, 2013: 43–63).

The collapse of the gold standard: the reality of contradictions

In Polanyi's account of the Hundred Years' Peace between the Napoleonic Wars and the First World War, the balance of power was important but so was the pattern of finance. If the balance of power operated without 'continuous war between changing powers' (6), this was because of the work of powerful agencies. The reactionary Holy Alliance had prevented wars 'with the help of instruments peculiar to it, the international kinship structure of the European aristocracy and the "voluntary civil service" that was the Roman Catholic Church. And by the mid-nineteenth century, it was assisted another "powerful social instrumentality … which could play the role of dynasties and episcopacies … and make the peace interest effective' (9). That instrumentality was *haute finance*.

This *sui generis* institution 'functioned as the main link between the political and economic organization of the world … as a permanent agency of the most elastic kind' (10). 'Independent of single governments, even the most powerful, it was in touch with all'. Though also 'independent of central banks, even of the Bank of England', no state 'would consider any long-range plan, whether peaceful or warlike' without its goodwill (10). In its heyday, haute finance was also, effectively, the Rothschild banking dynasty: 'subject to no *one* government; as a family they embodied the abstract principle of internationalism; their loyalty was to a firm, the credit of which had become the only supranational link between political government and industrial effort'. The world needed 'a sovereign agent commanding the confidence of national statesmen and of the international investor alike'; and 'the metaphysical extraterritoriality of a Jewish bankers' dynasty … provided an almost perfect solution' (10).

Through much of the nineteenth century, haute finance consistently served 'a new interest which had no specific organ of its own, for the service of which, no other institution happened to be available … namely peace' (12). It 'acted as a powerful moderator in the councils and policies of a number of smaller sovereign states' (14); secured their adherence to the gold standard and constitutionalism (14); provided '*de facto* administration for … troubled regions where peace was most vulnerable' (14). There were also a 'half dozen national centers [of finance] hiving around their banks of issue and stock exchanges. Each was a microcosm', differing from others in pattern and practice (11). International haute finance cooperated with national financial centres and through them, kept in touch with governments.

Eventually, however, the national overshadowed the international even in finance. Though finance had an interest in preventing 'general war between the great powers' (10), Polanyi also appreciated that haute finance made its fortune 'in the financing of war' and that, 'ultimately, it was war that laid down the law to business' (12). As tensions in Europe mounted, business became less international.

> International finance had to cope with the conflicting ambitions and intrigues of the great and small powers; its plans were thwarted by diplomatic maneuvers, its long-term investments jeopardized, its constructive efforts hampered by political sabotage and backstairs obstruction. *The national banking organizations without which it was helpless often acted as the accomplices of their respective governments, and no plan was safe which did not carve out in advance the booty of each participant.* (13, emphasis added)

By the 1870s, a shift towards nationalism and war appeared to have taken place and only colonial trade and investment preserved the semblance of cosmopolitanism. With industrialization of contender powers like Germany, the singular imperial expansion of Britain turned into a competition for markets and investment outlets between several nationally organized blocs of capital of comparable power: 'Economic imperialism was mainly a struggle between the Powers for the privilege of extending their trade into politically unprotected markets' (217).

As post-Bismarckian Germany asserted itself more uncompromisingly and entered a 'hard and fast' alliance with Austria-Hungary and Italy (19), room for balance of power manoeuvres narrowed. It disappeared after Britain's own 'counter-alliance' with France and Russia in the new century. The balance of power was displaced by 'two hostile power groupings' (19) and the path to war lay open. Now,

> an emotional change was noticeable, though there was no corresponding break in the dominant ideas. The world continued to believe in internationalism and interdependence, while acting on the impulses of nationalism and self-sufficiency. Liberal nationalism was developing into national liberalism, with its marked leanings towards protectionism and imperialism abroad, monopolistic conservatism at home. (198)

This new nationalism was only the final and most dramatic result of a 'long development within the most advanced countries which made the system anachronistic' and represented 'the failure of the market economy' (20). The drama of the interwar decades consisted precisely in the fact that 'a return to the nineteenth century system appeared the only way out' (21) even as that way was effectively barred. *TGT* is centrally about how this new nationalism emerged and how it changed the geopolitical economy of world capitalism.

The gold standard era is generally attributed an almost legendary stability, broken only by war, though Marcello De Cecco (1984) debunked this myth some time ago. Its real volatility is clear only, he argued, if we replace the Ricardian understanding of it with a Listian one, in which the state-led industrialization of the contenders behind protectionist walls, complete with regulatory and banking structures tailored for it, undermined Britain's manufacturing superiority (Desai, 2013: ch. 2, but see also Hobsbawm, 1968; Chang, 2002). Industrial competition sharpened, spilled over into imperial competition and led, as is well known, to the First World War (Hobsbawm, 1968). This turbulence also undermined the gold standard.

Two opposing processes made the gold standard volatile. Britain linked its colonies' currencies to sterling, directing their gold earnings to London which were then exported, thus sustaining Britain's position as the world's financial centre. India, Britain's lucrative colonial 'crown jewel', served as a model (this was what the young Keynes of 1913 not only demonstrated but advocated, in striking contrast to his mature views, as Desai, 2018a argues).

Only colonial and semi-colonial control gave the gold standard that semblance of universality Polanyi noted:

> In all matters relevant to the world monetary system, similar institutions were established everywhere, such as representative bodies, written constitutions defining their jurisdiction and regulating the publication of budgets, the promulgation of laws, the ratification of treaties, the methods of incurring financial obligations, the rules of public accountancy, the rights of foreigners, the jurisdiction of courts, the domicile

of bills of exchange and thus, by implication, the status of the bank of issue, of foreign bondholders, of creditors of all description. (205)

Independent countries, however, could and did exercise other options depending on the proclivities and abilities of their ruling classes. While some countries, such as the oligarchical primary commodity exporters, Austria-Hungary and Russia, remained with depreciating silver while gold appreciated (De Cecco, 1984: 51–52), others sought to escape the depreciation that occurred when India was forced off the silver standard and the rupee was linked to sterling, and yet others did so to obtain credit. Lastly, and most importantly, contender nations, beginning with Germany, sought to link their currencies directly with gold, on the model of sterling itself, as a challenge to Britain's financial and commercial pre-eminence and to gain international acceptability for their own currency as part of a drive to expand market share (ibid.: ch. 3). If, as Polanyi noted, 'the actual use of the gold standard by Germany marked the beginning of the era of protection and colonial expansion' (19), it was because Germany joined the gold standard not to accede to it but to challenge Britain's command over it.

This challenge made the period volatile well before the First World War when the gold standard is generally considered to have collapsed. After all, 'a stable gold exchange standard could exist only so long as the political sovereignty of the centre countries *vis-a-vis* the periphery remained unchallenged' (De Cecco, 1984: 57). So,

> the system was stable while it remained a Sterling Standard, and … it began to oscillate more and more dangerously, till its final collapse in July 1914, as Britain declined and other large industrial countries rose to greater prominence, and adopted the Gold Standard [i.e. sought to become key currency countries] as a form of monetary nationalism, in order to deprive Britain of her last power, that of control over international financial flows. (Ibid.: vii–viii).

This understanding pervades *TGT*, providing the substance of its richest passages. The gold standard assumed that member countries would be willing to impose punishing costs on themselves to abide by its principles. However,

> It was idle to expect that invariably the country whose currency slumped would automatically increase its exports and thereby restore the balance of payments, or that its need for foreign capital would compel it to compensate the foreigner and resume the service of its debt. Increased sales of coffee or nitrates, for instance, might knock the bottom out of the market, and the repudiation of usurious foreign debt would appear preferable to a depreciation of the national currency. (207)

When this happened, the market mechanism of civil society no longer sufficed and had to be replaced by the rude force of the state, exerted, inevitably, by the strong on the weak. No wonder such self-abnegation was rare outside the hapless colonies.

If force had to be deployed against defaulting countries, presenting them with the alternatives of 'bombardment or settlement', it was also equally effective in forcing 'colonial peoples to recognize the advantages of trade when the theoretically unfailing argument of mutual advantage was not promptly – or perhaps not at all – grasped by the natives' (207). Only colonies could be subject to the allegedly apolitical market mechanism. Even the smaller and weaker among the independent nations could be expected to deal with debt and payments crises through repudiation (207). The more 'political instruments had to be used in order to maintain equilibrium in the world economy' (208), the more the gold standard system came under strain.

If political power could be wielded to shore up the allegedly self-regulating market against weaker states, it was also used by powerful contenders to challenge that system. As unemployment strained the credibility of the self-regulating market, the liberal state could use repression or '[i]n the case of strong states, the pressure [of unemployment] might be deflected into a scramble for foreign markets, colonies, zones of influence and other forms of imperialist rivalry' (210–211). Polanyi saw the gold standard as perched precariously atop a world of social protection trying to maintain some vestigial semblance of the self-regulating market even as it required its abrogation in every field. From the 1870s onwards,

> the typical institutions of the market economy could usually be introduced only if accompanied by protectionist measures, all the more so because since the late 1870s and early 1880s nations were forming themselves into organised units which were apt to suffer grievously from the dislocations involved in any sudden adjustment to the needs of foreign trade or foreign exchanges. (214)

Thus it was that the gold standard, the 'supreme vehicle for the expansion of market economy' (214), was accompanied by social protection not only of central banking but also social legislation and agricultural tariffs (214).

Polanyi's view of what undergirded all this demonstrated his powerful insights into the nature of the nation-states system which consisted of imperial, colonized and contender states. All three required 'crustacean nations', though only the first and last had them. 'Crustacean' states were necessary to survive the industrial and financial might of other powerful capitalist countries once they had emerged. The 'paradox of imperialism', inexplicable in terms of conventional economic theory, was the need for 'crustacean nations'. Countries rejected free trade and, where possible, competed to acquire 'overseas and exotic markets' because it was clear that the alternative was the 'unspeakable suffering' of the 'exotic and semicolonial regions' where markets were 'imposed on a helpless people in the absence of protective measures'.

What made countries act in this manner was simply the fear of consequences similar to those which the powerless peoples were unable to avert. The difference was merely that while the tropical population of the wretched colony was thrown into utter misery and degradation, often to the point of physical extinction, the Western country's refusal was induced by the danger of a smaller peril but still sufficiently real to be avoided at almost all cost. (214–215)

The negative demonstration effect of the colonies reinforced the struggle of nations to avoid this fate at all costs. The colonies, in their turn, suffered for lack of 'crustacean nations' and fought to acquire them. While necessary to imperialist expansion, they were equally necessary to protection against it. That was why Polanyi considered 'crustacean nations' necessary to the prospects for socialism.

Conclusion

In trying to beat a path to socialism in the twenty-first century, we would do well to recall this conclusion and to adapt our understanding to the unfolding of the capitalist world since 1945 to reflect it. The master narrative of *TGT* emerges as a powerful account of the close relationship between capitalism and the nation-state form and its centrality to any path towards socialism. Polanyi appreciates deeply that the capitalist world must necessarily consist of a plurality of competing and struggling nations. He clearly saw through Wilson's ploy behind the League of Nations: it was an 'absurd device of the permanent disarmament of the defeated countries [which] ruled out any constructive solution. The only alternative to this disastrous condition of affairs was the establishment of an international order endowed with an organised power which would transcend national sovereignty' (22) and that was not possible without the abolition of 'universal capitalism'. Not only are nation states the principal sites for the organization of social protection in general but, by also organizing social protection against the commodification of money, they become effectively the necessary organizers of capitalist economies and, so long as powerful capitalist economies exist anywhere, of social democratic and socialist economies.

Notes

1 I would like to thank Fred Block, Gareth Dale, Michael Hudson and Kari Polanyi Levitt for their comments on previous drafts. They greatly improved the chapter. Any remaining problems must, of course, be laid at my door.
2 References with page numbers alone are to pages in *The Great Transformation* (Polanyi, [1944] 1957).

5

Double movement, embeddedness and the transformation of the financial system

Oscar Ugarteche Galarza

This chapter aims to use Polanyi's concept of embeddedness and disembeddedness in order to understand how the category of 'Too Big to Fail' (TBTF) financial institutions came into being through the double movement of market deregulation and social regulation. The concepts of embeddedness in social regulation and disembeddedness under market regulation permit an understanding of how, as a few TBTF financial institutions re-embedded themselves, becoming risk proof, the majority remained disembedded and subject to failure. We want to argue that, given this, the financial system may no longer be considered a system. 'The term "embeddedness" expresses the idea that the economy is not autonomous, as it must be in economic theory, but subordinated to politics, religion, and social relations. Polanyi's use of the term suggests more than the now familiar idea that market transactions depend on trust, mutual understanding, and legal enforcement of contracts' (*TGT*: xxiii–xxiv).[1]

In doing this, the chapter shares the view that 'Polanyi's arguments about money and its double movement [are] consubstantial … with the constitution of the world order of capitalism as a plurality of modern national economies and interventionist … states in competition and struggle" (Desai in this volume). The process of re-embeddedness happens in most countries with large financial institutions given that the political and the economic are more imbricated in one another and that they have grown to be the size of large countries.

This chapter is relevant for Polanyian scholars in so far as it helps to understand contemporary systemic financial problems. The analytical process using his concepts opens the way for a new understanding of systemic flaws in general and financial systemic flaws, in particular.

The chapter is divided into two parts. The first part revises Polanyi's concept of embeddedness/disembeddedness and reviews the concept of Too Big to Fail financial institutions. The second proposes the idea of a financial complex, as a derivation of those concepts, where some financial institutions TBTF are re-embedded while those the right size to fail (RSTF) remain disembedded. The contemporary usefulness of Polanyi's work for the analysis of such very complicated financial architecture is clear in this work.

'Market economy implies a self-regulating system of markets; in slightly more technical terms, it is an economy directed by market prices and nothing but market prices' (ibid.: 45). The opposite is where the logic of capital is socially embedded. This is what Ruggie refers to as 'embedded liberalism' (Ruggie, 1982). This distinction can be seen as one between financial institutions that came to be regulated by the market and the risk and return principle, by and large after the deregulation process ended in 1999, and a subset of 'too big to fail banks' which came into being in 1984. These institutions are considered too socially important to be allowed to fail on market principles: the results would be socially too damaging. Here the Polanyian idea that there is a double movement of disembedded economic liberalism on the one hand and the principle of embeddedness in the rubric of society and government on the other can be utilized to analyse the separation between TBTF banks and RSTF banks in the early 1980s. The TBTF concept was introduced in 1984 with the bankruptcy of Continental Illinois Bank (Hetzel, 1991; Moyer and Lamy, 1992; Hughes and Mester, 1993). Banks in this category are socially embedded while the rest are disembedded and left to competition and market rules.

The second point is that if the financial market contains two subsets of institutions, one subject to the disembedded market logic of risk and return and the other not, then the second subset can assume more risk than the first. However, together they will no longer add up to a system, as the two subsets do not follow the same rules. The liberal financial system was initially disembedded with the gold standard and self-regulation at its centre but this broke down in the 1930s bringing the gold standard and haute finance to its end.

To liberal economists, the gold standard was a purely economic institution; they refused even to consider it as a part of a social mechanism. Thus, it happened that the democratic countries were the last to realize the true nature of the catastrophe and the slowest to counter its effects. Not even when the cataclysm was already upon them did their leaders see that behind the collapse of the international system there stood a long development within the most advanced countries which made that system anachronistic; in other words, the failure of the market economy itself still escaped them (*TGT*: 21).

After 1934, with the Glass Steagall Act, re-regulation re-embedded the US financial sector, introduced the dollar/gold standard and terminated the gold standard.

This lasted until the demise of the dollar/gold standard (1971) when the dollar's gold backing was withdrawn and liberalized currency markets were introduced. Later, in 1980 general financial deregulation began to disembed the financial sector once again. Soon after, with the Latin American debt crisis, the concept of 'Too Big to Fail' was operationalized and broke through the usual boundaries between politics and economics. A group of banks were re-embedded to protect them from bankruptcy in 1984. It was the first time that the idea was launched. And it went with a historically unprecedented 'revolving door' between the TBTF institutions and the US Treasury: the best way to illustrate this is that whereas only three Secretaries of the Treasury *did not* come from the financial sector between 1980 and 2018, between 1960 and 1979, only two *came* from the financial sector (see Tables 5.1a and 5.1b).

The third point is that if the addition of the two subsystems does not constitute one system, it must constitute, then, a *complex*. The constitution of the US financial sector as a complex developed from the 1980s and was strengthened in 2008 when a new set of political relationships was created that reflected the operation of the complex based on the even greater government protection of the largest TBTF financial institutions. Since the 2008 crisis they have become even larger. This change provides for a significant change in the dynamics of embedded liberal capitalism and paves the way for a new 'riskless financial capitalism' with its own financial institutions TBTF.

Table 5.1a   Secretaries of the Treasury of the United States, 1961 and 1979
            Mostly from the productive sectors

Name	Period	President	Origin
Douglas Dillon, NY	21/1/1961–22/11/1963 22/11/1963–1/4/1965	Kennedy, LBJ	CEO Dillon Read IB*
Henry H. Fowler, VA	1/4/1965–20/12/1968	LBJ	Lawyer, public official
Joseph W. Barr, IN	21/12/1968–20/1/1969	LBJ	Economist, public official
David M. Kennedy, UT	22/1/1969–11/2/1971	Nixon	CEO Continental Illinois Bank*
John B. Connally, TX	11/2/1971–12/6/1972	Nixon	Lawyer, oil
George P. Shultz, IL	12/6/1972–8/5/1974	Nixon	Academic
William E. Simon, NJ	8/5/1974–9/8/1974 9/8/1974–20/1/1977	Nixon, Ford	Partner Salomon Brothers*
W. Michael Blumenthal, MI	23/1/1977–4/8/1979	Carter	CEO Unisys

Source: US Department of the Treasury. Prior secretaries at https://home.treasury.gov/about/history/prior-secretaries. Accessed 6 January 2018.
Note: *Exception to the rule of coming from the productive sector.

Table 5.1b   Secretaries of the Treasury of the United States, 1979 and 2017

Name	Period	President	Origin
G. William Miller, RI	6/8/1979–20/8/1981	Carter	CEO Textron Chairman Boston Fed
Donald T. Regan, NJ	22/1/1981–2/2/1985	Reagan	CEO Merrill Lynch
James A. Baker III, TX	3/2/1985–17/8/1988	Reagan	Lawyer, senior partner Baker and Botts*
Nicholas F. Brady, NJ	16/9/1988–17/1/1993	Reagan, G. H. W. Bush	CEO Dillon Read
Lloyd M. Bentsen, TX	22/1/1993–22/12/1994	Clinton	CEO Lincoln Consolidated Financial Services
Robert E. Rubin, NY	10/1/1995–2/7/1999	Clinton	CEO Goldman Sachs
Lawrence H. Summers, MA	2/7/1999–20/1/2001	Clinton	Financial advisor academic
Paul H. O'Neill, PA	30/1/2001–31/12/2002	G. W. Bush	CEO Alcoa*
John W. Snow, VA	3/2/2003–29/6/2006	G. W. Bush	Lawyer, president and CEO of CSX (railroad industry)*
Henry M. Paulson, Jr., IL	10/7/2006–20/1/2009	G. W. Bush	CEO Goldman Sachs
Timothy F. Geithner, NY	26/1/2009–25/1/2013	Obama	Public official, IMF, President New York Fed
Jacob J. Lew, NY	27/2/2013–20/1/2016	Obama	Citigroup, Public official
Steven Mnuchin, NY	13/2/2017–	Trump	Goldman Sachs

Source: US Department of the Treasury. Prior secretaries at https://home.treasury.gov/about/history/prior-secretaries. Accessed 6 January 2018.
Note: *Exception to the rule of coming from the financial sector.

Polanyi's concept of embeddedness/disembeddedness and TBTF

Polanyi's concepts of embeddedness and disembeddedness arise from his recognition that 'The human economy … is integrated and entangled in economic and non-economic institutions' (1971: 148). An example of this is the concept of haute finance. In chapter I of *The Great Transformation*, Polanyi says:

> *Haute finance* was not designed as an instrument of peace. This function fell by accident, as historians would say, while sociologists would prefer to call it by the law of availability. The reason for *haute finance* is profit. To achieve this, it was necessary to stay on good terms with governments whose goal was power and conquest. We can neglect at this point the distinction between political and economic power, and between economic and political purposes by governments. Indeed, it was the characteristic of nation-states in this period (1870–1910) that such a distinction was unrealistic, because whatever their objectives, governments endeavoured to achieve them through the use and increase of national power. (ibid.: 10)

Polanyi said of haute finance, 'this mysterious institution has hardly emerged from the chiaroscuro of politico-economic mythology' (ibid.: 10). For Polanyi, haute finance is a dark hole that must be understood in order to understand capitalism. He then proceeds to uncover some of the mystery. '*Haute finance*, an institution sui generis, peculiar to the last third of the nineteenth and the first third of the twentieth century, functioned as the main link between the political and the economic organization of the world' (ibid.: 10). Its role was not just that of financial intermediary, but also political intermediary. 'It supplied the instruments for an international peace system, which was worked with the help of the Powers, but which the Powers themselves could neither have established nor maintained' (ibid.: 10). The power-brokering role of international bankers during the nineteenth century and the early part of the twentieth was essential for the keeping of the Hundred Years' Peace between 1815 and 1914. 'Yet the secret of the successful maintenance of general peace lay undoubtedly in the position, organization, and techniques of international finance' (ibid.: 10). There was a very tight bond between diplomacy and finance. The Rothschilds are a good example of this. Having made their money through financing wars, their interest as a family was international peace and they knew how to obtain it without giving in to national allegiances but rather by keeping their loyalty to the firm.

> The Rothschilds were subject to no one government; as a family they embodied the abstract principle of internationalism; their loyalty was to a firm, the credit of which had become the only supranational link between political government and industrial effort in a swiftly growing world economy. In the last resort, their independence sprang from the needs of the time which demanded a sovereign agent commanding the confidence of national statesmen and of the international investor alike; it was to this vital need that the metaphysical extraterritoriality of a Jewish bankers' dynasty domiciled in the capitals of Europe provided an almost perfect solution. (Ibid.: 11)

Polanyi adds that international banking included the financing of governments, their wars, 'foreign investment in industry, public utilities, and banks, as well as long-term loans to public and private corporations abroad' (ibid.: 11). Haute finance as a centre, with international agents related to national agents, shows how the financial world works not only in terms of a system of expanded reproduction of capital, but also of the relationship with peace and diplomacy required at times for this end.

Given that financial institutions are rooted in particular societies while also being international, the issue is how can they be socially regulated and which society prevails over which? New questions arise from Polanyi's work in this field. Is it a matter of economic size? Military prowess? Political craftsmanship? All together?

These questions are definitive because the continuity of haute finance in other forms conserving its international characteristics and functions in 'unions and consortiums, foreign loans, financial controls or other transactions of an ambitious scope' (*TGT*: 12) is what generated the transformation of the international financial system during the 1930s and early 1940s. After the war, haute finance as such disappeared and was transformed into multinational banks, mostly regulated by the Glass Steagall Act, if they were American, and by similar laws in Great Britain, and into the creation of financial havens, to avoid those regulations.

Finally, money, though it operates in a market context, is simply a sign of purchasing power that, as a general rule, does not come into being spontaneously through the operation of the market, but comes into existence through the mechanisms of the state, banking and finance. It is one of the three fictitious commodities around which the argument of *The Great Transformation* revolves.

The crucial point is this: labour, land and money are essential elements of industry; they also must be organized in markets; in fact, these markets form an absolutely vital part of the economic system. But labour, land and money are obviously not commodities; the postulate that anything that is bought and sold must have been produced for sale is emphatically untrue in regard to them. In other words, according to the empirical definition of a commodity, they are not commodities. None of these is produced for sale. On the one hand, to describe them as commodities is entirely fictitious (ibid.: 75–76). On the other, Polanyi states that 'The extension of the market mechanism to the elements of industry – labour, land, and money – was the inevitable consequence of the introduction of the factory system in a commercial society. The elements of industry had to be on sale''' (ibid.: 78).

It is critically important that the idea of money as a fictitious commodity not be confused with Marx's idea of fictitious capital in the famous chapter 25 of *Capital*, Volume III. Fictitious capital refers to financial assets which are not backed by productive investment, whereas real capital is invested in production. Polanyi's argument is about money. Money is not a commodity because it is a social institution. It is not produced for sale. When, under capitalism, the commodity form is forced on it, as it is also forced on the two other elements of industry, land and labour, which are not produced for sale, it functions, like them, as a fictitious commodity. Money as a fictitious commodity and Marx's idea of fictitious capital intersect where, once money is commodified, one of the forms it can take is that of financial assets which are traded; assets that can constitute fictitious capital, though they may also constitute real capital. The commodification of money is therefore clearly tied to the emergence of fictitious capital and, at certain times, particularly when real productive investment slows down, the generation of fictitious capital takes on a logic of its own and dominates the financial sector, extinguishing its function of directing capital towards productive investment and turning it into a hive of speculation. The concept of the self-regulated market that Polanyi uses refers to the disembedded system whose essence is self-regulation.

A market economy is an economic system controlled, regulated and directed by market prices. Order in the production and distribution of goods is entrusted to this self-regulating mechanism. An economy of this kind derives from the expectation that human beings behave in such a way as to achieve maximum money gains. It assumes markets in which the supply of goods (including services) available at a definite price will equal the demand at that price. It assumes the presence of money, which functions as purchasing power in the hands of its owners. Production will then be controlled by prices, for the profits of those who direct production will depend upon them. The distribution of the goods will also depend upon prices, because prices form incomes, and it is through the distribution of these incomes that the goods produced are distributed among the members of society. Under these assumptions order in the production and distribution of goods is ensured by prices alone (ibid.: 71).

That is, the market is self-regulated in so far as it is a system and the money market is a money system or a financial system that incorporates real capital and fictitious capital. The physicist Von Bertalanffy (1968) states that to recognize systems as such, they must have mechanisms of self-feedback so they may self-regulate. Systems are self-regulated by definition. The market is a price system, for example. The thermostat is a system *par excellence* because it knows when to turn on and off in order to keep the temperature stable. In this sense, all systems self-regulate in some way or other and therefore, as the economy is self-regulated, we can talk about the economy as a system. The same is not true for the financial 'system'.

The problem begins with the exceptions; for example, monopolies and concentrated oligopolies. When the competition is monopolistic, or when there are power or information asymmetries between the agents, or when markets are fragmented, there is no self-regulation: the law of the strongest prevails. And the idea of TBTF introduced another type of exception. When banks seek government protection in order not to go bankrupt and, being seen as TBTF, they are rescued, they become re-embedded in social institutions and are insulated from the market. The TBTF idea, which had emerged in the 1980s, became significant again during the first decade of the twenty-first century as analysts tried to warn of what might happen with a major financial crisis (Stern and Feldman, 2004; Baker and McArthur, 2009; Zhou, 2010). It must be pointed out that, while the US is usually the focus of discussion of TBTF financial institutions, this happened in various countries without questions being raised about the size of the financial institutions, for example Japan, Great Britain, Spain, France and Germany, where few banks control over 80 per cent of all banking assets (see Table 5.4, p. 115). This became a matter of a return of the state in a national dimension in a global financial market.

Some large banks that were rescued because they were TBTF were absorbed entirely by the nine largest US banks. The resulting entities, measured by their asset value, were comparable to the GDP of some G7 countries. Great Britain nationalized its TBTF banks, Spain and Italy struggled with theirs, capitalizing them and then selling them. The German government became an important supporter of German banks, and Japan also rescued its major institutions. All this government action ensured that these institutions could no longer be disembedded in the market economy and compete on equal terms with others. Instead they have become even bigger, and competition between them and those who do not depend on society and government for protection, even more asymmetric. The choice of all governments to protect their TBTF institutions rather than breaking them up into smaller entities that would not be TBTF was due in part to state competition. Without a general agreement to split TBTF institutions, the first to do so would enjoy a 'first mover' advantage. It would be the first to enter the market for the purchase of the smaller institutions in its own and other countries. In the US, this anomalous growth and re-embeddedness was coordinated between the Secretary of the Treasury – a former banker – the Federal Reserve Bank (FED) and the thirteen major bankers themselves (Johnson and Kwak, 2010).

Being TBTF, these institutions do not compete on equal terms with disembedded banks that we may call the 'right size to fail' but have another logic. The RSTF financial institutions do not endanger society while those that are TBTF do. Yet, if in financial markets risk is conceptually the measure of profitability from a neoclassical angle, enterprises that take higher risk should be more profitable. But this re-embedding turns things on their head. Those that are TBTF take little risk but remain highly 'profitable'. This raises questions about how their profitability should be measured. It is not clear where their profitability comes from in the absence of risk. RSTF and TBTF financial institutions do not operate with the same rules or with the same rationality.

What has happened is that there are two subsets of institutions whose aggregation cannot constitute one financial system, as they are subject to two different sets of rules. This is not just a national issue but also an international problem of the global financial markets. In 2016, there were nine banks in the US that were 'too big to fail' (see Figure 5.1), which represented 0.1367 per cent of the total number of banks in the United States. These institutions have been closely imbricated into the

| TBTF 9 US banks 0.1367% of all US banks 73% US financial assets

EMBEDDED | *These two subsets have different laws of operation.*

TBTF banks do not follow the risk return principle and thus cannot go bankrupt. Embedded.
RSTF banks follow the risk return principle and can go bankrupt. Disembedded | RSTF 6,582 US banks 99.8633% of all US banks 27% US financial assets

DISEMBEDDED |

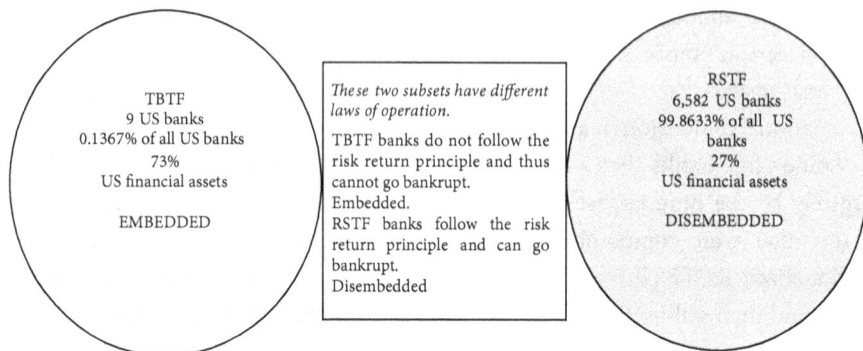

5.1. Subsets of the financial complex

structures of US political power since 1980 and are those that received most support from the so-called Troubled Asset Relief Program (TARP) in 2008: $426,400 billion out of $700,000 billion released by the Bush administration upon request of Treasury Secretary Hank Paulson, former CEO of Goldman Sachs. This generates the question 'relief for whom and problems for whom?' in a world where there are thirty of these banks out of a total of 30,000, where they constitute 0.00001 per cent of all banks but much more in terms of financial assets. The same is true for other countries.

A system is 'a set of rules or things so related or connected as to form a unity or organic whole; as a solar *system*, irrigation *system*, supply system' (*Webster's Dictionary*). A financial system, therefore, would be the total sum of banks, pension funds, investment funds, trusts, stock exchanges, commodity and exchange markets, and other financial institutions that contribute to the creation of money and credit markets, ideally in order to facilitate the movement of resources from surplus sectors to deficit sectors with the purpose of stimulating physical investment, production of goods and services, and consumption, though with deregulation since the 1980s such purposes have been superseded by speculative impulses.

Webster's Dictionary also defines a system as a set of rules or principles on a matter rationally linked together. This definition opens the question of whether any agglomerate with different rules for institutions within it can be called a system. Embedded TBTF banks with disembedded banks that can fail cannot, therefore, constitute a system as defined above. There would at least have to be subsystems of TBTF banks and of RSTF banks. These are two subsystems, one embedded of TBTF institutions, supported, protected and regulated by the state and that do not operate on risk and cannot fail, and one disembedded that operates on the risk return principle and that can fail. Both added together *do not* form a single system because they operate with different economic laws. In systems theory, what constitutes the system is partially its uniform rules for all its components. The principle of self-regulation is universal for all components of a system and its result is homeostasis. With two subsystems where one is protected and the other is not, by definition one is self-regulated and the other is not. Further, they cannot reach the same point of equilibrium. These two subsystems do not operate with the same set of rules nor with the same rationality; therefore they do not constitute a system (see Figure 5.1). The fact that TBTF banks and RSTF banks compete does not mean they belong to the same 'whole', or system. As systems theorist, Von Bertalanffy pointed out long ago: 'In the state of wholeness, a disturbance of the system leads to the introduction of a new state of equilibrium. If, however, the system is split up into individual causal chains, these go on independently' (Von Bertalanffy, 1968: 69).

With the onset of the 2008 financial crisis some institutions received massive US federal aid and others did not and went bankrupt. In total between 2007 and 2016, 547 banks went bankrupt, which were RSTF, this is 52.3 banks per year on average. Before that, 24 banks went bankrupt between 2000 and 2007, this is 3.5 banks per year, average. With the crisis, 15.3 times more banks went bankrupt per year than before the crisis (see Table 5.2). TBTF banks were protected by the state and went on independently from the others, creating for themselves a new equilibrium.

Table 5.2   *Total number of bankrupt banks, 2000–2016 in the United States*

Year	Number of bankrupt banks
2000–2006	24 (3.4 banks yearly on average)
2007	3
2008	25
2009	140
2010	157
2011	92
2012	51
2013	24
2014	18
2015	8
2016	5
2017	8
	Total: 555

Source: FDIC 'Failed Bank List', www.fdic.gov/bank/individual/failed/banklist.html. Accessed 7 August 2018.

The largest bankrupt banks were incorporated into ever larger banks with public resources as part of their re-embeddedness:

- J. P. Morgan purchased the investment bank Bear Stearns and Chase Manhattan Bank;
- Bank of America bought the brokerage firm Merrill Lynch and Maryland Bank of North America – the credit card business;
- Wells Fargo Bank bought Wachovia;
- Citigroup, which purchased Travelers Insurance in 1998, was capitalized;
- Goldman Sachs did not buy any other entity;
- Morgan Stanley bought Smith Barney, another investment bank;
- US Bancorp bought First Bank and Colorado National Bank;
- PNC Financial Services Group purchased National City Corporation, Sterling Financial, Yardville National Bancorp and Mercantile Bankshares Corporation;
- Capital One bought ING Direct and GE Capital's Healthcare Financial Services Lending Business;
- TD Group US Holdings bought Epoch Holding Corporation and Scottrade Bank.

As a result of bankruptcies and rescues (Figure 5.2), the sum of the value of assets of the nine largest banks in the United States indicated in the Table 5.3 is equivalent to 60.5 per cent of US GDP in 2016, according to the FDIC. TARP injected public monies and protected some banks: the two largest were Bank of America and Citibank; the other seven were operations with preferred shares, with a fixed rate

Number of bankrupt banks

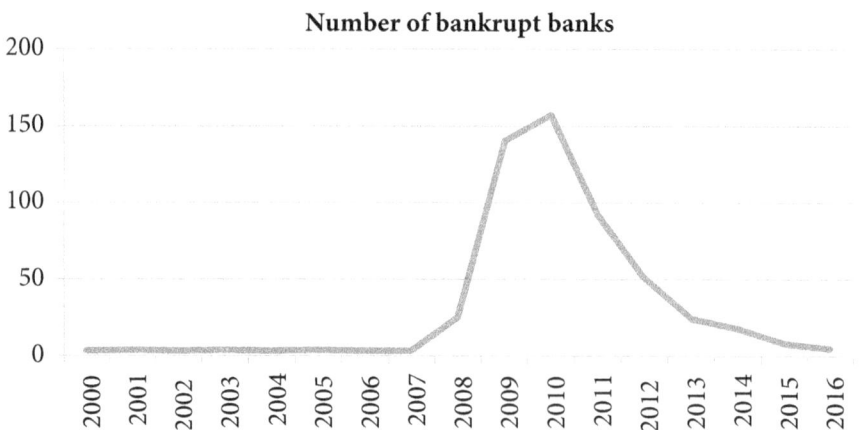

5.2. Time distribution of bank failures

Table 5.3 *The Too Big to Fail financial institutions in the United States, 2012–16 (to June)*

Name of bank	City of residence	Total asset value (US$ 2016)	Total asset value (US$ 2012)	Change (%)
Morgan Chase & Co.	NY, NY	2,490,972,000	2,359,141,000	5.6
Bank of America Corp.	Charlotte, NC	2,189,266,000	2,212,004,452	−1.0
Wells Fargo & Company	San Francisco, CA	1,930,115,000	1,422,968,000	35.6
Citigroup Inc.	NY, NY	1,792,077,000	1,864,660,000	−3.9
Goldman Sachs Group, Inc.	NY, NY	860,185,000	938,770,000	−8.4
Morgan Stanley	NY, NY	814,949,000	780,960,000	4.4
US BANCORP	Minneapolis, MN	445,964,000	353,855,000	26.0
PNC Financial Services Group, Inc.	Pittsburgh, PA	366,872,249	305,285,879	20.2
Capital One Financial Corporation	Mclean, VA	357,158,294	313,040,688	14.1
Total assets		11,247,558,543	10,550,685,019	6.6
Top 3		0.42	0.57	
Top 5		0.65	0.73	

Source: FDIC.

of return, that served as loans while solving the liquidity problems faced. There was a second form of financial assistance for TBTF banks, the Capital Assistance Program which, according to the Treasury, consisted of two basic elements. One was an exercise of supervision and prospective evaluation to determine if any of the large American banking entities needed a capital buffer during the period of greatest uncertainty. The other was giving qualifying financial institutions by the FED contingent common shares provided by the United States Treasury as a way of re-capitalizing them. The US government was a shareholder for a period until the bank could pay back the shares.

Let us put all this in a Polanyian perspective. As we have seen, the embedding of the US financial system within a system of strict state regulation after the various post-Depression Banking Acts, of which Glass Steagall is the most prominent, had begun to be upturned by the early 1980s. However, no sooner had this process begun than it encountered problems with the Third World Debt Crisis endangering the viability of important banks such as Continental Illinois. So, the US government began a process of *partially* re-embedding the financial sector by rescuing and 're-embedding' only what it considered the TBTF or systemically important banks. This was the process that reached a new peak when the intervention of the Treasury through TARP in 2008 took the state's role as regulator and guarantor in re-embedding the financial sector to new heights.

What we have seen is the creation of separate financial systems, one for a small number of TBTF institutions (Table 5.4) and another for the rest, the RSTF ones, and a union of the political and the economic spheres.

The banking complex

There are various approaches to the concept of the banking complex. We want to argue that the United States Treasury was taken over, from the 1980s on, by banking and finance sector agents, and that it acts on and defines public policy from this perspective and from there exerts influence on the IMF. This is a first step to the end of the system. This was the beginning of the TBTF concept. On the other hand, it is known that the Federal Reserve has historically been directed by commercial bankers.

Class A directors represent the member commercial banks in the District, and they are mostly bankers. Class B and class C directors are selected to represent the public, with due consideration to the interests of the agriculture, commerce, industry, services, labour and consumer sectors. Class A and class B directors are elected by member banks in the District, while class C directors are appointed by

Table 5.4   Global systemically important banks by country

United States	Canada	France
Bank of America	Royal Bank of Canada	BNP Paribas
Bank of New York Mellon	**Japan**	Group Credit Agricole
Citigroup	Mitsubishi UFJ FG	Société Générale
Goldman Sachs	Mizuho FG	**Switzerland**
JP Morgan Chase	Sumitomo Mitsui FG	Credit Suisse
Morgan Stanley	**Great Britain**	UBS
State Street	Barclays	**Germany**
Wells Fargo	HSBC	Deutsche Bank
China	Royal Bank of Scotland	**Netherlands**
Agricultural Bank of China	Standard and Chartered	ING Bank
Bank of China	**Spain**	**Sweden**
China Construction Bank	Santander	Norway
Industrial and Commercial Bank of		**Italy**
China LTD ICC		Unicredit Group

Source: Data from Financial Stability Board,www.fsb.org/wp-content/uploads/P211117-1.pdf. Accessed 27 August 2018.

the Board of Governors of the Federal Reserve System in Washington (Board of Governors of the Federal Reserve, 2019).

We want to suggest that from the 1980s onwards the banking system has gradually been replaced by the banking complex, in Eisenhower's sense of the term. Paraphrasing his farewell speech, replacing the words 'military' and 'industrial' by 'banking' and 'financial', one could say that:

> This conjunction of an immense banking establishment and a financial industry is new in the American experience. The total influence – economic, political, even spiritual – is felt in every city, every State house, every office of the Federal government. We recognize the imperative need for this development. Yet we must not fail to comprehend its grave implications. Our toil, resources and livelihood are all involved; so is the very structure of our society.
>
> In the councils of government, we must guard against the acquisition of unwarranted influence, whether sought or unsought, by the financial banking complex. The potential for the disastrous rise of misplaced power exists and will persist.
>
> We must never let the weight of this combination endanger our liberties or democratic processes. We should take nothing for granted. Only an alert and knowledgeable citizenry can compel the proper meshing of the huge financial and banking machinery of defense with our peaceful methods and goals, so that security and liberty may prosper together. (Eisenhower, 1961)

The notion of complex is defined by Eisenhower when he signals that there are economic interests that absorb the resources of the state using their influence both in academic and business research. They form an elite that captures public policy and skews the management of the state in its favour. To paraphrase Eisenhower: the complex joins together an immense financial establishment with a new banking industry. The three new components of the complex are the media, academia and credit risk agencies. As Johnson and Kwak (2010) have pointed out and Charles H. Ferguson underlined in the *Inside Job* documentary (2010), academia has become a part of the complex and provides it with dubious theoretical support, such as in the Black and Scholes model and their Long-Term Capital Management L.P. fund that lost $100 billion before being rescued by the US government in 2000. That was one of the largest financial rescues and it happened to two Nobel Prize winners long before the 2008 crisis. Indeed, fully one-third of Nobel Memorial Prizes in Economics (originally there was no Nobel Prize in Economics, one was created in 1968) have been awarded in the field of financial theory.

In order to determine whether or not an embedded banking complex exists in the United States, one must first examine the size of financial banking activities in the United States and how they have developed since the beginning of financial deregulation; that is to say since 1971, when the free exchange market was established bolstering commodity and securities markets. There are several ways to do this: by measuring the size of the banking financial value added; by measuring the financial assets in the GDP; and by measuring the scale of employment in the banking sector. Then the appearance of new instruments and institutions during the deregulation period can be reviewed. The increase in financial research during the period between 1980 and 2010 can also be reviewed. On the other hand, in order to see the impact on public policy, the presence of players from the sector inside the executive machinery and the impact on the United States Congress, and the reduction of public regulation and the increase of fiscal spending devoted to this sector, can be reviewed.

The weight of the financial sector, in the broadest possible economic definition that includes commercial banking, insurance, stocks, funds, real estate and financial leasing, doubled in the US GDP between 1970 and 2010 from 15 per cent of GDP to 31 per cent. More specifically, the proportion by which the weight of the financial sector increased was the same as the proportion by which the weight of the manufacturing industry and commercial sector declined. This means that the weight of the productive sector in the GDP compared with the stages prior to 1970 has shrunk compared with the growing weight of the financial banking sector.

According to the Final Report of the National Commission on the Causes of the Financial and Economic Crisis in the United States:

> The Commission concluded that this was an avoidable crisis. The crisis was a result of human action or inaction, not of Mother Nature or computing models gone crazy. The captains of finance and the public guarantors of our financial system did not heed

the warning and did not question, understand or manage the growing risks within the system, which is essential for the welfare of the American population. Theirs was a serious fault, not a mishap. Whilst the business cycle cannot be cancelled, a crisis of this magnitude did not need to happen. Paraphrased from Shakespeare, the fault lies not on the stars, but in us. (Financial Crisis Inquiry Commission, 2011: Conclusions, xvii)

Enough is said by recalling that Henry Paulson, former CEO of Goldman Sachs, while carrying out his duties as Treasury Secretary, forced investment banks, and all shadow banks that wanted to receive public support, to become bank holding companies. The reason for this was that bank holding companies' depositors are protected by the FDIC while investment and shadow bank clients are not. Bank holding companies are also covered by deposit insurance; have access to the FED discount window; and have access to a wide range of new FED mechanisms to give credit to the banking sector, while investment and shadow banks do not have any of these benefits. None of this would be possible while they remained part of the non-bank financial system. The public support he organized in the form of TARP was followed by Quantitative Easing policies, with the result that there was wider access to lower-cost credit in the United States, something that did not happen in the rest of the world.

It is not possible to look at what occurred within the United States financial sector without at least glancing at the effects on the rest of the world. *The National Commission on the Causes of the Financial and Economic Crisis Report* acknowledges that the financial sector (finance, insurance, real estate) is much more dominant in the twenty-first century than it was in the twentieth. The figures reveal that it is the dominant sector in the United States, expressing 21 per cent of total GDP in 2017, versus 10.3 per cent of US GDP in 1947. It is double the manufacturing sector, which amounted to a mere 11.2 per cent of US GDP in 2017 though it was 25 per cent in 1947.

Between the years 2000 and 2010, the weight of the financial sector increased further and the low-growth economy which actually declined in 2009 meant that the financial sector's weight was greater after the crisis it caused than before it. Put differently, the financial crisis that chiefly impacted the US economy and spread to the rest of the world did not significantly affect its growing weight in the United States financial sector, despite causing an entirely avoidable crisis and not owning up to its responsibility for it.

The US financial sector assets in the broadest sense increased from $3 billion to $36 billion between 1978 and 2007, or by more than twice that of the GDP of the United States in 2007. According to The National Commission on the Causes of the Financial and Economic Crisis, in 2005, 55 per cent of the financial sector's assets were held by the ten largest commercial banks in the United States, more than double what it was in 1990. According to the same Commission, this figure rose in 2012 to 73 per cent after an $11 billion loss, as we shall see later.

If the crisis failed to dent this industry's share of GDP, it was not only because the rest of the economy was in a low-growth phase and declined in 2009. It was also because the industry defended its performance and because the Federal Reserve purchased devalued assets from this sector in addition to pouring public resources and Federal Reserve credit into the ten banks that were TBTF, a benefit that no other sector enjoyed at this or any other time. This is telling of a split within the financial sector. Those banks regulated by the market went bankrupt, while those socially regulated because they were TBTF were injected with taxpayers' money. These two subsets of institutions have two different sets of rules and therefore do not constitute a system (Figure 5.3).

Looking carefully into the value added of the financial sector, which is very significant for the total value added of the United States, it must be observed that taxes have a low weight in its structure. Adding up all the subsectors of the financial sector already mentioned, taxes make up approximately 5 per cent of its total value added. Looked at another way, with the financial sector contributing 31 per cent of the total value added, of which taxes account for only 5 per cent, the financial sector contributes a mere 1.6 per cent of total US value added. The average of the US's tax burden at all levels (federal, municipal and state) is 24 per cent of GDP according to the OECD (OECD Statistical Database at https://stats.oecd.org/). In other words, the tax contribution of the financial sector, which reflects almost a third of total US production, is only 6.6 per cent of government revenues at all

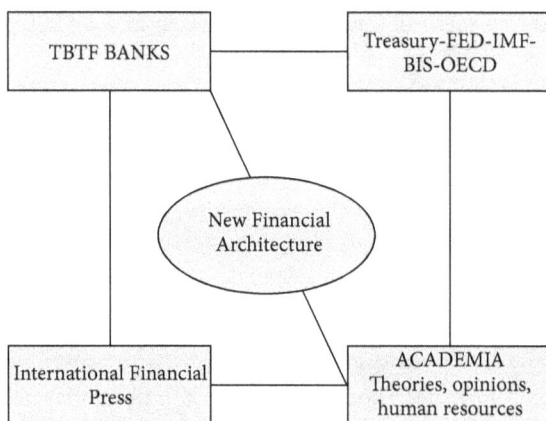

5.3. Power structure of the embedded financial banking complex

Table 5.5   Value added structure of the US financial banking complex, 2004–10

% GD	2004	2005	2006	2007	2008	2009	2010
Total banks, stocks, insurance, funds, real estate, rentals and financial leasing	100	100	100	100	100	100	100
Profits/GDP	79.77	80.23	80.04	80.08	79.90	80.68	80.27
Salaries/GDP	14.99	14.79	14.91	14.85	14.81	13.87	14.18
Taxes/GDP	5.24	4.98	5.06	5.07	5.29	5.45	5.56

Source: www.BEA.org, author's own calculations.

levels. This is the result of steps taken by the Legislative branch and the promotion of financial and tax havens whose aim is tax avoidance (see Table 5.5).

This very low tax burden, together with the financial support the sector received from the Treasury in 2008–9, possibly helped it to avoid the 2009 contraction and not lose its drive at the same rate as the rest of the economy during the 2008–9 crisis (see Figure 5.4). What is certain is that while it did not collapse with the rest of the economy it has followed a declining trend in growth, while the rest of the economy has painfully reversed the drastic fall of 2009.

The further component of the complex is the media. They help to create a common sense and repeat financial information from New York and London. World-wide the *Financial Times* and the *Wall Street Journal* can be read in most leading newspapers in all continents not because the GDP of the US and Britain are brilliantly growing with exemplary macroeconomic data but because the largest financial markets are there. Notably CNN and the BBC repeat this information on

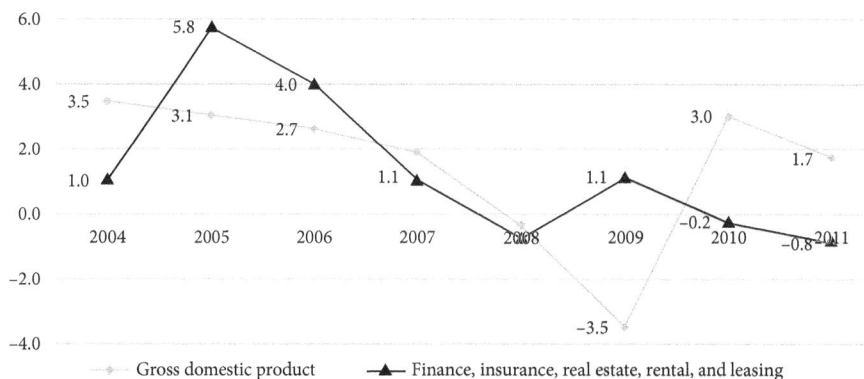

5.4. US GDP and finance, insurance, real estate, rentals and leasing (percentage growth rate)

cable television, and other sources are available on the internet such as Bloomberg and Yahoo. This fourth leg of the complex creates a common sense that the economy is managed in a particular way that favours the financial sector. The media have also demonstrated their ability to come out fighting if the macroeconomy is not handled in that particular way, a way that supports the financial sector and its unproductive activities. The attacks by the international financial press (see the *Wall Street Journal, Financial Times, The Economist* and the economics section of the *New York Times*) on Venezuela and Argentina between 2010 and 2014, and the reference to the Chinese recession and its looming crises, and the European boom over the 2010 to 2019 period, are cases in point.

Finally, the least visible but critically important side of the complex are credit-rating agencies, of which only three have US government approval. All three are American: Fitch's, Standard & Poor and Moody's. Arthur Andersen, the auditing firm and credit risk agency, was shut for corruption when the Enron case erupted in 2001.

To conclude

There is a double movement of economic liberalism on the one hand and the principle of protection on the other hand in the early 1980s, where TBTF institutions are created and protected and follow non-market rules, while the rest are left to competition and market rules. Too big to fail and right size to fail financial institutions constitute the financial complex.

The financial system that existed before instantiated embedded liberalism was the product of the 1934 Glass Steagall Act and its regulations. The process of financial deregulation started in 1980 and concluded in 1999. During the deregulation of the 1980s, a banking crisis erupted as a result of the Debt crisis, leading to the re-embedding of those very large institutions and the emergence of the concept of TBTF institutions as a guide to policy. This re-embedded a few very large institutions under government protection while most remained disembedded, subject to free market rules. What occurred at the time was that the separation between politics and economics was broken and a revolving door between TBTF institutions and the Executive power was established. Thus, there were two subsets of financial institutions, one TBTF and the other RSTF. The one with immense political power, the other, irrelevant.

The addition of these two subsystems, one embedded and one disembedded, does not constitute a system but a non-structured financial set or complex. The transformation from the system into the complex after the 1984 banking crisis made way for TBTF banks to strengthen and a new set of political relationships that reflect their privileges based on government protection. This change provides for a significant change in the dynamics of liberal capitalism where TBTF institutions hold strong political power for their own benefit. Polanyi's contribution to this understanding is invaluable and sheds light on the intricacies of the modern financial structure.

Note

1   All page references to *The Great Transformation* are to the [1944] 2001 edition.

Part III

The double movement and socialism

6

The reality of society[1]

Abraham Rotstein

As we commemorate the fifty years since Karl Polanyi's death, we may also recall the three people responsible for the fact that we are all here today: number one, Kari Polanyi Levitt, who invented this Institute; number two, Margie Mendell, who directed it all of this time; and finally, Ana Gomez who did all of the hard work. Today in their presence, I feel somehow that I was an also-ran.

The late Frank Scott, when he was honoured on a similar occasion, said with his characteristic touch of humour, 'I feel that this is a pre-mortem.' I have that sense as well. So permit me, as an ageing participant in this conference, a few reminiscences and recollections of the work that Karl and I were trying to do in that last decade of his life. The extended transcript of our discussions is available in the Polanyi Archive as the *Weekend Notes*. I am very pleased to say that, largely through Margie and Ana's doing, they are now available online along with all the archival records of the Institute.

I walked into Polanyi's class at Columbia University in September 1951. Coming from Brooklyn by subway, I was ten minutes late. I had no idea what to expect other than the fact that the course was called 'General Economic History' and there was a man called Polanyi whom I'd never heard of.

Why did I take this course in the first place? For all the wrong reasons. When I entered Columbia, the requirement for a Master's degree was a total of twenty-one points. Since every course was worth three points, you had, in effect, to pass seven courses. Polanyi's course, however, was a double course and so you could earn six points for it. I was enough of an economist to know that the economies of scale were probably at work here; I guessed that I wouldn't have to do twice as much work in a six-point course as I would taking two separate three-point courses, and I registered for it. Such are the trivial considerations that have lifetime consequences. So here we are this evening some sixty years later.

As I walked into class that first day, I was taken aback by the subject of Karl's lecture. I was at the time a refugee from the University of Chicago where I had been enrolled the previous year. I had fled before the year was out, not so much because Milton Friedman's lectures were 'right wing', but because of the school of economics being taught. It was the larger tradition he represented, the Austrian tradition that stemmed originally from Carl Menger. Frank Knight, the leading figure at Chicago, had studied in Germany and had carried forward that tradition. Towards the end of his tenure, Knight brought in Milton Friedman, who continued in the same vein. My objection was not political but that they had created an intellectual maze in which I felt trapped, a maze in which you scurried about looking for an exit but there was no exit.

This position was summed up in Lionel Robbins's essay 'On the nature and significance of economic science'. Robbins had done his graduate work in Vienna and brought the Menger tradition to England. The tradition turned on the existential 'fact' of economic life, namely 'scarcity'. We can't have all the goods we might want, luxury and otherwise, because the world had finite resources. Since there isn't enough for everyone's heart's desire, we needed a process of allocating what we do have. How do we do that? Lo and behold, it's the free market.

It meant that economic life itself was defined as this process of allocating these scarce goods to the best advantage. Such a process did have a mathematical validity which was unassailable. I knew, however, that the real world we inhabited and its economy were not about such a theorem.

The world of the 1950s was a post-colonial era; it was about newly developing countries such as India that had become independent, it was about income inequality globally and locally, it was about the fear of whether the Great Depression might return. Karl Marx had said that depressions were inherent in capitalism; studies of the business cycle at the time hovered at the edge of a similar conclusion. Keynes, in turn, claimed to have found a way out. Who was right and what was in store for us? This was the economy that I knew and cared about.

I spent much of my time in Chicago in the library. I was looking for every possible review of Lionel Robbins's book hoping to find an exit from the maze in which I felt trapped. If I didn't find an exit, I told myself, I would leave the profession entirely and go into psychiatry. And so, I became a refugee and migrated to Columbia.

I walked into the classroom that September morning and there it was. Polanyi was talking about that very theorem: scarcity, alternative uses, rational action with regard to scarce means and so on. He called his critique 'the two meanings of the word "economic"'. He distinguished theoretically the formal meaning that the Austrians employed from the substantive meaning related to the economic institutions of the real world. Polanyi had found the exit from the maze and I knew then that this course was important.

It was a peculiar course. It was about ancient Rome, ancient Greece, feudalism, about the anthropologist Melville Herskovits who had it right at the start but was then seduced by the marginal economists.

It was only after the course was over, during a casual conversation, that Polanyi said to me 'Why don't you have a look at *The Great Transformation*?' In the entire reading list of the economic history course there wasn't a mention of *The Great Transformation*. Unbelievable. I started to read it after the course was over, and that was when I had an intellectual earthquake. I was stunned by the depth and clarity of his account of the coming of the industrial revolution, a revolution that was in lockstep with the world of laissez-faire. And so began our correspondence and extended discussions.

I returned to Montreal. Our contact continued and in 1956 Karl suggested that I come to visit him. He was living in the hamlet of Rosebank about an hour outside of Toronto. The little house on the top of the hill had a steep drop at the back with a stream running below. In the front was a beautiful garden that Ilona had planted with many poppies and other flowers. In the living room was the round table that had followed the Polanyis from their time in Vienna.

As we sat around the table, Karl started to talk: he talked about the Cold War, international politics, the interdisciplinary project at Columbia, Robert Owen and a topic he called 'the reality of society'. It was a one-way conversation and I was taken with how important these comments were. I feared that they would disappear into thin air so I grabbed a pad and began to write. And I wrote and wrote trying to get it all down.

This was the beginning of many such visits. I had a job in Montreal at the time, with an office and a secretary. I could fly out on a Friday evening to Toronto and return on a Sunday night to Montreal. Karl talked freely about many subjects for hours on end. I had the occasional question and comment but kept writing away. The subjects varied and moved back and forth, so that when I returned to Montreal, I re-grouped them under the general headings for that weekend. I tried to keep all the *Notes* verbatim so that there were no personal intrusions. After some light editing, I had the secretary type up these *Weekend Notes*.

I revisited Karl in Rosebank on some twenty-eight occasions between 1956 and 1959. He had enormous energy and conviction and talked for hours on end.

It was not easy to keep up. I brought the typed *Weekend Notes* back with me from time to time so Karl could have a look at them. He approved of them and did make some pencilled corrections. (The copies with these corrections are in the Columbia University archives. There weren't many corrections.)

Karl had suggested that I should help him write the sequel to *The Great Transformation* and this became the main focus of our discussions. At first the sequel was to be called *The Great Transformation and America*. Later the title was changed to *Freedom and Technology*. Let me recall a little of what we were trying to do.

The whole drift of that sequel was to be completely different in its basic premises and in its tone from *The Great Transformation*. Let me talk about two of its features. First there is the question of how to understand Karl's turn from time to time, to a religious vocabulary. Terms like 'the three revelations', 'the work of Jesus', that 'man has a soul to lose'; these terms appear incongruous to readers of *The Great Transformation*. That book was built on a social sciences approach using institutional analysis. Except for the brief last chapter with some elliptic references, there was no sign of religious semantics.

How can this turn to a religious vocabulary be explained? Over the years, Karl had followed the work of Hegel, whose philosophy was studded with religious semantics. But these were qualified – Hegel's intent was expressed in the following sentence: *Wir die religiöse Vorstellung in Gedanken fassen*: We want to turn religious expression into philosophical thought. Much of what Karl was doing followed similar lines. One had to take religion seriously he thought, but to look beyond its outer trappings such as the ceremonials, the legends, the myths, the virgin birth, and the rest. The question was: Were there important truths that lay behind and beneath these beliefs and practices?

Put briefly, what Karl was looking for was an overview of the high points or stages in the evolution of human consciousness. Beneath the credos and the cathedrals there lay the inner kernel, the proximate clue to human consciousness. But this was not a calm and unbroken sea. Over time, such consciousness changed sharply and re-emerged on higher 'plateaus'. These high points Polanyi called 'the three revelations'. They aren't revelations in the sense of coming from Mount Sinai or from the angel Gabriel; they were a way of revealing to human beings who they really were, how their consciousness was grounded.

All civilizations, Karl maintained, are held together by some underlying ethos, a shared belief, a *raison d'être* that is axiomatic to its participants. Such a common consciousness might endure for a lengthy era, but not indefinitely. Decisive events or an interregnum might bring sharp breaks with the past and recast the mind formation and outlook of that society. This is what Polanyi meant when he appropriated the term 'revelations'.

The reality of society

In a brief schematic approach, Polanyi pointed to three high points in these shifts of consciousness in Western society. Using a simplified view of primitive, tribal society as a point of departure, we see it as encased in superstition, in myth, in a fixed role for each individual and absorbed in some form of a pantheistic religion. This might be accompanied by animal and occasionally human sacrifice. Actual tribal societies differed from each other and were more complex, but for heuristic purposes our discussion starts with this simpler view. Primitive man lived in a kind of torpor, a cyclical existence where he completely internalized the norms of his society.

What snapped man out of that torpor was his confrontation with the knowledge of death – the full realization that his existence was finite and that its termination was inevitable. This was filtered through his consciousness in the form of myth. There were many such myths but one of the most compelling was in the Old Testament. It was the story of the Garden of Eden and man's fall from grace. This legend helped to implant the sad inevitability of death in the Western consciousness and with it, a vital response.

This knowledge of death is what Polanyi called the first of the three revelations. Such a revelation was not an occasion for a benign or passive acceptance of this stark reality. You may resign yourself to the inevitable but you may also confront it with a legacy that you leave behind when you die. That was the challenge.

At a certain level of civilization, this became a pervasive response throughout much of the ancient world. These societies had their own legends of death and the hereafter. They accepted their mortality and embarked on the great edifices that would outlive them. The civilization of ancient Egypt pivoted on this knowledge of death. The very day the new Pharaoh ascended to his throne, he began to build his elaborate tomb and stake out his place in the Valley of the Kings. Pyramids, temples and great monuments followed. One may mention as well the hundreds of palaces and temples of the Khmer of Cambodia and the Forbidden City of the Chinese.

As this knowledge of death works its way through Western societies, the tangible marks of civilization appear. Churches, castles, fortresses and weapons of war become widespread. They are designed to far outlast their founders and to secure their family dynasties. New technology is developed to achieve and enhance these objectives and becomes widely diffused. Consciousness of death was implanted in the psyche of Western society and drove those societies forward.

Efforts such as Polanyi's to probe the content of one's consciousness face almost insuperable obstacles. It is not only the Pauline adage of seeing 'through the glass darkly' that confronts us. It is like trying to discover what lies at the other side of that mirror by continuing to stare at one's own reflection. Only the 'shadows' that our consciousness casts may be available to us. We must search beneath the *religiöse Vorstellung*, the outer vestments, to find evidence of the mind's imprint.

Likewise, the timing for the great shifts in consciousness remains its own mystery. This first revelation, the knowledge of death, was superseded by a second revelation linked to the coming of Christianity. There was something more vital and more precarious than our physical existence. We recognized that we had an inner life to attend to, call it a 'soul' or a 'conscience'. It was more precious and more precarious than our physical existence and it stood at risk; we might violate something vital and desecrate the essence of who we really were.

We walked with this abiding fear of a fateful misstep. In religious language, this might be called a fear of 'damnation'. Instead, we hewed to its opposite and sought for what we termed 'salvation' or 'eternal life'. These were the religious metaphors for what Polanyi termed the second revelation.

Man had a soul to lose; he was suspended between an abiding inner fear and the hope to which he aspired. This comes to us first in the New Testament with Paul and subsequently with others such as Luther. Polanyi did not refer to Luther directly in our conversations, but Luther's famous essay, *Von der Freiheit eines Christenmenschen*, 'On the freedom of a Christian', goes to the heart of the matter. Luther states that a Christian is free because he cannot be touched by the misery and all the pressures brought on by the world around him; he can stay above the fray and safeguard his unblemished conscience. His main duty is to serve and love his neighbour.

That was the source of 'Freedom' (capital 'F') as it came to us from the sphere of religion. That was what religion offered to the inner life of the individual: a clear conscience, untarnished and intact. This is what he aimed to preserve against the lingering fear of an empty, soulless existence. This existence was represented by its own myth of 'original sin'.

Freedom appeared first in its religious garb before acquiring its cherished secular status – our civil liberties. They are an offshoot of the original religious message. Their origin lies, Polanyi maintains, in the tacit recognition that everybody is walking the same tightrope; all of us are in common jeopardy when it comes to the integrity of our inner life. We share a tacit understanding and mutual sympathy in our common moral hazard. This is the 'cross that we must bear' and no one should be unduly burdened or obstructed in this personal quest. All of us walk in trepidation at the edge of this abyss. That is why we hew so closely to our concrete freedoms – freedom of the press, freedom of religion, freedom of assembly, and so on. These are assured so that everyone may have the best chance of finding his own way. The converse side of this ethos is not to oppress or constrain others – essential to maintaining a clear conscience.

We cannot explain why and when these revelations make their appearance, why the response to death suddenly permeates Western society (as it did in other societies before it) or why the burden of conscience (the 'soul') becomes a touchstone of our own identity. Momentous changes in consciousness appear suddenly; they exist everywhere at once and begin to reshape the whole of that society.

With the coming of industrial society, this moral landscape begins slowly to shift. Such a society knits all individuals more tightly together. By the twentieth century we become mutually dependent on the technological systems around which our lives have been built. Our lives would be shattered without that dense network of communications, transportation, electricity and water. As we realize the full extent of that dependence, our own vulnerability hits home: we realize that we must protect these arteries of our life at any price. We offer our tacit consent to hand over to our government the virtually unlimited power to do whatever is 'necessary'.

This is the enhanced world of *raison d'état* in our midst – the new world that Edward Snowden and Julian Assange have uncovered for us. It is the clandestine world that is flanked by the institutions of 'Homeland Security'. This is also the world where there are recurrent cyber attacks on our computers, where global epidemics threaten our health, where we are improvising new uses for the anonymous and guiltless technologies such as the drones. It is the world of 'Big Data' where discreet banks of computers now monitor what we think and anticipate what we want to do.

We don't know who is hit by this tight network of new technology and exhaustive bureaucratic surveillance. Such repercussions are widespread and anonymous. Yet, the responsibility for these events remains ours.

While Polanyi viewed the emerging scene from the vantage point of the 1950s, he was prescient in regard to the venue today. A new consciousness was making its way and began to render the previous moral challenge and its accommodations obsolescent.

Somewhere at the back of our mind we remember that it is our tacit consent that supports this entire apparatus but we also know that we cannot go into reverse. This new world writes *finis* to the stellar aspiration of a blameless and clear conscience. We may look away and go into denial; we may hide momentarily behind some refurbished idealism. But we must finally acknowledge that the basis of the old 'Freedom' – for example Luther's promise that nothing can touch our inner existence – is now eroded. The pristine conscience that we dreamt of has become a thing of the past.

This became the basis of Polanyi's third revelation. This concept was to be the centrepiece of the sequel that we were planning.

The 'reality of society' is a subtle concept and easily misunderstood. Here we have a radical shift in the connotation of the term 'society'. It now plays a totally different role from that played by 'society' in *The Great Transformation*. In some intuitive way, 'society' restrained the blind expansion of the laissez-faire world of the nineteenth century and stood up as a counterforce to the robotic drive of the market economy.

In 1944 *The Great Transformation* offered hope for the post-war world. Its message was that institutions were pliable, they could be altered and reformed. The market could be contained and made subordinate to the larger goals of society. Now that technology rather than market institutions is the main protagonist that we must encounter, our options shrink drastically. Technological systems form a medium of an entirely different kind, more rigid and not easily amenable to institutional containment.

A half-century ago Polanyi was prophetic when he described this emerging world with 'ribs of steel and nerves of electronic impulses'. The following paragraph offers a semblance of the sequel that we planned:

> What appears as the real world, all that is massive, impressive and discussed, is outside of us; heaped up in agglomerations of concrete, dynamos, terminal stations, hospitals, structured steel, motor cars, bulldozers and stocks of goods of endless variety. … Man exists now outside himself, he is externalized. His life is hedged in by roadblocks. Yet all this is but a symbol of the true change from inner freedom to loss of freedom. Automation and the mechanical brain are but visible imitations of the automatism and the mechanization of the human tissue of society. We are as helpless in the human world as we are in that of power and movement. For our consciousness has not adjusted to our lives, and may be never will; the shape of our lives may have to give in. But whatever the balanced result, if such there be, the external environment has ceased to be material and mechanical alone, it comprises a human structure – a complex society – which is an ultimate reality, ultimate in the metaphysical sense.

Living today within the depths of this modern leviathan, it seems clear that the old promise of a clear and blameless conscience is now forfeit. Polanyi is not alone in sensing that something of ultimate importance has been lost. During the same decade of the 1950s, the French existentialists were attempting to portray something similar. Theirs was a nameless despair with an intangible sense of loss. Recall Samuel Beckett in the famous line from *Waiting for Godot*, 'Nothing to be done', or Sartre in *La Nausée* or in *No Exit*. Albert Camus's *The Stranger* comes to mind as well. They share a sense of inarticulate sorrow and despair that something nameless has vanished.

For Polanyi, the mood was sombre as well but not one of total despair. The existentialists can despair, he maintained, but we must face up to it. We will never retrieve the unsullied conscience that was promised long ago in the second revelation. Its ethos and ideals are gone. We will never be released from the electronic bureaucracy that accompanies this new world nor can we eliminate the compulsion that makes it function. This is the society in which we are going to live and it cannot be reversed.

But a mature approach does not imply a passive acceptance of an untrammelled bureaucracy, a runaway technology nor the lack of recourse for the individual who has been victimized or ignored. We are mandated to search for better safeguards, for an iron-clad *habeas corpus*. We must search for the limits where we can draw the line to contain these systems. Only then can we resign ourselves to the fact that the technological society will always remain part of us.

Towards the last decade of his life, some dozen years after *The Great Transformation*, Polanyi is sombre but realistic about the outcome.

> Frustrations and alienation in technological civilization and the adjustment of life it requires may eventually lead to a recognition of a dwindling or loss of inner freedom which transcends the institutional sphere. There is thus a technological civilization, the adjustment of life, and thirdly, the loss of freedom, which may destroy those forms of adjustment, but we are uncertain whether we can survive it … there is here a danger of untrammelled idealism wiping us off the globe.

That was said in 1957. Now that we are well into our new millennium, we see such untrammelled idealism erupt in new quarters. We become increasingly desperate to recover the dwindling ideals whose time is past. And as all this seeps in, various forms of denial and sharp reaction occur. Dogmatic schisms within countries and within religions come to the fore. They have their diverse origins but are now amplified through technology, terrorism and war. Frequent cyber attacks remind us of the increasing vulnerability of our technological world. As the sponsors and defenders of that world, we are left with these difficult dilemmas of transition into this new reality.

In conclusion, you may ask why this sequel to *The Great Transformation* did not appear? The answer is that Polanyi would never let go of the *Dahomey* manuscript which he was still trying to complete. He was a perfectionist and worked at it continuously. I had moved to Toronto to work with him and discovered – fortunately or unfortunately – much new research material that was relevant such as the monographs of *L'institut français d'Afrique noire*. While we kept talking about the sequel, we continued to work on *Dahomey*. *Dahomey* eventually was finished; the sequel never was. When I think about this, I fall back on the closing line of Karl's essay on 'Hamlet': 'Life is a missed opportunity.'

Note

1   This chapter is the text of the transcribed speech Abe Rotstein, Karl Polanyi's long-time associate and prominent Canadian political economist, gave at the dinner held during the conference organized by the Karl Polanyi Institute of Political Economy in Montreal on 'The Enduring Legacy of Karl Polanyi' held on 6–8 November 2014, marking the fiftieth anniversary of Karl Polanyi's death and the seventieth anniversary of the publication of *The Great Transformation*. Most contributions in this volume stem from that conference. Rotstein's speech was spell-binding, at once dredging the depths of his memory and producing a practically sun-lit lucidity of understanding, one he shared with Polanyi. Very sadly, he passed away a few months later.

7

Fictitious ideas, social facts and the double movement: Polanyi's framework in the age of neoliberalism

Claus Thomasberger

Since the 1990s Karl Polanyi's *The Great Transformation* (hereafter, *TGT*) has become an important point of reference not only for activists and critical minds, but also for social scientists who feel uncomfortable with the current trends of economic globalization, liberalization, privatization and commodification. The increasing influence of the neoliberal creed on economic theory and policy since the 1980s has motivated numerous researchers to look for innovative categories and concepts in order to throw some light on the ongoing transformation of the economic and social environment. For many scholars, *TGT* affords a promising starting point for such an endeavor. Notions such as 'the self-regulating market system', 'fictitious goods', 'protection of society', 'double movement' and 'embeddedness' have become part of the standard repertoire, and not only in the critical discourse about globalization and neoliberalism. Starting from Mark Granovetter's 1985 article 'Economic action and social structure: the problem of embeddedness', the so-called New Economic Sociology also relies heavily on Polanyi's work.

Unfortunately, there is no consensus about how Polanyi's concepts can be used fruitfully in the social conditions prevailing today. In part, this may depend on the nature of the book. *TGT* is a complex book in which several trains of thought are interwoven and which is open to different interpretations. But this is only half of the truth. Too often, the socialist roots of Polanyi's approach are deliberately disdained or completely neglected. And sometimes it seems as if the authors pick out the categories which best fit their own line of reasoning. Little attention is paid to Polanyi's emphasis on the *exceptional* character, the *uniqueness* of the civilization of the nineteenth century. The fact that Polanyi underlined that nineteenth-century civilization was not only fundamentally different from what the world had seen before, but that it also presented 'a distinct stage in the history of industrial civilization' (Polanyi, [1944] 2001: 5), is ignored.

Some authors apply the idea of 'the institutional separation of society into an economic and a political sphere' (ibid.: 74) to all types of market societies. At the same time, the concept of the 'always embedded economy' downplays the differences between market and non-market societies. As the success of the recent publications of Carmen Reinhart and Kenneth Rogoff (2010), David Graeber (2011) and Thomas Piketty (2014) demonstrates, long-term approaches based on the universalization of modern economic categories have come back into vogue since the financial crisis. Paradoxically enough, and in spite of Polanyi's well-known critique of the 'economistic fallacy', Polanyi's categories are also arbitrarily applied to other historical periods.

I do not want to say that the tactics of limiting the reading of Polanyi's oeuvre to *TGT* and of isolating single categories cannot be fruitful. But I doubt that these approaches do justice to Polanyi's intentions. Hannes Lacher has pointed to the paradoxical result 'that we (and "critical" social theorists in particular) have come to embrace as the fulfillment of Polanyi's vision the very social order against which he warned so insistently' (Lacher, 2007b: 62). And I fear that important and valuable insights are lost. Therefore, I will try to discuss some categories which Polanyi developed in *TGT* in the wider context of his oeuvre.

The most important sentence for understanding *TGT* seems to me to be the first sentence of the book: 'Nineteenth-century civilization has collapsed' (Polanyi, [1944] 2001: 3). The sentence sounds trivial but has far-reaching consequences for understanding the book and for the possible modes of applying its findings to today's social conditions. It tells us that in *TGT* Polanyi is analyzing a civilization which no longer existed; which had become history. It is the story of the failure of this civilization. Indeed, none of the four institutions which Polanyi considers the defining institutions of the civilization of the nineteenth century – the balance-of-power system, the international gold standard, the self-regulating market system and the liberal state – had survived the great transformation. And Polanyi is not alone with this judgment. If we think of John M. Keynes, Walter Lippmann, Peter Drucker or Friedrich Hayek: they all regard the inter-war period as the end of the European liberal civilization of the nineteenth century.

The crucial point is this: in so far as Polanyi studies the European civilization of the nineteenth century, he is doing this from the point of view of an observer. He analyzes it from the outside. This is a clearly advantageous position. He can use insights, categories and ideas which were unfamiliar or even unknown to the scholars of the nineteenth century. But it has also the consequence that he cannot hope to exert influence on the course of the nineteenth century. He can only determine the facts. He does not take somebody's view, neither the part of economic liberalism nor the side of the counter-movement as such. Certainly he does not make a secret of his sympathy for the classes which suffered most. And he leaves no doubt that human freedom is the value that guides his research. He expresses his admiration for Robert Owen and other socialists. But he admits that the latter had had only a marginal influence on the course of the events. Basically, he tries to analyze in objective terms the institutional transformation which had been at the roots of the breakdown of the civilization of the nineteenth century.

At the same time, we have to take into consideration that Polanyi wants to exert influence and to contribute his share to what he calls the 'reform of human consciousness' (ibid.: 133) by writing a new narrative about the history of the nineteenth-century civilization. Polanyi cannot hope to influence the consciousness of the era which he is analyzing; this is only possible for another epoch, the one which represents his present or which is in the future. As he states in the introduction, he 'dwells on scenes of the *past* with the sole object of throwing light on matters of the *present*' (ibid.: 3; italics added). He cautions against reconstructing universal capitalism instead of regional planning (Polanyi, [1945] 2018) and against Churchill's plan to join England to America via the Bretton Woods System (Polanyi, [1947] 2018a), and he criticizes 'our obsolete market mentality' (Polanyi, [1947] 2018b). Polanyi does this because he is convinced that neoliberalism, after the failure of the classical form of the liberal creed, is trying to bring the outdated ideas back to life.

Therefore, whoever attempts to apply Polanyi's interpretation to the current conditions has to face the question of what we today can legitimately pick up of the analysis of a sunken age. What can we learn from the account of the transformation of the society of the nineteenth century for the understanding of our own civilization? In *TGT* Polanyi leaves the question without a concrete answer. And in his later works he gives only cautious hints. Which elements and categories are relevant for understanding and for exerting influence on the contemporary social context? Or better, how can we justify utilizing some of Polanyi's categories in order to make sense of our world at the beginning of the twenty-first century?

Most authors do not discuss the question explicitly. But whether ex- or implicit, the application of his categories supposes an answer. Let us take the popular vision of interpreting the transformation in terms of a double movement, driven by the principle of economic liberalism on the one hand and by the principle of protection on the other hand. Some authors enlarge the vision by drawing on the idea of embedding/disembedding, supposing that 'disembedding the market is similar to stretching a giant elastic band. … With further stretching, either the band will snap – representing social disintegration – or the economy will revert to a more embedded position' (Block, 2001: xxv). Others model some kind of 'pendulum' that swings between socially disembedded markets and socially re-embedded markets (cf. Beckert, 2007; Gills, 2008: 513–522; Mason, 2009: 171). Obviously, these interpretations – independent of their differences – assume that the current developments can be understood as a prolongation of the dynamics that Polanyi describes in *TGT*, notwithstanding the different concrete forms making up the institutional framework. Perhaps it is not by chance that some protagonists of the 'varieties of capitalism' project stick to this kind of interpretation. Therefore, we should not be astonished that they regard the first sentence of *TGT* as flawed. 'We know now, of course, that he [Karl Polanyi] was wrong', we are taught by Block and Somers (2014: 19), when he assumed that in the 1930s the ideas of economic liberalism were discredited.

The question remains: Can negligence of the differences between the European civilization of the nineteenth century and today be justified? And, if so, how? Are there good reasons for criticizing Polanyi and his contemporaries for deeply mis-interpreting the course of events in the 1930s and 1940s? Or is the fruitfulness of such an endeavor a sufficient criterion for applying some of Polanyi's categories to current social conditions?

The chapter is divided into six sections. In the first two sections, I shall recon-struct Polanyi's interpretation of the double movement. The following two focus on the very heart of Polanyi's analyses, the problem of freedom in a technological civilization and the limits of the counter-movement vis-à-vis the challenges of a complex society. In sections five and six I shall come back to the question of how to use Polanyi's categories in order to throw light on the post-war era and our society today.

Polanyi's interpretation of the double movement in the nineteenth century

In *TGT* the advancement and the breakdown of the European market society of the nineteenth century is described as the outcome of a double movement. It is no surprise that the idea of a double movement is one of the concepts most employed in the current debate. 'Polanyi's double movement thesis is intricately crafted and magnificent in scope. Its considerable influence is deserved', affirms Dale (2012: 9). Nevertheless, we are far away from a consensus of how to understand and apply it to contemporary social conditions.

Therefore, let us start with an attempt to answer some basic questions: What are the roots of the double movement? What (or who) are the driving forces? Who are the principal actors? What are their motives? Is double movement a category which describes a particular feature of the historical period under scrutiny? Or can it also be justifiably and profitably applied to other periods?

In order to answer these questions it is helpful to recall that the picture of a double movement is not Polanyi's discovery. He does not make a secret of the fact that he adopted it from liberal authors. 'Liberal writers like Spencer and Sumner, Mises and Lippmann offer an account of the double movement substantially similar to our own', Polanyi ([1944] 2001: 148) explains. According to the liberal view, impatient and shortsighted protective movements against the achievements of the industrial revolution were driving for reforms in the direction of social utopias, while the liberals defended reality against harmful and damaging regulations such as the Speenhamland system which until the 1830s prevented the establishment of a competitive labor market.

It seems to me essential to understand that the liberal interpretation does not simply refer to two opposing movements – one in favor and the other against the extension of the market logic – but to a utopian claim against the defense of social reality. From the beginnings, Malthus, Ricardo, Say and their followers fought against the vision that, since the Age of Enlightenment, had motivated and disturbed social thinking in the Western world, that is, the idea that human well-being can be increased by a conscious transformation of the institutions of society.

From Polanyi's point of view, the appearance of economic liberalism in the form of a new science pretending to be able to determine the limits of the creative power of man was groundbreaking. Ricardo had discovered, Polanyi underlines in *TGT*, 'the existence of a society that was not subject to the laws of the state, but, on the contrary, subjected the state to its own laws' (ibid.: 116). The industrial revolution had unleashed new potentials incomparable with everything humans had previously invented. Technical possibilities seemed infinite. Did this mean that 'anything goes'? What would be the effects on society? If not, what kind of limits had to be recognized?

From his early years in Budapest, Polanyi is concerned about the influence of the industrial revolution on Western culture and society. The issues which trouble Polanyi are not technical problems but cultural and, in a certain sense, ethical or moral questions. Polanyi welcomes the increase of productivity and technical progress but he is worried about the social and moral implication of mass production, the global division of labor and the increase of the amount of material goods. He is not interested in technology as such, but in its cultural implications, in the effects on human relationships and the way in which society (and the relationship between different countries) is affected. In his younger years in Hungary, he is concerned primarily with the question of the influence of the machine on man's consciousness. He concentrates on social and cultural change, ethical and moral transformation, and the reform of human consciousness. The increasing division of labor and large-scale industrial production require standardization of life and discipline. He fears that, under the conditions of organized industry, conformity is getting the upper hand over spontaneity and control over self-determination. He is afraid that human consciousness is becoming uniform and standardized, that bureaucratic management is dominating over personal initiative and that critical states of mind are regarded first as superfluous, then as repulsive and finally as immoral (cf. Polanyi, 01–06).

Western civilization had to find an answer to the challenges of the new epoch. Polanyi regards the emergence of the social sciences as a chance to increase human self-consciousness; he believes that the political economy could and should contribute to a better understanding of the possibilities and the limits of the machine age. In England, Joseph Townsend's *Dissertation* (1786) and Thomas Malthus's *Essay on the Principle of Population* (1798) paved the way, pointing to the limits of the means of subsistence. Both opposed the idea that institutional reforms could improve and perfect society by drawing attention to natural boundaries. The conflict between increasing population and limited means of subsistence would necessarily mean that 'the actual population [is] kept equal to the means of subsistence, by misery and vice' (Malthus, [1798] 1998: 44). By accepting the framework, Ricardo built his formulation of the laws of distribution, 'the principal problem in Political Economy' (Ricardo, [1817] 1984: 3), directly on the inexorable laws of Nature, that is, on two biological laws: the fertility of man and the fertility of the soil. It is crucial to understand the particular character of this argument and of its influence on the consciousness of the nineteenth century. Two aspects are critical.

The first aspect we may call 'naturalism'. Ricardo had discovered the existence of an industrial society. Society, he assumed, was governed by natural laws. This line of reasoning reinforced the position of economic liberalism vis-à-vis its antagonists enormously. Institutional reforms looked powerless compared with the laws of Nature. 'The circumstances under which the existence of this human aggregate – a complex society – became apparent', Polanyi underlines, 'were of the utmost importance for the history of nineteenth-century thought' (Polanyi, [1944] 2001: 121). It seemed that political norms could be derived immediately (and without further evaluation) from economic facts. The force of this line of reasoning enormously strengthened the idea of free trade and of the spontaneous identification of interests, that is, the simplified form of the Utilitarianism that Halévy ([1901] 1949: 514) called the 'Manchester philosophy', and contributed to its triumph over the doctrine of the parliamentary Radicals, the 'Westminster philosophy'. Any kind of social regulation that was in contradiction to the laws of Nature had to be avoided or abolished. Knowledge of the economic principles was regarded as a straight guidance on what kind of social reform would be desirable. Drawing on alleged natural laws and natural rights gave them a considerable advantage in relation to their opponents. All plans to raise living standards, to limit market forces or to redistribute property could be rejected a priori on the grounds that such policies were impracticable because they contradicted what was natural. The result was economic determinism, that is, the idea that society is principally constrained by economic laws, which can be attributed to Nature. The protagonists of economic liberalism used this new insight to attack any and every demand for protection. Thomas Carlyle appropriately characterized the liberal economic theory of the nineteenth century as a 'dismal science'.

The belief in naturalism explains the otherwise astonishing feature that the classical theory was not interested in institutions, not even in the institutional features of the market system. The classical value-theory, the theories of distribution and of accumulation can be understood without referring to the institutional characteristics of the market. The alleged economic laws, which the theories of the nineteenth century discovered, were not the laws of the market. They are not laws of any particular institution. Malthus, Ricardo or Say were looking for natural boundaries traceable to biological laws. In the classical theories, the market is taken for granted. Its properties remain in semidarkness. Supply and demand are considered the driving forces behind the daily fluctuations of prices around the exchange value. But the focus remains on value theory, not on the short-term fluctuations. The core of classical theories – the theories of value of exchange, of distribution and of accumulation and so on – can be elaborated without taking into consideration the features of markets in any detail.[1]

From today's perspective, it may be difficult to imagine what the influence of naturalism on the consciousness of the nineteenth century really meant. From today's point of view, we have difficulty conceiving what it means if you are convinced that *money is gold*; we have difficulty imagining an economic world in which categories such as inflation and deflation were used not to describe price fluctuations but changes in the proportion of circulating coins and bills relative to the amount of precious metal. Nevertheless, this was the case in the nineteenth century. As long as it is taken for granted that money is a good (gold), the price level seems to depend on the relative value of two sets of goods, the money-good (gold) on the one hand and the other goods on the other hand. Both values are beyond the reach of monetary policy. Therefore, central banks apparently do not have at their disposal instruments that would allow for keeping the general price level stable. Consequently, the monetary authorities were regarded as being in charge of stabilizing the financial system by guaranteeing the convertibility of coins and banknotes in gold (at a fixed rate). As long as central banks followed the 'rules of the game' and ensured convertibility, it seemed absurd to hold them accountable for the increasing or decreasing price level. Under these conditions, paper money simply appeared as a substitute for gold, which was used for reasons of convenience. In theory, the gold standard was considered a self-regulating system as long as banks guaranteed convertibility. The so-called 'price-specie flow mechanism' was expected to protect the national monetary system against disturbances from the outside. The 'belief in gold' was the indispensable tacit assumption on which the international gold standard rested.

Now we know that in reality the gold standard never worked as automatically as classical theory assumed. Especially in the last decades before the war when, as a consequence of democratization, increasing popular influence and political pressure, the central banks had to take into account national policy goals, the commitment to the gold standard began to shake (cf. Eichengreen, 2008). In any case, it is too easy to explain the proposals and decisions of the English economists of the nineteenth century by pointing to class interests and personal advantages alone. They acted out of conviction. When Ricardo fought for the abolition of the old Poor Law, he was convinced that he would contribute to the improvement of the living conditions of the capitalists, but also of the poor.

Secondly, we have to understand that the alleged natural laws were used, above all, to demonstrate what is *not* possible. I shall, therefore, call this dimension the impossibility theorem. In the twentieth century Karl Popper would make the impossibility theorem one of the cornerstones of 'critical rationalism': 'Every "good" scientific theory is a prohibition. It forbids certain things to happen. The more a theory forbids, the better it is' (Popper, [1963] 2006: 48). Classical political economy used the reputation of the natural sciences to demonstrate that certain social reforms such as the 'old Poor Law' or the disentanglement of the pound sterling from gold should not be undertaken because they were 'against nature'. The logic of the impossibility theorem is irresistible. If it can be proved scientifically that certain measures are doomed to fail, only misunderstandings and wrong-headedness can motivate the resulting proposals for reform. Their supporters can be denounced as dreamers who believe in utopian visions. The impossibility theorem is more than a rhetorical figure. It depends on the belief in social laws which can be established scientifically. The importance of the perversity thesis, the futility thesis and the jeopardy thesis, which Hirschman (1991) describes so vividly in his book *Rhetoric of Reaction*, was that they appealed not only to the material interests of the propertied classes, but also to the conviction that the proposals for social reform brought about by the counter-movement could be excluded on purely scientific grounds.

Why is it important to take a look at the consciousness of the nineteenth century? Why does Polanyi dedicate several chapters of *TGT* to the analysis of the liberal creed, even though he understands its flaws and weaknesses? The reason is that the liberal worldview was the main driver of the institutional transformation of the civilization under scrutiny. 'People's strivings are', Myrdal (1956: ix–x) underlined, 'among the most important social facts and they largely determine the course of history.' As I have demonstrated on another occasion (Thomasberger, 2012/13), Polanyi does not accept the separation of being and thinking, of material life-process and consciousness, which is taken for granted by the conventional theory of knowledge. Polanyi regards the liberal creed as part of social reality. The liberal utopia was the driving force behind the institutional transformation of nineteenth-century civilization. The belief in economic laws that determine the limits of the possible improvement of society was a constitutive element of the civilization of the nineteenth century. In Polanyi's explanation of institutional change, ideas do play an indispensable role. 'Not the material world but the conception of it that is the driving force (however false and erroneous this conception is)' (Polanyi, [1919] 2018: 266), he stresses as early as 1919. When Polanyi characterizes the civilization of the nineteenth century as an economic society, the reason for this particular feature lies in the dominating world view, the liberal creed. The nineteenth century believed in economic laws. The belief had real consequences. The market system expanded and it produced a fervent dynamic unknown to earlier generations; a new way of life which spread across the planet.

The belief in the economic laws which could be traced back to natural conditions had critical consequences. The first was laissez-faire. If social and economic progress is regarded as a natural development, it seems as if human intervention can only hamper the advancement of society unless it promotes what is natural. The laws of nature are beyond human control. They cannot be changed by political decisions. They are also a norm. The philosophy of natural law implies that teleology and causality are identified. The economic laws had to be understood and accepted as a guideline for political action.

Another important consequence of the belief in naturalism was the particular dichotomy characterizing nineteenth-century civilization. Society consisted of two spheres: the 'economic sphere' which was determined by the natural laws of production and natural rights, on the one hand; and a 'higher sphere' encompassing the 'rest' of society where man-made laws prevailed, on the other hand. Polanyi calls this separation disembedding of the economy from society. The rule of property and contracts were regarded as natural laws originating in the nature of things. Polanyi obviously refers to this division when he states:

> As regards man, we were made to accept the heresy that his motives can be described as 'material' and 'ideal', and that the incentives on which everyday life is organized spring from the 'material' motives. Both utilitarian liberalism and popular Marxism favored such views. As regards society, the kindred doctrine was propounded that its institutions were 'determined' by the economic system. (Polanyi [1947] 2018b: 198)

The liberal economists of the nineteenth century took for granted the existence of an economic sphere, which was controlled by natural laws and was, therefore, free from the jurisdiction of the state.

At this point it should be obvious why the notion of the 'always embedded economy' can be misleading. The question of whether the term 'self-regulating market system' should be regarded as a utopian experiment doomed to failure or as an existing system, an 'ontological reality', is missing the point. A utopia is only a utopia because it is unachievable. This is self-evident. The assertion that the economy, even in the nineteenth century, was not completely disembedded can thus be taken for granted. But this is clearly not Polanyi's point. His emphasis is on the particularity of the society of the nineteenth century. Never before in human history had the idea prevailed that human destiny depends on economic laws detached from moral and ethical considerations. Never before was the institutional transformation of society driven by a belief which separated society so completely from the moral world. Polanyi calls the economy 'disembedded' because the belief in economic determinism was a constitutive factor of the consciousness, and therefore the history, of the nineteenth century.

From the inter-war period: looking back to the future

The First World War and the Bolshevik Revolution marked a fundamental break in social consciousness. In the following decades, it came to be taken as self-evident that there have never been economic laws which determined society. After the war, Polanyi maintains, 'the omnipresent economic interest … proved to be not merely unreal and abstract to the point of sophistry but also mere economic superstition and empty fantasy' (Polanyi, [1919] 2018: 266). Antonio Gramsci even characterizes the Bolshevik Revolution as a 'revolution against Karl Marx's Capital' because it 'is based more on ideology than actual events' (Gramsci, 1917, author's translation). Not only for Polanyi, but also for Mises, Lippmann, Hayek and other 'new' liberals, it seems obvious that Ricardo and his followers had misinterpreted the existence of an industrial society. Classical economists had failed miserably because they mistook social laws for natural laws. The 'lapse into naturalism', as Polanyi ([1944] 2001: 121) suspects, might have been the consequence of what to nineteenth-century consciousness appeared as the 'apparently insoluble problem of pauperism' (ibid.: 121). But whatever the origins of the naturalist interpretation of laws which turned out to be essentially social in character, a fallacy had haunted the human consciousness for the greater part of the nineteenth century.

In other words, we must distinguish clearly between the self-consciousness of the actors of the nineteenth century and the worldviews which prevailed in the inter-war period (including Polanyi's reasoning). For the contemporaries of the nineteenth century, naturalism seemed real. From the point of view of the inter-war period, naturalism became the fallacy of the past. Polanyi is not alone with his critique of the naturalist belief. The 'new' liberals of the twentieth century not only share Polanyi's critique of naturalism, but also the political implications, that is, the repudiation of laissez-faire. Walter Lippmann (1937: 184) categorizes the doctrine of laissez-faire as one of the 'cardinal fallacies of nineteenth-century liberalism'. And Friedrich Hayek ([1944] 2001: 18) agrees: 'Probably nothing has done so much harm to the liberal cause as the … the principle of laissez-faire.' On this occasion, I do not have the space to discuss the question of why the naturalistic error collapsed in the inter-war period. It must suffice to recall that already in the nineteenth century some socialist thinkers, albeit with limited influence, had denounced the laws of nature as fictions. The counter-movement intervened, violating the alleged natural laws. Finally, the First World War and the Bolshevik Revolution had demonstrated to the world *in practice* that the idea of natural progress was an illusion and that conflicting social arrangements had become reality.

What does this shift in consciousness mean for the understanding of the liberal creed and the double movement? The liberals of the nineteenth century were convinced that they were defending reality against utopian struggles for social protection. From the point of view of the 1920s and 1930s, it was self-evident that, regarding the nineteenth century, the juxtaposition between realistic liberalism and utopian counter-movement could not be maintained. Ricardo and his followers had not defended reality against utopian claims, but they had fought for a fiction, the naturalist fallacy. In reality, the counter-movement which opposed economic liberalism was the one which defended social reality against a utopian project. The roles are reversed. Polanyi adheres to the impossibility theorem, but – as we shall see in a moment – not to naturalism.

By accepting the idea of a double movement, Polanyi inverts the impossibility argument and turns it against the liberal creed. 'While in our view the concept of a self-regulating market was utopian, and its progress was stopped by the realistic self-protection of society, in their view all protectionism was a mistake due to impatience, greed, and shortsightedness, but for which the market would have resolved its difficulties' (Polanyi, [1944] 2001: 148). Up to this point, Polanyi's reasoning seems obvious. Indeed, from the point of view of the inter-war period, the inversion of the argument does not call for any particular justification. It is more plausible than the liberal case!

The more interesting aspect is perhaps that Polanyi does not invert the model completely. He never argues that the counter-movement 'would have resolved [the market's] difficulties'. He never pretends that the counter-movement offers a solution of the problem of freedom in a complex society. And more than that, he points out the limited character of the counter-movement. This has to do with the principal task of the counter-movement. The factors of production – or the 'fictitious commodities', as Polanyi calls them – are the obvious starting points of the counter-movement. There are three characteristics which distinguish the fictitious commodities from ordinary goods:

- They are indispensable for the working of the self-regulating market system. Without the factors of production, no self-regulating market system is possible.
- The prices of the fictitious commodities form the incomes of the principal classes of society. Wages, interest and rent derive directly from the sales of labor, money and land.
- In so far as labor, money and land are not produced, they have neither production costs nor supply functions comparable to ordinary commodities.

Certainly all kinds of markets suppose the existence of a legal and institutional framework. Nevertheless, in the case of the fictitious commodities, this is not sufficient. In the case of the fictitious commodities, political intervention cannot be limited to setting a framework. Economic liberalism is guided by the utopian idea of *simulating* the existence of supply functions by establishing rules that *feign* economic scarcity. In the case of money, this can mean keeping the supply of money artificially scarce by linking it directly to commodities (such as gold, silver and so on) or by limiting its quantity by law (monetary rules). In the case of land, the right of appropriation has always been a reason for political struggle. In the case of labor, wage levels have to be fought over by labor unions and defended by intervention against the pressure of the artificial market.

Therefore, the counter-movement has good reasons to oppose the liberal initiatives. But opposing market pressures does not mean developing answers to the question of how to organize a technological civilization. The counter-movement is mainly concerned with the problems of capitalism, not with the problems of a complex society. Its aim is defense against exploitation, social injustices, marginalization, loss of dignity, and so on, but this does not mean that it develops a plan, an idea, a real solution to the problems that a technological society has to face. When Polanyi states in *TGT* that, 'while laissez-faire economy was the product of deliberate State action, subsequent restrictions on laissez-faire started in a spontaneous way. Laissez-faire was planned; planning was not' (ibid.: 147), he not only opposes the liberal interpretation. He also underlines the limited character of the counter-movement, that is, the fact that during the nineteenth century protection was for the most part defensive, if also pervasive. The counter-movement had no plan of how to respond to the conditions of a technological civilization. Right on the second page of *TGT*, Polanyi warns of the negative and disruptive side effects of a counter-movement that focused on protection against the market system. It 'impaired the self-regulation of the market, disorganized industrial life, and thus endangered society in yet another way. It was this dilemma which forced the development of the market system into a definite groove and finally disrupted the social organization based upon it' (ibid.: 4). And in the last chapter of *TGT* he underlines once more the co-responsibility of the counter-movement for the disintegration of the nineteenth-century civilization.

What is the origin of the dilemma to which Polanyi refers in the quoted paragraph? The short answer is: Polanyi is convinced that the counter-movement remained trapped within the logic of the liberal society. On the one hand, the counter-movement was necessary because the self-regulating market system, left to itself, would have destroyed society. On the other hand, since it expressed itself mainly as a protective movement, it depended on economic liberalism. As the term indicates, a counter-movement cannot stand alone. According to Polanyi's interpretation, the counter-movement was a reaction to the liberal utopia, which made it an integral part of this civilization. It was born with the civilization of the nineteenth century, and it was destined to die with it. The deeper questions then are: What is the character of the relationship between the two unequal forces which drive the double movement? Why does Polanyi consider socialism, but not the counter-movement, the real alternative to economic liberalism? In order to answer these questions, we have to turn to the advancement of liberal reasoning after the First World War, Polanyi's critique and his understanding of the challenges of a technological civilization, the problem of 'freedom in a complex society' (ibid.: 257).

The industrial revolution and the problem of freedom in a complex society

As underlined above, the question of the consequences of the industrial revolution for human society can be regarded as the main thread running through Polanyi's work. He addresses the challenges of the machine age already in Hungary, but finds a precise definition of the issue only after the First World War while participating in the 'socialist accountancy debate' and Austro-Marxist discussions about the possibility of a socialist reorganization of society. What is the issue?

Ludwig von Mises launched the 'socialist accountancy debate' in 1920 with the article 'Economic calculation in the socialist commonwealth' (Mises, [1920] 1935). While also assuming that the naturalist fallacy was a story of the past, Mises posed the question of the institutional organization of economic relations in a complex society. Superficially, the issue seemed to be 'market versus central planning'. However, Mises's article and the following book *Gemeinwirtschaft* (1922, later published in English under the title *Socialism* (cf. Mises, [1922] 1951)) did not only attack central planning. The real importance of the debate is that Mises pointed to the problem of an industrial society in order to criticize the 'communist fiction'.[2] Mises understood that the latter was the cornerstone of both, of the idea of central planning and of the notion of 'social value', which was in turn a cornerstone of the welfarist schools. Indeed, even if at first glance Mises's contributions seemed to attack Otto Neurath's (1919) proposal for 'planning in kind', they were no less directed against Friedrich Wieser's notion of a 'simple economy' ([1914] 1927: 9), the Lausanne School (Walras, Pareto) and welfarism in general. Mises realized that all these models had a common ground, in so far as they start from the assumption that society is essentially the result of human will aiming at social well-being.

The starting point of Mises's argument is the distinction between a household economy and a modern, complex and technological civilization. Under the conditions of 'the narrow confines of a closed household economy, it is possible throughout to review the process of production from beginning to end', Mises explained. 'This, however, is no longer possible in the incomparably more involved circumstances of our own social economy' (Mises, [1920] 1935: 103).[3] Mises insisted on the insight that the analysis of an industrial civilization cannot be based on the model of a community or household because modern society has to face a problem, which, in a household, does not exist. Under the conditions of a modern society, rational economic planning is impossible because no single person and no central authority is able to have the overview and knowledge that would be necessary for rational economic planning.

Consisting of two steps, Mises's reasoning is quite simple yet fundamental. First, he defines the problem of an industrial civilization, arguing that in a complex industrial society human relations are necessarily opaque and non-transparent. Under these conditions, it is impossible for a single person to gain an overview of the consequences of his/her decisions and to take responsibility for his/her actions. Therefore, the model of a household or a community, even if it seems attractive, is totally misleading. The problem of overview cannot be resolved by reverting to a communist fiction. Rational economic planning is impossible because nobody can have the knowledge which would be necessary. This is the principal social problem of a technological civilization, and it cannot be resolved by any kind of technical device. An alternative solution has to be found. In other words: Mises draws on the impossibility theorem but, in opposition to Ricardo, not on the basis of natural laws. In his line of reasoning the problem of a complex society is substituted for the laws of Nature.

In the second step of his reasoning, Mises purports to offer the answer. If in a complex society overview is impossible and direct human relationships few, then the market system provides the solution, he claims. The market achieves what community is unable to accomplish! Mises's contributions to the socialist calculation debate are still relevant today not because they taught anything about accounting, but because they laid the foundation for a new meta-theoretical belief, the *neoliberal fiction*. Just like the naturalist fiction (or the communist fiction), the neoliberal fiction has the character of an assumption, a prejudice or a superstition. Mises never explains how the market accomplishes this task.[4] He simply assumes that there are only two alternatives: household/community and markets. And he takes for granted that the second is the only possible answer, if it can be proven that the first is a false and misleading analogy. If under modern conditions a world-wide human community is inconceivable, he assumes that only 'the market' accomplishes the task. The market system, he maintains, achieves what central planning is striving for in vain. Markets are regarded by Mises as a *substitute* for overview and direct human relations.

Karl Polanyi is one of the first to understand the crucial importance of the line of reasoning brought forward by Mises. Polanyi publishes a paper (1922) presenting his own position and giving a rejoinder (1924; Polanyi, 2018e) in the same journal in which Mises's article appeared. He accepts the question posed by Mises. He recognizes that a complex society cannot be understood in terms of a community: 'We consider it impossible to solve the problem of accounting in a centrally administered economy' (Polanyi, [1922] 2016c: 398). But he rejects the idea that the market provides a solution. In other words, Polanyi accepts the first step of Mises's reasoning but not the second. He accepts the impossibility theorem as well as Mises's rejection of naturalism. But he regards Mises's defense of the market system as no less utopian than the naturalist fallacy.

Participating in the discussions on the fringes of Austro-Marxism, Polanyi explores the possibilities of a guild-socialist solution, which goes beyond the alternative 'central planning versus market'. He adopts a broader perspective than Mises in so far as his principal concern is not the problem of economic rationality but the problem of freedom, that is, the difficulty that in a complex technological society single actors cannot gain an overview of society, and cannot understand the social consequences of their actions. So they cannot decide freely and with responsibility towards others. In a lecture he gave some years later exploring the relationship to Marx's analysis of the Fetishism of Commodities (Polanyi, [1927] 2018), he raised the question in more philosophical terms. How can a person be free in conditions of modernity if he/she cannot comprehend the consequences of his/her actions? How can he/she take over responsibility for his/her decisions if in a complex technological society he/she is unable to have an overview of what the consequences are for other people? And how might a really free society look? Polanyi discusses at length not only the problem of external, but also internal, overview (human needs, work-related suffering). Overview, he argues, cannot be substituted by a soulless mechanism like the market system. Organizational reforms are required, which help to *increase* overview in reality (Polanyi, [1922] 2016c, [1925] 2018, [1927] 2018, 2005d). In speeches and articles, he explores how the organizations of the socialist and the labor movements – labor unions, associations, socialist municipalities, direct democracy – can contribute to an expansion of overview in a technological society.

Polanyi never accepts the alternative 'market or community'. He never agrees with the idea that the problem of freedom can be handed over to the market system. Polanyi's understanding sees overview, freedom and responsibility as human values, not facts. They have to be defended against whatever soulless systems assail them. Even if it is true that institutions are unavoidable in society, no institution can be expected to solve the problem. Human norms and ideals can only be made true if we recognize them as a task, as our mission.

Over the years, Polanyi realizes that the problem industrial civilization had laid bare is not limited to the liberal age. It is the far more fundamental problem of human society as such. In his later work, instead of the term 'problem of overview', he prefers the notion 'problem of freedom in a complex society'. In time, Polanyi learns to recognize that there may be no perfect solution to the problem of freedom under modern conditions. On the one hand, self-regulating institutions cannot replace overview without making free and responsible human decisions impossible; on the other hand, impersonal institutions are unavoidable in complex societies. Therefore, we can only compare different social settings from the point of view of *how much* freedom they allow. Perhaps Polanyi's oeuvre is understood best as a lifelong search for answers to the challenges of a technological civilization from the point of view of human freedom and responsibility.

Polanyi has been characterized as one of the most important institutionalists of the twentieth century, together with John K. Galbraith, Karl W. Kapp, Adolf Löwe, Gunnar Myrdal, François Perroux and J. Ron Stanfield (Cangiani, 2011). This classification is, I think, completely correct. Polanyi considers institutions a third realm beneath nature and human will. As he points out in the manuscript, *On Freedom*:

> In every large society based on division of labor, no direct socialization of people is possible. The unity of the whole can only be perceived here if certain social phenomena continuously appear and are mediated between persons. These social phenomena form a kind of third realm that stands between the realm of Being and of Consciousness. ... It is the actual object of sociology. Its wealth of phenomenal forms is no less than that of nature or of the human soul. Alongside near-corporeal organs like state and market, they include laws that assert themselves with causal inevitability, such as those which govern price formation in capitalism. (Polanyi, [1927] 2018: 317)

Even though it may sound paradoxical, institutions stand centre stage in Polanyi's research because he considers them to be indispensable for life in society, but at the same time a threat to personal freedom and autonomy. In modern societies, the most important institutions deal in power and economic value. In discussions with the Christian Left, he maintained that

> Power and value are inherent in society; political and economic coercion belong to any and every form of human co-operation. It is part of the ineluctable alternative of human existence that we can choose only between different kinds of power, and different uses to which to put it, but we cannot choose not to originate power or not to influence its use once it has been created. (Polanyi, [1937] 2018b: 152)

In *TGT* he comes back to this argument when he speaks of a necessary 'reform of human consciousness to be reached through the recognition of the reality of society' (Polanyi, [1944] 2001: 133). 'No society is possible', he stresses, 'in which power and compulsion are absent, nor a world in which force has no function' (ibid.: 266). And finally, at the end of the 1950s, he recapitulates: 'Society's invisible tissue did not truly come to light before it had been dyed through contact with machinery. Technology thus partly created, partly revealed the existence of an interpersonal structure around us that had a consistence of its own – not any more an aggregate of persons, nor even a Hobbesian Leviathan built of human maggots but reality, not in its changing forms but in its abiding existence as unshakable as death' (Polanyi, 37–06: 1). Society, that is, the existence of an institutionalized, interpersonal structure of human relations, is a *reality* that can only be recognized. No technical progress and no institutional innovation can overcome the limits that are defined by the conditions of the machine age. Humanity cannot go back in history; it is beyond human will to reverse the industrial revolution. But it is within the realm of human will to decide *how to respond* to the challenges of a technological society.

It is an irony that Polanyi, who since his days in Budapest and until the end of his life opposed the communist fiction vehemently, after the Second World War was accused by several reviewers of romanticizing and idealizing community in his writings. Polanyi is not only familiar with the distinction made by Tönnies ([1887] 1957b) between *Gemeinschaft* and *Gesellschaft*, but he is also interested in the institutional particularities of ancient societies exactly for the opposite reason, that is, because he knows that 'no society can be the realisation of community' (Polanyi, [1937] 2018b: 152). It is true that he uses the idea of community as a regulative idea.[5] Overview, personal freedom and responsibility are norms for which he strives. However, in his writings he never confuses norms and facts, community and the reality of society.

The challenges of a technological society and the counter-movement

If the problem of freedom in a complex society is the underlying challenge, the question arises: How does the counter-movement respond? Does it develop its own solution to the challenges posed by the machine age? Or does the counter-movement accept the liberal claim that there is no alternative to the market system and limit itself to protection against the negative side effects of the market mechanism? Polanyi's assessment is obviously that during the greater part of the nineteenth and twentieth centuries, the latter is the case. The counter-movement remained trapped in the liberal worldview. It certainly rejected the proposition that the result of the blind market system is beneficial for everybody. It recognized that the market system threatens human dignity, nature and even the stability of the economic system itself. But as long as the counter-movement did not search for alternatives to the market mechanism, it remained stuck in the logic of economic liberalism.

This explains why in *TGT* Robert Owen is Polanyi's hero. Owen tried to understand and to adapt to the conditions of a complex society. Owen accepted the challenges of the machine age. He welcomed technological progress. But at the same time he was looking for (and experimenting with) new institutional arrangements which increased overview, enlarged the possibility of men and women to participate in social life, and improved the opportunities of the inhabitants of New Lanark to shoulder responsibility and determine their destiny. He did not fall back or seek refuge in the self-regulating mechanism of the market. He was one of the few who really transcended the limits of nineteenth-century civilization. What distinguished Owen was his quest to find creative answers to the question of how to combine the recognition of a technological society with the aspiration to uphold personal freedom and responsibility.

Socialism (and fascism) are not simply part of the counter-movement. Though socialists accept that under modern conditions, markets are at least to some extent necessary institutions, they uphold the claim to freedom and search for alternative answers to the challenges of a technological society. In other words, awareness of the challenges of a technological society is the crucial point. This is precisely the weakness of the counter-movement in the nineteenth and twentieth centuries: its protagonists struggled for protection, but they accepted the liberal assumption that concerning the problem of technological society there is no alternative to market solutions. This also explains Polanyi's doubts about the struggles of the working class. He expresses them in one of the Bennington Lectures when he states (referring to the conditions in the nineteenth century): 'While the working people had been fighting against economic liberalism under the lead of Owenism and Chartism, they gave up the struggle in the Fifties and turned whole-heartedly to liberalism themselves. Not they, but rather the owning classes represented the interests of a partly conservative, partly social protectionism' (Polanyi, 1940a: 3).

As long as the counter-movement enforced protective measures while essentially accepting the liberal answer to the challenges of a complex society, there was a further danger. The objection of the protagonists of economic liberalism that interventions in the mechanism of supply and demand constrained the flexibility of the market mechanism is not unfounded. Interference in the market, without seeking an alternative answer to the challenges of a technological society, runs the risk of falling into a dead end. The 1930s demonstrated that this was not a theoretical issue but that it had enormous practical significance.

The interpretation that the counter-movement was progressive and/or in open opposition to the market has little to do with Polanyi's description of the transformation of civilization of the nineteenth century. It is certainly correct to criticize some sociologists at the end of the twentieth/beginning of the twenty-first century who, drawing on Polanyi, 'tend to idealize social protection' (Fraser, 2012: 5). But you cannot blame *TGT* or other writings of Polanyi for the same fallacy. Under the conditions of the nineteenth century, social protection was unavoidable. However, it remained a rather limited endeavor.

To sum up, the double movement cannot be depicted as some kind of a meta-physical development or as a trans-historical tendency that can be observed in all epochs of history. It was the outcome of a particular political struggle – a utopian project referring to alleged laws of nature on the one hand and realistic, but limited, counter-movement on the other hand. It cannot be generalized without examining the concrete conditions prevailing at the time. Polanyi applies the notion of the double movement because in the nineteenth century a utopian creed, masked as alleged realism and opposed by defensive counter-movements, became the power-house of institutional transformation. Polanyi never uses the term to describe, for example, the conditions in Austria in the 1920s with its strong socialist movements. He is well aware of the fact that the double movement came to an end in the inter-war period. As Polanyi makes clear, not only in the last chapter of *TGT* but also in numerous articles during the 1920s and 1930s: fascism and socialism cannot be regarded as counter-movement. Both represent alternative models of society which aspire to supersede and to take the place of the liberal civilization of the nineteenth century.

The breakdown of the naturalist fiction in Europe during the inter-war period opened the possibility of overcoming both the liberal creed and the limitedness of the counter-movement, and to lay bare the challenges of a technological civiliza-tion. Polanyi regards the breakdown of naturalism as a chance in so far as in some European countries it opens the possibility of a reform of human consciousness based on a true understanding of the problem of a technological society. 'Much of the massive suffering inseparable from a period of transition', he states in *TGT*, 'is already behind us. In the social and economic dislocation of our age, in the tragic vicissitudes of the depression, fluctuations of currency, mass unemployment, shiftings of social status, spectacular destruction of historical states, we have expe-rienced the worst' ([1944] 2001: 258–259). But he is also well aware of the fact that there is no automatism which leads to a socialist and democratic society.

When Polanyi drafts *TGT*, he knows that in the inter-war period the fiction which had dominated the thinking of the nineteenth century in Europe was passé. He regards the breakdown of the naturalist vision as progress in so far as it opens up the chance for substituting a more realistic vision of society for the liberal utopia. At the same time, Polanyi is skeptical concerning the future, not only because fascism was a serious danger which threatened Western civilization, but also because eco-nomic liberalism was still alive. Mises was not alone. The protagonists of economic liberalism did not acknowledge defeat and abandon the field. Instead, Raymond Aron, Friedrich Hayek, Louis Rougier, Jacques Rueff, Alexander Rüstow and Lionel Robbins in Europe, and Walter Lippmann, Henry Simons, Aaron Director and many others in the US joined their forces, organized influential think-tanks and engaged in developing new justifications for the market system which would be able to take the place of the naturalist fallacy.

Is it true that Polanyi is overoptimistic concerning a socialist future after the Second World War? In his writings he never excludes or underestimates the dangers of a restoration of economic liberalism. Moreover, if he really had fallen victim to false optimism, the writing of *TGT*, which was directed mainly against the liberal utopia, would have had little sense. And even if in the first years after the Second World War he detects, starting from Europe, a general tendency in direction of regional planning, he warns of the contrary influence issuing from the United States of America:

> The United States has remained the home of liberal capitalism and is powerful enough to pursue alone the Utopian line of policy involved in such a fateful dispensation … the United States has no alternative. Americans almost unanimously identify their way of life with private enterprise and business competition – though not altogether with classical laissez-faire. This is what democracy means to them, rich and poor alike … the stupendous achievements of liberal capitalism appear to Americans as the central fact in the realm of organized society. ([1945] 2018: 232–233)

As we shall see in a moment, Polanyi's fears were justified: based on the dominant position of the US in the Western world, economic liberalism witnessed resurgence after the Second World War.

Post-war era

At this point, we have to return to our original questions: What can we learn from Polanyi's analysis for the post-war era? How can we make use of his approach to cast light on the recent transformation of society? Is it justified to assume that the dynamic prevailing before the wars continues after the Second World War? There are at least three reasons to question a research program that builds on the supposition of continuity.

First, at the end of the Second World War, as we have shown above, the institutional framework on which the civilization of the nineteenth century had rested had collapsed. Secondly, faith in the natural development of society had come to an end. Laissez-faire had lost its premises.

Thirdly, Europe was defeated. After the war, America (the US) took over the lead and the role of the world's trendsetting continent. Compared with European nations the US was a quite different society with its own institutions, its own traditions and its own identity. Wouldn't it be much more plausible to expect that the international post-war system would rely on the US model rather than on European traditions?

In other discussions about the history of the twentieth century, the shift of power from Europe to America is recognized as a deep break. Moreover, it is observed that US society differed fundamentally from nineteenth-century civilization in Europe. Recall that the US was born out of a revolt *against* Europe. Actually, US society was the result of the American Revolutionary War, in which the Thirteen Colonies had triumphed over the old colonial powers. As several economic historians have demonstrated, the US never adopted the naturalist vision of society, which had shaped the European vision. Laissez-faire did not dominate in US politics, neither in the nineteenth century nor in the 1940s. 'The founding fathers ... were not proponents of laissez-faire' (Schlesinger, 1989: 219–220). 'There was in the new nation no real consensus for true laizzez-faire, either in the private sector or in the government' (Prince and Taylor, 1981: 114). Without going into the details, it is reasonable to maintain that from the beginning the social and economic conditions in the US were rather different from those in Europe (to list only the most important aspects: establishment of the US as a society, not as a state; 'free land' in the west; 'rivalistic state mercantilism' (ibid.; Scheiber, 1966: 5–6); the constitution, which until the 1930s prevented the establishment of a federal state with substantial internal power). Polanyi was well aware of the difference: 'While America was founded and carried on as a society, which only quite recently started to develop a state in the strict sense of the term, European countries at least since the 16th century possessed a state power on which the actual social system rested' (Polanyi, 1940b: 2). Another feature of US society (as opposed to Europe) was the reciprocal interaction (and not the opposition) of business and politics. Interventions served society by seeking a balance between the interests of producers and consumers – an aspect that Polanyi considered crucial in order to understand why the US did not find itself in a dead end which in Italy, Germany and other European countries had made possible fascist revolutions. In Europe, Polanyi explains, 'the alternative was between an integration of society through political power on a democratic basis, or, if democracy proved too weak, integration on an authoritarian basis in a totalitarian society, at the price of the sacrifice of democracy. The American social system is, in my conviction, not faced with this tragic dilemma' (Polanyi, [1940] 2014: 219). All these divergences have nothing to do with socialism. Undoubtedly, the US was a market society, but a market society of a different kind compared with the European civilization of the nineteenth century. In contrast to Britain, the political forces in the US aimed at preventing the emergence of a self-regulating market system within the country. Externally, the US economy was protected by customs and controls. Only with the New Deal did Washington take responsibility for economic well-being, which up to the Great Depression was in the hands of the single states. And only after the Second World War, when its leading position in the Western world was undisputed, did the US move on to some kind of free trade policy with the rest of the world.

How can we suppose that all these differences played no role? Isn't it reasonable to expect that the US did indeed attempt to impose on the Western world the type of society which in the US model had been created after the New Deal: a) a central state (Washington) that fostered economic growth, employment and social welfare; and b) an international system that favored free trade and open markets (Bretton Woods, IMF, GATT, and so on, directed against the privileges granted to colonial trade by European countries)?

Such a model could certainly find allies in Europe. From a theoretical point of view, Keynes's ideas fitted quite well into the picture. Even if Robbins (1932) had forcefully criticized the idea of social welfare as scientifically worthless, Keynes's break with the classical school offered a chance. During the inter-war period, Keynes had paved the way by highlighting the goals of price stability (1930), employment (1936) and external balances (1942–44). After the war, by focusing on inflation/ deflation, unemployment and external imbalances, his followers were able to integrate some of the problems that had been topical issues of the nineteenth-century counter-movement. Keynesianism recognized that the market system could not be left to itself and that it had to be augmented by macroeconomic policy. The central authorities (government, central banks) should take over the task of steering the economy. In the industrialized countries of the Western world in the 1950s and 1960s, Keynesianism was able to resolve – or at least considerably reduce – some of the most pressing problems of capitalism revealed by the inter-war period. However, recall that neither the US model nor Keynesianism attempted to tackle the challenges of a technological society.

If we recall Polanyi's concern about freedom in a technological civilization, we should not be surprised that welfarism was reaching its limits at the beginning of the 1970s, when the international system threatened the national economic policy space not only in the European countries but also in the US. The conflict within a system which was built on the belief in an open unregulated international market system on the one hand, and the capacity of national governments to protect society against the socially disruptive consequences of the former on the other hand, was no less utopian than the belief in the self-regulation of the international gold standard had been. Both arrangements had in common that, in the end, they depended on the utopian creed that the problem of freedom in a complex society can be resolved by a blind mechanism, the international market system. Welfarism was not sustainable because it did not offer an independent answer to the problem of freedom in a complex society. By limiting itself to the problems of capitalism while ignoring the more fundamental problem of a technological society, welfarism collapsed, becoming a utopian dream. Polanyi's concern about the return of the market utopia after the Second World War under the guidance of the United States proved to be true.

When the conflict between the international market system and national protection broke out in the 1970s, destroying the Bretton Woods exchange rate system, neoliberalism was prepared while the political left was not. As we have seen above, Mises had laid the foundation of neoliberalism in the 1920s. In the meantime, an army of economists, organizations and research projects from the London School of Economics to Chicago, from the Mont Pelerin Society and the Free Market Study Project to the Heritage Foundation, the Centre for Policy Studies and various other think-tanks had refined the approach. With astonishing clarity, Milton Friedman described the long-term objective of his efforts as keeping 'options open until circumstances make change necessary. ... Only a crisis actual or perceived produces real change. When that crisis occurs, the actions that are taken depend on the ideas that are lying around. That, I believe, is our basic function: to develop alternatives to existing policies, to keep them alive and available until the politically impossible becomes politically inevitable' (Friedman, 1982: 7). The key ideas that Friedman was to propose refer back to Mises: Welfarism was doomed to failure because without offering a solution to the problem of a technological society its promises were empty.

Karl Polanyi today

What remains? Why should we study Polanyi's works? Doesn't this mean that Polanyi's insights are interesting only as historical artifacts and worthless in shedding light on the transformation that is taking place at the beginning of the twenty-first century? Now, if we try to make use of *TGT* today, we have to be aware of the fact that we are not focusing on a civilization which has collapsed, but on our society; not on history, but on the present. We do not have the possibility to explore our society from the outside, for we are insiders. We are observers and actors at the same time. We want to exert influence on what we are studying. Research and participation cannot be separated. At the center of our studies are social struggles in which we want to support some protagonists and weaken others. Therefore, our concern with the social forces is completely different from Polanyi's relationship with both the economic liberalism of the nineteenth century and the counter-movement. We are not in the advantageous position of being able to use insights and categories which may be invented after our civilization has become history. We have to base our reasoning on current ideas and worldviews; and we can make use of ideas and insights of the past, that is, as far as we refer to *TGT*, of Polanyi's ideas of the inter-war period. Again, why should we refer to Polanyi? Could it be that in the inter-war period insights and notions had been developed that were then lost? Is it possible that the scientific discourse in sociology and economics during the neoliberal epoch has flattened and become superficial, so that Polanyi's analysis might reintroduce depth and meaningful understanding? Can we really rule out the possibility that the neoliberal fiction is hampering scientific thinking, similar to how the naturalist fallacy misguided classical political economy? If we refer to Polanyi's work today, we are obviously convinced that he has something to teach us which contemporary theories do not offer.

What are the most important insights? At the beginning of the twenty-first century, Polanyi's analysis is topical first because in our days a utopian belief, masked as realist insight, has again become the main driving force of social change. Again, this fiction is used in order to favor market solutions and reject (as far as ever possible) the claims of social protection. Just as the nineteenth century considered self-evident the alleged economic laws, neoliberalism believes in the market as the only solution of the problem of society which is compatible with personal freedom. Today the neoliberal fiction is as real as the naturalist fallacy was in the nineteenth century. It motivates political reforms and, therefore, determines the direction of the institutional transformation. Neoliberalism has real consequences. It is the real driver of social change. It threatens man, nature and the future of the Western civilization no less than earlier forms of economic liberalism in Polanyi's times.

Yet again, the protagonists of the neoliberal fiction refer to the impossibility theorem and the limits of human reason to justify their refusal of social protection. Again, social reality and fiction are turned upside down. Again, the market system is proposed as a solution to the problem of a technological society. Again, the fiction is veiled behind the mask of alleged realism and supported by contemporary economic sciences. And both employ an analogous rhetoric. The protagonists of neoliberalism draw on the problem of society to reject claims for institutional reform and social protection in a way similar to Ricardo's irrefutable laws of nature. While classical liberalism taught that protection is against nature, neoliberalism declares that protection is against the laws of the market, the only institution that offers an answer to the problem of a technological society without destroying personal freedom and falling back on dictatorship over needs.

Last but not least: Polanyi directs our attention to the fundamental problem revealed by the industrial revolution: the problem of freedom in a technological society. It may be seen as a paradox that economic liberalism refers to and abuses the problem without making any serious attempt to resolve it. It exploits the problem of society so as to strengthen its own position, but at the same time it obscures the challenge and the possible solutions. Polanyi is a contemporary witness to the birth of the neoliberal fiction. He discovers and lays bare the fallacy while it is still under construction. He understands the relevance of the impossibility theorem and turns it against the neoliberal reasoning. And he shows how the problem can be faced, if we strive to safeguard personal freedom and democracy.

However, we cannot simply 'transfer' the results of Polanyi's analysis to our times. There are significant differences between nineteenth-century civilization and our own era that we have to take into consideration. First of all, neoliberalism recognizes the problem of society as a social problem (instead of treating it as a natural condition). This difference is crucial in so far as neoliberalism accepts that society is a human product. Society is regarded as being based on human action and not on laws, which are beyond human control. Human action aims to realize purposes and intentions. As Robbins recognized: 'All economic life involves planning. To plan is to act with purpose, to choose; and choice is the essence of economic activity. ... The issue is not between a plan and no plan, it is between different kinds of plan' (Robbins, [1937] 1972: 3–6). Laissez-faire has lost its grounding. As long as the naturalist fiction prevailed, liberalism could polemicize against the idea of aiming at human goals with the simple argument that this was against the nature of things. Since the defeat of naturalism, the conditions for the defense of liberal principles have changed profoundly. Laissez-faire has been replaced by 'planning for the market' or 'planning for competition' (Hayek, [1944] 2001: 43).

Now, the protagonists of neoliberalism question whether the goals and the instruments proposed are compatible with the alleged solution of the problem of a complex society, that is, if they are in conformity with the logic of the market system. Hayek is well aware of the fact that at the end of the twentieth century, the conditions for the defense of liberal principles have changed profoundly. Arguing 'against the welfare state' he explains, 'we shall see that some of the aims of the welfare state can be realized ... others can be similarly achieved to a certain extent, ... and that, finally, there are others that cannot be realized in a society that wants to preserve personal freedom' (Hayek, [1960] 2009: 225–226). If planning for competition is regarded as necessary, a strong state is needed in order to organize markets. Neoliberal economists accept that markets for the fictitious commodities have to be planned because of the lack of a supply schedule. In order to stabilize the labor market, even Hayek proposes the introduction of a state-guaranteed 'equal minimum income for all' (Hayek, 1960: 226, cf. also Hayek, [1944] 2001: 120). And the question of how to create a global monetary system became one of the most discussed and most controversial issues not only between Keynesians and their opponents, but also between the Austrian and the Chicago currents of the neoliberal creed.

And a further difference between the conditions in the nineteenth century in Europe and the neoliberal age is important. As we have seen earlier, in the nineteenth century the naturalist fiction meant that society was divided into two spheres: an economic sphere which was governed by natural laws and natural rights and the rest of society where human decisions prevailed. If, as in the case of the neoliberal creed, the problem of society and not the laws of nature are regarded as the essential limit of the scope for human decision-making, the division collapses. Society as a whole is regarded as a result of human will under the constraint of the coordination problem of an industrial society. The necessity of coordination is not limited to a specific sphere. The problem of how to deal with the fact that in a complex society the actors are unable to gain an overview of the consequences of their actions touches all areas of human activity. This means: if competition is proposed as the solution, it applies to human behavior as such.

In other words, if the market is presented as a solution to the problem of society, the vision presupposes certain assumptions concerning human behavior. Maximization of income, wealth or utility is part of the story. However, in so far as there is no reason to limit these behavioral assumptions to any specific sphere of society, it can, and it has to be (in order to be coherent) applied to all forms of human activity. The imperialist aspirations of economic sciences towards other social sciences are based on the idea that the separation of economy and society on which the liberal creed of the nineteenth century was built must be left behind. Gary Becker expresses the idea of an all-encompassing market society when he states:

> I am saying that the economic approach provides a valuable unified framework for understanding all human behavior. ... The heart of my argument is that human behavior is not compartmentalized, sometimes based on maximizing, sometimes not, sometimes motivated by stable preferences, sometimes by volatile ones, sometimes resulting in an optimal accumulation of information, sometimes not. Rather, all human behavior can be viewed as involving participants who maximize their utility from a stable set of preferences and accumulate an optimal amount of information and other inputs in a variety of markets. (Becker, 1978: 14)

When Habermas ([1981] 1987, vol. 2: 318–331) refers to the 'colonization of the life-world', when he criticizes the invasiveness of the instrumental rationality of market forces, he clearly discusses a problem which is the consequence of the neoliberal as distinct from the liberal creed of the nineteenth century. From the neoliberal point of view, the market is the model for an ever-increasing area of social relations. Exploitation turns up as one aspect of the far vaster problem of commodification and commercialization of life, which appears not only as a menace to economic well-being, but also as a threat to the cultural legacy of the Western world.

Polanyi characterizes the society of the nineteenth century as one in which the economy was disembedded from society. This was certainly a particular feature of that society compared with all earlier societies. Disembedding was the consequence of the influence exerted by the naturalist fiction. Under the current conditions, the situation is worse. If we want to apply Polanyi's notion, it is not sufficient to speak either of disembedding or of re-embedding the economy in society. On the contrary, today society runs the risk of being 'embedded in the mechanism of its own economy', as Polanyi (1977: 9) characterized the market society in a posthumously published book. The neoliberal fiction includes the claim that society as a whole is subordinated to the rules of the market mechanism.

This means that the negative consequences of the market fiction are more encompassing than in the nineteenth century. The area where the neoliberal fiction exerts influence is not limited to the fictitious commodities. Economic rationality and institutional reforms seeking to implement new forms of markets and competition are not limited to the economic sphere as they were in the nineteenth century. The commodification of life does not spare culture, education, family and other personal relations. The institutional transformation driven by the neoliberal creed encompasses society as a whole. Conflicts emerge on different fronts. The range of the opposing forces also broadens. Opposition is more heterogeneous than in nineteenth-century Europe and encompasses new conflicts which have their roots in the increasing commodification of life as such. This helps to overcome the economic blinders, but at the same time it makes it more difficult for the struggling movements to comprehend the common ground.

Up to now, opposition to economic globalization and the neoliberal creed seems to be again directed, in the first place, against the problems of capitalism, neglecting the fact that behind the questions of a market society lurks a far bigger challenge: the problem of freedom in a technological society. Under these conditions, it is not sufficient to denounce power, coercion and oppression in all spheres of society and call for broader and more ambitious goals so as to overcome them. It is also essential to recognize the dangers posed by genetic engineering, biotechnology, nuclear energy, digitalization and artificial intelligence and to search for possibilities to defend personal freedom and democracy under these conditions.

It is at this point that immersion in current social and political affairs can turn out to be an obstacle to a realistic vision of the questions which have to be faced today. Whoever is engaged in a social struggle wants to discover, above all, how to achieve the movement's goals. He or she does not develop the same enthusiasm for a study of the obstacles and the limits of the endeavor. An attentive reader will notice a difference not only in style but also in the line of reasoning between the writings Polanyi drafted during the period of his active participation in the social struggles in Red Vienna, and his later works in America. Studying the transformation of society from the outside makes it less problematic to focus on the obstacles and limits of what could or can be achieved. Therefore, today a certain distance would be advantageous in comprehending the weakness of welfarism. The 'reform of human consciousness to be reached through the recognition of the reality of society' (Polanyi [1944] 2001: 133) called for by Polanyi is understood more easily from the point of view of the observer than from the perspective of the activist. The grandeur of *TGT* lies in Polanyi's capacity to combine both; a recognition of the reality of society together with the upholding of the claim to freedom in an industrial civilization.

Notes

1 This remains true even for the founding fathers of the theory of marginal utility. The whole approach of Walras, for example, revolves around the price relations which are necessary in order to achieve the maximum of utility. But he is not interested at all in the institutional conditions which are more or less favorable for reaching this goal. Walras's maximum of utility is consistent with any degree of government intervention.

2 I use the term 'communist fiction' in the same sense as Myrdal ([1930] 1965) does to refer to the idealizing assumption that an entire economy can be seen as a massed unit, a household or a community directing its forces to a common goal.

3 In the German original text, Mises uses the verb *übersehen* (to gain an overview) instead of 'review'. I mention this difference because in his articles Polanyi uses not only the same verb, *übersehen*, but also the nouns *Übersicht* and *Übersichtsproblem* (problem of overview). See below.

4 Hayek feels the weakness of Mises's reasoning. He undertakes several attempts – ultimately without success – to bridge the gap (cf. Hayek, 1937, 1945).

5 From this point of view, Polanyi's approach shows striking similarities to Myrdal's remark that 'there is no way of studying social reality other than from the viewpoint of human ideals. A "disinterested social science" has never existed and, for logical, reasons, cannot exist. … It is … on account of scientific stringency that these valuations should be made explicit' (Myrdal, 1956: 336). Compare Thomasberger (2015).

8

Multilinear trajectories: Polanyi, *The Great Transformation* and the American exception

Hannes Lacher

Karl Polanyi's seminal *The Great Transformation* (*TGT*) is widely read as a call for regulated capitalism and a historical and theoretical exposition of the case for the welfare state. The institutions of the Bretton Woods system, and the domestic mechanisms of public macroeconomic management, labour market regulation and income redistribution are usually considered the concrete forms through which the world-wide 're-embedding' of capitalist markets envisaged by Polanyi was achieved after 1945 (Esping-Andersen, 1990; Boyer and Hollingsworth, 1997; Streeck, 2011). This narrative is frequently linked to theories of hegemony, which posit the central-ity of American power and purposes in the making of the order of 'embedded liberalism' (Ruggie, 1982). On this view, it was the New Deal that laid not just the foundations for the socioeconomic and military dynamism that allowed the US to reconstitute the international political and economic order; but also provided the model for the post-war Western reconstruction of social relations and economic institutions that underpinned the subsequent 'golden age' of capitalism.

But the widespread appropriation of Polanyi's *TGT* for such conceptualisations of the social and international transformations of the mid-twentieth century faces two significant anomalies. First, the US played barely any role in *TGT*; neither America's domestic reconstruction, nor its emergent international role, are given much consideration. The New Deal, most importantly, merits only a few remarks in passing.[1] The overwhelming empirical focus of *TGT* deals with developments in Britain and Central Europe. Secondly, Polanyi's published and unpublished writ-ings and speeches from the mid-1940s are characterised by an overt and visceral hostility to the emerging Bretton Woods system and to the American world order project, which he considered driven by the aim of restoring the 'liberal utopia' (cf. Lacher, 2007a).

Based on a systematic review of the materials collected in the Karl Polanyi Archive (at Concordia University, Montreal), I shall argue that the post-war order represented, for Polanyi, not the realisation, but the frustration of his expectations of a re-embedding of markets. Indeed, almost as soon as he had submitted the manuscript of *TGT*, Polanyi began to insistently warn his audiences that the re-embedded future he had until then taken for granted was now in danger of being aborted by an American foreign policy bent on re-imposing 'universal capitalism' on Europe and the rest of the world. For the USA, Polanyi (18–25) now argued, '[t]he restoration of the pre-1914 world became the tacitly accepted but nevertheless axiomatic war aim', including even the return of the gold standard.

This strategic aim was, in Polanyi's view, rooted in the nature of American society itself. For the New Deal, he maintained, had done little to challenge the marketing principle and the rule of the profit motive. In its foreign policy, there-fore, the 'United States has no alternative. Americans almost unanimously identify their way of life with private enterprise and business competition – though not altogether with classical *laissez-faire*. … The Great Depression of the early thirties left this predilection unimpaired, and merely dimmed the aura of adulation which surrounded *laissez-faire* economics' (Polanyi, 1945: 87). For Polanyi, it was essential to recognise that the US was set on a unique trajectory. Whereas Europe was bound for a fundamental socialist transformation, Polanyi believed, he considered social-ism an impossibility in the US, given its entirely different history and constitution. Ultimately, Polanyi concluded, the 'US fits into one pattern, that of nineteenth century society, while all other powers, including Britain herself, belong to another, which is in course of transition to a new form' (ibid.: 86).

Almost up until he submitted *TGT*, Polanyi assumed that the very uniqueness of America's societal trajectory would prevent the US from playing a significant role in post-war reconstruction – much like in 1919. Europe would move towards social-ism, he assumed – and to the extent that the US defied this world-historical process, it would be left behind as a lonely capitalist outpost. (In this inimical environment, the US might ultimately find a path to socialism; but for Polanyi that was neither an immanent tendency nor a pressing concern.)

But in mid-1943, Polanyi realised with increasing trepidation that the obverse might happen: the American exception might become the basis for post-war recon-struction and threaten the future of the great transformation. The United States, he argued in 1945, 'has remained the home of liberal capitalism and is powerful enough to pursue alone the Utopian line of policy involved in such a fateful dis-pensation' (ibid.: 87). America might thus emerge as the lode-star for pro-capitalist forces elsewhere, and strengthen their resolve and ability to thwart the socialist transformations Polanyi had envisaged in the final pages of *TGT*.

And so it was. What today we celebrate as the realisation of the Polanyian vision and project in the form of 'embedded liberalism' was, for Polanyi, the defeat of his vision of a society in which the market would be re-embedded, labour would cease to be a commodity and the profit motive would no longer guide decisions over investments. In reconstructing Polanyi's understanding of the distinctive nature and trajectory of the US, we can gain a better appreciation for the social and international struggles and alternatives of the mid-twentieth century. We also gain a better understanding of Polanyi's theoretical and political project, and the purposes of *TGT*.

Polanyi's general theory of modern history

In some respects, Polanyi's interpretation of the American path to modernity fits squarely within the broad tradition of writers who focused on the absence of a strong socialist working-class movement and party. Indeed, we shall see that for Polanyi this absence was the single-most critical factor distinguishing the US from Europe in the 1930s and 1940s. It also helped Polanyi to answer the question that ultimately concerned him far more than Werner Sombart's ([1906] 1976) question regarding the absence of socialism in America: why, Polanyi asked, is there no *fascism* in the United States? Though it clearly rearticulates long-standing tropes, Polanyi's take on American exceptionalism is, ultimately, highly idiosyncratic. In some ways, he comes close to anticipating Daniel Bell's later reformulation of Sombart's question, namely 'Why *Should* There Be Socialism in the United States?' (Bell, [1952] 1996: 197). To understand Polanyi's framing of the American trajectory, we have to set it in the context of Polanyi's conceptualisation of the rise and unravelling of 'nineteenth-century civilisation'.

Teaching and writing in the aftermath of the Great Depression, Polanyi was convinced that democratic, liberal capitalism had run its course. From now on, capitalism could only persist if it was 'freed', by way of fascism, from the accumulated encumbrances imposed on market-economy by decades of social legislation. The choice confronting modern societies, he asserted, was between fascist capitalism and democratic socialism. What had brought them to this point was the peculiar operation of the 'double movement' that was set in motion with the 'dis-embedding' of the market in the 1830s. In plain contrast to what most modern interpreters have attributed to him, Polanyi did not consider the counter-movement an adequate and stabilising response to the liberal utopia; for while it was necessary to protect the political, social, cultural and environmental integrity of society, it contributed, he insisted throughout *TGT*, decisively to the catastrophic unravelling of 'nineteenth-century civilisation' in the 1930s (cf. Lacher, 2019).

The reason, Polanyi argued, was that the market-constituting measures of the initial phase had made the economic reproduction of society, and of most of its members, a matter of incomes (from profits, wages, interest, etc.) that had to be realised in the market. That market was regulated through two immanent mechanisms in particular: the decision over investments on the grounds of calculations of profitability; and on the fluctuation of prices on the basis of supply and demand. On their operation now depended jobs, incomes and livelihoods. But the consequences of allowing these mechanisms to operate freely would have wreaked havoc on the very possibility of humane existence – it would have required the subordination of every aspect of social existence to the dictates of the market. No society was willing to tolerate these consequences, and so, increasingly, they interfered with the 'self-regulating market'.

Thus was set in motion the increasing contradiction between society and the market, with ultimately catastrophic consequences. For the interventions and protective measures, which became increasingly numerous and far-reaching after the 1870s, did not undo the profit-calculation-based allocation of investments, they merely interfered with the prices and conditions under which land, labour, money and products would be bought and sold – and thus with the underlying calculations on which the whole system depended. As long as land and labour were still being bought and sold in the market, protective measures would and could not 're-embed' the market; they would merely 'impair' it, Polanyi asserted. Land and labour were here still treated and traded as if they were commodities, even if their prices were no longer fully determined by supply and demand, but increasingly by political decisions (cf. Lacher, 1999b). In the end, people would still have to sell their labour in the market in order to make a living. Their livelihoods would still depend on the willingness of the owners of industry to deploy their capital and to employ them. But with distorted prices and impaired markets, that could no longer be presumed, Polanyi argued.

Why, then, did nineteenth-century civilisation not collapse in the late nineteenth century and instead keep going, in an increasingly chaotic form, until the 1930s? Polanyi argued that under the largely non-democratic conditions that prevailed in most of Europe until the First World War, protective measures, and their market-disorganising effects, remained fairly shallow. Factory legislation improved the conditions under which labourers worked, for instance – but protectionism was advanced *on behalf* of the working class, not *by* it. The initial European responses to social pressures for protection – from working-class organisations, but also from land-owners and the churches – were filtered through state institutions, and through statesmen, who sought to stabilise their societies even while committing them to further capitalist expansion and deepening (Polanyi, [1944] 2001: 212–214). They contributed to a creeping 'impairment' of market mechanisms (as prices increasingly reflected political determinations), and 'strains' between the institutions of society, but they did not yet generate pervasive socioeconomic crises. Capitalism became increasingly 'dis-organised', Polanyi argued, but not yet fatally so.

This dynamic changed decisively, Polanyi (ibid.: 139–140) argued, with the enfranchisement of the subordinate classes in most European countries after 1918. Now, the European working-class parties (usually in alliance with other parties, especially those representing various agrarian groups) were able to *directly* legislate measures to the benefit of their constituents. The inherent tensions between capitalism and democracy – which liberal thinkers had recognised all along when they argued for the permanent dis-enfranchisement of the poorer strata of society (cf. Polanyi, 18–8) – now became fully actualised: 'At a definitive point in their development these two came into conflict, notably in Europe. The post-war situation developed into an immediate danger to society as a whole; the danger of a *deadlock* of the political and the economic system' (Polanyi, 12–7; cf. [1944] 2001: 140, 218, 245 and 252).

Polanyi's analysis of the social conditions that prepared the ground for the 'cataclysm' of the following decade has rarely found entrance into the interpretations of, or applications by, today's Polanyi industry – perhaps because it is so starkly at odds with the prevailing story of the 'double movement' as the solution to the ills of 'liberal' capitalism. But it is the critical point to which all his concepts and theories lead. It is his attempt to make sense of the crisis and collapse of an entire social order. Polanyi argued that the fundamental institutions and functions of society, the political and the economic in particular, were working at cross-purposes. Parliaments during the 1920s had become the stronghold of the working class while industry remained under the control of capitalists.

Institutional paralysis followed (Polanyi, [1944] 2001: 244). For parliaments could impose political conditions and determinations of the use of labour – and even on the deployment of machinery. But they could not force capitalists to invest if they did not see a possibility for the *profitable* use of machinery and labour under those conditions. In the process, workers lost their employment and incomes. Sharpening economic crises thus gave rise to a general crisis of social reproduction, Polanyi argued. The very existence of society was at risk as a result of the institutional dysfunction between capitalist economics and (tendentially) socialist politics.

It was the ability of Fascists to propose a coherent – if violent and destructive – way out of the economic crisis that allowed them to gain the upper hand during the 1930s. Fascists promised to re-establish the institutional coherence of modern societies by destroying the democratic mechanisms that had allowed socialists to gain influence in parliaments, municipalities and in factories. The democratic alternative would have required the opposite: bringing the economy in line with socialist politics by way of revolution. But, Polanyi noted, the socialist parties proved unwilling or unable to take that step. As a result, the working-class parties were vanquished without much resistance (12–7). Indeed, significant elements of the working class even joined in the fascist onslaught in the hope that the restoration of profitability would also lead to renewed investments by capitalists, and thus restore wage incomes (even if in a diminished form).

With the impending military defeat of fascism, Polanyi hoped that the door would open to the second solution: the reintroduction of political democracy in continental Europe, along with the adoption of socialist forms of production. Profit calculations would no longer decide over the if, where and when of investments; decisions would instead be taken by 'democratic planning'. But this result would not come by itself. Deeply ingrained working-class illusions about the malleability of capitalism could lead to the misguided resurrection of social democratic arrangements. The task now, Polanyi believed, was to step outside the self-defeating and destructive historical dialectic of liberalisation and protectionism. This, ultimately, required the working classes to challenge capitalism itself.

> The challenge is to an order of things which resists the subordination of the property system to the requirements of human values. The aim is to adjust the industrial civilization of our time to the requirements of those values. ... [T]he mission to lead society onwards on the road to freedom falls to the working people. For their position under the economic system recalls to them continuously its limitations, while their lack of property in the means of production keeps them from acquiring a vested interest in the preservation of that system. Hence the responsibility of the working class for the future of mankind. (Polanyi, 18–33: 16)

The New Deal and the place of the US in modern history

In *TGT*, the socioeconomic reorganisation of the US during the 1930s makes only two important appearances. In one of those, Polanyi notes that, after the Great Depression, 'Russia turned to socialism under dictatorial forms. Liberal capitalism disappeared in the countries preparing for war like Germany, Japan, and Italy, and, to a lesser extent, also in the United States and Great Britain. But the emerging regimes of fascism, socialism, and the New Deal were similar only in discarding laissez-faire principles' ([1944] 2001: 252). In the absence of a substantial engagement in *TGT*, we may get a better grasp on Polanyi's understanding of the New Deal from his 1930/1940s notes, lectures and presentations.

Ironically, considering the dearth of direct pronouncements, Polanyi's presumed take on the New Deal has come to play a surprisingly prominent role in current attempts to reconstruct the meaning and social purposes of Polanyi's social theory, and of *TGT* in particular. Many scholars would probably consider uncontentious the notion that, for Polanyi, the 'only viable road after the War, at least for the West, could be an extension of the New Deal, the development of a fully-fledged social democratic welfare state' (Szelenyi, 1991: 233). This notion is largely shared by Fred Block and Gareth Dale in their influential reconstructions of *TGT*; despite important differences, they agree on the New Deal as the realisation, or at least close approximation, of Polanyi's vision of a re-embedded society (though they may disagree with Szelenyi in regards to its characterisation as 'social democratic').

In Fred Block's influential narrative of a 'theoretical shift' that Polanyi supposedly underwent during his three years in Vermont, the direct experience of the New Deal he gained there seems to play a critical role. Block argues that Polanyi had, during the 1930s, adhered to a Marxist understanding of historical processes and social choices – which precluded him from recognising that there were no objective limits to the regulation of markets for various social purposes. Capitalist fascism and socialist planning seemed to Polanyi the only choices available at this point *because* he was a Marxist (Block, 2003: 277–278). But, living in New Deal America from 1940–43, Block suggests, Polanyi grasped the possibility of democratically regulating markets for the purposes of stability and equality, *without* resorting to command economics. Under the impression of 'both the real political and social achievements of Roosevelt's New Deal, as well as the anticipated social legislation of England's Labour Government', Polanyi thus came to see state intervention and regulation as compatible with private property and markets – and indeed as a historical universal (ibid.: 298). Having arrived rather late during his Bennington stay at this insight, Block suggests, Polanyi was unable to express it fully in *TGT*. Combining old and new elements, Polanyi's book thus remained incompletely realised and indeed self-contradictory (for a systematic critique of all these claims, see Lacher, 2019). Finally, Block (2001: xxxv and 2003: 298) argues, Polanyi had, by the mid-1940s, given the term 'socialism' a meaning that was compatible with the realities of – or at least with the more far-reaching aspirations for – the New Deal.

Block's chronology does not sit well with Polanyi's actual evaluations of the New Deal before or after his arrival at Bennington. For someone supposedly under the spell of Marxism, he adopted, during the 1930s, a rather positive stance towards the efforts of the first two Roosevelt administrations to reorganise America's economy, society and state – despite understanding fully that those aimed at the reform, not the transcendence, of capitalism. Meanwhile, while this appraisal persists during his initial years at Bennington, sometime during 1943 Polanyi's view of the New Deal became far more circumspect. Polanyi's actual stances towards the New Deal run directly counter to what Block's narrative would lead us to expect.

Gareth Dale, on the other hand, recognises clearly Polanyi's positive appraisals of the New Deal during the 1930s. Indeed, he suggests that the policies Roosevelt adopted after 1935 came close to realising Polanyi's vision of a re-embedding of the market (Dale, 2016a: 146–170). For Dale, this is evidence that Polanyi's socialism, even during his London years, was far from revolutionary (and the fact that Polanyi maintained his support even as the New Deal lost its radical edge after 1936 may indicate a further moderation in Polanyi's politics). On Dale's view, Polanyi had, since the 1920s, embraced the reform-socialist expectation that a socialist society could be realised by peaceful, parliamentary and gradualist means (Dale, 2016b: 282). With socialists gaining political sway, with capitalism becoming increasingly 'organised' and production 'socialised', the state would become a critical agent of this transformation. With some allowances, the New Deal might indeed seem to fit the reform-socialist bill. However, it fits rather badly with the actual argument of *TGT*, in particular Polanyi's insistent emphasis on the deleterious consequences of protectionism and interventionism throughout the 1930s and 1940s (not to mention the almost complete omission of the New Deal from Polanyi's book).

Ultimately, Dale's evaluation of Polanyi's political purposes seems to end up in a place not far removed from Block's. And yet, in a recent exchange, Dale (2017) and Block and Somers (2017, 2018) charged each other with mistaking Polanyi for a social democrat when, really, he should be considered a 'socialist'. Some may consider this an indication that we have reached peak-Polanyi, and that any further attempts at reconstructing *TGT* are unlikely to be productive. I would suggest, to the contrary, that the case of the US provides us with an excellent opportunity to fundamentally re-evaluate claims, assumptions and presumptions regarding Polanyi's social theory that Dale and Block and Somers share with most (neo) Polanyians. It allows us to see, first, that *Polanyi was not the sort of socialist who considered the New Deal socialist*. Secondly, it reveals that Polanyi long subscribed to a fundamentally multilinear understanding of the European and American trajectories – past, present and future – which neither Dale nor Block and Somers has recognised. Thirdly, it enables us to conclude that Polanyi was a revolutionary socialist in the European context, but a proponent of regulated welfare capitalism in the US. In conjunction, these propositions allow us to approach *TGT* in a new light.

Observing the New Deal from afar: pre-1940

In the 1930s, as Polanyi started to develop the themes and theorems that would culminate in *TGT*, he was well aware that America fit his general developmental scheme, and his diagnosis of the crisis of his time, rather badly (16–10: 4). Increasingly, he gravitated to the view that the historical choice between fascist capitalism and democratic socialism was limited to Europe and did not apply to the US. But why was there no fascism in America? Because, Polanyi maintained, there had previously been no (or little) socialism in America. For the absence of a strong working class had allowed the US to avoid the institutional deadlock he considered the essence of the crisis in Europe. There, he thought, a socialist transformation would be necessary, and perhaps inevitable. In America, Polanyi maintained, a socialist transformation would neither be possible, nor even desirable, for a long time to come.

The US was not, of course, the only capitalist country that had elided the fascist trend. Britain, Polanyi argued, was similar to the US in certain respects, but it constituted at best a partial exception to the general trend pitting fascist capitalism against democratic socialism (16–10). Britain's distinctiveness, Polanyi suggested, could be attributed to the historical rootedness there of a conception of freedom that was more libertarian than the egalitarian conceptions prevailing on the continent. This mitigated the challenges posed to capitalism in Britain relative to continental Europe. But Polanyi expected the British working class to emerge with greater strength and confidence from the war. This would eventually force the choice between capitalism and socialism onto the agenda there, too. The US, by contrast, stood *entirely* apart from the main currents of European history; here, a somewhat redeployed form of capitalism could persist. The reasons for this contemporary divergence, Polanyi argued, reached back to the very founding of the USA.

> The Covenanters founded a *society* not a *state* or a *nation*. In the USA the *political state* is banished by the Constitution to a remote corner in society. It exists only on sufferance and on condition that it will on no account try to gain powers and competences similar to those enjoyed by the European States. Thus society in the USA exists without the props of the political state. The American does not think of society as being supported by or based on the power of the state or of any kind of force whatever. The USA Federal Government has no police powers, in fact no effective powers in home affairs whatever. There is no police. Society is supposed to look after itself. *Anarchy* is here realised. (Polanyi, 19–26: 4)

For Polanyi, the US was unique in this respect, and 'probably the only instance known in history that such a task has been deliberately undertaken or even conceived of' (18–14: 4). This constitutional framework, Polanyi suggested, engendered '*the extreme plasticity of American society*' in which individuals were directly and without institutional mediation related to society (19–26: 5). With society thus overshadowing the state, Polanyi argued, the United States developed a uniquely clear-cut separation of politics and economics that was not – as it had become in Europe since the end of the nineteenth century – increasingly breached. Politics in the US 'have remained a peripheric and subsidiary sphere in the great American experiment' (18–14: 5; cf. Mills, [1951] 2002: 10). Not until the 1930s, Polanyi maintained, would demands for societal protectionism in America become politically (and economically) relevant. For the ability of the dissatisfied parts of the settler population to go off in search of land meant that socialist ideologies and movements could not gain hold. Agrarian populism in the late nineteenth century had done little to change that: 'American radicalism did not ask for social rights but for *space*' (16–12: 41; cf. Fay, 1933: 34). Though America had become a democracy long before any European state, the difficulties of collective action in this context prevented the use of state institutions by the mass of the population for the purpose of social legislation and the protection of labour.

Despite the absence of redistributive mechanisms, Polanyi noted, American society became more prosperous than even the most advanced European societies. Under these conditions, the US was for long able to elide the European problems of increasing market impairment. 'Given a free supply of coarse labour, land and money, market-economy worked successfully in America up to 1900' (Polanyi, 20–2). And even after the turn of the twentieth century, the state remained far too small and ineffectual to have a significant economic and social impact; labour legislation was 'abhorred', and rejected by courts as an infringement on individual liberty (Polanyi, 8–3). And yet, Polanyi suggested, society and culture in America were in some respects more 'social democratic' (8–3) during this period than in most European societies – and particularly in Britain. 'American democracy embodies the idea of *liberty* to a much greater degree than England, and the idea of *equality* to a much greater degree than Europe. But the *efficiency of the national government* is very slight indeed' (16–12: 33). Most importantly, in America definite differences in wealth did not turn into rigid differences of social status. 'In common human appreciation both on the side of the rich and the poor *equality is a fact*. So is equality in *speech, manners, behavior* for some 80% of the population (excluding the Negroes). The rich man does not feel socially superior to the not rich, the common citizen does not feel socially inferior to the rich' (19–26: 2).

Indeed, Polanyi argued that contemporary Americans did not see their society as based on power of any kind, whether of the state or of class. To some extent,

Polanyi was even inclined to agree with that assessment. 'Occupation is not class', he argued, adding: 'In the USA, there are no clear-cut upper and lower classes, but rather farmers, factory workers and so on' (16–16: 5). By the 1930s, the US had moreover obtained a thorough-going system of mass education that allowed poorer members of society to obtain a degree of knowledge and self-respect impossible in Britain, where education was *class* education (18–14: 5).

Polanyi's perspective on America's societal divergence relied rather heavily on Werner Sombart's seminal 1906 book. (Sombart himself had drawn on the frontier thesis of Frederick Jackson Turner, published thirteen years earlier, in his efforts to explain the distinctive character of American radicalism.) Sombart's influence also shaped Polanyi's understanding of American labour and class relations: 'Because of the democratic system of government, universal education, and the higher standard of living of the worker [in America], there is genuinely a lesser social distance between the individual strata of the population, and – due to the effect of the customs and perceptions described – this distance becomes even smaller in the consciousness of the various classes than it really is' (Sombart, [1906] 1976: 10). Indeed, even Polanyi's first-hand reporting on his American experiences during the 1930s echoed rather directly Sombart's distillation of his own experiences some three decades earlier:

> Anyone who has ever observed, even only fleetingly, male and female American workers as they carry on their life outside the factory or the workshop, has noticed at first sight that they are a different breed of people from German workers. [...] There is nothing oppressed or submissive about him. He mixes with everyone – in reality and not only in theory – as an equal. ... The bowing and scraping before the 'upper classes', which produces such an unpleasant impression in Europe, is completely unknown. (Ibid.: 109–110)

Polanyi's reference point was the British rather than the German worker, but his evaluation largely coincided with Sombart's. For Sombart, as for Polanyi, moreover, this situation helped explain the lagging of working-class organisation in America behind that of Europe. Not only was American capitalism the most 'pure' and complete anywhere in the world, untainted by feudal elements, but it could also rely on a stabilising divorce of class and social status. As a result, American workers had not only adopted a largely benign understanding of state institutions (in as much as they existed) and forms of authority, both private and public, but, even more, they had developed a uniquely favourable attitude towards capitalism, Sombart argued:

> I believe that emotionally the American worker has a share in capitalism: I believe that he loves it. Anyway, he devotes his entire body and soul to it. ... Hence, only rarely do we hear complaints about the lack of adequate protection against dangers at work;

174

instead, the American worker is ready to go along with these dangers, if protective arrangements might diminish his earnings. (Ibid.: 20)

And yet, after all this, Sombart famously turned around, in the last paragraph of his book, and declared that the American worker was now getting ready to shake off their 'condition of slavery' and 'escape into freedom' (ibid.: 115). For

> *all the factors that till now have prevented the development of Socialism in the United States are about to disappear or to be converted into their opposite, with the result that in the next generation Socialism in America will very probably experience the greatest possible expansion of its appeal.* (Ibid.: 119)

That same year (1906), the leader of the Industrial Workers of the World (IWW), Daniel De Leon, declared that capitalism was perhaps more ripe for revolution in America than anywhere in Europe: 'If my reading of history is correct, the prophecy of Marx will be fulfilled and America will ring the downfall of capitalism the world over' (quoted in Lipset, 1985: 189). In 1929, Josef Stalin suggested that time had drawn close. Warning against the 'fundamental error of exaggerating the specific features of American capitalism', he proclaimed: 'the moment is not far off when a revolutionary crisis will develop in America. And when a revolutionary crisis develops in America, that will be the beginning of the end of world capitalism as a whole.'[2]

Polanyi was having none of *that*. In the midst of the Great Depression, he was convinced, American society was still held together, not by coercive institutions but by a shared belief in the 'fundamental righteousness of [its] social order' (19–26: 3).[3] Drawing on experiences gained during several month-long visits to the USA between 1935 and 1937, he noted:

> The general belief [in] the ultimate validity of the principles of this society is its only support. It *is* delivering the goods: an unprecedented standard of life and a great equality of chances. [...] [T]he vast majority are the best fed, best clothed, best housed, and on the average certainly the best educated, people in the world. (The economic crisis although it has made an indent on the minds and thoughts of the people has not yet decisively changed this appreciation). This is the outcome of the experiment started by the Covenanters. It has not yet come to an end. It still continues. (19–26)

In Polanyi's lived experience, Sombart's descriptions of the pre-twentieth-century American workers' (supposed) attachment to their social order were just as applicable to the 1930s.[4] Neither the period of increasing growth and prosperity, nor the subsequent period of crisis and depression, had given rise to a widespread socialist reorientation of American workers. In its absence, the politically driven socioeconomic reconstruction of the New Deal since 1932 could lead to a significant shift in – but not a radical break with – America's societal pattern and capitalist constitution. As we shall see, in Polanyi's view, that was for the best.

From capitalism to socialism with Roosevelt?

At no time did Polanyi observe the American scene more keenly or deliberately than during the period from the crash (1929) until the end of Roosevelt's first administration (1936). During his tenure as editor (and, until 1936, London correspondent) of *Der Österreiche Volkswirt*, Polanyi regularly wrote about the socioeconomic crises and political struggles in the US. A collection of his articles on these issues was published in 1936 as a special issue on the TVA (Polanyi, 3–14). His extended lecture tours of the US in 1935 and 1936, sponsored by the WEA/IIE, afforded him the opportunity for closer observation and reflection (19–26: 1). Throughout this period, Polanyi attended to the New Deal experiments with considerable sympathy. Indeed, it was in a mid-1930s lecture in (and on) the US that Polanyi first referred to a 'great transformation' (he had previously invoked, frequently but more narrowly, the 'fascist transformation'): 'Out of the depression 1929, a great transformation in the USA is growing out' (Polanyi, 8–3: 1).

In Europe, Polanyi considered the long-term effects of societal protectionism (and especially of the 'parliamentary socialism' of the 1920s) to have been contributory to the protracted depression of the 1930s. In the US, by contrast, economic collapse was the result of the strength of big business, not of the working class, Polanyi argued. Prior to the 1930s, with trade unions weak and state institutions lacking sovereignty and efficacy, real political interferences with private interests and with the market had remained relatively minor. The 1929 collapse of Wall Street could therefore not be attributed to powerful unions and interventionist government. Instead, 'the leaders of finance and big business [stood] discredited' (15–2: 44). This, and the fact that unions posed no real threat to capitalist interests, undermined any fascist efforts to reconstruct the US economy by handing political power over to business interests. Instead, 'the movement is towards the dictatorship of political powers (called New Deal)' (ibid.: 44).

If these conditions continued to prevail, Polanyi argued in 1936, the US might be able to reform capitalism under democratic conditions – unlike any European society, he was convinced (18–14: 7). However, the battle was far from over. In 1937, he warned: 'In the USA, Big Business [is] undermining the authority of political bodies by all means' (21–11: 3). This might yet lead to fascism in the US even absent a mass movement. Fascism, for Polanyi, meant political rule for and by capitalists; a fascist 'corporative state' might emerge if capitalist power occluded popular government (15–2: 44). The realisation of this tendency in the US, however, was being thwarted by Roosevelt's strengthening of democracy 'by cutting loose from Wall Street; artificially fostering the CIO, by deliberately strengthening popular education' (Polanyi, 17–19: 4).

For Polanyi, the prospects for the democratic reform of capitalism in the US (after it had been so brutally defeated in continental Europe, and nowhere more so than in his own 'Red Vienna') would depend not just on the strength of Big Business or the electoral support for the New Deal administration; this was, above all, a question of labour and trade unionism in the US. In this regard, however, Polanyi's position was not at all what neo-Polanyians might expect:

> As far as I can see the future of the States is being now shaped for a long time by the manner and the conditions under which the new Unionism is born. Continental society, British society were fatefully determined by this: at what juncture and by what forces was the unionization of labour carried through? In Central Europe it was the function of the *political* working class movement [...] thus making this movement vital to the development of capitalism & at the same time, strengthening, in the short term, the mass organizational basis of the prol[etarian] party (*Soc[ial] Dem[ocratic]* and partly Communist). At the same time this proved a fatal weakness of the prol[etarian] working class movement, in the long run, since the Trade Unions could only be successful in the period of a rapidly advancing private capitalism. When this passed – the Unions became a nuisance to society and no help to their own members. In England, Unionism was a non-political movement (pre Labour Party, making the latter dependent upon the Trade Union System ...). English Unionism tried to stabilize a phase of *imperialist boom*, basing the Unions on a guild footing, which was feasible to society as a whole only on condition of permanent national super surplus being made at the expense of a colonially mishandled world. Thus English Unions became the real cancer in the body social, the cause of the ultimate downfall of the community.
>
> American unionism is taking shape to-day. It is entirely different in its origins. It is non-political ... but at the same time almost state-made, a creation of the enlightened absolutism of Rooseveltian (New Deal) democracy. (Polanyi, 47–8)

To understand what Polanyi was getting at here, we must place this quote in the context of his general theory of modernity and crisis. Polanyi's relationship with trade unions in England and continental Europe, particularly during the 1930s, was characterised by deep misgivings. With their demands for higher wages and protection, they had contributed to the 'impairing' of the market system. That may have been bearable in times of economic prosperity, but in a time of systemic crisis such demands had become a 'nuisance' to society. Polanyi's stance, of course, had a radical intent: his argument was that at this point the unions should have abandoned their redistributive and protective goals, and organised for a socialist revolution. This, he held, was the only alternative to fascism in Europe – the restoration of the institutional and functional unity of society by extending democracy from the political to the economic sphere. But in this historic task, the European unions and working-class parties had utterly failed. The socialist movement had proven strong enough to disorganize capitalism, in other words – but not strong enough to replace it. For Polanyi, the critical task was to enable the European working classes to understand that conundrum, and thus lay the foundations for the decisive replacement of capitalism by socialism. *TGT* was his effort to live up to that task.

But in America, things were different. There, Polanyi was convinced, the working class was in no conceivable position to even consider the possibility of revolution. What *was* possible in America, precisely because there was no strong working class, was the democratic reform of capitalism towards social ends. That depended on the moderation of demands for social protection and (as in Europe in the 1870s) on the successful arbitration of competing social interests, and their incorporation into a deliberate strategy that would serve both the needs of the capitalist market and the democratic polity. Such 'plasticity' might ultimately allow the US to develop an 'organised', stable capitalism with broad-based prosperity quite different from Europe's 'disorganised' capitalism. But, in Polanyi's view, this depended on Roosevelt's ability to both mobilise *and* contain the working class. The 1935 Wagner Act had significantly strengthened union rights and powers, and generated critical support for the New Deal. Roosevelt's landslide re-election in 1936, and the significantly expanded Democratic majority in Congress, seemed to herald a radicalisation of the New Deal. Indeed, industrial workers now organised themselves more directly in the newly founded CIO, as well as in increasingly militant sectoral unions like the United Auto Workers, whose forty-four-day sit-down strike in 1937 won them union recognition at General Motors.

To Polanyi, this posed a risk to the American experiment of social and democratic capitalism: America's unions might retrace the European experience and, in pressing their claims too far, not only impair the market but also provoke a fascist counter-mobilisation in the US (which they would be even less capable of withstanding than their European counterparts). The challenge for Roosevelt was, Polanyi believed, to maintain the unions in a dependent and subordinate position – strong enough to provide him with the means to keep Big Business at bay, but not so strong that they could undermine American capitalism's recovery at a time when the economy seemed to slide back into recession.

In fact, even while Polanyi's letter to his friend Peter Drucker was still in the mail, Roosevelt broke with the CIO leader, John Lewis, in an interview on 29 June 1937, and refused to throw his support behind peaceful picketers as they were being viciously attacked by police and company-controlled para-military forces (Derber,

1975: 127). It marked the end of the 'radical' New Deal. As Dale rightly notes, Polanyi maintained his support for it in the following years – but, as we have seen, because of its moderation, not despite it. Moreover, this support does not lend itself to the conclusion that Polanyi envisaged Europe's post-war reconstruction along the lines of the New Deal, radical or otherwise. It was, for Polanyi, a specific solution to the specific problems of American capitalism. In Europe, a far more thorough-going transformation would have to overcome capitalism itself.

Living in (post-)New Deal America, 1940–43

Did Polanyi's evaluation of the New Deal in America – and his perception of a necessary choice between fascist capitalism and democratic socialism elsewhere – undergo a fundamental shift as he experienced New Deal America first hand from 1940–43? Did he begin to see the American experiment of democratically regulating capitalism as a model for the reorganisation of European societies – a model quite distinct from more traditional socialist aspirations (his own prior ones included) of abolishing capitalism altogether? Fred Block suggests, along these lines, that America showed, to Polanyi and to the rest of the world, the possibility of liberating social life from the dictates of the market mechanism; it thereby opened the way to 'subordinate both national economies and the global economy to democratic politics' (Block, 2001: xxxv; cf. Block and Somers, 2014: 95).

> Polanyi saw Roosevelt's New Deal as a model of these future possibilities. Roosevelt's reforms meant that the U.S. economy continued to be organized around markets and market activity, but a new set of regulatory mechanisms now made it possible to buffer both human beings and nature from the pressures of market forces. (Block, 2001: xxxv)

But if so, why does the New Deal only make the most marginal of appearances in *TGT*? Strikingly, Polanyi's lack of concern with the New Deal there is matched by a dearth of sources from his Bennington years indicating *any* effort to grasp the details of the emerging social institutions and mechanisms in America. While Polanyi continued his pre-war habit of collecting the most arcane details of the social development and the domestic and international politics of European states and societies, his engagement with the realities of American society falls far short of that he had shown during the 1930s. To be sure, Polanyi read numerous books on American history while in the US, but those mostly concerned the eighteenth and nineteenth centuries (11–9). His analysis of the developmental trajectory of the US remained largely unchanged by these readings. Much like in the mid-1930s, he noted in 1941:

> The New Deal … was fundamentally democratic and political, but less concerned with the transfer of property rights than socialism; it reflected the two closely related basic facts of American social history: the absence of a traditional state power and the presence of free land, which, for a long time, had made a market-economy a signal success. (Polanyi, 1941: 8; cf. 17–3: 13)

The question of how to make sense of the *current* trajectory of the US clearly continued to bother Polanyi. In one of his initial lectures at Bennington College, which anticipate the argument of *TGT* to a great extent, Polanyi summarised his general theory of the great transformation – and pointed to the peculiarity of the US:

> In post-war Europe the separation of economics and politics developed into a catastrophic internal situation. The captains of industry undermined the authority of democratic institutions, while democratic parliaments continuously interfered with the working of the market mechanism. A state of affairs was reached when a sudden paralysis of both the economic and the political institutions of society was well within the range of the possible. The need for re-integration of society was apparent. This was the critical state of affairs out of which the fascist revolutions sprang. The alternative was between an integration of society through political power on a democratic basis, or, if democracy proved too weak, integration on an authoritarian basis in a totalitarian society, at the price of the sacrifice of democracy. *The American social system is, in my conviction, not faced with this tragic dilemma.* But if loss of freedom should be avoided, it will have to take two steps at the same time: accept the need for integration and achieve it through democratic means. (Polanyi, 1940a, emphasis added; cf. Polanyi, 8–11)

Taking up the issue again in a subsequent lecture, titled 'Is America an exception?', Polanyi (1940b) warns against the temptation of seeing the future of the US as a retreading of Europe's past. For while Europe's states had developed sovereign and effective forms of state power ever since the sixteenth century, Polanyi maintained, it 'was only as recently as the beginning of the 'Thirties that the federal government struck out on a line directed towards the establishment of a political state with real powers in internal affairs' (ibid.). These conditions circumscribed the possible roles for the American state – as a potential fascist apparatus but also as an instrument of effective reform. Ultimately, Polanyi cautioned:

> It would be too early to say whether America has already achieved a plastic society, i.e., a society which can be shaped by the political state and other conscious social factors without danger of a fatal stoppage. If so, this would be mainly due to the absence of the control of the financial market over the credit of the state itself. […] The basis on which the future integration of state, industry and other independent social factors will have to proceed in America is still far from clear; yet it might well be the case that the fatal condition of a helpless society has been finally overcome in this country. (Ibid.)

Over the following years in Vermont, Polanyi added little to this diagnosis (and the underlying analysis). It is clear, however, that his stance on the New Deal remained fundamentally positive during this period, as the only *TGT* passage of any significance on this topic shows:

> A decade of prosperity in the twenties sufficed to bring on a depression so that in its course the New Deal started to build a moat around labor and land, wider than any ever known in Europe. Thus America offered striking proof, both positive and negative, of our thesis that social protection was the accompaniment of a supposedly self-regulating market. (Polanyi, [1944] 2001: 211)

Had Polanyi then, by the time he completed *TGT*, settled on an answer to his question of American society's unique 'plasticity'? In a private letter, written early in 1943, Polanyi was even more emphatic, suggesting that the New Deal might have overcome the interplay of market-making and protectionism, and reached the point at which a genuine re-embedding of the economy had become possible (if not yet a reality):

> I believe in a New Deal which relies on a clear conception instead of opportunistic, unresolved, confused and unprincipled intervention in everything. I would set up my formula like this: since today neither money, nor land, nor labour are under the laws of the market any more, the best thing would be openly to take the three out of the market. (Polanyi, [1943] 1991: 259–260)

The American experience showed, in Polanyi's view, that the 'question of property has no priority any more' (ibid.: 259). Money had become managed, he maintained, and the TVA and other New Deal mechanisms had shown that 'land can't be surrendered to the market' (ibid.: 259). With respect to labour, Polanyi (ibid.: 260) noted that the 'present trade-union situation plus social policy has taken the labour organization out of the market' (but added, echoing his earlier concerns: 'the present situation is characterized by the trade union's abuse of their authority'). And yet, as soon as Polanyi returned to Britain, questions of class and property returned to the centre of his analyses. For there, socialism – rather than the reform of capitalism – remained the only viable path forward, in Polanyi's view. In *TGT*, Polanyi noted the obstacles posed by capitalist property relations to efforts to subordinate the market to society:

> Socialism is, essentially, the tendency inherent in an industrial civilization to transcend the self-regulating market by consciously subordinating it to a democratic society. It is the solution natural to the industrial workers who see no reason why production should not be regulated directly and why markets should be more than a useful but subordinate trait in a free society. ... From the point of view of the economic system, [socialism] is [...] a radical departure from the immediate past, insofar as it breaks

with the attempt to make private money gains the general incentive to productive activities, and does not acknowledge the right of private individuals to dispose of the main instruments of production. This is, ultimately, why the reform of capitalist economy by socialist parties is difficult even when they are determined not to interfere with the property system. ([1944] 2001: 242)

Whatever the possibilities for reform in the US, in Britain the impending efforts of working-class organisations to gain even moderate steps towards greater social security were bound, Polanyi thought, to quickly run up against that limit of private property: 'That such a transformation cannot leave the property system untouched is fairly obvious. And that is why socialists advocate a change in the property system, primarily in respect to the means of production' (Polanyi, 16–1b).[5] That the New Deal was not 'socialist' was – *pace* Fred Block – as clear to Polanyi in the early 1940s as it was in the mid-1930s. In a 1943/44 lecture back in Britain, Polanyi pointed out (much as he had done a decade earlier and in 1941) that fascism 'attempts to solve the problem of market-economy, or capitalism, by handing over government to industry; Socialism, on the contrary, is [the] tendency to hand over industry to a democratic government; the New Deal is more akin to socialism, but it leaves the property system unaffected' (Polanyi, 15–8: 18).

Socialism, for Polanyi (it bears repeating), 'cannot leave the property system' – but the New Deal did just that. While closer to socialism than to fascism, even the most generous interpretation of the New Deal as the tentative solution to the problems of American capitalism could not, for Polanyi, yield a model for European post-war reconstruction (nor obviate the need to finally abolish capitalist property as the historic task of the newly resurgent working classes there). But even with respect to the US itself, Polanyi's evaluation remained subject to revision. By mid-1943, he had begun to worry that the 'New Deal might continue but not develop'. Even more importantly, Polanyi started to wonder just how much of a transformation had indeed occurred there:

Private enterprise is popular in America. The Great Depression has not shattered its prestige. Big-Business still stands high. ... To imagine that post-Depression America had lost its faith in liberal capitalism would be to misread utterly the basic beliefs of the American people. The New Deal, as one can learn from Henry Wallace, is not meant to supersede private enterprise, but on the contrary to save it from monopoly and modernize its working. (18–25: 4)

Never mind socialism in America – had the New Deal even overcome *liberal* capitalism? And if not, Polanyi now asked himself, what would be the consequences for the rest of the world – and for socialism in Europe?

Capitalist universalism and democratic socialism, 1943–49

As a possible solution to the problems of American society, Polanyi placed considerable hope in the New Deal; as a conceivable solution to the devastating problems of Europe, none at all. Up until about mid-1943, Polanyi remained broadly optimistic that the US might be embarked on an independent path beyond liberal capitalism. But Polanyi *never* considered the New Deal to be a variant of socialism (though even less one of fascism); nor did he think that the New Deal was embarked on a journey *towards* socialism.[6] America was a historical exception whose social composition and political constitution had not only precluded the emergence of an organised, socialist working-class movement there in the past, but would also preclude a socialist reconfiguration of its social institutions in the foreseeable future. If the US eventually became socialist itself, it would be the result of the successful socialist transformation of Europe which at some point might provide the US with a model of social transformation and existence (and an increasing constriction of the room needed for the persistence of such a 'capitalism in one country').

But over the course of 1943, Polanyi came to realise that he might have had it all backwards. Far from an outlier with little relevance abroad, the US might indeed turn itself into a model for (and dominant actor in) Europe's post-war reconstruction – a model that would undercut any momentum towards democratic socialism there. 'The U.S. made her social and industrial system the crucial issue of the war; it was on the strength of her "way of life" that she claimed leadership', Polanyi (20–2) now recognised. America's

> foreign policy still finds itself tied to the pre-1914 system. Even though at home the New Deal might mean the beginning of an independent solution of the problem of an industrial society, abroad America must insist on the economics of the gold standard and free trade, these primitive 'Trotskyist' forms of capitalism. The contradiction between her domestic and her external economics may for a considerable time, though not indefinitely, be bridged by virtue of her great political and economic strength. The USA represents the temptations of an universalist line of policy. (Polanyi, 20–2: 16; cf. Polanyi, 1945: 87)[7]

The persistence of (liberal) capitalism in the US, Polanyi feared, might become the basis for a project of European restoration that would put Metternich's to shame. In a speech titled 'America 1943', Polanyi identified Pearl Harbor as the moment when the US shifted decisively from domestic to global restructuring:

> The dominating change was the realization of the need for foreign policy; and that its natural aim must be the restoration of a world in which the United States has grown wealthy and powerful. The world had, unaccountably and for not good reason,

changed. She herself had not changed and could not change. Consequently, the only possible war aim was the restoration of the old world. Democracy and its American way of life were now finally identified with liberal capitalism at home and abroad. The Gold Standard and Free Trade were established as the corollaries of democracy and as the esoteric meaning of the Atlantic Charter. (18–25: 2)[8]

Polanyi's growing trepidation deepened further once the contours of the post-war international economic order envisaged by the US (and Britain) became more clearly visible. In particular, his notes and lectures during his second London period (1943–47) show an unremitting hostility towards the Bretton Woods system. Far from embodying the principles and rules which would make democratic socialism possible, Bretton Woods, for Polanyi, represented the defeat of the hopes and aspirations that he had been working towards since his departure from Austria in 1933.

> The Americans fervently believe that freedom and liberty are identical with capitalism; in making the world safe for democracy Woodrow Wilson assumed that this involved private trading and the gold standard. Bretton Woods proclaims the same principles; in insisting on the abolition of preference in Empire trade the Americans are only consistent; they equally strongly insist on the restoration of liberal capitalism in Germany and on unplanned trade along the Danube. (19–8: 13)

Polanyi was, as yet, far from ready to resign himself to capitalist restoration in Europe. He remained optimistic that there, the convulsions of the last decades could finally be overcome; for those had been the result of 'market-economy, which existed during the 19th century but which – with the exception of the United States – is in our time rapidly disappearing' (35–8: 111). Polanyi's choice of terms here is significant. While he had, up until mid-1943, considered the New Deal one of the modalities through which liberal capitalism and market-economy had been overcome, his writings over the next half-decade reflect a profound re-evaluation of the limits of the New Deal. Despite the New Deal, Polanyi at this point had come to classify the US, once more, as a market-economy. And that capitalist US seemed now to be hell-bent on stopping the disappearance of market-economy elsewhere in its tracks, including – and especially – in Britain.

Britain, in Polanyi's view, was the country in which the prospects for a democratic, socialist transformation were most advanced at this historical moment. But even here, everything was still up for grabs. Not only did pro-capitalist *domestic* social forces seek to undermine further moves towards socialism; but financial and military pressures from the US also sought to deflect what Polanyi considered Britain's destiny. Already in late 1943, he had warned: 'The American retrospective utopia of a restoration of the pre-1914 world is not as fantastic anymore once one puts one's self into the place of the Americans. If England can be won over or coerced over, the plan is feasible. Germany, Italy, France do not exist anymore, and the USSR then might be forced to give in' (18–25). The issue of the Soviet Union served as a critical wedge issue in this regard, Polanyi recognised. Even significant elements in the Labour Party considered the Soviet Union an ideological enemy and a strategic rival. They consequently sought to tie Britain into a permanent post-war alliance with the US directed against the perceived threat from the Soviet Union – even as that clearly required Britain to give in on American demands on financial and economic issues. Thus, a foreign policy turn towards the US held the 'danger of cramping Britain's own development at home, as this happened during the Napoleonic Wars. … Then, England for a long time lost her chance of becoming a democratic country; today she might lose the chance of becoming a socialist country' (19–8: 13).

Subsequent events bore out Polanyi's fears, as he recognised only too well. Though he continued to hope that transformative socialist policies might gather pace, he was under no illusion that, on the whole, Britain was still far from a socialist country. For a short moment late in 1946, Polanyi's optimism surged, as Labour back-benchers challenged their own leadership. They articulated the interests of the 'poor people of England [who] could never be persuaded to overcome their suspicion of the American Loan, coupled, as it was, with Bretton Woods' (18–34). But to carry forward this 'Westminster Revolt against Wall Street rule of England' (18–34) would require more than a shift in the domestic balance of power and the reorientation of Labour policies, Polanyi argued.

> But very much must depend on the response of the American New Dealers. It will need an effort on their part to realize the importance which a controlled foreign economy holds for British socialism. Britain must remain free to manage her currency, she must be free *to plan her foreign trade, and free to cooperate industrially with any other country*. Wall Street is determined to cut these life lines of a socialist Britain. If New Dealers will help to *fend off Republican free trade imperialism*, then the people of Britain may be able, not only to establish democratic socialism at home, but also to carry its principles into all dealings of the Commonwealth. (18–34)

None of Polanyi's hopes would come to be realised in Britain. The 'Westminster Revolt' remained a minor stumble on the path to 'the erecting of a world bastion of Anglo-Saxon capitalism' (18–34). In the US, meanwhile (to which Polanyi had returned early in 1947), Republican congressional victories threatened what remained of the New Deal. In a letter to Christian Socialist friends of old, Polanyi noted:

> The 'Back to GOP!' move is born by a deep mass feeling of reversal to business and the traditional American philosophy; for the time being it dominates everything. I am

thankful to God for my insensitivity but for which I'd feel like cancelling my course. … It is a miracle that I can make [my students and colleagues] take kindly to a voice in the wilderness, and even be amused by it. Of course to some it is as a life belt to a drowning man. (56–13)

America's capitalism, in the end, did become a 'model' for European reconstruction. The American-led restoration of global capitalism put an end to the great transformation. Would Polanyi find it amusing, today, that many consider the New Deal to be the embodiment of 'democratic socialism', the post-war welfare states the realisation of his call for the 're-embedding of the market', and the Bretton Woods system the overall (if temporary) triumph of his vision?

Conclusions

Divergent perspectives on the political purposes over *TGT* have a long existence. Over the last decade, this debate has intensified and been pursued with increasing depth, based on a systematic engagement with archival sources. Polanyi himself noted in 1945 that his book was 'meant as a new foundation of the outlook of democratic socialism' (47–15) – but that has merely fanned controversies over Polanyi's understanding of that term. In this chapter, I have argued that Polanyi's central aim was indeed to provide an innovative analysis of the contradictions of capitalism in order to aid the British and European working classes in their historical task of overcoming it. In Britain, Polanyi hoped that the liberal heritage that had saved British capitalism from fascism would ultimately become the foundation for a democratic socialism which would plan the economy with a view to enabling the full realisation of individual rights and capacities beyond their capitalist limits. In this role, Britain could then guide the reconstruction of a Europe freed by military power from fascist (and particularly Nazi-German) oppression. With *TGT*, Polanyi sought to demonstrate the need, and the possibility, of a systemic transformation that would go beyond previous efforts to tame capitalism from within, which had, in Polanyi's view, contributed to the present existential crisis of humanity. Most importantly, it sought to stimulate the *will* to overcome capitalism, which the European working classes had so sorely lacked during the previous decades – and which had exposed them to defeat by fascist forces in country after country.

Drawing almost entirely on European experiences, *TGT* was mainly addressed to the continental – and especially the British – working classes. But it could not speak *only* to them. Written in America, Polanyi's book also had to find a US publisher and an American audience. Towards the end of his life, Polanyi noted that '*The Great Transformation* had a twofold objective: to transplant into the English labour movement the spirit of the Austrian militant socialist workers' culture; [and] to give wings to Roosevelt's New Deal by an up-to-date critique of capitalism' (29–8: 12). This balancing act helps to explain the vagueness of Polanyi's political programme in the last chapter of *TGT*; writing for two very different social contexts, Polanyi chose abstraction. The apparent ambiguities of *TGT* are the result of Polanyi's decision to leave things somewhat ambiguous. It is not, as Block has suggested, that *TGT* embodies deep theoretical tensions as Polanyi, supposedly moving from Marxist socialism to social democracy, could not tie things up properly. Nor is it the case, as Dale maintains, that Polanyi, as a supposed 'reform-socialist', oscillated between revolution and reform. The book's conclusion, rather, was (slightly) vague because Polanyi was a (non-Marxian) revolutionary socialist on Britain and Europe, but less than a social democrat on America.

Despite the book's overwhelming focus on the European trajectory – past, present and future – it may seem tempting to conclude, then, that a reformist reading of *TGT* is as valid as a revolutionary one. But the fact remains that, for Polanyi, the universalisation of the American 'solution' to the global crisis of capitalism represented the defeat of the socialist aspirations to which he had dedicated his life. Instead of socialism overcoming capitalism in Europe and then spreading to the rest of the world (including, eventually, America), American capitalism vanquished the socialist future that Polanyi had, in Europe, sought to help usher in with *TGT*. Market-economy once again became the basis of social and global organisation.

Notes

1 See Polanyi ([1944] 2001), p. 24 (in passing, as one of the post-laissez-faire patterns in the 1930s); p. 31 (in passing); p. 211 (a short but important passage); pp. 236–237 (in passing, on the gold standard); p. 252 (another short but important passage).

2 Speech delivered in the American Commission of the Presidium of the Executive Committee of the Communist International, 6 May 1929, https://www.marxists.org/reference/archive/stalin/works/1929/cpusa.htm. Accessed 7 August 2019.

3 Polanyi added: 'In a sense this is true. Thus the American, *disregarding the very important qualifications* of this truth, *believes* in society and upholds it as the fulfilment of God's purpose on earth' (29–26: 3).

4 But perhaps Polanyi's 'lived experience' was at least partly a product of the conceptual reference points he brought to bear on his encounters with the 'common men' of America. For, as Michael Mann (1993) points out, the first two decades of the twentieth century were marked not by class harmony, but by increasingly militant conflicts. Indeed, Mann maintains, America was *not* born exceptional; rather, 'it became extreme' in those decades (ibid.: 658).

Up until 1900, Mann suggests, the constellations of union strength and militancy were similar in the US and in Western Europe. After 1900, a new wave of mobilisation set in which culminated in the establishment of the IWW and the Socialist Party of America, and their success could have cemented the parallels with European developments. They were met, however, with 'ruthless, righteous repression' (ibid.: 657), and were largely defeated by the end of the First World War. Even apparent gains – such as the 1914 Clayton Antitrust Act, which had declared that the 'labor of a human being is not a commodity or article of commerce' and posited the legality of trade unions – could not prevent that court-sanctioned anti-union injunctions actually increased during the 1920s (ibid.: 652).

The increasing prevalence of the craft union type of labour organisation (amidst a turn to sectionalism) thus represented, Mann concludes, an enforced adaptation to the tightening limits of the possible, imposed by multi-pronged forms of repression. This, more than any internalised individualism and endorsement of capitalism, accounted for the weakness of socialist ideas and organisations at the beginning of the 1930s (though the American Federation of Labor's leader, Samuel Gompers, certainly took delight in disparaging socialism).

These social struggles of the first quarter of the twentieth century barely entered Polanyi's conceptualisations of America's societal development – and this should give rise to questions. Was it really the case that the attitudes he encountered were almost identical to those Sombart described, despite those two decades of intense struggle that followed Sombart's own stay in the US? Had the defeats of the 1920s brought the 'common men' back precisely to where they had been in the first years of the century? Or did Polanyi fail to recognise significant changes in social realities and attitudes *because* he approached his environment through the lens of Sombart?

5 This document was written in Britain, either before 1940 or after 1943. It is undated, but the contents suggest a date around 1944. Its reference to World War I indicates that it was written *after* Polanyi's return from the US for two reasons: only after about 1941 did reference to a Second World War become widespread (and thereby make reference to a *First* World War meaningful); moreover, 'World War I' was, at this point, a definite Americanism.

6 My interpretation here differs from Block and Somers (1984: 61); Dale (2010b); and from my own earlier suggestion that Polanyi expected the New Deal to lead towards socialism in the US; cf. Lacher (1999a).

7 This set of documents, titled 'Tame Empires', is dated by the Karl Polanyi Archive to 1938/39. Reference to the Atlantic Charter (14 August 1941) makes that dating impossible. It is more likely one of the variations of a 'topical' book Polanyi proposed in March/April 1943.

8 In a related course proposal entitled 'America 1943' (16–5), Polanyi planned to include lectures on 'The return of big business' and 'New Deals or Old?'.

9

This freedom kills:
Karl Polanyi's quest for an alternative to the liberal vision of freedom

Michael Brie

The idea of being responsible for our personal share in the life of 'others', that is, in social realities, and incorporating it into the realm of freedom cannot be realized in the bourgeois world. But it is just as impossible to renounce and thus to arbitrarily limit our responsibility and thus our freedom. The bourgeois world's idea of freedom and responsibility points beyond the boundaries of this world.

Karl Polanyi (Polanyi, [1927] 2018: 304)

Perhaps one day this attempt to give a new meaning to the concept of freedom will turn out to be the most far-reaching aspect of Polanyi's work.

Michele Cangiani and Claus Thomasberger (2002: 42)

Karl Polanyi is arguably the best-known unknown intellectual of the twentieth century. His ideas of the double movement between the attempt to create self-regulating markets and society's efforts to protect itself from them are repeatedly quoted in the mass media. The great financial crisis of 2009, the growing doubts about the neoliberal project of global market radicalism, rising ecological and security concerns, and the rise of a New Right have brought these central theses of his work back to consciousness. An increasing number of conferences are dedicated to Karl Polanyi. In May 2018 the International Karl Polanyi Society was founded in Vienna.

Karl Polanyi's growing fame, however, stands in striking contrast to the profound ignorance of his work beyond *The Great Transformation*. Karl Polanyi's work was not only received internationally in reverse order to its creation, but was also largely separated from the author's intentions. One reason for this is that only in the last two decades have his writings from the 1920s and 1930s become more accessible (and this initially in German and only recently in English) (see Polanyi, 2002, 2003, 2005a, 2018a; Brie and Thomasberger, 2018). The Hungarian articles written before and after the First World War are even less known (see in English Polanyi, 2016). And it was not until 2016 that a first fairly comprehensive biography appeared in English (Dale, 2016a).

Karl Polanyi was, above all, an intellectual who posed important questions backed by strong normative ideas and based on new categories and methodological approaches. That is his strength. But he is perceived as someone who had answers, answers above all to the market radicalism of the liberal age. He is regarded as the prophet of movements against this market liberalism: he is held to have believed that every wave of progressive marketization will face counter-trends that seek to bring social regulation back to the centre; that the unleashing of market forces would always be answered with the 'protection of society'. There would always be new efforts to embed markets into society. In this understanding, the movement of the history of capitalism is pendulum-like. However, such a view is less and less tenable today when the historical tendency appears increasingly to point in the direction of a subordination of society to markets (Streeck, 2009: 27). Social democratic and conservative projects, left-wing and right-wing populism are regarded as expressions of movements against this subordination to markets and Polanyi appears as their advocate. There is even the accusation that he more or less neglected questions of freedom and emancipation (see Fraser, 2013; and the critique in Brie, 2017). It is this Polanyi of the double movement, or a 'Polanyi lite', that determines the reception of his work. It is more or less forgotten that Polanyi was firmly convinced that the society in which such a double movement occurred was condemned to degenerate into fascism if it does not advance towards socialism.

Great social thinkers have a lasting impact for three key reasons. First, their work is guided by a question that links fundamental moral concerns to existential problems and challenges the ruling *Zeitgeist*. Polanyi's guiding question was formulated through ethical insight into the problems of ordinary people. Secondly: philosophically and morally based guiding questions only become scientifically meaningful if these thinkers develop their own research prism. This must combine an original methodology with illuminating categorical constructs and an independent elaboration of concrete objects. The scientific work proceeds as light of the guiding questions passes through this prism. Thirdly, as it does so, it disperses into the individual works revealing new narratives of hitherto unexploited possibilities, both utopian and dystopian. They are textual actions that construct identities and realities. Explicitly or implicitly, they call for action, are performative. These three elements – guiding question, research prism and narratives – often develop in a cyclical process (Figure 9.1).

Polanyi dealt very consciously with difference between formulating existential philosophical questions and conducting scientific analysis. He criticized the tendency to privilege science and to derive existential orientations from the investigation of objective facts. In a manuscript written between 1920 and 1922, also known

9.1 Guiding ideas, research prisms and narratives as components of scientific and philosophical work

as *Behemoth*, he wrote: 'we have to turn to ethics for counsel', 'when what is at stake is the direction of our own lives and our relation to our fellow human beings and to the past and the future' (Polanyi, 2018b: 268). He stressed that moral insight and scientific knowledge are in no way equivalent: '*First* come the counsels, derived from life itself, of the ethical What-ought-to-be and *then*, and *only where* scientific knowledge has *proven* its validity can it also claim validity' (ibid.: 269).

In the late 1930s, as he was preparing to write *The Great Transformation*, Polanyi returned to the relationship between existential questions and scientific investigation. In his manuscript 'How to make use of the social sciences', written after 1939, he reflected very precisely on why science so often detaches itself from the actually decisive questions. First, he assumed that questions would be addressed to science. These questions would form the 'matrix' in which science is embedded. This matrix, however, is soon differentiated into the 'metaphysical questions' that are *external* to science and the part which science can internalize because it is amenable to treatment by the methods it has refined. However, this part of the matrix, as a consequence, becomes independent of, even alien to, the part that stands outside science and deals with existential human questions:

Man's innate interest in his environment is the starting point of all the sciences. But every science necessarily restricts its subject matter to such elements in the context of its environment as are susceptible to its method. Consequently the subject matter of the sciences will deviate from the original subject matter of the innate interest – the matrix. That is why physics, chemistry, and psychology do not 'add up' to the model of a cat; nor can mathematics and botany, between them, produce the complete pattern of a meadow. [...] Method is the key to what science can do and what it cannot; it is the general rule applicable to the operations constituting a particular science. That which is selected as its subject matter and that which is eliminated from it as 'unscientific' matter are differentiated by method. It is to method that sciences are indebted for their definitions, and therefore for their grip on the elements selected, as well as for the rejection of that part of the matrix which now appears as 'metaphysical'. Science is, by method, out of matrix. The birth of a science destroys the matrix in which it was conceived. (Polanyi, 2014b: 109f; see also the reflection on science in 2014c)

Polanyi's work cannot be understood without reconstructing the guiding existential questions that are an indissoluble part of the 'matrix' for him which also contains the central contradictions that shaped his thinking. Kari Polanyi Levitt refers above all to the relation between freedom and reality, the empirical and the normative, community and society, science and religion, efficiency and humanity, technological and social progress, and, last but not least, institutional requirements and personal needs (see Polanyi Levitt, 2018: 44–46).

According to Polanyi, *The Great Transformation*, written against the background of the fundamental civilizational crises of the middle of the twentieth century, aimed to ask the right questions and to develop methods, categories and fields of research adequate to address the questions it raised such that the narrative that emerged could support an emancipatory solution of the crisis. One should keep in mind that Polanyi's work became so influential not least because it arose from the conversation, from the constant dialogue with the 'ordinary people' he taught in Great Britain or the US. As Claus Thomasberger writes: '*TGT* is written as a defence of *common people's realism* against the utopian vision of the liberal economic elite' (Thomasberger, 2018: 54).[1] Polanyi himself formulated the requirements for such a narrative:

This story should tell in simple language how it all started ... This story should be *ruthlessly frank*. ... This story should be *consistent*. ... The story should be *intelligent*. ... The story should be *true*. ... This story should be *complete*. ... This story should be *practical*. ... This story should be the story of the *common man*. ... This story should be about the *unsolved problems of our time*. (see in detail Polanyi, [1943] 2017: 89–91)[2]

With reference to Karl Polanyi it can be said that he was able to formulate a guiding question that is still challenging today – the challenge of freedom in a complex society – and to develop a convincing narrative of a new great transformation that would create the conditions for the realization of such freedom. He realized that the transformation of consciousness, the overcoming of 'our obsolete market mentality' is the condition for the transformation of social reality. As he wrote in 1947, he was convinced that in a truly democratic society, the problem of industry would resolve itself through the planned intervention of the producers and consumers themselves. Such conscious and responsible action is, indeed, one of the embodiments of freedom in a complex society. But, as the contents of this chapter suggest, such an endeavour cannot be successful unless it is disciplined by a total view of man and society very different from that which we inherited from market-economy (Polanyi, [1947] 2018b: 211).

The methodological and categorical approaches to the analysis of capitalist market societies developed by Karl Polanyi on this basis are more relevant today than ever before. The multifaceted crisis of globalized financial market capitalism has prepared the ground for Polanyi's questions and directions of research and the resulting narrative of a completely new 'view of man and society'. This chapter aims to reconstruct Polanyi's existential guiding question. Only on this basis can his research prism and his narrative be understood. I concentrate on sketching the emergence and formulation of Polanyi's guiding question in its barest outline. It is described as a path that led him to and beyond his main work, *The Great Transformation*.

The origin of the guiding question (1909–19): freedom as responsibility

It may seem pointless to ask what existential motives guided the researcher. No matter how great his or her impact on social discourses, only the results and consequences seem to matter. However, thus isolating the results of the research from the intentions and motives of the research constitutes a very instrumental relationship to science and deprives one of an understanding of alternative possibilities that have since emerged for achieving the same goals. Especially when the guiding questions have a truly existential dimension, their interpretation often goes far beyond the realized work. This seems to be the case with Karl Polanyi, who constantly renewed his connection with the existential or metaphysical dimension and never regarded it as finished. Ironically, however, the reception of Polanyi's work is an illustration of what happens when ideas are detached from the guiding questions, the research process and the narratives. They lose their real content, because a sentence can only be understood if one understands the language in which it is embedded and which must be understood as a 'form of life' (Wittgenstein, [1953] 2009: 11). Without understanding the existential guiding question underlying Polanyi's lifework, without understanding what he wanted to say, his work is deprived of the meaning he sought to give it. Of course, the importance of the work cannot be reduced to this meaning. It only becomes accessible through communication and thus changes with every wave of reception. Real communication, however, requires trying to grasp the meaning that the speaker was pursuing. So, what was the purpose of Polanyi's work? What was the guiding question pushing it forward?

In a letter of 1934, thirty-eight-year-old Karl Polanyi distinguished two periods of his life – the period until 1919, and the period in Vienna – before he left for his second exile, in Great Britain. He wrote: 'Although nearly all my published writings falls into this second period ... the first, the Hungarian period, forms the real background of my life and thought' (quoted in Dale, 2016c: 1). It was the Hungarian time, the time before the First World War, during it and immediately after, in which Polanyi began to formulate his guiding question and tried to give meaning to his further work. This time was above all marked by the reception, processing and critical questioning of those positions which he found in the environment of the critical intelligence of Central Europe and, above all, Hungary. That is why I shall go into Polanyi's views from this period in such detail, since they express in a radical, often starkly clear form, the question and search direction to which he adhered in the decades that followed.

It should be noted that Karl Polanyi as a social researcher was, in the strict sense of the term, a latecomer. It was only at the age of fifty, in exile in England, that his career picked up speed. Previously, Polanyi concentrated primarily on social-ethical interventions, journalistic activity and education, as well as on the problem of socialist economic systems. Looking back in 1950, he wrote in a letter that since his youth he had been a prophet awaiting the redemption of his prophecy of a renewal of the idea of freedom proclaimed early in his article 'The crisis of our ideologies' ([1910] 2016): 'I now see that, ever since then, I was waiting for the actuality of the prophecy. This is the simple, melancholy and comprehensive explanation of the lack of realism that I exhibited in the middle part of my life, the root cause of my theoretical and practical barrenness. From 1909 to 1935 I concluded nothing. I strained my powers fruitlessly: in a one-sided idealism, its soarings disappearing into the void' (Polanyi, [1950] 2016: 228).

The Jewish part of the bourgeoisie of the Habsburg Empire and its intelligentsia experienced a tremendous social ascent in the second half of the nineteenth century. They were winners of liberalization and bourgeois-capitalist development. But these processes came to a standstill before the First World War. Especially in Hungary, the contradiction between their interests and those of the peasant classes and the workers became particularly palpable. Fearing these claims and the demands of suppressed nationalities, the bourgeoisie refused further steps of democratization. Freedom was declared the privilege of the educated and well-off.

The Galileo Circle, shaped by Karl Polanyi, and the Radical Bourgeois Party, also inspired by him, broke with this attitude and sought cooperation with social democracy, albeit under the hegemony of the bourgeois forces (Polanyi, [1913] 2016a). The convenient idea that capitalism and individual rights of freedom and democratic participation would progress hand in hand had become suspect.

Like others, Karl Polanyi drew a radical conclusion from this crisis of liberalism and its spiritual foundations: freedom is not a privilege of the individual; it cannot be separated from social responsibility. He merged English liberal and Russian social revolutionary influences in an original way. He assumed the freedom of the individual as a matter of fact and demanded an orientation of the freedom towards social duty. He assumed 'that .... the will is free, and that this freedom is, at the same time, the highest social obligation' (Polanyi, [1913] 2016b: 59). The twenty-five-year-old intellectual wrote in 1911:

> We who believe in the self-determination of man thereby accept a duty. There is no tradition the antiquity of which can absolve us from self-determination; no authority whose loftiness can eliminate the consequences of our behaviour. Behind us lies the bridge, which we have burned, along which one can could [sic] have escaped to safe shores, choosing the cowardly but comforting path of refusing responsibility. ... Our morality is not a compromise between credulity and the phantasms of our imagination but is the governable assumption of responsibility for the consequences. (Polanyi, [1911] 2016: 51)

The First World War transformed this tension between moral rigorism and the existing social relations and tendencies into a stark divide. There was an existential crisis, which Polanyi addressed in his 1954 'Hamlet' essay. Unlike so many contemporaries, Polanyi accepted his personal responsibility for not being able to prevent the original catastrophe of the twentieth century, the First World War. In 1918, in the midst of the upheavals at the end of the war, of revolution and the struggle for its direction, Polanyi wrote the article 'The calling of our generation' and stressed: 'What became evident to us was not how we could have avoided the war but that everything that we had done until now had contributed to making it unavoidable. What we perceived was not who was to blame: that we all were' (Polanyi, [1918] 2016a: 71). According to him the current historical hour was a point of departure comparable only to the time of the Crusades or the Reformation. One must bear witness 'to the shame of the present' to 'find the true path' (ibid.: 73). In this exaggerated situation of guilt and shame Karl Polanyi found his central theme – the contradiction between the freedom of the individual to make clear decisions and the senselessness and absurdity of the complex relationships that lead to civilizational catastrophes:

man cannot live in a world whose meaning he can only search for in vain. Individual man, dumbfounded, kept gazing at the colossal catastrophe. There he stood, in its very midst, unaware of its cause and unable to search for its purpose; not knowing of himself whether he was an actor in it or a mere spectator, and whether it had been enacted for or against him. One thing and one thing only he knew with unsurpassed clarity: the existence or non-existence of the war in no way depended upon his own volition – yet, throughout the war, everyone was constantly invoking himself and his will. The hero on the front line was carrying out his will, and the enemy, when justifying his actions, referred to his will; the fate of the whole world, it seemed, depended upon his will. In vain did he sense that this was sheer delusion and had no reality at all; that he could have neither intention nor will within a world which for him had no meaning. Yet, he himself no longer knew what he wanted and whether his actions were the outcome of his own will or that of others, and if of others, who were they? … 'Not only can we not live in a world devoid of meaning, we cannot even adequately describe it. Better ages to come shall never learn the simple truth, that one of the gravest afflictions of the Great War, both in the hinterland and in the trenches, was boredom – the *boredom* of a world without meaning' (ibid.: 67).

Karl Polanyi's first exile began in 1919. During these years, his central question took shape. He reversed the terms of faith and unbelief. Those who referred to the scientifically recognized laws of society and claim to derive the goals and means of politics from them, he called adherents of unbelieving politics, Marxists and conservative forces alike. The former wanted to radically change society, the latter to maintain it. If the Bolsheviks lost their Marxist faith in the laws of society from which they derive the means of their struggle, 'humankind will be free once again to determine its goals' (Polanyi, [1918] 2016b: 90).

From the cataclysms of the First World War and the revolutionary period, Polanyi drew the following conclusion: 'For we only believe that we are materialists. In reality, there is today no more decisive political factor than ideas; they are central to people's consciousness, and they revolve around a single invisible axis: the question of where the truth lies' (Polanyi, [1919] 2016: 95). Polanyi has subordinated all his further work to this conviction that it is important to change ideas in order to transform the world. He was strongly convinced of the effectiveness of alternative visions. The question is only which vision can prevail – a humane or inhumane one. With a view to the civil war in Russia and Hungary he wrote: 'He who is victorious but without humanity loses the battle that he has won. For he cannot be in the right' (ibid.: 97). For Polanyi, socialism was above all a moral imperative of social transformation that could not be 'derived' from the scientific analysis of social reality. The latter can only inform about the possible means. This also explains his difference with the Marxism of the Second International, namely with Karl Kautsky (Polanyi, [1921] 2016: 107).

The 1921 paper 'Believing and unbelieving politics' marked the end of the preparatory phase of the formation of Polanyi's guiding question. Freedom and the reality of society, moral reflection and individual scientific knowledge, ideals and interests were still put against each other in an abstract way. This changed with Polanyi's post-war intrusion into the contradictions of socialist politics, the intensive discussion of the various wings of socialist theorists and politicians.

The formulation of the guiding question (1920–34)

In the years after the First World War, society seemed pregnant with socialism, not only in Soviet Russia but also in Central Europe. Even though social-revolutionary struggles had died down and the comprehensive economic-democratic plans for socialism had largely lost their political relevance, socialism seemed on the agenda, not least as a reform project, as in Red Vienna governed by the social democrats, where Karl Polanyi lived between 1919 and 1934. Comprehensive changes took place in many areas of public services and, above all, in housing construction and culture (see Jahn, 2015). But this socialist era encountered obstacles and was fatally challenged – intellectually by the neoliberalism with Ludwig von Mises and politically by the emerging fascism. Karl Polanyi responded to both challenges and, from these responses, emerged a new understanding of freedom. Let's start with the intellectual challenge.

The intellectual challenge of Ludwig von Mises

In 1922 Mises's book *Socialism* was published. It was preceded by two writings that sought to argue that in a socialist community rational accounting is impossible (see Mises, 1920a, 1920 b). On the one hand, Mises assumed that he and his contemporaries would live in 'The Epoch of Socialism': 'for more than a generation the policies of civilized nations have been directed toward nothing less than a gradual realization of Socialism' (Mises, [1922] 2010: 25). On the other hand, his verdict was clear: the formation of prices necessary for any rational economic accounting could not take place under socialism. In his view pricing is linked to capitalism, based on private ownership of the means of production: 'it is not possible to divorce the market and its functions in regard to the formation of prices from the working of a society which is based on private property in the means of production and in which, subject to the rules of such a society, the landlords, capitalists and entrepreneurs can dispose of their property as they think fit' (ibid.: 137–138) Mises reversed the socialist critique of capitalism. Until then, the socialists had accused capitalism

197

of making a rational structuring of the economy impossible – Mises claims this in relation to socialism. He described socialism as an inherently destructive and irrational project.

In direct opposition to Engels (Engels, [1876] 1983: 323; see also Marx [1867] 1996: 89) and all other socialists, Mises argued that the attempt to consciously control the process of social reproduction by concentrating the rights of disposal over the means of production in the hands of a monosubject ('society') cannot lead to increased rationality and control, but only to complete irrationality and irreversible disintegration of society, losing control altogether: 'Socialism has not consciously willed the destruction of society. It believed it was creating a higher form of society. But since a socialist society is not a possibility every step towards it must destroy society' (Mises, [1922] 2010: 497). In the preface to the second German edition, Mises wrote that those who advocate socialism are 'helping thereby to bring about the inevitable decline of civilization. ... And so we must inevitably drift on to chaos and misery, the darkness of barbarism and annihilation' (ibid.: 23). Polanyi, for his part, in *The Great Transformation* will turn the tables on liberalism, blaming the quixotic attempt at self-regulating markets which, precisely because it was an impossible utopia, led to its destruction, including the rise of fascism and the collapse of civilization.

Here is not the place to deal in detail with Mises's positions and analyse Polanyi's disagreement with them (see Cangiani, Polanyi Levitt and Thomasberger, 2005: 29–42; Bockman, 2013; Bockman, Fischer and Woodruff, 2016). What is important in this context is that Polanyi took over a central assumption from Mises: social rationality does not arise from the actions of a monosubject. Rational behaviour is only possible on the basis of the interaction of a plurality of interrelated actors. Rationality is an outcome of a communicative process. Polanyi sought a solution to the problem of socialist accounting at the beginning of the 1920s on the basis of guild socialism by Cole (1920) and functional socialism by Otto Bauer ([1919] 1976). The various functions of social individuals– 'production, consumption, neighbourly relations, intellectual life and their flourishing' (Polanyi, [1922] 2016a: 122) – should each be represented by independent self-governing organs, the guilds. Individuals would behave towards each other in different functions and achieve forms of solidarity in carrying out different interests. This idea unites the plurality of actors in a commonality based on solidarity.

In guild socialism a variety of guilds would represent the interests of the same group of individuals, but in different aspects, in relation to their various activities. Until then, the reality of society was a rather abstract concept for Polanyi. In the years he devoted to this problem of socialist accounting, it became clear to him that a consciously designed society is confronted with the problem of complexity and unintended consequences. As soon as a plurality of free actors acts to realize their interests a complex network of relationships emerges that cannot be completely identical to the intentions of the actors. It is the freedom of the actors that creates the very complex web that is the 'reality of society'. In turn, it cannot be directly traced back to the intentions of those who have created it.

Karl Polanyi worked for years on a convincing solution to the problem of rational accounting in a plural socialist society (see Cangiani, Polanyi Levitt and Thomasberger, 2005: 40), convinced that 'Humanity will only be free when it understands what it must pay for its ideals' (Polanyi, [1922] 2016b: 422). Without an overview of causes and effects, costs and benefits, free decisions cannot be made. Polanyi increasingly dissociated himself from the idea that a socialist economic order would exclude all markets and market-shaped exchange processes. He approached the later position that labour and raw materials should not be treated primarily as commodities. A democratic framework of prices on these goods should be established. In a paper of the late 1920s he speaks of 'framework goods'. This concept implied critical changes in existing markets: '1. restricting the market by withdrawing framework goods on the one hand and essential goods on the other from it... 2. purposeful domination of the market thus constricted by public service supply and even an equally public service demand ... As a result of this functional change, the so-called market loses its "natural law like character"' (Polanyi, 2005b: 128–129). Unlike many traditionally Marxist-oriented theorists, Polanyi realized in these years that man's economic needs are different when considered as a private individual and when considered as a 'member of society', 'as an isolated being' and 'as a social being'. The capitalist market economy lacks 'the organ to express the needs of people as social beings' (ibid.: 133). The reality of complexity is the price of freedom and can only be destroyed with it.

According to Polanyi himself he never achieved a satisfactory result in the accounting debate. But in this discussion he succeeded in formulating the central guiding question that was to determine his research process over the next four decades and made him one of the most original, but in this regard almost unknown, philosophers of freedom in the twentieth century. In a letter to his friend Rikárd Wank in 1925 Polanyi wrote:

> During these years my ideas on social issues have found passionate expression. The social sciences, activity, but above all the possibility of freedom of thought on social issues. *How can we be free, in spite of the fact of society?* And not *in our imagination only,* not by abstracting ourselves from society, denying the fact of our being interwoven

with the lives of others, being committed to them, but in *reality*, by aiming at making society as something its members can oversee [*übersichtlich*], as a family's inner life is, so that I may achieve a state of things in which I have done my duty towards *all men*, and so be *free* again, in decency, with good conscience. (Polanyi, [1925] 2000: 317)

From now on his guiding question was: How is freedom possible in a complex society?

The political challenge of fascism

The rise of fascism represented a deadly political challenge for socialism. It was linked to the crisis processes that worked themselves out after the First World War. The great global economic crisis starting in 1929, the rise of fascist forces and the new wave of wars revealed the enormous structural problems that shaped the economic-political and international system after the First World War. From the analysis of this crisis, Karl Polanyi gained central insights, which then became part of *The Great Transformation*. In his article for the *Österreichischer Volkswirt*, Polanyi was able to show early on how democratic concerns about the defence and expansion of social rights by social democratic governments and the imperatives of economic stabilization and rationalization were in deep conflict with each other under the given conditions. The so-called 'double movement' of marketization of the society on the one hand, and protecting society on the other, took forms that threatened liberal civilization as a whole. In 1932 Polanyi wrote in the article 'Economy and democracy':

A chasm has opened between the economy and politics. These scant words give the diagnosis of the times. The economy and politics, two manifestations of the life of society, have declared their autonomy and wage unceasing war against each other. They have become slogans under which political parties and economic classes pursue their opposing interests. Things have reached the point that right and left feud in the name of economy and democracy, as if these two basic functions of society could be embodied in two separate parties within the state! Behind the slogans, however, lurks a terrifying reality. The left *is* rooted in democracy; the right *is* rooted in the economy. As a direct result, the current functional breakdown between the economy and democracy is stretching into a catastrophic polarity. The realm of political democracy gives rise to forces that intervene in the economy, disturbing and constraining it. In response, business mounts a general attack on democracy as the embodiment of an irresponsible hostility towards the economy that is devoid of objectivity. There is no contemporary problem more worthy of the attention of well-intentioned people than this one. A society whose political and economic systems are in conflict is doomed to decline – or to be overthrown. (Polanyi, [1932] 2018: 61)

The overthrow came shortly afterwards with the transfer of power to the National Socialists in January 1933 in Germany. Now, Polanyi concluded that fascism and socialism were the only two alternatives. According to him both are revolutionary answers to the crisis of liberal civilization, but pointing in opposing directions: *'Fascism is that form of revolutionary solution which keeps Capitalism untouched.* … Obviously, there is another solution. It is to retain Democracy and abolish Capitalism. This is the Socialist solution. For, just as Capitalism needs Fascist politics as its complement, so Democracy needs Socialist economics as its extension' (Polanyi, [1934] 2018a: 127).

In this context, the radical political character of Polanyi's insistence on freedom in confrontation with liberalism and fascism becomes clear: 'Commitment to "material interest" could lead to the downfall of the workers' movement; the ideal of freedom could be "bought" from it. *Where there is only material interest, there is easily a balance, a compromise possible. But where freedom or rule, faith or unbelief in man and the meaning of history are at stake, there is only place for a decisive struggle to the last'* (Polanyi, 2005c: 220). If fascism becomes a direct attack on freedom and therefore overrides elementary democratic institutions and turns to open terror, then, according to Polanyi, the society that triggered this disastrous dynamic, in which democracy and economy are incompatible, must be overcome by a socialist transformation. For Polanyi, socialism was the only possible way of realizing both individuality and freedom. However, this requires the extension of democracy to the whole of society, especially the economy: 'Socialism is preformed in Democracy. For Socialism is but Individualism with a different emphasis' (Polanyi, [1934] 2018b: 85). All this opened the way to the research agenda underlying *The Great Transformation*: How can the collapse of the liberal civilization of the nineteenth century be explained and on what basis does responsible freedom in the complex society created by this civilization become possible?

Already in the early 1920s he stressed: 'Freedom of will is neither existent nor non-existent; it is a task for the human being. The validity of values is neither existent nor non-existent; it is a task for the human being. Even the objective reality of human society [identified with alienated objectivations] is neither a given nor a non-given, but its transcendence, overcoming it, is the task of human beings' (Polanyi, 2018c: 290). He remained true to these orientations in the following decades.

The philosopheme of the murdered Chinese

Polanyi's reflections on freedom during his time in Vienna culminated in a lecture entitled 'On freedom' from 1927. It expresses Polanyi's mature understanding of freedom. His main criticism of capitalism – and here he follows essential insights of Marx concerning fetishism – is in the reification of people's social relationships to each other. According to Polanyi, socialism is not primarily a 'stomach question' or a question of justice, but goes beyond them. Socialism aims at freedom. There could also be 'dictatorial justice' (Polanyi [1927] 2018: 301), contrary to socialism. Moral progress, progress towards freedom, would only be possible through democracy.

The existential dimension of freedom in a market society was expressed by Polanyi using the 'philosopheme of the murdered Chinese':

> You have probably all heard of the 'philosopheme of the murdered Chinese,[3] which goes as follows: If we were given the possibility of immediately having every wish granted by simply pressing a button, but on condition that at each press of the button one of 400 million Chinese people would die in far-off China, how many people would abstain from pressing the magic button? ... This odd philosopheme gives us a true allegory of the situation in which even the best person finds himself in relation to his co-citizens. Anyone who is able to offer an appropriate price on the market can promptly conjure up everything that humanity can create. The consequences of this trick take place *on the other side of the market.* He does not know anything of these; he cannot know anything of them. Today, for every single one of these human beings, all humanity consists of nameless Chinese whose life he is ready, without batting an eye, to snuff out in order to fulfil his wishes, and this is what he in fact does. Here, moreover, we see the importance of an attitude that is unconsciously immanent in socialism but has never been clearly expressed. This is the *finiteness of the human world* and thus the limitlessness, but *finiteness*, of the task that socialism confronts. This is where the essential progress of the socialist conception of humanity over the bourgeois conception resides. (ibid.: 308)

Polanyi's position is clear: freedom in a civil society founded on so-called 'free markets' is inevitably irresponsible and deadly. The 'blessings' and the 'horrors' of market society are the unintended result of a certain freedom. It is the freedom of individuals who pursue their interests unmindful of their consequences on others and for which they cannot reasonably be held responsible. Such a freedom creates the fatal reality, Polanyi wrote, 'that each workplace accident has occurred for our own well-being, and the coal that we have just thrown onto the stove, the light with which we now see, contains a part of human life. However, this recognition is the price that we have to pay for our freedom. So even after we fully overcome the shameful injustice of our condition, our full freedom will not drop into our laps' (ibid.: 309).

From the actions of individuals, based on their free decisions as market participants, buyers and sellers, wage earners and capitalists, lenders and borrowers, regulated by law, guarded by the state, reified relationships emerge: 'Social institutions, laws, reifications, all these phenomenal forms of social objectification have in common that they insert themselves between Man and Man, on the one hand, and between the diverse volitions of one and the same person on the other. In that they separate human beings from human beings, they prevent an unmediated personal community between them' (ibid.: 318). The freedom of the individual as a selfish individual, depending on his market power, is opposed to his impotence as a member of a community. As an individual, he creates relationships that he cannot control. Polanyi uses Rousseau's distinction between bourgeois and *citoyen* (Rousseau, [1762] 1994: 56).

The individuals as bourgeois condemn themselves as *citoyen* to powerlessness:

> the individual life itself is split, that the part of our life which produces the cause of the objectifications is split off from the part that represents its effect. ... The result is the monstrous concept of two humanities as thing-like realities: of an egoistically active humanity that limits the other helplessly passive humanity in its freedom and pushes it into misfortune – without the ability of the theoretical knowledge to counteract against this semblance, that what is involved here is just two directions of intent of one and the same humanity. (Polanyi, [1927] 2018: 318–319, see for his understanding of Rousseau: Polanyi, [1953] 2018; Dale, 2018: 134)

The abolition of capital relations and the overcoming of alienated statehood are for Polanyi not the goal, but the means to create the social conditions of responsible freedom. The horizon of transformation points beyond justice to the realm of freedom. It is the combination of injustice and lack of freedom in capitalism that Polanyi criticized (see [1927] 2018: 316). For this reason, Polanyi's vision went beyond any reformism whose goal is to reduce structural inequality. Nor did he flee into etatism, which delegates all responsibility to the state. He was concerned with a non-capitalist and non-bourgeois society in which everyone can and must take responsibility for the impact of her or his free actions on the lives of others. This is not a comfortable socialism of passive well-being, but a challenge for the transformation of both society and the individual: 'Being free therefore no longer means, as in the typical ideology of the bourgeois, to be free of duty and responsibility but rather to be free *through* duty and responsibility' (ibid.: 304). For him, freedom is freedom as solidarity, and the only society that could make this freedom possible, but also require it, is socialism.

Polanyi understood freedom in the lecture as the practical task of dissolving society in 'the direct relation of human being to human being' (ibid.: 301). As a result 'the social relations ... become clear and transparent, as they are in fact in a family or in a communist community' (ibid.: 306). The horizon of a society as a community arises. However, this formulates a strong utopia that can be aspired to but never realized. This utopia is not a fixed state, but rather an ideal reference point from which concrete options are evaluated. The totality of all relationships that people enter into with one another must at the same time be, directly, at all times and everywhere, the expression of the free will of each individual and at the same time form an inseparable whole that encompasses the whole humanity and constitutes it as a single subject. This utopia is above all a guiding orientation. In his lecture, 'On freedom', Polanyi tried to meet this challenge through reflections that refer to guild socialism and assume that a socialist society is built from the bottom up, always resulting from the most free, immediate and self-determined democratic socialization of the people. Concluding this lecture, Polanyi stresses that this is 'an unlimited task that appears only at the beginning of socialism, whose accomplishment however must remain an eternal task of humanity, an asymptotic goal to be approached and never completely reached' (ibid.: 315). An attempt is made to construct a non-utopian utopia (Block, 2018a: 174). The impossibility of an ideal society should not be understood as resignation but, as Thomasberger writes, as the opening of a space of possibilities that can be responsibly designed. There is 'a variety of ways how to increase freedom in complex societies' (Thomasberger, 2018: 61; see also 2009).

The dialogue with Christian Left: freedom, community and the reality of a complex society

The years of British exile subsequently proved to be years in which Polanyi finally formed the concepts on which *The Great Transformation* was based. The analysis of radical changes in the 1930s, National Socialism, the New Deal and the rapid industrialization of the Soviet Union, the wars in Europe and Asia that prepared the path for the Second World War offered the contemporary material. Polanyi's studies of English history in connection with his work in worker education became the historical basis. His lecture tours in Great Britain and the USA helped him to develop an increasingly consistent and convincing 'narrative'. Here, however, I shall deal with another aspect that made a significant contribution to understanding how Polanyi connected his understanding of freedom to what he called 'the reality of a complex society' from here on. It was through the dialogue with the Christian Left in Great Britain.

As early as the 1920s, Karl Polanyi drew on the distinction between community and society, developed by Ferdinand Tönnies, to understand the phenomenon of modern socialism (see Tönnies, [1887] 2001). Polanyi's participation in the book *Christianity and the Social Revolution*, for which he wrote the chapter, 'The essence of Fascism', and his participation in the Christian Left led to a sharpening of his understanding of socialism in relation to the terms 'community' and 'society'. Polanyi finally broke with the idea that social relations in complex societies can be dissolved totally into relations between individuals. This idea, he wrote, is 'the complete denial of the objective existence of society' (Polanyi, [1937] 2018a: 154). Polanyi's renewed examination of Marx's legacy, based on the publication of Marx's early writings (in particular the so-called 'Economic and philosophical manuscripts' of 1844), contributed to this sharpening of positions. Society, Polanyi wrote, is 'an aggregate of functional institutions conditioned by geophysical, technological and other environmental factors' (ibid.: 155) and not a community. Polanyi recognized that 'So-called community for community's sake is a poisonous beverage that makes us dream of the things it prevents us from achieving' (Polanyi, [1937] 2018b: 153). From now on, the poles of Polanyi's socialist vision of freedom are relations of concrete communities in which individuals can act responsibly and with sufficient overview of the results of their actions on the one hand and the vision of a universal community of free people as a horizon for action on the other. Complex societies should be democratized and transformed in a way which diminishes unintended destructive tendencies.

Under the heading 'No perfect society' Polanyi wrote:

Community transcends society. Not because man is evil, but because society is necessarily imperfect, no society can be the realisation of community. Power and value are inherent in society; political and economic coercion belong to any and every form of human co-operation. It is part of the ineluctable alternative of human existence that we can choose only between different kinds of power, and different uses to which to put it, but we cannot choose *not* to originate power or *not* to influence its use once it has been created. ... The ideal society is that which makes fully responsible human existence conceivable by throwing the responsibility of our choice on ourselves and, where no choice is possible, by allowing us to shoulder consciously the inevitable burden of our responsibility for coercing and interfering with the lives of our fellows. The measure of true freedom is the measure in which we are free to choose where choice is possible. Where and when it is not, to take our share in the common evil. There is no contracting out of society. But where the limits of the socially possible are reached, community unfolds to us its transcending reality. It is to this realm of community beyond society that man yearns to travel. (Ibid.: 152)

Freedom in a complex society: an outlook

In the already quoted letter to Oscar Jaszi, Karl Polanyi wrote in 1950: 'I was fifty years old when circumstances in Britain led me to study economic history. When a teacher, I earned my bread from it. Because I was born for this vocation. At that point I did not even conceive that I could have another vocation, even as I was engaged in its precursory stages. Some three years later, again seemingly under the pressure of circumstances, I wrote a book, another attempt to analyse the era – essentially on the foundations of 1909. But this time I also added an economic-historical perspective to my argument. This was in 1940, ten years ago' (Polanyi, [1950] 2016: 229). Time and again, the article, 'The crisis of our ideologies', published in 1910, is the point of reference. The original thesis of 1909 was: 'The ruling ideas of capitalist society are in crisis, for the first, transitional phase of capitalist epoch is *drawing to a close and the next period*, which is in gestation, *will give rise to a different set of prevailing values*' (Polanyi, [1910] 2016: 83). Over thirty years later, Polanyi wanted to contribute to this new set of values and ideas with his work *The Great Transformation*.

Reading *The Great Transformation* one should keep in mind the existential question to which he referred. His already mentioned confrontation with Shakespeare's tragedy *Hamlet* was always in the background (see Polanyi, [1954] 2017). The desperate cry of the Danish prince 'The time is out of joint. O cursed spite/ That ever I was born to set it right!' resonates all the time:

> It is precisely the socially feeling person, the ethical person, who is today in danger of having his inner personal freedom completely cancelled out by this ethical orientation itself. For his social feeling opens his eyes to the endless mutual entanglement of human life and thus a series of unforeseeable responsibilities which he unintentionally brings upon himself. He feels that he must, he can, indeed he should free himself from the destinies of others and, in a sense, reassert his personal freedom, despite the reality of general socialization; but the only way in which he can do so without damaging his own true personality– and he feels this no less clearly – is by paying the full price for it, that is, by taking full account of all responsibilities to which social being gives rise. But he sees no means of doing so, no path. (Polanyi, [1927] 2018: 305)

It is no coincidence that *The Great Transformation* concludes with the section *Freedom in a complex society*. The basic condition to achieve this freedom is, according to Polanyi, to shift the 'industrial civilization onto a new nonmarketing basis' (Polanyi, [1944] 2001: 258). Polanyi focused on the expansion of individual freedoms and comprehensive economic democracy. His position was very clear: 'An industrial society can afford to be free. The passing of market-economy can become the beginning of an era of unprecedented freedom. Juridical and actual freedom can be made wider and more general than ever before; regulation and control can achieve freedom not only for the few, but for all' (ibid.: 264–265). In a few pages he outlined the basic elements of a civilization transcending the capitalist market society: the basic goods of economic life (labour, land and money) are to be excluded from the market system, so that it loses its self-regulating character. He expected a fundamental change in civilization, which would open up the possibilities of different cultures in independent 'tamed empires' ([1943] 2017: 93; see his article of 1945: [1945] 2018). The concrete understanding of 'freedom in a complex society' developed in *The Great Transformation* goes beyond this article.[4]

As Cangiani, Polanyi Levitt and Thomasberger write: 'The core and basis of Polanyi's thinking is the idea of a polar relationship between *human freedom* and *market institutions*, between *the responsibility of the individual* and the objective, impersonal *social mechanisms* that characterize modern civilization, or between *democracy* and *the market economy*' (Cangiani, Polanyi Levitt and Thomasberger, 2005: 16) The relationship between freedom and machine society, between a meaningful life in freedom and mass society became increasingly significant for Polanyi during this period. He continued his work on these issues in the 1950s.

To summarize the concept of freedom in a complex society Karl Polanyi developed in the decades before the writing of *The Great Transformation*, one can recognize four aspects. The basis is first his understanding of freedom as responsibility or as *freedom based on solidarity*, as a duty. This is the heritage of Rousseau and Kant. Secondly, freedom is defined as a joint effort to control the processes of a complex society. One could speak of *democratic freedom*. Thirdly, Polanyi combines freedom with the goal of a meaningful and fulfilling life, embedded in a diversity of cultures and rich nature. Polanyi integrated the legacy of progressive romantic criticism of capitalist civilization. This refers to the concept of *substantial freedom*. In his lecture, 'On freedom', he formulated this threefold concept of freedom in the following way:

> In that highest ideal condition of social freedom, in which all three requirements are simultaneously fulfilled, both the mastery of the necessary consequences of socialization and the universal goal of humanity, which includes ultimate responsibility for all social effects of our existence – in this situation the personality is free in a way that it could never be either in ideal anarchy or in bourgeois anarchy. (Polanyi, [1927] 2018: 307)

There is a fourth aspect of Polanyi's concept of freedom: he formulated his questions from the point of view of ordinary people. Never did he forget the liberal and Marxist disregard for the peasants in the Hungarian Revolution of 1918. From then on, he insisted on the heritage of popular movements. He is convinced that those who seek freedom for everyone must address the social question. *Social freedom* is the fourth cornerstone of Polanyi's understanding of freedom.

Polanyi's entire work in social philosophy and social science was aimed at con-tributing to this 'highest ideal state' of fourfold freedom. Until the end of his life he was convinced: 'The way to prevent freedoms from disappearing is to expand them' (Polanyi, [1957] 2018: 322). The multiple crisis of the capitalist civilization in the early twenty-first century has put this task back on the agenda. How solidarity-based democratic, substantial and social freedom can become possible has once again become an existential challenge for each and everybody and for all of us together. Polanyi's guiding question must be answered anew. The light of the search for responsible freedom must be refracted by new research prisms with new metho-dologies, new categories and new empirical research fields. New narratives must be formulated.

Notes

1 Margaret Somers developed a brilliant critique of this 'utopian vision' (Somers, 2018).
2 Polanyi wrote directly against the narratives of neoliberalism (see Block and Somers, 2014: 98–113).
3 For details of this philosopheme see endnote 6 in Polanyi ([1927] 2018: 319).
4 A more comprehensive analysis of various aspects of this last chapter of *The Great Transformation* by various authors is given in Brie and Thomasberger (2018).

Part IV

Elective affinities

10

Polanyi's democratic socialist vision: Piketty through the lens of Polanyi

Margaret R. Somers and Fred Block

2014 was a remarkable year for political economy. It was the seventieth anniversary of *The Great Transformation* (*TGT*), Karl Polanyi's groundbreaking volume which is now recognized as one of the most influential works of twentieth-century social science. Unlike most other books, Polanyi's becomes ever more indispensable because of the destructive consequences of the market fundamentalism that he critiques. But 2014 also marked another milestone in the revival of interest in political economy with the publication of Thomas Piketty's *Capital in the 21st Century* (*C21*). An unexpected bestseller, *C21* is a highly intelligible economic and social history, accompanied by graphs and tables that document and explain the trajectory of inequality since the eighteenth century.

Piketty's data on the dramatic rise of income and wealth inequality since the 1970s have been essential in demonstrating the increasingly oligarchic nature of the US and the UK with parallel but weaker trends in other developed market societies. Piketty's work represents a return to political economy's historical concern with distributional equity and social change, and its broad impact has increased public awareness of the fragility of mainstream economic ideas and the pressing need for heterodox alternatives.

Although many have noted the glaring absence of any reference to Polanyi in *C21*, the two works complement each other. Indeed Piketty's study in many ways picks up where *TGT* left off. In 1944, Polanyi seemed hopeful that belief in the self-regulating market had been routed by the devastations of two world wars and a global depression. Seventy years later, Piketty's study confirms that for the *trentes glorieuses* (1945–75), Polanyi's optimism was correct; lower levels of income and wealth inequality were maintained through this period in the major market economies. However, Piketty also shows that the post-war political economy that Polanyi hoped would be enduring proved fragile and temporary, and it was replaced starting in the late 1970s with a system that has returned inequality to nineteenth-century levels.

The complementarity of the two works as well as the problem of explaining the post-1970 rise in income and wealth inequality suggest the value of putting these two works into conversation with each other. We highlight three especially important insights and contributions that emerge from looking at *C21* through the lens of a Polanyian perspective. First, we focus on those aspects of Polanyi's theoretical apparatus that can correct for a number of *C21*'s limitations. As much as Piketty stresses the importance of institutions and politics in driving varying levels of inequality, his famous r>g 'law of capitalism' naturalizes the market as a self-activating economic mechanism and effaces the centrality of power at its heart, which Polanyi identified as the foundational deceit at the core of economic liberalism and classical political economy. Secondly, we look critically at how Piketty explains the decline in income and wealth inequality that occurred between 1914 and 1970, and we suggest that Polanyi provides a more compelling explanation for that disruption in the historical pattern. Finally, we argue that Polanyi's substantivist focus on what an economy actually produces is a more useful angle of vision than Piketty's implicit argument that changes in production are irrelevant for understanding the core economic processes of capitalism.

Conceptualizing and politicizing the relationship between the economy and politics

The complementarities and commonalities between Polanyi's book and Piketty's are notable as both authors express a deep skepticism towards mainstream economics. Polanyi believed that it was precisely the hegemony of classical political economy and neoclassical economic liberalism that contributed so mightily to the calamity of twentieth-century civilization that is the subject of *TGT*. Piketty, with a PhD in economics, distances himself from mainstream economics that so valorizes abstract mathematics that it completely misses and obscures the crises of social maldistribution at the center of his analysis. Both works seek to understand the present in terms of long-term historical processes that need to be traced back to earlier centuries.

Nevertheless, the two books diverge in the way they understand the relationship between the economy and politics, and analyzing this difference allows us to develop a deeper appreciation of Polanyi's theoretical framework. The difference emerges as Piketty makes his central analytical claim that there are 'two laws of capitalism' that result in income and wealth being concentrated in the top 1 percent.

He formulates the most significant of these laws as 'r>g' – the average annual rate of return on capital investment tends to exceed the annual growth rate of the economy.

Piketty's originality and remarkable data collection should not obscure the fact that his argument rests on some standard assumptions about the economy and the state. Piketty accepts the premise that there is a fundamental structural separation between the economy and the government. From this follows the distinction between 'primary' market outcomes in income and wealth (so-called 'pre-tax'), which are the product of endogenous economic processes, and secondary 'after-market' outcomes (post-tax), which are the product of redistributive governmental tax policies. This distinction makes primary income distributions the result of 'natural' free market forces that are conceptualized as being pre-political, free of the influence of political power and driven by impersonal economic forces. For Piketty that impersonal force is r>g; for most economists, it is competition, globalization and technological development. In either case, these are self-propelling market forces that are deemed beyond our control. The government, in contrast, is the site of political power, which can readjust those primary economic outcomes after the fact based on normative standards of social justice, Keynesian demand theory or arbitrary coercive political calculations that violate natural market justice – depending on one's political viewpoint (Somers, 2008, 2018).

This assumption is evident in Piketty's analysis of the rise of inequality since the 1970s, which he attributes to neoliberal policies that undermined the social state so as to allow the laws of capitalism to again dominate. The system's own endogenous mechanisms are now unhindered by the state, so that the newly deregulated free market economy returns to the inequitable outcomes generated by the law of r>g. Piketty's basic framework puts him firmly within a standard approach to economics, which theorizes that market inequalities can only be corrected by using the state to adjust for the most extreme instances of income inequality.

Polanyi's critique of social naturalism

Polanyi's innovation was to disrupt this dualistic conceptual landscape through his critique of social naturalism, the philosophy invented by the classical political economists that declared the economy to be equivalent to an autonomous biological organism that is self-propelled and free of power, institutions and human artifice (Somers, 2008: ch. 7). They viewed the state, by contrast, to be a political entity driven by arbitrary rules of power, hierarchy and coercion, whose interference in the economy poses a fundamental threat to market self-regulation. Polanyi ridiculed classical political economy's biologization of any part of the social world. While he recognized the social facticity of the nineteenth-century belief that the economy and the state were two separate entities, he challenged its empirical reality.

He called his method 'the institutional approach to the economy', a political economy which rejects the idea that the economy can be a pre- or non-political naturalistic entity because the economy is itself an institutional complex of political economic rules and policies constituted by power and coercion (Polanyi, 1957a). According to Polanyi, government power cannot be an external 'interference' in the autonomous sphere of economic activity; there simply is no economy without its constitutive structure of legal and governmental rules, institutions and coercive powers. These include rules and practices that economic liberalism treats as natural to markets, including legal contracts at the heart of all market exchange; degrees of monopolization over market power; the rules for what constitutes property and how it is to be bought and sold; the rules that determine rates of unemployment and thus the bargaining power of labor and capital; the supplies of money and credit; and ultimately the institutional mechanisms designed to enforce the prevailing rules, regulations and powers (Block and Somers, 2014; Reich, 2015; Baker, 2016; Stiglitz, 2016).

We propose to use the term 'predistribution' to convey the Polanyian insight that what appear to be autonomous voluntary and 'free' market forces are in fact constituted by government policies and institutional powers, which by definition entail structures of rule and domination (Hacker, 2011).[1] Whereas much of the progressive agenda has advanced redistributive tax and benefit policies that reshuffle income to overcome market inequalities, predistribution focuses on government policies and power that influence the levels of inequality produced within markets, such as the government-orchestrated consolidation of the financial services industry and government enabling of huge increases in executive compensation. Predistribution rejects the binary that limits politics and power to the sphere of government, and freedom and contractual 'equality' to the market. It instead shines light on the distributive power 'inside' the economy that determines original market income prior to taxation. These are powers that can structure market pathways to drive the bulk of income to the top 1 percent, or they can generate a more equal distribution of wages and wealth, as was the case in earlier decades.

Predistribution plays on the term 'redistribution', which, as discussed above, is used to refer to government tax and benefit policies by which market incomes are subject to government taxation that 'redistributes' that initial income according to 'social needs' determined by legislative bodies. The conventional use of redistribution identifies two sequential and substantively opposed moments of income distribution – the first, primary market distribution, derives from wages and capital earnings based on impersonal market forces and/or effort and merit; the second, redistribution, in which the government takes a politically determined percentage of that primary income and uses it to fund the government and social programs. In this model, unequal incomes at the primary level of pre-tax earnings are not caused by power and domination but by neutral market distribution which reflects the non-political impersonal dynamics of free market processes – freedom of contract, and voluntary exchange of effort for equivalent earnings.

The concept of predistribution challenges this binary by demonstrating that both pre- and post-tax outcomes are determined by political power and policy rules: whereas the 're' in redistribution refers to policies that will distribute after gross income and profits have already been earned, the 'pre' of predistribution refers to political rules and coercive policies that determine the amount and dis-tribution of those earned wages and profits in the first place. It aims to draw an equivalence between explicit government practices of redistribution that rearrange those original primary market incomes, and those government practices that take place beneath the radar within the sphere of economic processes and markets. The concept is designed to lay bare that no less than government redistribution, what appear to be purely economic processes and natural market outcomes are products of government policies, rules and institutional arrangements, the content and effect of which reflect the distribution of power in society, not the endogenous workings of a free market.

The concept of predistribution denies the existence of a self-governing economy whose market outcomes reflect purely economic factors or capitalist laws that are independent of policy. Although he did not use the term, the concept of predistri-bution is a direct legacy of Polanyi's project to develop a transformative socialist political economy, which rests firmly on his argument that there is no such thing as a 'free market' driven by natural forces (Somers, 2008, 2018). All actual markets are constituted and sustained by government actions, especially the markets in the key inputs into the economy, or what he calls the 'fictitious commodities' of land, labor and money – fictitious because they are non-economic in origin.

Indeed it is because they are fictitious and not actual market commodities (they were not produced for the purpose of buying and selling) that they must be politi-cally and economically coerced into the market and subjected to being bought and sold as if they were in fact commodities. Like Marx, Polanyi understood land and labor to exist partially within and partially without the economy, and that it is coercion – not neutral market forces – that explains this bifurcated existence.

Indeed, for Polanyi the ultimate predistributive act was the creation of a 'free' wage labor force through the imposition of the New Poor Law (Block and Somers, 2014: ch. 6).

Predistribution is a term that also builds on the classical insights of the legal realists (Hale, 1923; Fried, 1998; Block, 2013; Rahman, 2014) who argued that legal rules shape the relative bargaining power of labor and employers through laws affecting the rights and capacities of unions. The outcome of political battles influences the way that market exchanges provide different rates of return to employees and employers, tenants and landlords, consumers and firms through mechanisms of predistribution that are able to move wealth and income upward towards the rich through structures of domination operating under the guise of the free market. So, for example, all modern economies have central banks whose job it is to manage the supply of money and credit. And the specific policies chosen by the central bank, such as the Fed's bias towards fighting inflation over full employment, have had enormous consequences for the bargaining power of labor and thus for the distribution of income. Hence former Director of the Fed, Alan Greenspan, famously justified his anti-inflationary policies by stressing the importance of maintaining a continuous level of job insecurity among workers to prevent them from becoming overly confident about their bargaining power over wages (Woodward, 2001: 168).[2] These policies contributed to the stagnant wage levels since the 1980s. Central bank policies are part of the political apparatus of predistribution whose success in keeping wages stagnant for decades is instead passed off as the result of impersonal natural labor market forces that are beyond our control, such as inflation, globalization and automation (see also Baker, 2016).

There are several caveats to be noted. First, there is some ambiguity in Polanyi's approach to the relationship between the state and the economy. At times he appears to argue that as an empirical reality, what made the nineteenth century unique was the separation of the economy from the government into two distinct spheres. At other times, he insists that the separation was ideological, as the very idea of an economy independent of government and political institutions is utopia: 'The utopian nature of a market economy explains why it never could be really put into practice. It was always more of an ideology than of an actual fact … the separation of economics and politics was never carried completely into effect' (Polanyi, 2014a: 218).

What brings coherence to his approach, however, is that even if the split between government and the economy is only ideational, Polanyi is adamant that ideational power has empirical institutional effects ([1944] 2001 [hereafter *TGT*]: 124–125; Block and Somers, 2014: 106–107). These compel social conformity to the needs of a socially factitious self-regulating market, such as the commodification of humans, nature and exchange into labor, land and money as central factors of production, regardless of the societal destruction this induces. It also compels a legal and political firewall between economy and politics, which is used in the name of market efficiency and autonomy to prevent the demands of labor and popular democratic constituencies from influencing distributional practices in the economy. This has been enshrined in American constitutional law and reflected in the anti-democratic policies in both traditional economic liberalism and modern neoliberalism (Hayek, [1939] 1980; Buchanan and Tullock, 1962; Crouch, 2011; Streeck, 2014a; Burgin, 2015; MacLean, 2017). That this same 'firewall' is so readily breached in the service of capital, such as the financial bailouts in 2008–10 and in the unquestioned hegemony of government patent and copyright laws which ensure corporate monopolies, attests to the ideational nature of the split (Baker, 2016).

A second caveat: Polanyi's emphasis on the predistributive power of the state in shaping putatively neutral market outcomes should not be mistaken for an argument that the state is neutral. Polanyi emphasized the dynamics of the nineteenth- and early twentieth-century state in the context of furthering the project of building markets through its powers of coercion:

> [T]he introduction of free markets, far from doing away with the need for control, regulation, and intervention, enormously increased their range … even those who wished most ardently to free the state from all unnecessary duties, and whose whole philosophy demanded the restriction of state activities, could not but entrust the self-same state with the new powers, organs, and instruments required for the establishment of laissez-faire. (*TGT*: 147)

One of Polanyi's signature contributions to modern political economy is the argument that the state is not only critical to the successful rise of market societies, but it is equally critical in maintaining the economic foundations of market societies: 'The road to the free market was opened and kept open by an enormous increase in continuous, centrally organized and controlled intervention' (ibid.: 146). At the same time, Polanyi also acknowledges that under certain conditions nineteenth- and twentieth-century counter-movements of resistance successfully compelled the social state to become a necessary ally in the form of statutory labor regulations, such as the 1847 Ten Hours Act (Somers, 1997).[3] Even in these instances it is arguable, as Marx ([1867] 1977) demonstrated, that by restricting the ability of employers to exploit workers to death, the government saved capitalists from themselves. Moreover, the same government that passed the Ten Hours Act imposed the draconian New Poor Law, the most anti-working-class, pro-business Act of the nineteenth century (*TGT*: 82–88, 143–146; Block and Somers, 2014: ch. 6).

There are clearly no autonomous state interests at work here but predistributive ones. Thus, in some of the most memorable words of *TGT*, Polanyi gives us a classic case of predistribution by emphasizing how much pitiless coercion was necessarily exercised by the state under the guise of 'freedom of contract':

> To separate labor from other activities of life and to subject it to the laws of the market was to annihilate all organic forms of existence and to replace them by a different type of organization, an atomistic and individualistic one. Such a scheme of destruction was best served by the application of the principle of freedom of contract. In practice this meant that the noncontractual organizations of kinship, neighborhood, profession, and creed were to be liquidated [by the state] since they claimed the allegiance of the individual and thus restrained his freedom. To represent this principle as one of [government] noninterference, as economic liberals were wont to do, was merely the expression of an ingrained prejudice in favor of a definite kind of interference, namely, such as would destroy noncontractual relations between individuals and prevent their spontaneous reformation. (*TGT*: 171)

Viewed through the concept of predistribution, Piketty's focus on r>g thus misses how much of the maldistribution of income is not the result of an internal law of capitalism but a result of politics and policy operating to shape original market outcomes. Indeed, from a Polanyian perspective the very fact of r>g is not a natural law but is itself a product of actions that consistently drive up the rate of return on capital in relationship to a lagging growth rate. So, for example, government antitrust policies have a sizeable impact on the rate of profit of large corporations. When antitrust policies are nonexistent or weakly enforced, established firms can extract monopoly profits by arbitrarily bidding up their prices. Those firms can claim, as big Pharma firms do today, that they are so profitable because they are superbly managed, but the reality is that predistribution is occurring. Their heightened profits reflect the power of 'law and economics' judicial policy to turn antitrust law upside down so it now condones and facilitates monopolies and oligopolies in the name of the Orwellian concept of 'consumer welfare' (Piraino, 2007; Crouch, 2011; Somers, 2012; Rahman, 2014, 2016;).

Polanyi's work corrects for *C21*'s chief analytic flaw, which ascribes to r>g – the causal force in generating inequality – the status of a fundamental economic law of capitalism. For Polanyi there are no economic laws of capitalism because capitalism is a political economic entity, which by definition is continuously co-created by historically variable political and economic powers. The concept of predistribution pierces the heart of neoliberalism's foundational deception that obscures the fact of power and coercion within the black box of the 'free market'.

Polanyi's political critique

But Polanyi is not merely a source of analytical insight; equally important, his socialist political economy, which includes the concept of predistribution, is also a necessary political corrective to *C21*'s failure to provide a convincing political strategy to combat massive inequality and a necessary weapon in the battle against neoliberalism more generally. In condensed form, one way of characterizing these differences is to contrast Polanyi's democratic socialism, with its clear goal not to tweak the effects of market inequality but to eradicate the malignancies at the core of the capitalist economy, against the classic weaknesses of Piketty's political program, which aims less at transforming the market itself and more at using government to correct its flaws after the fact.

One way that Polanyi's approach provides a more powerful challenge to neoliberalism than Piketty's is in the conceptualization of democracy. As an unabashed critic of egregious inequalities Piketty, like Polanyi, puts great stake in the power of democracy to combat both inequality as such and market fundamentalism more generally. Thus, while capitalism 'automatically generates arbitrary and unsustainable inequalities that radically undermine the meritocratic values on which democratic societies are based', Piketty expresses the hope that there are 'nevertheless ways democracy can regain control over capitalism' (*C21*: 10). But because his main proposal for regaining control is limited to using governments' redistributive tax capacities to impose a global wealth tax, Piketty restricts the mobilization of democratic forces to the public sphere and downplays their potential to exercise power inside the market itself. In this way, he inadvertently reproduces the conservative attack on democracy as a threat to the necessary firewall between politics and the economy, and thus defangs the real potential of democratic empowerment.

Polanyi's democratic socialist commitments manifest very differently. For him, 'Socialism is, essentially, the tendency inherent in an industrial civilization to transcend the self-regulating market by consciously subordinating it to a democratic society' (*TGT*: 242–243). Some of the ways that Polanyi envisions the power of democracy to disrupt and dethrone the putatively untouchable price mechanism at the heart of the neoliberal market include his ideas of guild socialism, socialist accounting methods and employee participation in the governance of the workplace as has been developed in systems of collective bargaining, works councils and codetermination, all of which challenge and 'violate' the fictitious firewall between market dynamics and democratic organization. To oppose monopoly, for example is to support an independent democratic citizenry against financial autocracy (Rahman, 2014). Despite the various strategic approaches in his socialist project, for Polanyi they all aim to strike at the heart of the market economy by decommodifying the fictitious commodities of labor, land and money, and removing them from being subordinated to the forces of marketization (*TGT*: 259–262; Block and Somers, 2014: ch. 8).

Thus, in his incisive rejection of the free market conception of 'freedom' (*TGT*: ch. 21), Polanyi argues that ideological demystification is a critical instrument of socialist critique. This is especially true in the case of predistribution. With so much at stake in the claim that market outcomes reflect impersonal natural market forces, the reality of a politically organized economy has been fiercely guarded from public scrutiny. Indeed, the unfamiliarity of the term 'predistribution' testifies to the successful depoliticization and naturalization of so-called primary market inequalities. Because they take place not in the public sphere of government 'coercive' agencies such as the Internal Revenue Service that collects taxes in the US, but inside the black box of the 'prepolitical' market, predistributive political practices effectively go unrecognized and market outcomes continue to be attributed to forces beyond our control.

One of predistribution's great political assets is precisely its demystifying capacity. It reveals how the singular focus on redistribution limits the presence of political coercion to the site of government, and thus falsely naturalizes unequal power in the market, a naturalization that can manifest in any argument from r>g to the impersonal forces of globalization, technology and automation. By demonstrating how it is free market advocates who peddle the myth that freedom depends on an economy unfettered by the yoke of governmental power, Polanyi helps explain the right wing's otherwise puzzlingly tenacious appeal: it offers an ideal of a world free of 'coercive' constraints on economic activities while it fiercely represses the fact that power and coercion are the unacknowledged features of all market participation.

Polanyi thus anticipates the critical power of predistribution to unveil the deception behind the self-serving claim on the part of economic liberals that markets are superior mechanisms of efficiency as well as of morality and freedom because they operate in a space free of power, coercion and domination. It is not nature but the invisible power and coercion of government that accounts for the disproportionate rewards going to a small sector of the population. Polanyi can then be mobilized to point to the predistributive government-driven war on unions launched by Reagan and Thatcher as setting the stage for the rapid increase in the share of income and wealth going to the top 1 per cent that Piketty and his colleagues have documented.

An essential political strategy to make this argument persuasive is to challenge the concept of 'deregulation', which is the watchword for those who celebrate the freedom they claim to be found in the sphere of the non-political free market. The conceit of deregulation is that there is a prepolitical market that if not for exogenous political interference would self-regulate efficiently like an organic entity. Deregulation then becomes defined as a project of *restoration* that frees the market to return to its natural state. But if we accept that predistribution is constitutive of all economies, then there is no such thing as a prepolitical market to be restored, and deregulation is impossible. What is possible, however, and what deregulation actually entails, is the replacement of more egalitarian regulations by alternative regulations that serve a different, distinctly inegalitarian purpose, such as protecting the claims of developers or corporate predators.

Taking Polanyian political economy seriously means using predistribution to redefine deregulations as re-regulations (Block and Somers, 2014). Because just as redistributive tax policies can be designed to advantage wealth and oligarchy or to foster more equality, even more so can predistributive policies be calibrated to guarantee that greater profits and earnings go either to the top of the economic ladder or to a more equitable structure of incomes. If regulations and predistribution are always necessary components of markets, the question becomes what kinds of regulations do we prefer? Do we want those designed to benefit wealth and capital? Or those that benefit the public and common good? Similarly, since the rights or lack of rights that employees have at the workplace are always defined by the legal system, we must not ask whether the law should organize the labor market, but rather what kinds of rules and rights should be entailed in these laws – those that recognize that it is the skills and talents of employees that make firms productive? Or those that rig the game in favor of employers and private profits?

A final way in which the Polanyian concept of predistribution provides a more powerful weapon against neoliberalism than Piketty's redistributive strategy is in its ability to puncture the moral high ground that has been monopolized by economic liberalism. Conservative and neoliberal political actors have peddled the myth of market meritocracy. This ideology posits that whatever the market produces in the way of income, wage or wealth inequalities is equivalent to differences in contributory effort and worth. In other words, people are paid in precise proportion to their level of hard work, effort and productivity, and thus earn exactly what they deserve. In the conservative playbook, unequal market outcomes thus represent a 'market justice' that is merit-based and not subject to the distorting powers of government coercion or political special interests. By contrast, it attributes the state's redistributive policies to calculations of 'social justice' that are entirely arbitrary, driven by envy of the rich, subject to the excesses of democratic entitlement as spelled out by public choice theory (Buchanan and Tullock, 1962) and ultimately coercive. And because redistribution entails government policy that violates the original merit of market justice, they view it as deeply illegitimate as well as an economically danger-ous distortion of market dynamics (Somers, 2017, 2018).

In this context a political strategy focused on redistribution reinforces the image of an economy free of political meddling whose market earnings accurately reflect the distribution of worth and desert. And while it is empirically the case that since the 1980s the majority of redistributive tax policy has redistributed upwards and vastly favored the highest earners, the language of redistribution is associated almost exclusively with the transfer of wealth from 'hard workers' (mostly white) to the 'lazy poor' (mostly minorities). This is decried as the government punishing – even stealing from – those whose often only minimally higher earnings reflect greater work effort, only to reward those whose low incomes indicate their lack of contributory worth. In the popular jargon of neoliberalism, the state illegitimately taxes the 'makers' to give to the 'takers' (Foroohar, 2016; MacLean, 2017; Somers, 2017). The strength and wide reach of this conservative assessment of redistributive taxation as little short of theft, combined with the overwhelmingly disproportionate political power of wealth, reveals that as a political attack on neoliberalism Piketty's global wealth tax flounders on the moral high ground of market meritocracy.

With its ability to burst the self-serving fiction of market meritocracy, Polanyi's socialist alternative once again benefits from the political power of predistributive analysis. Once we accept his argument that market outcomes are shaped not by individual effort, merit and desert but by politics, rules and power, it is much easier to understand his carefully constructed thesis that wealth and income are in fact not individually but collectively produced. This means that the privileges long associated with the control of wealth must ultimately be subject to Polanyi's deconstruction of their illicit foundations (*TGT*: 262–267).

Accounting for historical shifts in income distribution

Piketty recognizes that the period from about 1910 to 1970 was an exception to the trend of ever-growing inequality of income and wealth. His data clearly show a marked decline in both forms of inequality in the United Kingdom, France and the United States during these six decades. His explanation for this unusual pattern centers on disruptions caused by two world wars. His key explanation appears to be that the destruction of physical capital in the wars combined with war-induced budgetary and political shocks meant that the normal pattern of returns on capital investment could not be maintained (Piketty, 2014: 147–148).

Polanyi used institutional analysis to suggest a very different explanation that again centers on how government policies, including particularly predistributive policies, changed the nature of the economy from within. He demonstrates that the efforts in the last decades of the nineteenth century to organize a self-regulating global market through the gold standard created a powerful counter-movement in the form of a mass movement of working people organized through trade unions and socialist parties (*TGT*: 183–186). One of the main targets of this movement was the existing distribution of income and wealth and by 1910 these movements began exerting influence on policy-makers to enact policies to reduce economic inequality. This influence became particularly serious with the success of the Bolshevik Revolution and the continuing strength of the working-class movement in the decades before and after the Second World War.

Moreover, in the three decades immediately after the Second World War, the replacement of the gold standard with Bretton Woods created a global context in which governments had much greater leeway to enact policies that improved the distribution of income and wealth. In Europe and the US, both predistributive and redistributive policies in this period produced more egalitarian outcomes. However, with the shift from fixed exchange rates to floating exchange rates in 1973 and huge increases in international capital flows, that benign context disappeared and egalitarian policies were scrapped, so that income and wealth inequality started to climb again (Block and Somers, 2014).

In short, there is a political explanation for the changed pattern in the distribution of income and wealth that Piketty describes that is more compelling than his focus on the disruptions of war. Moreover, this alternative political explanation highlights the rise and fall of socialist movements and their trade union allies, an approach that is important in thinking about any possible challenge to the current pattern of increasing inequality. The fact that social movements were effective in the past in reducing the level of income and wealth inequality provides some grounds for imagining that they might be able to do the same thing again in the future. In contrast, Piketty's explanation offers little hope since nobody would be foolish enough to favor global warfare as the route to greater equality. Piketty's call for a global tax on wealth ends up sounding abstract and unrealistic, since he has failed to identify any actors who might have the capacity to overcome a logic that is built into the current economic system.

There is also a second Polanyian point that has to do with explaining the origins of the two world wars. Rather than seeing these as exogenous events, Polanyi sought to explain both wars as a consequence of choices made about the organization of the global economy. Polanyi rejected the Leninist argument that powerful financial interests drove Britain and Germany into imperialist expansion that ultimately made war inevitable. In fact, Polanyi argued on the contrary that global banking interests had served as a 'peace interest' that had worked assiduously to discourage a general European war during the Hundred Year Peace from Waterloo to Sarajevo (*TGT*: ch. 1).

Polanyi's alternative explanation for the First World War focuses on connections between a rising working-class movement and the mechanism of the international gold standard. Under the pressures of the gold standard, European powers could not afford to make significant concessions to the rising industrial working class either in the form of higher wages or protections against the periodic waves of unemployment that came during business cycle downturns. Instead, some governments chose to insulate their economies from the pressures of the gold standard by imposing tariffs on foreign goods. Even this was not enough; virtually all the major European powers in the last decades of the nineteenth century turned to colonialism as another strategy of protection. Those colonies with resources could produce a revenue stream that could help stabilize the home economy and the colonies also provided safe markets for domestic products. In Polanyi's argument, the rush to empire at the end of the nineteenth century was an effort to manage the growing class divide at home.

The search for lucrative colonies brought Germany into direct conflict with Britain and the result was an arms race as each of these powers sought to intimidate its opponent. The antagonism also froze Europe into two competing alliances that disrupted the balance-of-power mechanism that had kept the European peace for a century. In this account, the assassination in Sarajevo was just the spark; the European war was an inevitable consequence of the growing class divide within Britain and Germany that could not be ameliorated because the gold standard had taken on the status of a virtually necessary fact of nature.

Polanyi went on to argue that after the First World War, European leaders made the horrendous mistake of trying to restore the gold standard. This deeply flawed decision led directly to the Great Depression, the rise of fascism and the Second World War (ibid.: ch. 2). So, in Polanyi's view, the exceptional period that Piketty identifies from 1910 to 1970 can be seen as a direct consequence of the rise of the industrial working class and the pressure it was able to exert on political elites to pursue both predistributive and redistributive policies that shifted income away from the top 1 percent.

Moreover, this alternative Polanyian context highlights the importance of political interventions such as the decision to abandon the Bretton Woods regime of fixed exchange rates in 1973 that worked to tilt national politics away from social democrats and towards market liberals. It was in this different global context that Margaret Thatcher and Ronald Reagan were able to change tax, regulatory and social policies in ways that shifted both pre-tax and post-tax income towards the wealthiest households. The impact of these policies, including the rapid growth of the financial sector, continues down to the present.

Transformations in what the economy produces

While Piketty provides many trenchant criticisms of the weaknesses of mainstream economics, there is yet another way in which his mode of analysis replicates these shortcomings. Conventional economic analysis pays very little attention to what a market economy produces; the assumption is that whether the principal product of an economy is foodstuffs, automobiles or computer chips is irrelevant. Production is production; whatever the product, it requires some mix of capital, labor and raw materials and those details do not matter in understanding the important questions. Piketty basically follows this same logic when he uses an umbrella concept of capital that includes land, slaves, machinery, factories and a wide range of different financial instruments.

But Polanyi insisted in *The Great Transformation* that it was the shift from agriculture to manufacturing in the early decades of the nineteenth century that drove the momentous transformation in the role of markets in society. He argued that markets had existed throughout most of human history, but what was new and unique in Britain in the nineteenth century was the creation of a self-regulating market system to govern the production and sale of all commodities, including the fictitious commodities of land, labor and money. For Polanyi, the project of creating a self-regulating market system was indelibly connected to the rise of factory production itself. For him, the reality of industrialization was central to the dynamic he was describing (ibid.: ch. 6).

The Great Transformation was published in 1944, probably the year in which the industrial working class in the US reached its peak size and far too early for any discussions of a post-industrial era. But in a newly available manuscript from 1958, Polanyi (2014a: 32) explicitly uses the term 'postindustrial' – around the same time that others including Daniel Bell and David Riesman were initially using this term (Bell, [1973] 1976: 37). From the context, it seems that Polanyi was using the term in reference to the tightening interconnections among science, technology and production.

The timing is not surprising since the late 1950s saw a great deal of debate about automation and the potential for job loss. From our current vantage point, the factory automation of that time appears quite primitive. However, the advances made it possible for a constant or declining industrial workforce to produce an

225

ever-expanding flow of goods. Moreover, these early steps towards automation pointed towards a future in which the industrial working class would shrink in size and lose much of its political clout. While this single reference is hardly enough to recruit Karl Polanyi as a theorist of postindustrialism, his approach to analyzing the economy indicates that for him the question of what is being produced is of central importance. This is what motivates Polanyi to make his critical distinction between the formal and the substantive meaning of economics (Polanyi, 1968: ch. 7). The former focused on the problem of economizing scarce resources while the latter analyzed how human communities secured their livelihoods. It followed that whether people were hunter-gatherers or engaged in settled agriculture or secured much of their food from the sea or depended on factory jobs made a huge difference in how their societies were organized.

Building on this insight today requires understanding distinct economic periods that occur as a market economy adjusts to changes in technology and production. One of the most useful theorizations along these lines is the argument developed by Social Structures of Accumulation scholars (Gordon, Edwards and Reich, 1982; Kotz, McDonough and Reich, 1994). Building on the analyses of long cycles of Kondratiev and Schumpeter, they make the argument that as the outputs of a market economy change over time, earlier social structures become obsolete and turn into barriers to further economic development. This happened with the global economic crisis of the 1930s. The rapid advances in industrial productivity in the US in the 1920s helped precipitate the crisis as the combination of electrification and the assembly line facilitated the mass production of consumer durable goods such as automobiles and appliances. These capacities erupted in an economy that had not yet created the institutions required for a mass consumption economy, and the result was the deep crisis of the Great Depression (Block, 2015).

The New Deal and post-Second World War reforms created new social struc-tures of accumulation and the results were the *trentes glorieuse* – the thirty years of global economic growth from 1945 to 1975. This was based on a mass consumption economy in the developed nations that relied heavily on individualized household consumption through suburbanization, the automobile and the purchase of vari-ous other appliances. While the resulting pattern of growth intensified pre-existing inequalities of gender and race, it did not involve the upward trend in income and wealth inequality that would characterize the period from 1980 onward (ibid.).

However, this mass consumption structure of accumulation had begun to reach its limits by the mid-1960s. One set of problems centered on the structure of employ-ment as the need for factory labor began to shrink as a consequence of technological advances such as automation. Another set of problems were environmental since the suburban pattern of growth was wasteful and energy-intensive. There were also cultural shifts that influenced demand as women revolted against the homemaker role and young people rejected the suburban lifestyle. Finally, the business class in the US was disoriented as it suddenly faced intensive competition as a result of the successful rebuilding of the European and Japanese economies.

The resulting crisis in the 1970s provided an opportunity for the long-time critics of Keynesian fiscal policy and New Deal social policy to claim the high ground. There was a period of heated debate about the types of restructuring that would be necessary to restart growth. Some liberal analysts talked about a postindustrial transition and the need for new forms of social and economic planning to redirect investment in more productive ways. But the political forces behind progressive reform were divided and weakened by the extent of the economic crisis, and they were unable to win support for their approach. In the context of continuing economic difficulties, the emerging neoliberal right was able to step in and offer a much simpler and business-friendly solution. They argued that tax cuts, reduced government civilian spending and laxer regulation of business were all that was needed to restore economic growth. With the electoral victories of Margaret Thatcher and Ronald Reagan, neoliberalism or market fundamentalism became enshrined as the dominant policy for the next forty years (Block and Somers, 2014: ch. 7).

It was a policy designed to squeeze additional life out of the mass consumption social structure of accumulation while using both redistributive and predistributive measures to reverse the more egalitarian distribution of income that had made the New Deal settlement effective. So, for example, thanks to continuing tax incentives for home ownership, single-family residential homebuilding continued to be one of the main drivers of the economy even while the trend towards urban living accelerated. At the same time, the long-term decline in unionization rates accelerated and government spending on civilian services was squeezed at both the federal level and at the state and local levels.

Logically, this economic strategy should not have worked at all, and, in fact, on most measures the performance of the economy was considerably worse than it had been in the thirty post-Second World War years. There were economic expansions in the 1980s and 1990s, but by the 2000s expansion had become much weaker. Two factors are most important for explaining why this contradictory economic policy had some successes. First, to sustain demand economic growth became far more dependent on increases in consumer debt, primarily through increased home mortgage borrowing. This was, of course, facilitated by a continuous rise in home prices that made this 'privatized Keynesianism' of increasing household indebtedness appear to be sustainable (Schwartz, 2009; Crouch, 2011). It was not, of course, and the severity of the crisis that unfolded between 2007 and 2009 was a consequence of the huge number of homeowners who owed more on their houses than the post-downturn market price.

Secondly, the expansion in the 1980s and 1990s was facilitated by the positive shock of the emergence of the personal computer and the internet as drivers of both consumer and business demand. Both of these technologies were products of the 'hidden developmental state' in the US (Block, 2008). Years of under-the-radar government funding of research and early-stage technology companies had nurtured these technologies. Moreover, the huge global advantage that came to the US from being the first mover in these markets has helped to sustain the US economy ever since.

Nevertheless, the severity of the 2007–9 global financial crisis indicated that the strategy of trying to squeeze additional life out of an exhausted social structure of accumulation had reached its limits. Moreover, since the crisis there has been no significant shift in public policies; if anything, economic policies have intensified distributional inequity. This is most evident in the global economy that has teetered at the edge of renewed recession for more than ten years since the crisis.

The problem of growing income and wealth inequality is therefore closely linked to the absence of new economic policies to support a new period of sustainable global growth. Since the 1970s, conservative resistance to building a new social structure of accumulation has driven the spectacular and continuous growth of income and wealth inequality. Moreover, without reversing the current trend of income and wealth inequality it is going to be almost impossible to address the problem of how to renew growth.

The implications are that Piketty's preferred policy proposals, including redistributive taxation, would gain greater resonance if he analyzed the post-1970s trend in inequality in relation to a theory of changing social structures of accumulation. The reforms of the 1930s and 1940s were implemented precisely because they simultaneously addressed the injustice of entrenched economic inequality *and* the need to restore economic growth. This combination made it possible to construct an unstoppable pro-growth coalition that stretched from the poor to some parts of the business class. Constructing such a coalition is the urgent task we face today with the additional complexity that such a coalition must be committed to immediate and radical action to halt and reverse global climate change (Block, 2018b).

Finally, adding a Polanyian dimension to Piketty alerts us to the danger in our current circumstances. The dystopia that Piketty warns against is an entrenched global oligarchy that is able to control an ever-growing share of the planet's wealth. But Polanyi's analysis of the 1920s and 1930s tells us that when established business and political elites are unable to protect populations from high levels of economic instability and uncertainty, the threat of fascist movements, authoritarianism and war becomes increasingly severe (*TGT*: 245–268). And indeed, in the few years since Piketty's book was published, the global retreat from democracy has accelerated and neo-fascists are on the march around the world.

Conclusion

To recap, our initial concerns are that Piketty's discovery of r>g as an inherent feature of a capitalist economy obscures an essential dimension of the inequality he seeks to explain, namely the predistributive political policies and practices that take place inside that economy. Politically, we worry that Piketty's adoption of the standard picture of an autonomous economic dynamic inadvertently reinforces the dominant belief that market outcomes, however unequal they may be, nonetheless derive exclusively from natural market forces and contributory merit. For the state to then act in the name of 'social justice' to redistribute what has been meritoriously earned is thus convincingly represented as the coercive powers of an unjust arbitrary government, which in turn generates a radical anti-statist reaction against the 'takers'. This perception, despite resting on specious foundational assumptions about the impersonal market sources of primary income distribution, makes support for Piketty's global wealth tax almost inconceivable.

Our intention in subjecting *Capital in the 21ˢᵗ Century* to a Polanyian critique is not to demean Piketty's remarkable achievement; even less is it to suggest that Polanyi had the answers to all important questions of political economy. However, Polanyi's institutional analysis is an absolutely indispensable tool for the urgent project of developing a critical political economy, one that can break through the mystification that endows the economy with natural powers that must, at all cost, be walled off from the 'distorting' influence and 'coercion' of governmental, politics and social norms – in short, the *demos*. It is absolutely essential, even for progressive analyses such as Piketty's, to analyze economic processes and primary market outcomes not independently of politics and power but as fundamentally constituted and determined by them.

While it remains essential to advocate for redistributional policies such as taxes on wealth to correct for the market's profound distributional inequities, this approach, by itself, is not however sufficient. We must instead follow Polanyi all the way into the heart of the economy to find the source of that maldistribution in an institutionalized complex of deeply regressive but unrecognized rules and relations of power. Only by forcing those to the surface and out of the shadows can we regain the moral high ground by asking not the question of whether we prefer government or market solutions, but rather what kind of predistributive policies do we want to shape economic processes. Do we want the political organization of the market to advantage only the 1 percent, or do we want it to advance the common good?

Notes

1 For an extensive discussion of how Polanyi's theory of market utopianism lays the groundwork for the modern concept of predistribution, see Somers (2017b).
2 We are grateful to Radhika Desai for this reference.
3 The state's support for the Ten Hours Act was also the subject of Marx's famous chapter on 'The working day' in Volume One of *Capital*.

11

Karl Polanyi as a precursor of world-systems theorists: an investigation of the theoretical lineage to Giovanni Arrighi

Chikako Nakayama

This chapter investigates the theoretical borrowings made by Giovanni Arrighi, one of the world-systems theorists, from the main work of Karl Polanyi, *The Great Transformation* (hereinafter *TGT*), published in 1944. The theoretical borrowings appear in Arrighi's later work including *The Long Twentieth Century* published in 1994, *Adam Smith in Beijing* published in 2007, several articles from the 1990s and his collaborative works with Beverly J. Silver or with other – including East Asian – collaborators around the same time. Arrighi's last two books contributed much to understanding of the structure of the world economy and conflict within it, and they have been translated and read world-wide, including in the East Asian countries.

We focus on Arrighi's statement that those familiar with Polanyi's classic explanation of the rise and demise of nineteenth-century laissez-faire capitalism 'cannot help but be struck by its anticipation of present arguments about the contradictions of globalization' (Arrighi, 1999a: 57). Much earlier, Arrighi and Silver had commented on how *TGT* had been 'attracting a growing number of admirers in the context of late twentieth and early twenty-first century "globalization"' (Silver and Arrighi, 2003: 325).[1]

While Arrighi's work has drawn on many sources aside from Polanyi, and it is possible to exaggerate Polanyi's influence, we find it worthwhile to clarify what Arrighi borrowed from Polanyi in the context of world-systems theory, of which Arrighi was a principal representative, along with Immanuel Wallerstein, the main organiser of the discipline (Yamashita, 2011: 590), Andre Gunder Frank and Samir Amin.

Goldfrank had already underlined Polanyi's influence on world-systems theory when, in his discussion of the intellectual sources of world-systems theory focusing on Wallerstein's education in the intellectual atmosphere of Columbia University in the 1950s, where Polanyi also taught, he pointed out that 'economic anthropologist,

Karl Polanyi, made a … fundamental contribution to world systems analysis' (Goldfrank, 2000: 161).[2] He compared Polanyi's contribution to those of Josef Alois Schumpeter, Max Weber and the German Historical School. According to him, the German Historical School, the Annales in French historiography and Marxism were three major traditions in Western social science 'in opposition to the dominant strain of Anglo-American liberalism and positivism' (ibid.: 160). In fact, Wallerstein himself expressed his indebtedness to Polanyi as one of his inspirations, along with Braudel, Karl Marx and several Marxists (Wallerstein, 2004: ch. 1).

In contrast to Wallerstein, Arrighi did not have any personal contact with Polanyi. According to his autobiographical interview (Arrighi, 2009a), Arrighi first studied neoclassical economics but was gradually influenced by social anthropology and Marxism. He went to Rhodesia early in his university teaching career but became political there and was expelled. That was when he met Wallerstein in Tanzania in 1966, though they did not begin working together on world-systems theory until 1979. Before that, Arrighi returned to his native Italy at the end of the 1960s and committed himself to politics as one of the founding members of Gruppo Gramsci and Autonomia, until he moved to the United States in 1979. In the treatise he published the year before (Arrighi, 1978), we see many quotations from *TGT*, though we do not have biographical evidence of exactly when Arrighi became acquainted with Polanyi's writings.

In this chapter, we distinguish two stages of Polanyi's influence on Arrighi. In the first stage, Arrighi borrowed from Polanyi's attention to haute finance and backward regions, as well as from his consideration of imperialism and uneven development, In Arrighi's 1978 treatise, *TGT* was one of the important references. The second stage of influence began after Arrighi's decisive encounter with Braudel. Taking Braudel's perspective into consideration, Arrighi re-examined the intellectual resources of economic sociology and rediscovered the potentiality of Polanyi's ideas for world-systems theory.

Recently, Gareth Dale numbered Arrighi among the social scientists influenced by Marx and Polanyi, stating, 'In my view the most impressive and unquestionably the grandest attempt to knit Polanyian concepts into a systematic analysis of modern history is his [Arrighi's] *The Long Twentieth Century*' (Dale, 2010a: 222). While not many other works have traced this relationship, Desai's *Geopolitical Economy* is sympathetic to the works of Polanyi as well as Arrighi and world-systems theorists, and Desai found Polanyi's contribution to be part of 'the political economy on which geopolitical economy must rest' (Desai, 2013: 30). It would be safe to say that this indirectly endorses our assertion.

Problems around the concept of imperialism

As Arrighi himself attested, there was an important turning point in his research interests around the end of the 1970s. Later, he recalled his discontent with the confusion around the concept of imperialism: 'I was disturbed, at that time, by the terminological confusions that were swirling around the term "imperialism". My aim [in *The Geometry of Imperialism*] was to dissipate some of the confusion. ... But as an exercise on imperialism, yes, it also functioned as a transition to the concept of hegemony for me' (Arrighi, 2009a: 70). A later explication reinforces this point: 'It follows from this argument [of 1978] that the very theories of "imperialism" that had been most successful in predicting trends in the first half of the twentieth century had become hopelessly obsolete' (Arrighi, 2003: 35). In this way, Arrighi made a close inspection of Hobson's idea of imperialism and came to recognise the importance of the concept of hegemony, which led him to analysis within the framework of world-systems theory. In this section, we are going to examine some of the catalytic roles Polanyi played in this transition.

The role of haute finance and non-economic influences on backward regions

Imperialism was one of the key concepts for the Marxists among Polanyi's contemporaries, pre-eminently for Lenin. And for that reason, this concept was also important for Polanyi. However, Hobson, one of the social liberals of their time, was apparently not as important. Though Hobson's book on imperialism (1902) exerted much influence on Lenin it did not emerge in *TGT* much, except for one humble appearance in a footnote about 'Finance and peace' (Polanyi, [1944] 2001: 275–276).

Nevertheless, this connection is important given Polanyi's emphasis on 'the influence of Wall Street on developments in the 1920s' (ibid.: 276) and, generally, on the importance of international finance and its complex relationship to peace in *TGT*. Polanyi had been investigating this connection since the 1920s, when he was much influenced by the English guild socialists Hobson was close to through his involvement in the peace movement.

Peace being sought for its own sake, then, became one of the main concerns of *TGT*,[3] so that we can see at least some resonance between Polanyi and Hobson.

Polanyi used the term 'imperialism' several times in *TGT*. In it, the term referred to 'colonial crimes' (ibid.: 16) as well as a general 'stranglehold on backward regions, in order to invest in railways, public utilities, ports, and other permanent establishments on which their [the Western Powers] heavy industries made profits' (ibid.: 16). Polanyi noted that Lenin held that finance capital was 'the chief instigator' (ibid.: 16) of colonial crimes and distanced himself from such 'popular Marxism' (ibid.: 158),[4] in which 'imperialism was explained as a capitalist conspiracy to induce governments to launch wars in the interests of big business' (ibid.: 158). Against them, he asserted that 'Actually, business and finance were responsible for many colonial wars, but also for the fact that a general conflagration was avoided' (ibid.: 16).

Polanyi admitted that colonial wars were caused by finance capital but argued that haute finance also contributed to maintaining peace between the last third of the nineteenth and the first third of the twentieth century. 'They were anything but pacifists. … But their business would be impaired if a general war between the Great Powers should interfere with the monetary foundations of the system. By the logic of facts it fell to them to maintain the requisites of general peace' (ibid.: 11).

According to Polanyi, such peace was the by-product of increasing international free trade in the nineteenth century. However, after the end of the First World War, the League of Nations, proposed by American President Woodrow Wilson to ensure peace, appeared 'to have realized the interdependence of peace and trade, not only as a guarantee of trade, but also of peace. No wonder the League persistently strove to reconstruct the international currency and credit organization as the only possible safeguard of peace among sovereign states, and that the world relied as never before on haute finance, now represented by J. P. Morgan instead of N. M. Rothchild' (ibid.: 23). He indicated that the post-war international institutions were attempts to re-establish a pre-1914 system and that 'belief in the gold standard was the faith of the age' (ibid.: 26).

Here lies the connection between Polanyi and Arrighi. The crisis of the gold standard in the 1930s thus signalled the great transformation. And this crisis was an important theme for Arrighi's treatise in 1978. Furthermore, in 1994 it was examined by Arrighi as one of the central elements of his analysis of the twentieth century from a longer historical perspective, which we will examine later.

Polanyi's focus on backward regions in the capitalist system was another connection with Arrighi. Polanyi referred to the ensuing destruction and degradation as a social calamity (ibid.: 164), whose outlines he first traced in his consideration of English society around the time of the Poor Laws, followed by concrete cases of cultural debasement of South African tribes and of the exploitation of India and American Indians (ibid.: 300–303). This part is important as not only the germ of an economic anthropological analysis but also as the essence of Polanyi's understanding of imperialism.

The case of India in the second half of the nineteenth century deserves particular attention. Polanyi argued that Indian people 'did not die of hunger because they were exploited by Lancashire … The three or four large famines that decimated India under British rule since the Rebellion were … simply a [consequence] of the new market organization of labor and land which broke up the old village without actually resolving its problems' (ibid.: 167–168). He judged that 'Economically, India may have been – and, in the long run, certainly was – benefited, but socially she was disorganized and thus thrown as prey to misery and degradation' (ibid.: 168).

Just as his focus on the market organisation of society, particularly the three fictitious commodities, contested the Marxist conception of exploitation, so Polanyi also privileged market organisation as the explanation for India's suffering. He considered the theory of exploitation an economistic prejudice. While Polanyi's focus remained on the rise and decline of world capitalism, his analysis did not neglect backward regions and the general structure and character of capitalistic domination. As we shall examine later, Polanyi seemed to have already nurtured this idea in the 1930s.

Arrighi's investigation of imperialism

Arrighi's 1978 treatise was explicitly an exploration of Hobson's theory of imperialism and its limits. In a relatively long introduction, starting with a short examination of Lenin's term 'monopoly stage of capitalism', Arrighi indicated that it failed to account for fundamental differences in the socioeconomic formation of each case and that the notion of a constant tendency to war and rivalry between capitalist countries on a politico-military level no longer appeared relevant. Arrighi indicated that 'diverse terms (imperialism, monopoly capital, finance capital, etc.) come to designate different, and even antithetical, phenomena: war and peace, suppression and reactivation of market competition, portfolio and direct investment, and so on' (Arrighi, 1978: 17), making it necessary to go beyond Lenin.

Arrighi went into a detailed investigation of Hobson, who 'referred especially to late nineteenth century England' (ibid.: 24), and of Hilferding, who mainly analysed the European continent, particularly Germany, both of whom were sources of Lenin's work. Noting that the former focused on supranational finance and the latter on national, he decided to take a stance closer to Hobson, and Polanyi had a hand in this decision as well. Arrighi stated that 'I am referring to Polanyi's authoritative account which stresses, like Hobson's study, the supranational character of high finance, but … defines it as the principal factor of peace operating among the

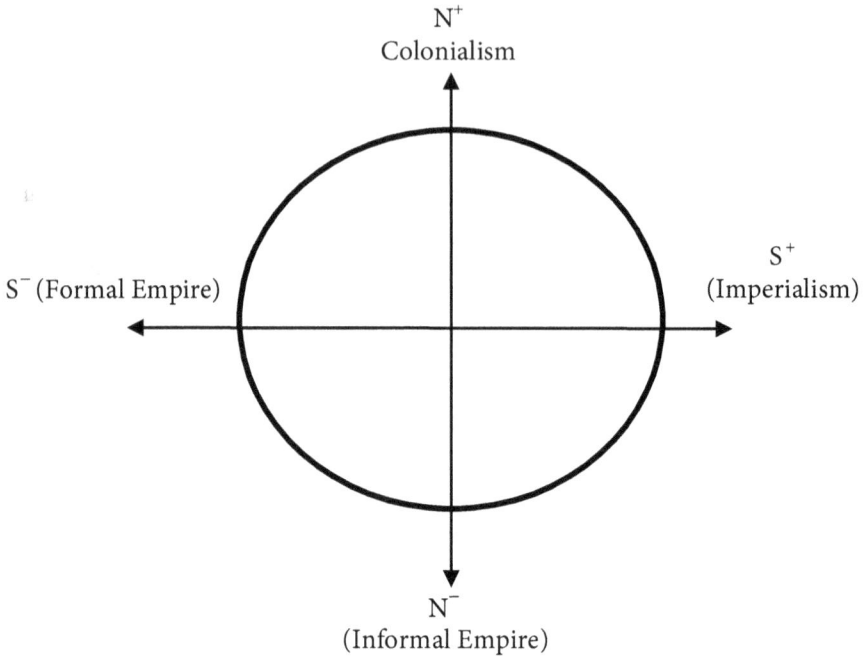

$$N^+$$
Colonialism

S^- (Formal Empire)

S^+
(Imperialism)

$$N^-$$
(Informal Empire)

11.1. The coordinates of Arrighi's 1978 analysis of imperialism and hegemony

Source: Adapted by the author from Arrighi (1978, Figures 1:43 and 3:51).

great powers in the second half of the nineteenth century' (ibid.: 121). Here, we see Polanyi's deliberation on peace revived in Arrighi's thought.

Further, Arrighi inspected Hobson's diagnosis of a tendency for under-consumption, comparing it with Lenin's idea, and attempted to prove the validity of Hobson's idea through his unique geometrical tool, which he devised to over-come the problem of historical and empirical validity of concepts and theories (see Figure 11.1). Arrighi considered this device a Weberian ideal-typical construction of a genetic nature, drawing on historico-empirical materials and utilising four elements of Hobson's analysis – colonialism, formal empire, informal empire and imperialism – as 'distinctions and oppositions … to be conceived as co-ordinates of a topological or structural space' (ibid.: 27–28).[5] In this way, he disassembled several aspects of imperialism. Focusing on the case of England in the nineteenth century, he carefully analysed their mutual relations and conflicting natures.

Plotting them along two dimensions, he showed the internally contradictory elements in the idea of imperialism. Arrighi defined the x-axis as the positive and negative extensions of states and the y-axis as those of nations. For the indicator

of the negative direction of the y-axis, he replaced Hobson's element of internationalism with 'informal empire', which meant economic interdependence, or 'an
informal order among free and independent nations, assuring their harmony of
interests through peaceful interchange of goods and ideas' (ibid.: 40) in a world
dominated by nationalism. In addition, the element of inclusion of migration was
considered here. In contrast to these, the indicator of its positive direction was
shown as colonialism, whose image was antagonistic expansion of a single nation
with 'dictatorial political rule' (ibid.: 38), accentuating exclusivism or 'the exclusion
of an old local culture' (ibid.: 42) and xenophobia. These were signs of national
expansion of opposite directions.

The x-axis was used for improving Hobson's image of imperialism. Its positive
direction corresponded to imperialism in the sense of 'expansion of the State' (ibid.:
44), which was counter-posed 'to Formal Empire by virtue of that anarchy of its interstate relations which tends towards universal war' (ibid.: 44). He then added brief
explanations of some concrete, historical changes and progress in several examples,
from Habsburg and the Ottoman Empires to Britain, the United States and Germany,
with the centrifugal and centripetal vectors of both axes. In this way, Arrighi laid a
geometrical foundation for understanding the various ways in which a given power
may act in the 'assertion of its *hegemony* over the international system' (ibid.: 50).

Then, Arrighi analysed historical descriptions of Hobson, using trajectory lines
and quadrants in the basic figure for the change of English world hegemony. Each
chapter of his treatise, the articulation, the reduplication and the dissolution,
respectively, discussed English imperialism, then the catching up of the United
States and German imperialism and then the destruction of this competing structure. We notice that the whole structure of this treatise was devoted mostly to the
analysis of English hegemony until its declining phase in the inter-war period,
which overlapped with the theme of *TGT* considerably.

Arrighi's emphasis was on demonstrating the prescience of Hobson's analysis;
that is, even though Hobson's book was published long before the critical phase
of dissolution in the 1930s, Hobson foresaw what would happen in the next stage
of the inter-war period: 'Hobson was proposing that England should anticipate
the time of its inevitable decline as a great power, to avoid exacerbating politico-
military rivalry between states' (ibid.: 79). In explaining the significance of Hobson,
Arrighi quoted Polanyi's *TGT* several times. This might have been because Arrighi
found the collapse of the gold standard to be 'the central event of this process [the
definitive breakdown]' (ibid.: 75).

Aside from Arrighi's emphasis on the importance of finance capital, referring to
TGT in this analysis is remarkable. In the last chapter, Arrighi introduced a third

dimension into the coordinates, the element of finance capital or high finance, which was, in Hobson's view, a 'supranational entity lying outside the plane defined by the expansion of the nation-state, while … it nevertheless influences [the plane] in a critical manner' (ibid.: 117). Arrighi designated it in the geometry as the z-axis. Quoting Hobson's idea of finance capitalism, he saw the investors 'both politically and economically … formed only the cat's paws of the great financial houses' (ibid.: 116). Arrighi explained that Hobson had evaluated these financial houses or high finance as the real governors of the imperial engine and as the supranational entity.

Clearly, the important concept with which Polanyi had struggled was highlighted by Arrighi via the analysis of Hobson. Though Arrighi initially contrasted Polanyi and Hobson, he went on to reconcile them: 'The contradiction between these two points of view reflected an effective contradiction within high finance itself' (ibid.: 122).

At this stage, Arrighi was shifting his focus from imperialism to the concept of hegemony, which led him to fruitful research and collaboration with other world-systems theorists in the 1980s. Later, in the 1990s, he gradually came back to this theme and re-read Polanyi's *TGT* with a deeper perspective than before and with consideration of a longer time span than *TGT* itself.

Embeddedness in analysing the declining hegemony of Britain

So, how did Polanyi see the decline of British hegemony? From the late 1920s to the middle of the 1940s, he wrote and published many short articles on topical matters, especially on the situation of British politics and economy, as well as on its international relations. These observations made by Polanyi were integrated into the analysis of *TGT* published in 1944 and then revised in 1957.

Arrighi might not have directly examined those articles, but he did investigate *TGT* for his treatise in 1978, so Polanyi's observations would have been indirectly known. We focus on the point that Polanyi had found the embeddedness of economic factors in a society through these observations and also put this concept in the analysis of England in *TGT*. This concept, then, played a decisive role in Arrighi's analysis later in the 1990s.[6] As indicated by Dale (2010a: 191), Polanyi first used this concept in German in an article on Lancashire published in 1934, where he explained that 'no labor condition could be grasped without the social condition in which it lies embedded' ([1934] 2002c: 239).[7] This concept shows the uniqueness of each society, its culture and its morals, and hence its different way of carrying out its economic activities.

Polanyi's articles on Lancashire in *Österreichische Volkswirt*, written shortly after he emigrated to England,[8] might have been contemporary reports as a correspondent for the journal, but they vividly showed Polanyi's recognition that British liberal capitalism was undergoing profound changes. Lancashire had been the symbol of the British origins of free trade. It had specialised in the cotton industry since the industrial revolution, but around the 1930s it confronted an uncomfortable declining phase as competition from new producers, especially India and Japan, stiffened. Polanyi argued that Britain would have to change the economic system and hence its hegemony, thus also ending 'a period of the most meaningful economic history' (Polanyi, [1934] 2002a: 231).

Certainly, the post-First World War period witnessed India progress towards independence and Lancashire losing its hold over India. Around the 1930s, the problem of Indian constitutional reform was discussed (e.g. Dewey, 1978: 36; Wurm, 1993: 236–237), and India's economic catching-up and anti-colonial resistance was threatening the hegemonic order of Great Britain. And for India, the rise and presence of the Japanese cotton industry indirectly meant the improvement of Indian bargaining power (Kitani, 2006: 657–658). Polanyi did not seem to be fully aware of this structure of mutual interdependence, but did mention both India and Japan and knew that Lancashire's problems came more from India than from Japan: 'the biggest blow against Lancashire's export was, as everyone knows, led not by Japan but by India' (Polanyi, [1934] 2002c: 247).

How was Lancashire to face this competition? One option was to adopt the competition's techniques. This was where the concept of embeddedness came in. Polanyi warned that it would not be wise to transplant or graft the Japanese system of labour onto Lancashire, even if the productivity of the former should far surpass that of the latter (Polanyi, [1934] 2002b: 232–233).[9] While Polanyi noted the great productivity of Japan, its imperviousness to crises, its backup system for labourers through the clan or the family-like organisation with some kind of collective consumption (Polanyi, [1934] 2002c: 239), he argued that Japanese labour conditions were embedded in their culture, ethics and civilisation and could not simply be separated and grafted somewhere else.

Rather than using the 'Japanese threat' as an indolent excuse to avoid confronting the reality of the declining economy (Polanyi, [1934] 2002b: 231–232), Polanyi felt England needed to radically overhaul its technical equipment and undertake radical change in the organisation of production in the factories (Polanyi, [1934] 2002c: 238). While he cautioned against promoting American or other methods of innovation and automation (ibid.: 241), he also noted that in comparison to technical innovations in machines and automation in America, as well as Japan's rapid adaptation of them, the British cotton industry was far behind (ibid.: 240). He found the problem of finance more serious, and still worse was the fact that it was not discussed in England (ibid.: 246).

One work about the industrial situation of the time discusses a speech by the then president of the Manchester Chamber of Commerce and points out that 'British cotton manufacturers were convinced that they were faced with a competition based on foundations which were wholly different from those of the West' (Wurm, 1993: 205). Polanyi was likely aware, if not of the speech, at least of the conviction it expressed, when he asked whether the social organisation of the Orient might possibly be superior in the late capitalistic phase (Polanyi, [1934] 2002c: 236).

The purpose of these reflections was not to highlight any conflict between the West and the Orient but, rather, to formulate this problem as one for the whole of humanity. This was evident in the title of the article, 'Lancashire as a question of humanity' (ibid.). In its conclusion, Polanyi emphasised that it was critical for Japan as well as European countries not to fall into political degeneration in the face of the severe crisis of the liberal capitalistic system of Europe (ibid.: 247–248).

As Polanyi saw it, the indispensable element for sustaining English hegemony, India, was slipping from its grasp, and other powers, like Japan, were emerging. Polanyi also became more sceptical of the merits of Western culture in general, as many unpublished papers and memos of the time show. Finally, in 'For a new West' (Polanyi, 2014a: 29–32) after the Second World War, he indicated 'the barrenness of the cultural West in its encounter with the world at large' (ibid.: 29), explaining that 'what matters here is not the level of its achievements in science or the arts … but the weight of its mind and life values as measured by the rest of mankind' (ibid.: 29). Arrighi expressed a similar view around the turn of the twentieth century.

Reconstruction in the context of globalisation

We now turn to Arrighi's rediscovery of Polanyi. While the decisive factor was arguably his encounter with Braudel, this was strengthened by two further elements: Arrighi's elaboration of the third category in the centre–periphery structure of world-systems theory, the semi-periphery, and the end of the Cold War, which integrated his East and South into a new area. Arrighi's strong sympathy for those two areas motivated him to revise his own version of world-systems theory.

During his years of collaboration with Wallerstein and other world-systems analysts, Arrighi put considerable energy into elaborating the 'intermediate position' (Arrighi and Drangel, 1986: 9) between the centre (hegemony) and the periphery, the semi-periphery. This category contained many different regions. On the one hand, it could contain a potentially rising centre that was increasing its power to become the next hegemon, as America had against the British hegemony, and then Asian countries against the American hegemony in the 1980s. This category was important for Arrighi's investigations of the mechanism of shifting hegemony.

On the other hand, there were more humble regions confronting the risk of falling into the periphery, which brought him to investigations of the persistent or growing inequality within the world system. In order to ground these ideas, he also used quantitative methods to compare historical data on GNP and other measures. In one article, for example, he examined the West–East divide and the North–South divide (Arrighi, 1991: 39).[10] In conducting such examinations, he came to be closely acquainted with East Asian researchers.[11]

Though he had already placed the former USSR and the Eastern Bloc in the category of semi-periphery in 1986 (Arrighi and Drangel, 1986: 10), the end of communism came as a blow to Arrighi, as it did to all those who had any serious concern with Marxism, socialism or communism. Arrighi contributed to the reflections on the future of socialism and communism that followed in many symposia and seminars. However, he was cautious about the emerging catchword of 'globalisation', claiming that 'it has in fact been a recurrent tendency of world capitalism since early-modern times' (Arrighi, 1999a: 53). This was the angle from which, Arrighi felt, world-systems theory could contribute to the analysis of 'globalisation', even though the mainstream interest had 'a different genealogy and thrust' (Arrighi, 1998: 115).

We now turn to the decisive influence of Braudel on Arrighi, and then the deepening of Arrighi's consideration of the semi-periphery into some comparative studies within the framework of economic sociology.

Decisive influence of Braudel

It is clear from Arrighi's writings that he was decisively influenced by Braudel's trilogy on the modern world, *Civilization and Capitalism*. In it, Braudel distinguished between everyday life or material civilisation as a first layer, the world of market economy as a second layer and capitalism as a third layer.[12] This led Arrighi to a new stage of analysis, first in collaboration with Wallerstein and then, gradually, independently. And as he began to explore rich sources of economic and social theories, he rediscovered Polanyi.

Wallerstein had noted that Braudel's influence on world-systems theorists was twofold. First, they accepted his sharp distinction between the sphere of the free market and the sphere of monopoly in which only the latter was considered capitalism. The related point that capitalism was anti-market 'marked a direct assault, both substantively and terminologically, on the conflation by classical economists (including Marx) of the market and capitalism' (Wallerstein, 2004: 18). Secondly, Braudel's insistence on 'the multiplicity of social time and his emphasis on structural time – what he called the *longue durée*' (ibid.: 18) became central to world-systems analysis.

While Wallerstein thus acknowledged Braudel's influence, as Arrighi pointed out later, there was a crucial discrepancy between Wallerstein and Braudel concerning the origins of the world capitalist system that was never sorted out since the two never entered into debate.

The discrepancy concerned the emergence of the European-centred capitalist world economy: Braudel located that origin in the city-states of northern Italy in the thirteenth century, while Wallerstein located it in north-western Europe in the sixteenth century. This difference reflected, Arrighi argued, the 'very conceptualization[s] of capitalism' (Arrighi, 1998: 125) in the sense that Braudel attached much importance to the organisation of long-distance trade and high finance, while for Wallerstein agricultural production and a mode of production for a trade-based division of labour were more essential (ibid.). Arrighi added that Braudel's conception of capitalism was underlain by the intermediate layer of market economy and the bottom layer of the non-economy of material lives. Arrighi's conception stood closer to Braudel's than Wallerstein's, a point of pride for Arrighi (Arrighi, 2009a: 71).

Braudel's longer time frame also became Arrighi's in his analysis of the twentieth century in 1994, when he explicitly stated that Braudel's contention that the essential feature of historical capitalism over its *longue durée* – that is, over its entire lifetime – was 'the starting point of our investigation' (Arrighi, 1994: 4). He emphasised that Braudel had put forth his theory to oppose the conventional view in the social sciences, political discourse and the mass media 'that capitalism and the market economy are more or less the same thing, and that state power is antithetical to both' (ibid.: 10).

Consequently, the conception of the capitalism of the West as a unique fusion of state and capital became central for Arrighi. Following Braudel, Arrighi included the whole range of capitalists – wholesalers, the rentiers of trade, the commission agents, brokers, money-changers, bankers and capitalists invested in production – in the category of capitalists and believed that only in Europe, owing to the interaction of state and capital, did these scattered elements become concentrated into a powerful mix. It enabled 'the territorial conquest of the world and the formation of an all-powerful and truly global capitalist world-economy' (ibid.: 11). Here, we see some development or slight shift of the problem's setting, from the origin of world capitalism to the conquest of the world economy by Europe. Arrighi explained that capitalist elements could also be seen in the Eurasian trading system that existed from Egypt to Japan and was not uniquely Western. What was unique to the West was the fusion of state and capital (ibid.).

Arrighi's focus on the financial aspect of capitalism is also Braudelian. However, in the introduction to his 1994 book, *The Long Twentieth Century*, he also cites Marx's argument about the role of the system of national debt pioneered by Genoa and Venice in the late Middle Ages in capital accumulation to support his choice, also emphasising that such financial expansion and the flows of capital from declining to rising centres repeatedly played a role in history, a phenomenon he linked to 'Marx's abridged formula MM' (ibid.: 8).[13]

Arrighi stressed not only the importance of finance capital in the transitional phase of hegemony but also important deviations from the pattern: in the early 1990s, the financial expansion of Japan and East Asian states 'diverge[d] from this pattern' (ibid.: 15). Arrighi also thought that the conquest by the West that Braudel pointed to should be complemented by the resurgence of the non-West. In retrospect, this idea seemed to be further elaborated and later became the main theme discussed much more comprehensively in his last book, *Adam Smith in Beijing*, in 2007. But already, in the analysis of *The Long Twentieth Century*, he began to seek his unique way of analysing the *longue durée*, blending the methodologies of many different authors of economic and sociological thoughts together with those of Braudel.[14] This was the context in which Arrighi rediscovered Polanyi's contribution.

Contextualisation of Polanyi in economic sociology

We can find references to Polanyi in some important pieces of Arrighi's since the 1990s. Most prominently, in an article in 2001 calling attention to the contribution of Braudel, Arrighi constructed a genealogy including Polanyi. The theme was the economic sociology that emerged at the beginning of the twentieth century in reaction to the metaphysical nature of academic economics (Arrighi, 2001: 107).

The genealogy went back to Werner Sombart and proceeded thence through the German Historical School, Max Weber and Joseph Schumpeter, and culminated in 'two radically different versions: Talcott Parsons' "structural functionalist" … and Karl Polanyi's "substantivist"' version (ibid.: 107). Here, with the use of the term 'substantivist' for Polanyi, we notice Arrighi's grasp of Polanyi as an economic anthropologist.

Arrighi argued further that the genealogy he traced was that of the old economic sociology, which he contrasted with the new one starting in the mid-1980s. Arrighi indicated that the only commonality between these two lay in the strong dislike of 'economicism' (ibid.: 108), real or imagined, liberal or Marxist, and emphasised that the characteristics of new economic sociology lay in the analysis of markets 'embedded in social networks' (ibid.: 107), the main weapon used to criticise economists' belief in self-regulating markets. Here, we clearly see the strong influence of Polanyi's conceptions.

Arrighi showed his sympathy with the new economic sociologists in the sense that 'economic sociology seems to me the most likely interlocutor of Braudel's work' (ibid.: 109). Acknowledging that his articles in 1998 and 1999, as well as *The Long Twentieth Century* and his collaborations with Silver and also with Hui and Hung in 1999 all dealt with historical capitalism through a dialogue with Braudel (ibid.: 111), Arrighi warned that the main tendency of new economic sociology had been to keep silent on Braudel and capitalism, two indispensable elements for analysis, he thought.

Braudel's three claims – that the essential feature of historical capitalism and its persistence was its flexibility, that financial capital was its defining element and that historical capitalism was closely identified with states, which was the secret of its world triumph – implied a strong critique of the new economic sociology, which focused mostly on the analysis of micro objects over a short period. This implied that it was important to go back to the old economic sociology, including the versions from Polanyi and Parsons.

Here, the question arises of whether Polanyi and Braudel are theoretically compatible. A negative answer is suggested if we take into account Braudel's criticism of Polanyi in the second volume of his trilogy.[15] In a discussion of Polanyi's and his pupils' methods of locating markets in societies for a comparative analysis of markets in the 1950s (Braudel, 1979: 223–230), Braudel found their definition of exchange and market too narrow.

However, Braudel also cited Douglass North's praise of Polanyi for offering 'an alternative analytical framework to account for past and present institutional organization' (North, 1977: 704) for understanding transaction costs, and this, as we shall see, also influenced Arrighi. Moreover, Braudel referred to Polanyi's project at the very beginning of his volume in relation to the aims of his own research:

> After all, the genesis of capitalism is strictly related to exchange. ... There is no simple linear history of the development of markets. In this area, the traditional, the archaic and the modern or ultra-modern exist side by side, even today. ... The ideal field of observation would cover all the markets in the world, from the very beginning to our own time – a huge area tackled with iconoclastic zeal by Karl Polanyi. ... I am not convinced that such a thing is possible. (Braudel, 1979: 26)

World systems' Polanyian inspiration

While Braudel did not adopt the same method as Polanyi, the intention and scope of Braudel's analysis certainly overlapped with Polanyi's.

Additionally, it is evident that Polanyi's contribution was not restricted to his joint work with his pupils and colleagues in the 1950s, even though Braudel only referred to this. As we know, the embeddedness that Braudel mentioned in his work was important for Polanyi. This coincidence implied the potentiality of their common research interest, which was apparently attempted by Arrighi.

Rediscovery of Polanyi's contribution

We can finally turn to Polanyi's influence on Arrighi in the 1990s. We have seen how Arrighi was influenced by Braudel when he proposed that financial expansion and the debt of rising centres to the declining centres was a cyclical occurrence in capitalism. The 'long' in the title *The Long Twentieth Century* indicated that the twentieth century had a long prehistory. More importantly, it indicated that the cycles of financial expansion through which declining powers financed rising ones had ended. With hegemony shifting outside of the West into the non-West or East Asia, either Japan or China, the hegemon no longer financed the new rising powers. Arrighi's central question was thus how the American hegemony had failed as a successor of the tradition of world systems. It simultaneously meant that the British hegemony was substantially the last one, and this supported Polanyi's thesis in *TGT* that a great transformation was occurring with the decline of the British hegemony in the inter-war period.

Furthermore, Arrighi also argued that the development of Western capitalism was as concerned with war-making as with state-making (Tilly, 1985), and this was his distinctive elaboration of hegemony. This connection could be self-destructive: in analysing the influence of the Vietnam War on America, Arrighi stated that 'the military and legitimacy crises of US world power were two sides of the same coin. In part, they were the expression of the very success of US rearmament ... in turning the systemic chaos of the 1930s and 1940s into a new world order. ... In part, however, the joint military and legitimacy crises of US world power were the expression of the failure of the US military-industrial apparatus to cope with the problems posed by world-wide decolonization' (Arrighi, 1994: 320). Let us take a closer look at his reasoning here.

The last, and main, chapter of *The Long Twentieth Century* began with an explanation of transaction cost. Arrighi referred to Ronald Coase, and we remember that in 1977 Douglass North also utilised this concept in analysing economic history, attributing such methodology to Polanyi. With this concept, Arrighi put forward the idea that British hegemony pursued the strategy of 'internalizing transaction cost' (ibid.: 239) as illustrated by the East India Company, which served as the external centre of this internalisation of transaction cost, which served for the maintenance of British hegemony. Arrighi concisely described this process and then the phase of industrial revolution, quoting much of Polanyi's conceptions of fictitious commodities and double movement in *TGT* (ibid.: 258).

In this connection, the meaning of India for British state-making and war-making was discussed. Already, in an earlier chapter, he had stated that, in British hegemony, the situation of non-Western peoples as well as the property-less masses of the West who had fought in vain for their rights to self-determination and a livelihood, began to change around the end of the nineteenth century because of the 'industrialization of war' (ibid.: 64). It was due to this industrialisation of war that the 'ever increasing number, range and variety of machinofactured mechanical products were deployed' (ibid.: 64) and 'the productive efforts of the propertyless … became a central component of the state-making and war-making efforts of rulers' (ibid.: 64).

Here, mentioning Marx and many other sources, Arrighi clarified that 'the large surplus in the Indian balance of payments became the pivot of the enlarged reproduction of Britain's world-scale processes of capital accumulation and of the City's mastery of world finance. … Equally critical was another pivot of the enlarged reproduction of British wealth and power: the Indian surplus of military labor which came to be organized in the British army' (ibid.: 263).

Thus, he concluded that the 'British "industrial revolution" was from the very start a global industry dependent for its competitiveness and continuing expansion on the external economies afforded by the procurement of inputs and disposal of outputs on foreign markets' (ibid.: 261). He explicitly indicated the dependence of British industry: 'The spread of machinofacture from spinning to weaving dates from this period of the British cotton industry's increasing dependence on the Indian market' (ibid.: 262).

That is why the decline of Lancashire, and thus the decline of British hegemony, in the 1930s was a structurally natural consequence. Once the flow of surplus from Indian money and labour stopped, Lancashire, or Britain in general, could not enjoy its hegemonic stance any more. This condition became reality in that period. Arrighi quoted Polanyi's criticism of the concept of exploitation with the example of Lancashire in *TGT* and added that 'Lancashire did something quite different and worse than exploit the Indian masses: it deprived them of the cash flows essential to their reproduction' (ibid.: 263).

What followed, then, in Arrighi's analysis was the rise of the industrial-military power of Germany as a real threat for the entire international system under British hegemony and the destruction, the great transformation, in the 1940s, which was signified by the abandonment by Britain of the gold standard, the New Deal, German National Socialism and the Five Year Plan in Russia. 'By 1940 every vestige of the international system had disappeared and, apart from a few enclaves, the nations were living in an entirely new international setting' (Polanyi, [1944] 2001: 24; Arrighi, 1994: 274). Arrighi added that 'this [military] confrontation was translated into the establishment of a new world order, centered on and organized by the United States' (Arrighi, 1994: 274). He characterised this new world order of state- and war-making with Bretton Woods, Hiroshima and Nagasaki, the San Francisco treaty and the UN Charter (ibid.: 274–275).

In this way, Polanyi's analysis in *TGT* was framed in a new context and longer historical perspective of several centuries in Arrighi's work. What mattered was not a shift of some hegemony any more. It was, rather, the shift of research interest into the labour factor to sustain hegemony.[16] This perspective was shared by Polanyi and Arrighi. Even after the end of hegemonic cycles, this viewpoint would remain applicable in further investigations. In fact, Arrighi indicated the fundamentally unstable character of American hegemony, which had already become apparent in its crisis in the 1970s. Shown in his analysis in *Adam Smith in Beijing*, American hegemony could not enjoy such advantages as Britain had. 'The United Kingdom had the Indian Army; the United States does not' (Arrighi, 2007: 138). He described the phase where America fell into crisis owing to its quagmire of the Vietnam War.

> Coercive control over the surplus of India's balance-of-payments enabled Britain to shift the burdens of its own persistent trade deficits onto Indian taxpayers, workers, and capitalists. In a post-colonial world, in contrast, no such blatant coercion was available. The United States faced the stark choice of either balancing its trade and current-accounts deficits through a drastic downsizing of its national economy and expenditures abroad, or alienating a growing share of its future incomes to foreign lenders. (Ibid.: 138)

In this sense, the decline of the British hegemony in the 1930s was, in substance, the crucial end of the hegemonic cycles of world systems centred in Europe, or, as Polanyi called it, the great transformation.

Conclusion

This chapter has investigated the theoretical and historical relationship between Karl Polanyi's *TGT* and Arrighi's representative work in 1994, *The Long Twentieth Century*. Though Arrighi was already acquainted with Polanyi's analysis in the 1970s when he criticised Marxian analyses of imperialism, it was only afterwards, after he became conscious of the vital importance of Braudel's work and of economic sociology in understanding historical capitalism, that he rediscovered Polanyi in the discussion of globalisation around the turn of the twentieth century. Putting and analysing Polanyi's discussion of the rise and decline of British hegemony in the long historical perspective and in a more complex structure, Arrighi has accomplished a very unique theoretical contribution to the globalised world of our age.

Notes

1   In this article dealing directly with Polanyi's concept of double movement deployed in *TGT*, Arrighi was the second author. We have to admit that it is difficult to separate his ideas from those of the article's lead author, B. J. Silver.
2   In this connection, Goldfrank also emphasised the importance of attention to Terence Hopkins, who worked in the research group under Polanyi and later collaborated with Wallerstein. This point was indicated also by Block and Somers (2014: 245), who made some comparisons of the methodologies of Polanyi and Wallerstein (ibid.: 68–69).
3   I once investigated the meaning of peace in *TGT* in some detail (Nakayama, 2018). Hobson's influence on Polanyi in the 1920s was indicated also by Cangiani and Thomasberger (2003: 19–21) and Cangiani, Polanyi Levitt and Thomasberger (2005: 27–28). They made reference to Hobson's 1917 book, *Democracy after the War*, not the 1902 book, in this connection.
4   Desai listed Marxian and non-Marxian investigative works of imperialism and made a close inspection of them (Desai, 2013: 43–53). Smith argued that the differences between Marx, Luxemburg and Lenin were in their grasp of imperialism as a production and reproduction of space (Smith, [1984] 2008: 126–131).
5   Here, Arrighi made reference to an article by G. Deleuze and stated that his analysis resembled also the ideal-typical constructions of the French structuralists, mentioning Piaget together with Deleuze, in the footnote (Arrighi, 1978: 28).
6   Still later, in an academic symposium on the concept of embeddedness, Arrighi was also invited as a speaker, according to the symposium's documentation (Krippner et al., 2004). Though he did not talk much, he defined the economy in a Polanyian sense in that it concerned 'the procurement of means of livelihood and the cooperation that such procurement involves' (ibid.: 125–126).
7   There is also an issue whether this concept stemmed from Thurnbald, but we do not go into detail.
8   Related essays from Polanyi ([1934] 2002a, [1934] 2002b, [1934] 2002c) were compiled in one part of an anthology of Polanyi's writings, 'Restructuring and democracy in England'.
9   Certainly, the Japanese cotton industry gradually showed an indisputable strength around that time. Historical data tell us that Japanese textiles had accounted for barely 2 to 3 per cent of world exports of cotton piece goods on the eve of the First World War (e.g. Wurm, 1993: 199). Another investigation elucidated that Japanese competitiveness began to threaten Lancashire around the end of the First World War (Dewey, 1978: 47). In 1933, the volume of Japan's cotton exports exceeded Britain's for the first time (Wurm, 1993: 202). This research indicated that many authors ascribed Japan's success to 'low wages and the availability of cheap labor' (ibid.: 200), even admitting the roughness of data of such international comparisons of labour costs.

10 In a review of the book *Empire* by Michael Hardt and Antonio Negri, Arrighi critically discussed their 'idea of Empire as a "smooth" space' (Arrighi, 2003: 30). Arrighi picked up their argument of the intermingling of the First and the Third World since the disappearance of the Second, examining their discussion on the labour and multitude, and criticised their optimism and lack of empirical evidence (ibid.: 32). Further, he refuted their comment on his 1994 book. While Hardt and Negri found Arrighi's analysis of the 1970s in his 1994 book vague and contradictory to his treatise in 1978, Arrighi insisted on his consistency and continuity, saying that he had been 'advancing a thesis about the crisis of the 1970s for thirty years' (ibid.: 34).

11 At the fifteenth annual conference on the political economy of the world-system at the University of Hawaii in 1991 (28–30 March), Arrighi made a presentation with S. Ikeda and A. Irwan on 'The rise of East Asia: one miracle or many?' Its final documentation is found as Arrighi, Hui and Hung(1999). Further, we should not forget Arrighi's mutual influence with Andre Gunder Frank, who was another representative of world-systems theory and published *Re-Orient* in 1998. He was also decisively influenced by cultural and economic anthropology in settling his research agenda and became a harsh opponent of neoliberalism, led by Milton Friedman, in the 1970s. Arrighi's book in 2007 was dedicated to Frank (Arrighi, 2007: xiii).

12 The first part of this trilogy by Braudel, *The Structures of Everyday Life*, was originally published in French in 1967, and its English translation came in 1973. But then, after an extensive revision of the French text, an English translation of the whole trilogy, including the second part, *The Wheels of Commerce*, and the third part, *The Perspective of the World*, was published in 1979.

13 Certainly, it was important for Arrighi to formulate two phases of hegemony in *The Long Twentieth Century*. By making use of Marx's general formula of capital, MCM' with Braudel's frame, Arrighi defined the epoch of financial expansion (CM') as the successive phase after the epoch of material expansion (MC), both of which consist of the 'systemic cycle of accumulation' (1994: 9). Arrighi quoted Braudel's insight that the stage of financial expansion after material expansion announced the maturity of capitalist development and that it was 'a sign of autumn' (ibid.: 6, 162) when capital accumulation by the hegemonic power entered the financial phase. When this phase of autumn reaches its limit, we naturally expect winter, which means the final end of such capital accumulation, which he defined as the 'terminal crisis' (ibid.: 215).

14 Arrighi might have wanted to leave some room for further stages. We can realise such an intention in the following retrospective statement: 'Braudel is an incredibly rich source of information about markets and capitalism, but he has no theoretical framework. Or more accurately, he is so eclectic that he has innumerable partial theories, the sum of which is no theory … you easily get lost if you just follow Braudel, because he takes you in so many different directions' (Arrighi, 2009a: 71).

15 For example, Salsano indicated that Braudel did not rely on Polanyi any more in his analysis of market and society (Salsano, 1990: 142). But we know that the November/December 1974 issue of *Annales*, the journal of his research group of which Braudel was one of the main editors, was devoted to the history of economic anthropology, and the main focus was on Polanyi's thought. This endorses Braudel's interest in Polanyi.

16 Arrighi admitted in his last interview that he could not include the analysis of labour in his 1994 book (Arrighi, 2009a: 73–74). He said that he conducted further research after 1994 to make up for this problem.

12

Polanyi in space

Jamie Peck

Introduction: placing Polanyi

The purpose of this chapter is to uncover something that for too long has been hidden practically in plain sight. It offers an exploratory appreciation of Polanyi's potential as a *spatial theorist*, albeit a somewhat closeted one – that is, as a pioneering and creative analyst of geographically variegated economies. The pluralisation of this latter word is anything but casual, since Polanyi's name has long been associated with the position that (all) economies are socially embedded and heterogeneously constituted, and that they are variably instituted or regulated, as well as with principled repudiations of (market) universalism, (stagist) teleology and (explanatory) monism (see Polanyi, 1957a, 1977; see also Gudeman, 2001; Burawoy, 2003; Hann and Hart, 2011). His is a body of work, furthermore, that by force of circumstances was produced under lifelong conditions of dislocation and displacement. It bears the hallmarks of a scholarly and indeed personal life lived in a somewhat stressed and liminal manner, the consequences of which included an elevated sensitivity to (historical and geographical) context and a somewhat paradoxical appreciation for the role of 'embeddedness' (see Dale, 2016a). Quite distinctively but hardly coincidentally, it is also a body of work founded on the recognition that pathways of socioeconomic development – past, present and future; real and imagined – are neither unidirectional nor singular. Having avoided the 'fallacious assumption that all societies [have] operated on the same economic principles' (Block and Somers, 2014: 65), Polanyi can be considered to be one of the original theorists of the hybrid, heterogeneous and pluralised economy, one that by definition is subject to uneven spatial development and contestable modes of regulation, to disequilibrating forces and endemic restructuring.

The claim that Karl Polanyi was a critical economic geographer *avant la lettre* is therefore not quite as far-fetched as at first it may sound. His was an expansive, rich and open-ended conception of *the economic*, one that was informed and inspired by the revealed truths of ceaseless historical transformation and persistent geographical difference. So it was that when Polanyi was teaching at New York City's Columbia University, in the 1950s, the demanding task that he set for his students amounted to nothing less than an exploration of the comparative historical geography of economic institutions, his lectures endeavouring:

> to define the *meaning of the 'economic'*;
> to classify economic systems in a manner that *does not prejudge the issues*;
> [and] to illustrate the *changing place of the economy* in human society through historical examples. (Polanyi, 2014a: 143, 147; see also Fusfeld, 1994)

While a case might be made for Polanyi to be recognised as a proto-economic geographer – at least in the sense that his programmatic concerns included the exploration and explanation of the irreducible diversity and sociocultural specifics of economic life – it has taken a while for the discipline with that name to get any sort of measure of him. The engagements of economic geographers with Polanyian texts, concepts and precepts have been rather fickle, episodic and selective – a somewhat exaggerated manifestation of a wider condition, it has to be said, evident across the heterodox economic sciences.[1]

Ever since economic geography's (re)birth, as a vibrantly heterodox field, in the late 1970s, Polanyi has been an enigmatic and occasionally inspirational presence, although in some respects he has remained an elusive if not rather cryptic figure. One of his first appearances came courtesy of regulation and state theories, beginning in the mid-1980s, where he served as an avatar for a raft of arguments concerning the necessity for (and contradictory effects of) social regulation and economic governance, the politics of crisis management (and resolution), and the vulnerability of welfare-statist economies to programmes of market-formatted transformation. This neo-Marxist appropriation of Polanyi would soon be eclipsed, after the early 1990s, by a neo-Weberian turn towards network sociology, in the wake of Mark Granovetter's influential (if restrictive) recovery of the embeddedness metaphor. Characteristically, these economic-sociological 'translations' often invoked what Gareth Dale (2010a) has called the 'soft' Polanyi, the theorist of social embeddedness and institutions, formulations that in various guises have since passed into mainstream conceptions of economic geography's purpose, object and approach (see Hess, 2004; Gertler, 2010; Peck, 2012).

Somewhat later, Polanyi was discovered once again in the context of millennial mobilisations against neoliberalism, this time as a prophetic critic of free market globalisation, aggravated financialisation and socioecological commodification (see Block, 2001; Peck and Tickell, 2002; Fraser, 2013). This hailed a 'harder' Polanyi, a trenchant critic of deregulated capitalism and an advocate for socialist transformation. In the field of economic geography, the suggestive notion of the 'double movement', a metaphor for societal reflexes against the contradictions and overflows of marketisation (including under the guises of neoliberalisation and globalisation) would find a place alongside embeddedness as part of an evolving disciplinary lexicon. More specifically, in the period since the Wall Street crash of 2008 and the Great Recession, Polanyi's work has found urgent relevance as a generative critique of austerity politics, financialised discipline and crisis-driven restructuring – notwithstanding his own conviction that the follies of nineteenth-century laissez-faire would surely never be repeated, and his abiding belief that 'the experience of the 1930s had [permanently] discredited the ideas of his free market opponents' (Block and Somers, 2014: 19).

Beyond these episodic encounters, there are still other economic-geographical readings of the plural and polysemic potential of Polanyian formulations, some yet to be fully articulated, including emerging lines of work on the variegation of markets and the political economy of financialisation, as well as contributions to the interdisciplinary programme of comparative economy (see Berndt and Boeckler, 2012; Peck, 2012; Muellerleile, 2013; Peck and Zhang, 2013; Zhang, 2013). This said, truly sustained engagements – not only with Polanyi's legacy but with the still-to-be-realised potential of Polanyian methods and approaches – have been relatively few and far between in the field of economic geography. While many have been drawn to Polanyi by the seductiveness of his metaphors, by the polemic force of his writing or by the encyclopaedic reach of his more-than-capitalist worldview, those seeking explicit methodological templates, unambiguous theoretical injunctions or models of case-study exposition will probably have been frustrated.

Yet there are profound complementarities here that invite further exploration and elaboration. In a sense, economic geography and Polanyian economics can be said to share the same object of inquiry – the culturally inflected, institutionally mediated, politically governed, socially embedded and heterogeneous economy, one subject neither to self-governing equilibrium nor to incipient convergence, but to restive restructuring and divergent development. These projects have recourse, moreover, to an overlapping methodological repertoire, generally favouring the qualitative, closely focused and experiential analysis of grounded and contextualised economic formations, often quite thickly described but always with an eye to emergent, more-than-local theory claims. And they have both been engaged, in various ways, in 'the search for general principles of economic organisation in our world, [given] the need to explain not only the common form, *but also its infinite variation*' (Hann and Hart, 2011: 147, emphasis added; Clark, 1998; Peck, 2012).

True, in (neo)Polanyian hands, 'variation' tends to be associated with much wider registers of socioeconomic difference – certainly historically, if not spatially – than has hitherto been the case in economic geography, the concerns of which have been characteristically preoccupied by the 'restructuring present', along with a marked Anglo-American and Western bias (see Yeung and Lin, 2003; Pollard et al., 2009). This said, economic geographers and Polanyians each wrestle with what amounts to a similar problematique, that of *placing economy*, subject to the analytical maxim that 'no economy–society configuration is permanent or natural' (Rankin, 2013: 1654; Harvey, 2010). No 'local' arrangement of economic affairs, it follows, should be mistaken for a universal pattern.

With these affinities in mind, the chapter proceeds in two parts. It begins by con-textualising Polanyi's work in relation to the shifting locales and vantage points that shaped its production. If Polanyi was a man 'of another time [and] of another place' (Cangiani, 2002 translated in Resta, 2014: 1), this part of the chapter asks, in effect, where his approach, method and worldview *came from*. It seeks to uncover, in other words, aspects of the geographical constitution of Polanyi's own intellectual (and social) formation, disclosing some features of the world that shaped his worldview. Next, the discussion turns to the question of the *potential* of Polanyi's research programme – incomplete as it understandably was – for the conceptualisation and exploration of economic geographies. The goal here is to sketch some of the ways in which Polanyian approaches might be put to work in economic geography and other space-sensitive modes of economic inquiry. Here, there is considerable virtue in the fact that the Polanyian project remains 'open to multiple interpretations' (Block and Somers, 2014: 8), since this permits its creative (and pluralist) mobilisa-tion as a moving system of thought, rather than as a fixed framework. In this spirit, the chapter closes with a brief reprise of the predicates, principles and potential of Polanyian economic geographies.

Displacements

Polanyi lived what he would come to see as 'a "world" life' (quoted in Dale, 2013: 1643). This twice-exiled cosmopolitan was denied anything approaching tenured security. His was a lived experience, in fact, profoundly shaped by the extended aftershocks of the great transformation. As a result, Polanyi possessed not only a critical eye but also a visceral feel for histories (and politics and geographies) always in the making, while also being especially sensitive to the shifting geographical land-scapes of cultural, institutional and political difference. Just as the contested present was understood to be humanly made and socially shaped, socioeconomic futures were consequently always open, never mechanically preordained or deterministically foreclosed. Polanyi retained a strong commitment to finding and building more humane forms of livelihood and more sustainable modes of development, but this would never calcify into dogmatism.

Polanyi's corpus, and his analytical and political worldview more generally, were themselves products of embodied and 'emplaced' practices, forged in the course of a life buffeted by the tectonic twentieth-century movements of fascism, liberal capitalism, state socialism and cold warfare. This was 'the great forge that shaped Polanyi's work', the scope, standpoint and indeed silences of which cannot be abstracted from their conditions of production, since these were 'interwoven with the story of his life' (Catanzariti, 2014: 221). A restless polymath, this nonconformist thinker 'defies academic pigeon-holing' (Hann and Hart, 2011: 55), having fashioned an extradisciplinary and transnational career out of less-than-freely chosen transitions between political journalism, workers' education, academic instruction and even a little poetry. There is some irony in the fact that the symbolic father of embeddedness should have led such a disembedded life, displaced from Vienna and the 'functional socialism' that remained an inspiration, to a somewhat precarious existence forged between England, Canada and the United States. Rarely an insider or even a 'local', his was a cumulatively acquired 'pattern of thought' repeatedly positioned 'against the stream' (Polanyi Levitt, 1990b: 1).

While the achievements of Red Vienna, the Russian Revolution and early-twentieth-century gyrations of liberal capitalism together constituted the 'mainspring' of Polanyi's scholarly project (Humphreys, 1969: 169), his subsequent work as a journalist generated a real-time interpretive critique of the contested present, including the wavering fortunes of British socialism, the rollout of the New Deal in the United States, and the descent into fascism and war in Europe. Polanyi's writings from the turbulent 1930s served as the working notes for *The Great Transformation*, while also reflecting a tension characteristic of all his work, 'between a certain utopianism and an acute sensitivity to the actual historical and political context' (Cangiani, 1994: 16). No fatalist, he identified both intellectual and political opportunities in the crises of these times, particularly in the wake of the demonstrated inability of orthodox economics to explain or contain the great economic dislocations of the inter-war years, which in principle, if less so in practice, 'opened the field to eclectic searches in comparative economics for new doctrines' (Humphreys, 1969: 173). These eclectic searches would animate Polanyi's work during and after the Second World War, along with his evolving analytical framework, yet they too would remain somewhat idiosyncratic creatures of context.

The concept of embeddedness may have been Polanyi's 'most famous contribution to social thought', but it has also been 'a source of enormous confusion', the subject of ongoing disputes around both its lineage and implications (Block, 2001: xxiii; Cangiani, 2011; Dale, 2011; Gemici, 2008; Krippner et al., 2004). It works as an indicator of (local) context in some formulations, as a metaphor for social entanglement in others; it is mobilised as a microsociological device in some renderings but elsewhere as a more structural or institutional concept. At root, the concept indexes Polanyi's enduring scepticism concerning the autonomy of the economic in orthodox analysis as well as free market ideology, encapsulating his counterclaim that all economies are socially placed, culturally hosted, politically mediated and institutionally regulated. Polanyi maintained that economic forms, behaviours and relations are inescapably embedded in 'instituted' social forms, behaviours and relations. Critical of the reductionism, absolutism, essentialism and symbolic violence wrought by orthodox visions of the market economy, Polanyi's work was founded not on abstract theories but on the recognition of historical, geographical and sociocultural difference, his goal being substantively to *position* economies in this variegated context. While Dale (2011) has traced the origins of the embeddedness concept to extended engagements with Thurnwald, Tönnies and Marx, Block (2001: xxiv) has ventured that 'it seems plausible that Polanyi drew the metaphor from coal mining', following his extensive work on British economic history during the 1930s. In this vein, Ilona Duczynska Polanyi would recall that 'stronger than any intellectual influence was the trauma which was England', and what would prove to be her husband's auspicious

> encounter with full-fledged capitalism. … [The] houses which Engels had described were still standing; people still lived in them. Black hills of slag stood in the green landscape of Wales; from the depressed areas, young men and women who had never seen their parents employed, drifted away to London. (Duczynska Polanyi, 2006: 311)

In an experiential sense, history and geography therefore really made a difference to the way that Polanyi understood processes of social, economic and environmental transformation – hence the many resonances of 'embeddedness'. Confusion was later sown by his sparse and rather variable deployment of the resonant term, however, sometimes historically, at other times analytically. Most notably, the observation that the British model of nineteenth-century capitalism had been associated with a 'disembedding' process, such that the principles of market exchange were raised to the status of governing ideology, at enormous social cost, enabled the (mis)interpretation that there was the potential for ('deregulated') markets to be self-acting, autonomous and self-regulating – a claim that appears on the face of it to contradict the plenary principle of the inseparability of the economic and the social (see Barber, 1995; Krippner, 2001). It also begged the question of whether *all* economies are socially embedded, always and everywhere (Block, 2001; Peck, 2005), or whether there is a sliding scale of 'marketness', some being purer/freer than others. Is it possible to weigh or quantify embeddedness, as if it refers to differences of degree (or 'deviations') from free market perfection? Or instead, should the concept be taken to signal a qualitative and necessary condition of all markets, marked by differences 'in kind' rather than on a singular spectrum?

Once again, finding answers to these questions involves situating the notion of embeddedness in relation to the uneven development, not only of socioeconomic conditions but also of the Polanyian project itself. Cangiani (2011: 178) maintains that the concept must be understood in the context of Polanyi's incomplete plan to build a 'comparative theory of economic systems and institutional change', the metaphorical formulation 'only [being] meaningful within his wide-rang[ing] comparative analysis of economic systems'. Furthermore, the fuller meaning of 'embeddedness' only becomes apparent in light of Polanyi's distinctive approach to institutionalism. His historical explorations had yielded the conclusion that the ascendancy of 'market society' represented an irreversible, Rubicon-crossing moment, after which market relations began to define society itself. The 'cultural containment' of the economic was, in effect, a pre-capitalist condition; in modern, 'machine society', the excesses of marketisation and commodification would have to be managed (somehow) by institutional and political forces, Polanyi believed – hence his interest in transformative episodes like the New Deal and his abiding concerns with institutional reform and economic democratisation (ibid.; Polanyi Levitt, 2013a). The identification of 'disembedding' tendencies in market societies does not mean, therefore, that Polanyi had somehow fallen for the orthodox conceit of a self-regulating, perfectly competitive market, as if oblivious to his own critique of that same formulation; rather, it spoke to his acute appreciation of the capricious character of capitalist development, the proclivity of markets to overflow into crisis, and their contradictory coevolution with all manner of social reflexes, cultural conditions and institutional 'interventions'. And just as the double movement never implied a simple pendular dynamic, so it followed that there was not to be found some enduring sweet spot of socioeconomic harmony (or institutional equilibrium): in their own ways, the market and the social were both understood to be sites of turbulence, conflict and contestation.

His historical and anthropological inquiries, coupled with his own lived experiences, had convinced Polanyi that while economies will often *contain* markets, they do not eternally oscillate around some market 'norm', and neither can they be lined up on some conveyor belt towards 'full' marketisation. It follows that actually existing or real markets, in all their variety, warrant attention not as special cases, nor as deviations from a pristine model, but as particular modes of economic coordination among others, displaying a variety of 'local' configurations and conditions of (co)existence. The very fact that markets cannot exist on their own (except, apparently, in the orthodox economic imagination) calls attention to their complex interrelationships and interdependencies with other forms of socioeconomic coordination, such as state regulation or the domestic sphere. In Polanyi's distinctive style of non-essentialist, social-constructivist economics, difference-finding manoeuvres (thinking comparatively, among different spatial-historical forms, and intra-regionally, across modes of economic organisation) were coupled with a commitment to relational holism (tracing the mutual relationships that make up hybrid formations at a regional or national scale, positioned within a moving universe of revealed conjunctures and political possibilities). Again, this did not lend itself to singular prognostications, but instead to the embrace of a differentiated and multi-polar economic ontology, properly combined with a pluralist and heterodox epistemology. Singularity and convergence were features neither of the past nor the present; visions, plans and imaginaries of the socioeconomic future should likewise not be constrained or preordained.

For these and other reasons, the programmatic aspiration to develop a truly interdisciplinary and deeply institutionalist project of *comparative economy* animated much of Polanyi's post-war research and writing. He lived out the final decades of his life in North America, in an environment decidedly 'less liberal' than his previous experiences in Europe (Humphreys, 1969: 175). Teaching economic history at Columbia required the 'visiting' professor to commute long distances from a home made in rural Ontario – due to the intolerance, south of the border, of Ilona Duczynska Polanyi's previous political associations. Lewis Coser (1984: 171–172), who counted Polanyi among the foremost intellectual 'refugees' in the United States, observed that the 'witch-hunting atmosphere during the Cold War' had consigned him to an existence 'perpetually in transit', a state of dislocation and circumspection that eventually seems to have tempered what had once been an impeccable 'instinct for the jugular'. It is surely no coincidence that Polanyi's post-war writings are notably more cryptic and circumspect, yet they also contain the seeds of a much more radical programme.

Along with a coterie of junior collaborators, Polanyi spearheaded a Ford Foundation project on 'Economic aspects of institutional growth', the ambitious goal of which was a cross-cultural, historical analysis of the 'place of economy' in a wide range of social systems, from Ancient Greece to an array of more contemporary, but usually non-Western or 'tribal' societies (see Polanyi, Arensberg and Pearson, 1957; Polanyi, 1977). Conspicuously absent in the research programme of the post-war Polanyi, especially for one whose previous work – both as a journalist and in *The Great Transformation* – pivoted so powerfully around the critique of liberal capitalism, was any serious engagement with the advanced capitalist economies of the time and indeed place. This, to be sure, was a rather curious (self?) limitation, which some have traced to a side effect of the inhospitable environment of McCarthyism (Halperin, 1984; Isaac, 2005). Fatefully, there were those that (mis)took this possibly calculated lapse to mean that the Polanyian approach was really only valid for antique, non-Western, idiosyncratic or so-called 'primitive' economies. If this was not problematic enough, no less pernicious was the flipside implication: that the apparatus of formal economics might suffice for the purpose of analysing advanced capitalist economies.

Polanyi was sceptical of formal economic theorising, derived only from the 'logical character of the means–ends relationship' and the singular problem of choice under scarcity, opting instead for what he portrayed as a *substantivist* alternative: grounded in a more ecosocial understanding of the economic, rooted in 'man's dependence for his livelihood upon nature and his fellows', this proceeded from the contention that '[p]rocess and institutions together form the economy' (Polanyi, 1959: 162; 1960: 329). Born under constrained circumstances, the potential of the substantivist alternative – like the project of radical comparativism with which it was associated – was never fully realised. The debate that Polanyi was instrumental in triggering, between formalist (or neoclassical) and substantivist (or realist-institutionalist) approaches to economic analysis, was subsequently conducted in largely defensive terms, and in no small part on the terrain of the premodern economy, soon being reduced to a forlorn objection to neoclassical imperialism, whispered from the (geographical) margins (Kaplan, 1968; Löfving, 2005). Yet if markets were, for Polanyi, a special case rather than the universal paradigm, he can be faulted (Cold War caveats aside) for sowing some measure of confusion around this issue, both by neglecting advanced market economies in his post-war investigations and by elsewhere appearing to concede limits to the substantivist method:

> the substantive meaning should be consistently adhered to throughout the social sciences, with the single exception of market phenomena, where the formal or scarcity definition can lead to an effective theory. (Polanyi, 2014a: 58–59)

Analytically, Polanyi's post-war project may have ended up provincialising itself, while barely checking neoclassical universalism. Affinities with radical critiques of modern, market economies, especially Marxian ones, were left untended by

Polanyi, only to be more actively spurned by his immediate successors, who themselves would be subject to attacks from some Marxist positions in the 1970s. George Dalton, for example, maintained that Marxian treatments of the economy and those more 'humanistic' approaches with which late-Polanyian work had been associated represented 'rival' theories (Dalton, 1990; cf. Jenkins, 1977; Dowling, 1979; Burawoy, 2003). Barry Isaac (2005: 20) reckons that Polanyi would have been 'deeply shocked' to learn of the largely self-administered methodological exile some of his key followers in the 1960s and 1970s (after the McCarthyite moment had passed), who chose not to contest the hegemony of neoclassical economics in its own backyard – the 'market economy' of the United States – despite the fact that the express objective of his post-war programme had been to establish 'a truly universal framework for comparative economics'. Nevertheless, the spaces nominally reserved for critical Polanyian analyses of contemporary market economies were to remain mostly unoccupied.

Polanyi's may have been a life of displacements, and no doubt many disappointments, but it was also one of hope. He recognised and confronted hegemonic powers, never losing sight of alternatives – both real and imagined. As a result, the Polanyian framework was constructed with a view to always open horizons; it remained in a state of progressive (re)construction, even if for practical and maybe political reasons it could only be assembled in pieces. This should be a caution against foreshortened or fossilised readings of Polanyi's project derived exclusively from *The Great Transformation*. In order fully to appreciate the potential of the Polanyian project, it is necessary not only to 'consider the entirety of his output' (Resta, 2014: 3), but to take account also of some of the missing links and neglected elements in this suggestive yet incomplete corpus. Viewed in such terms, for its creative provocations and constructive possibilities, the Polanyian agenda can be read as a bold licence for an institutionalist mode of comparative socioeconomics, opening a methodological path for an expansive, relational analysis of (and between) variegated economies, capitalist and otherwise (Peck, 2012; Rankin, 2013).

Departures

One of Polanyi's defining convictions was that there was much to learn from *the full range* of revealed (and potential) arrangements for the organisation of human affairs, lessons that could be recovered from the careful, critical and comparative study of economies old and new, near and far. This entailed a serious (mostly historic) engagement with 'market utopias', but it most certainly could not be confined to constrained analyses of (or in) the 'market pattern'. Notwithstanding the somewhat truncated nature of his post-war research programme, and those diplomatic remarks about the coexistence (or partitioning) of substantive and formalist approaches, Polanyi refused to accept the subordination of all socioeconomic forms to the 'market shape of things' (Polanyi, 1977: xl). Inquiries should properly embrace actually existing markets, and indeed market imaginaries, but they should not be reduced to these forms of integration. What Polanyi memorably portrayed as the 'economistic fallacy' involved the equation of the 'human economy in general with its market form' (ibid.: 6). His alternative to market reductionism, substantivism, instead took as its object the diverse, hybrid and variegated economy – 'the human economy in general' – combining situated local studies with recursive theorising across (moving) parts of the (malleable) whole. Against improper formalism, 'scarcity economics' and the presumed centrality of the self-regulating market, Polanyi argued for a

> substantive definition of 'economic' ... permits a redefinition of the main economic institutions that does not take as its frame of reference the market. ... The substantive meaning of 'economic' thus opens up the road to an institutional analysis that eliminates the market assumption from the picture—and therewith also its modernizing and economistic associations. (2014a: 61)

This entailed a theoretically informed (and informing) style of thick description intended to 'rid us of the incubus of an economistic or modernizing misinterpretation of the past' (ibid.: 60). What would later evolve into the project of comparative economics represented a somewhat idiosyncratic but nevertheless revealing form of geoeconomic history, no longer confined to 'the study of economic data of the past together with their changing background, but [instead interrogating] the place occupied by the economy in society as a whole, in other words the changing relation of the economic to the noneconomic institutions in society' (ibid.: 133). To borrow the subtitle from one of Polanyi's edited collections, this called for far-reaching explorations of 'economies in history and theory' (Polanyi, Arensberg and Pearson, 1957).

Holding to the Aristotelian position that the whole precedes the part, Polanyi contested both the concept of *homo economicus* and its downstream consequences, challenging the orthodox view that invariant and individual, if not *primal*, rationalities established enduring (micro) foundations for universal and invariant economic laws. Instead, social institutions effectively come first. 'Acts of exchange or barter on the personal level produce prices only if they occur under a system of price-making markets', Polanyi (1959: 170) argued, 'an institutional setup which is nowhere created by mere random acts of exchange'. Working across various levels of abstraction, Polanyi 'chose to focus his analysis at the level of concrete institutions' (Block and Somers, 1984: 69), the 'main methodological instrument' of his brand of substantivism being 'institutional analysis' (Polanyi, quoted in Dale, 2011: 317). This, in turn, entailed reading across institutions, across modes of integration and across actually existing economies – the manner in which Polanyi combined a commitment to holism with a subtle form of relational analysis:

> By adopting a holistic approach, Polanyi arrives at a methodological principle [which] suggests that the nature of a market economy is determined *through the particular relations it has with other social institutions*, not because it is separated from these institutions. ... [This] is derived from a holistic view of society, from looking at the various ways economic life is structured and shaped by economic institutions and relations [thereby inviting] the researcher to look for the social processes that structure and shape economic life. However, embeddedness itself is not a causal force or mechanism, nor does it specify how economic activities are structured by social factors. (Gemici, 2008: 24, 27, emphasis added)

Polanyi's methodological approach entailed an iterative engagement with actually existing (or formerly existing) *real economies*, understood in terms of their prevailing patterns of institutionalisation, applying, interrogating and refining mid-level concepts along the way. This is a receipt for reflexive theorising with, and between, concrete cases in a manner especially sensitive to socioinstitutional situation and context. Economies are 'emplaced'; investigations of their placement and positioning is an ongoing and never-complete task. Economic behaviour is always situated behaviour; it does not take place on the head of a pin. 'The substantive economy is situated in both time and place', is how Halperin (1994: 209) chose to characterise the approach; 'The formal economy, by contrast, operates in a time and space vacuum.'

The formal economics of the rational-choice logicians was therefore sharply (and less than favourably) contrasted with the substantive economics of the institutionalists, approaches separated as if 'opposite directions of the compass', with the singular, deductive model of the former being derived purely 'from logic', while the variegated and more inductive conceptions associated with the latter were shaped 'from fact' (Polanyi, 1959: 162–163). For Polanyi the 'fount of ... substantive concepts is [consequently] the empirical economy itself', on which he grounded a programmatic concern with 'study of the manner in which the economic process is instituted at different times and places' (ibid.: 166, 168). This is certainly not, however, a blindly inductive mode of analysis. It is an approach that combined exploratory empirical investigations with the ongoing (re)formulation of concepts and mid-level theory claims.

Terms and definitions constructed without reference to factual data are hollow, while a mere collecting of facts without a readjustment of our [theoretical] perspective is barren. To break this vicious circle, conceptual and empirical research must be carried forward *pari passu* [side by side]. Our efforts shall be sustained by the awareness that there are no shortcuts on this trail of inquiry. (Polanyi, 1977: liv–lv)

For Polanyi this 'trail of inquiry' took the form of a programmatic investigation (across multiple cases, contexts and indeed centuries) of what he portrayed as institutionalised modes of economic integration: 'I prefer to deal with the economy primarily *as a matter of organization*, and to define organization in terms of the operations characteristic of the working of [those] institutions' (Polanyi, 1960: 330, emphasis added). It follows that the 'substantive definition of the economy necessarily serves to place the economic back in the context of the social whole' (Block and Somers, 1984: 63); since markets come in 'many variants', a minimal methodological reach must encompass that 'wider frame of reference to which the market itself is referable' (Polanyi, 1959: 182, 184).

Underscoring the scope of this project, Polanyi (1957a: 244) later observed that 'only the substantive meaning of "economic" is capable of yielding the concepts that are required by the social sciences for an investigation of all the empirical economies of the past and present'. Since economic understandings and actions are always mediated by institutional forms, these (variable) institutions provide entry points for understanding historically and geographically variegated economic formations. Correspondingly, Polanyi's instituted economy is a multilogical one. He identified three (and occasionally four) distinctive 'modes of economic integration' on the basis of historical and comparative investigations – reciprocity, redistribution and exchange, with the fourth being householding – thereby extending his critique of market monism to a pluralist ontological principle. As such, modes of integration are found in a wide array of heterogeneous combinations and localisations. These local combinations are governed by politics, by patterned institutions and by social struggles, not by deterministic laws. And even where one mode of integration is evidently dominant, that dominance may be co-dependent on other (ostensibly subordinate) forms. This non-reductionist understanding of economic formations and relations as combinatorial 'alloys', rich in variety and endemically prone to uneven development, is deeply resonant with approaches in economic geography (see Massey, 1995; Peck, 2017a).

Polanyi repeatedly emphasised that a 'wide variety of combinations was possible' (Fusfeld, 1994: 4), the clear implication being that economies are not simply differentiated by degree (say, of marketisation or modernisation, as if these were one-dimensional axes), but in qualitative or in-kind form (Halperin, 1994; Peck,

2005). Polanyi was emphatic that the different modes of integration should 'not [be taken to] represent "stages" of development. No sequence in time is implied. Several subordinate forms may be present alongside of the dominant one, which may itself recur after a temporary eclipse' (Polanyi, 1957a: 256). In fact, he had no time at all for those mechanical stage theories that, for all intents and purposes, seemed to be 'based on some kind of railway timetable of social development' (Polanyi, 2014a: 40). This position is consistent with his rejection of both Marxian teleology and neoclassical equilibrium.

From this perspective, economies are understood to be 'internally' heterogeneous, conjuncturally constituted phenomena; real markets are present but in variegated and variably institutionalised forms; particular modes of integration should not be expected to secure monopoly positions within actually existing economies, which are marked by hybridity and complex coexistence; economic logics and rationalities are plural, warranting parity of analytical esteem across modes of integration. Ironically, the Polanyian notion of market exchange may have been the most incomplete (see Krippner, 2001), since for the most part the market was analysed historically and in a manner that left open multiple (mis)interpretations, for example concerning whether markets might be 'more' or 'less' embedded (as opposed to *differently* embedded). If notionally 'less' embedded or less regulated markets are contrasted with (more) intensively instituted markets, a hypothetical and idealised notion of purity remains in place as the (universal) template against which earthly conditions, institutional interventions and other 'distortions' are being judged. The problem here is that the embedded market cannot but hail its 'disembedded' other, setting a contrast with what is not merely a bad abstraction but an ideologically loaded ideal type.

It is fair to conclude, however, that a Polanyian take on markets (like other modes of integration) should be grounded in a social ontology: markets are constituted through instituted processes; markets necessarily coexist and comingle with other (often enabling) forms of integration, usually in co-dependent and contradictory ways; and to the extent that markets display disembedding tendencies, far from being the prelude to equilibrium or the attainment of 'purity', these are themselves predictably disruptive, provoking a range of social and institutional responses or double movements. In this respect, 'the' market is neither singular nor is it a stable form, and it is certainly not self-regulating; rather, an array of market(-like) forms may be present within actually existing, heterogeneous economies. And rather than existing above, beyond or outside politics, markets exhibit an inescapably political form, their 'place' being contingent and contested.

This said, the scope for analysing *spatially* variegated economies in such terms has only been fitfully realised (Peck, 2005; Grabher, 2006; Peck and Theodore, 2007; Harvey, 2010). If there is a Polanyian injunction here it is that explorations of this unevenly developed, heterogeneous economy should be conducted systematically, with a view to theoretical recalibration and reconstruction; it is not an invitation to grant institutional integrity or causal efficacy to every 'local' configuration, or to wallow in shallow, contingent or surface-level economic-geographical differences in some theoretically unprincipled manner, simply for their own sake. The purpose of such substantivist investigations ought to be to probe underlying logics and institutionalised rationalities, together with characteristic forms of social embeddedness, *across cases*. It should not lead, therefore, to the proliferation of freely relativised 'local' models of economy, since variegation must be explored in the context of rigorously cross-cultural and comparative methodological matrices (see Pålsson Syll, 2005), with analyses that 'cross and criss-cross between differently organised economic processes' (Halperin, 1994: 10), both in situ and between places. This kind of approach is compatible, for example, with category-stretching explorations across and beyond 'varieties' of liberal-market capitalism at a range of scales (see Peck and Zhang, 2013; Zhang and Peck, 2016).

A premium is therefore placed on what one might call 'terrain-level' theorising, executed not from emblematic centres but across unevenly developed landscapes (see Peck, 2016, 2017b). Moving in this direction, Polanyi's post-war project was concerned to widen, rather than narrow or foreclose, the 'areas of fruitful comparison' (Dalton, 1965: 2). Polanyi was a rigorous and restless critic of both economic determinism and economic solipsism. He took methodological issue with the reflexive orthodox resort to the 'market shape of things' challenging the proclivity of neoclassical 'formalists ... to see an abstract individualism everywhere' (Polanyi, 1977: xl; Hann and Hart, 2011: 70). Beyond critiques of the 'market mentality', this entailed conceptually (and politically) generative accounts of alternative forms of economic coordination, like redistribution or reciprocity, understood both in their own terms and relationally, among their mutually constitutive others. Applying a Polanyian method, however, must entail more than the thick description of distinctive local economies, represented in commonsense categories, since the latter (and their accompanying empirical gaze) may be prone to ethnocentricity (Halperin, 1984; Gudeman, 2001). The knowing interrogation of always-revisable extra-local concepts and proto-theories must therefore play a central role in the evolving methodology of comparative economics. Comparison, in this context, performs the function of a methodological lever, opening up ways of seeing anew the economic-familiar, while expanding the repertoire of alternative arrangements, both achieved and imagined.

Because Polanyi's project of pancultural comparative economics was incomplete, never being extended – in practice – to an engagement with some of the more proximate forms of contemporary capitalism, the full implications of socioeconomic variegation have remained somewhat implicit within his conceptual schema. The subsequent ascendancy of neoliberalised capitalism, of course, means that this unfinished business must now be addressed, and explicitly rather than obliquely. Difference-finding and difference-*explaining* methodologies are therefore called for, which not only span but exceed the archipelagic and arterial formations of globalising capitalism (Burawoy, 2003; Peck and Theodore, 2007; Haberly and Wójcik, 2017; cf. Block, 2012). Statically comparative approaches, such as the varieties of capitalism rubric, might provide a point of departure here, but more suggestive are those that combine the recognition of difference with the exploration of dynamic interdependencies (see Peck, 2016). Neo-Polanyian approaches to comparative socioeconomics – heterodox economic geographies by another name – will consequently value creative and border-crossing methodological investigations that acknowledge, work with and seek to explain both multi-polarity and mutuality. These will not only need to extend across the revealed geographical variety of actually existing capitalist formations, but they will also need to map more-than-capitalist worlds, in terms of both their distinct rationalities and their co-constitutive relations. Likewise, spatially sensitive explorations of the instituted character, contextual constitution and situational variability of real markets is called for, albeit not in isolation (or under conditions of presumed dominance) but taking due account of their respective positioning and placement. This need not be seen, however, as some immodest 'correction' of Polanyi's project, but more a contribution to its ongoing fulfilment. All along, this demanded exhausting investigation and creative theorising *across difference*, not separating out markets or advanced capitalism as special cases, or as premonitions of a convergent future, but as economic formations 'located' among their diverse and coexistent others. 'Nothing could be more detrimental to a genuine comprehension of Polanyi's work', Gérald Berthoud (1990: 171) once remarked, than some artificial separation between the 'theoretician of primitive and archaic societies' and the 'radical critic of our economic modernity'.

Conclusion: for Polanyian economic geographies

The objective of this chapter has been to call attention to the (still substantially unrealised) potential of Polanyian approaches in the analysis of geographically variegated economies – to unhide Polanyi the critical economic geographer. Polanyi's was an analytical framework designed to recognise and *work with* difference. It was addressed to differently instituted economies, both historically and geographically, in that there was no expectation of a teleological end point or gravitational centre. It explored different modalities of socioeconomic organisation, such that even dominant modes of organisation, like markets, were understood to be coexistent with and co-dependent on others, like redistributive or reciprocal systems. And, perhaps above all, it reserved a space for differently imagined futures, in the sense that economic pathways are socially and politically moulded, not fixed, pivoting as they do around heterogeneous or 'mixed' configurations, in a multi-polar socioeconomic universe, rather than trekking towards some singular or ultimate form.

In conclusion, it can be suggested that an emergent form of Polanyian economic geography might be shaped around the following convictions. First, it must entail a forthright commitment to historical and comparative analysis, engaging with and reanimating the long since submerged project of comparative economics. Secondly, it must seek to stretch and interrogate registers of difference *within* local economies, across modes of integration, like exchange and redistribution or state–market relations, exploring not only their distinctive logics, but their intersections and interactions, tensions and tolerances, contradictions and complementarities as well. Thirdly, it must be institutionalist all the way down, being sceptical of economic reductionism and market essentialism in all its manifestations, exposing social constructions and institutionalised patterns, while seeking to enrich the political imaginary through the purposive investigation of alternative socioeconomic arrangements. And, fourthly, it must explicitly confront, and then work with, the tensions between holistic, integral modes of analysis and those difference-finding manoeuvres that yield exceptional or disruptive cases.

This amounts to a different way of thinking about the relationships between the general and the particular with regard to economic formations and transformations. It means placing the critical investigation of local economic practices, including alternative and experimental practices, in dialogue with probing analyses of the 'global', the extra-local and the macro, including transnational economic interdependence, corporate deepening and monopolisation, financialisation, informalisation and (splintering?) neoliberal hegemony. As the archaic boundaries between economic geography and development studies are gradually dismantled (Murphy, 2008; Roberts, 2012), as postcolonial critiques challenge the practice of theorising primarily from metropolitan centres (Radcliffe, 2005; Pollard et al., 2009), as the case for extending the ethnographic reach of the field is made and heard (Dunn, 2007; Werner, 2015), and as new research agendas evolve around the problematics of diverse, variegated and unevenly developed economies (Peck and Theodore,

2007; Gibson-Graham, 2008); so there is potential for economic geographers to make common cause with the re-energised project of Polanyian economics in the pursuit of more richly relational, truly translocal forms of socioeconomic analysis. Intriguingly, any such conversation would throw into sharp relief the methodological questions of how to theorise socioeconomic diversity across and within heterogeneous 'local' economies, and between capitalism and its others.

Polanyi is regarded by many to be an inspirational but somewhat idiosyncratic theorist. His analytical admonitions are invariably provocative and often generative, but they can also be cryptic and inconsistent. He may have walked the walk of substantivist, comparative economics, but this was a journey that he never got to complete. Polanyi made the case for enriching the repertoire of socioeconomic analysis by way of ambitious, category-stretching comparisons, both historically and geographically, even if the critical edges of his contemporary, up-close investigations were somewhat blunted with time. The argument in this chapter has been that, while it is important to recognise these foibles, in as far as they speak to a wider programme that for various reasons was frustrated, there is no reason that this should continue to hinder contemporary elaborations or extensions of the neoPolanyian project; hence the approach adopted here of reading Polanyian legacy in a cooperative and creative spirit, not for iron-clad rules and finished formulations, less still to dwell upon limits or lapses, but for its methodological and analytical *potential*.

This is anything but a bloodlessly technical exercise, it should be underlined. Polanyi held resolutely to the view that it is politics that ultimately shape economies, not the other way around (Block, 2012). In this spirit, the search for more humane and sustainable ways of living can be facilitated not just by the trenchant critique and denaturalisation of current circumstances, but also with the aid of creative explorations of the political economy of alternatives – from the wide array of actually existing real economies, or what might be called economies *elsewhere*, to the renewal of economic imaginaries and 'real utopias', or what might be termed economies *otherwise*. Polanyi's programmatic project of comparative economics was only realised in incomplete outline. It is one that he was still attempting to advance with the launch of the journal *Coexistence*, in the final years of his life (see Dale, 2016a). Arguably, it is needed now, maybe even more urgently than before. This is a project in which economic geography may well have an active part to play. For their part, economic geographers may come to find that working under the sign of Polanyi is not only conducive to the field's pluralist disposition, it also promises to animate new projects, indeed to open up new horizons.

Note

1 For a selection of Polanyian currents in economic geography, see Gertler (2003), Hess (2004), Peck (2005, 2012, 2013a, 2013b), Grabher (2006) and Rankin (2013). The remainder of this chapter draws selectively on several previously published papers and commentaries: Peck (2013a, 2013b, 2015).

Bibliography

Documents written by Karl Polanyi and held at the Karl Polanyi Archive, Concordia University (Montreal)

01–06, Nézeteink válsága (The Crisis in our Ideology), *Huszadik Század*, 1909.

3–14, TVA – Ein Amerikanisches Wirtschaftsexperiment, 1936.

8–11, The Democratic Alternative: Is America an Exception, ~1943.

8–3, Political and Economic Experiments in Our Time – USA and New Deal, ~1935–36.

11–9, Notes on Reading, 1934–46.

12–7, Essence of Fascism, 1941.

15–2, Conflicting Philosophies in Modern Society, 1937–38.

15–8, Course on 'Government and Industry', 13 October 1943.

16–1a, Morley Lectures in International Affairs, 1945–46.

16–1b, Is a Better World Obtainable?, ~1945–46.

16–4, The Theory of Politics, ~1938.

16–5, Course Proposal on 'America 1943', 1943.

16–10, Conflicting Philosophies in Europe, 1937.

16–12, Lecture Notes on Modern European History, 1937–38.

16–13, Modern European History (Part 2), 1938–39.

16–16, Rochester Lectures on International Affairs, 1939.

17–1, Canterbury Lectures on Democracy and Culture, 1938–39.

17–3, Social and Political Thought, 1939.

17–19, Versailles and After, 1938.

18–8, The Fascist Virus, ~1944.

18–14, Observations on Education for Politics in England and the United States, 1936.

18–25, America 1943, 1943.

18–33, Socialist Education in the Labour Movement, 1945/46.

18–34, British Labour and American New Dealers, *The Leeds Weekly Citizen*, 10 January 1947.

19–5, Origins of the Cataclysm, Version A, ~1943.

19–8, The Meaning of Parliamentary Democracy, ~1945/46.

19–26, Experiences in Vienna and America, 1936–37.

20–2, Tame Empires, ~1943.

21–11, The Nature of the Present World Crisis, 1937.

21–20, Fascist Economics, mid-1930s.

29–8, Bibliography, annotated by Karl Polanyi, ~1960.

Bibliography

35–8, Whither Civilisation, 1946.
37–06, The Machine Age and the Discovery of Society, 1957.
37–11, Galbraith's Farewell to Poverty, 15 January 1959.
47–8, Letter to Peter [Drucker], 24 June 1937.
47–15, Letter to Oscar Jaszi, 28 August 1945.
56–13, Letter to Irene Grant, February 1947.

Secondary sources

Amin, Samir. 1990. *Delinking: Towards a Polycentric World*. London: Zed.
_____. 2017. 'From Bandung (1955) to 2015: old and new challenges for the states, the nations and the peoples of Asia, Africa and Latin America', *Interventions*, 19:5, 609–619.
Arrighi, Giovanni. 1978. *The Geometry of Imperialism: The Limits of Hobson's Paradigm*. Trans. P. Camiller. London: New Left Books.
_____. 1991. 'World income inequalities and the future of socialism', *New Left Review*, 189, 39–65.
_____. 1994. *The Long Twentieth Century: Money, Power, and the Origins of our Time*. London: Verso.
_____. 1998. 'Capitalism and the modern world-system: rethinking the non-debates of the 1970s', *Review*, 21:1, 113–129.
_____. 1999a. 'Globalization, state sovereignty, and the "endless" accumulation of capital', in D. A. Smith, D. J. Solinger and S. C. Topik (eds), *States and Sovereignty in the Global Economy*. London: Routledge, pp. 53–72.
_____. 1999b. 'The world according to Andre Gunder Frank', *Review*, 22:3, 327–354.
_____. 2001. 'Braudel, capitalism, and the new economic sociology', *Review*, 24:1, 107–123.
_____. 2003. 'Lineages of empire', in G. Balakrishnan (ed.), *Debating Empire*. London: Verso, pp. 29–42.
_____. 2007. *Adam Smith in Beijing: Lineages of the Twenty-first Century*. London: Verso.
_____. 2009a. 'The winding paths of capital' (interview by David Harvey), *New Left Review*, 56, 61–94.
_____. 2009b. 'Postscript', in *The Long Twentieth Century: Money, Power, and the Origins of our Times*. 2nd ed. London: Verso.
_____. 2010. *The Long Twentieth Century: Money, Power and the Origins of our Times*. Miamisburg, OH: Verso.
Arrighi, G. and J. Drangel. 1986. 'The stratification of the world-economy: an exploration of the semiperipheral zone', *Review*, 10:1, 9–74.
Arrighi, G., P. K. Hui and H.-F. Hung. 1999. 'Historical capitalism, East and West', revised version of a paper, 'The rise of East Asia: 500, 150, 50 years perspectives', Institute for Global Studies, Johns Hopkins University, 4–5 December.
Austin, P. E. 2007. *Baring Brothers and the Birth of Modern Finance*. London: Pickering & Chatto.
B20. 2012. *B20 Task Force Recommendations: Concrete Actions for Los Cabos*. June, http://b20.org/documentos/B20-Task-Force-Recommendations.pdf. Accessed 9 September 2012.
Bairoch, P. 1995. *Economics and World History: Myths and Paradoxes*. Chicago: University of Chicago Press.
Baker, Dean. 2016. *Rigged: How Globalization and the Rules of the Modern Economy Were*

Structured to Make the Rich Richer. Washington, D.C.: Center for Economic and Policy Research.

Baker, Dean and Travis McArthur. 2009. 'The value of the "too big to fail" big bank subsidy', *Center for Economic and Policy Research (CEPR).* CEPR Reports and Issue Briefs, January.

Barber, B. 1995. 'All economies are "embedded": the career of a concept, and beyond', *Social Research*, 62:2, 387–413.

Bauer, O. [1919] 1976. 'Der Weg zum Sozialismus', in O. Bauer, *Werke, Bd. 2.* Wien: Europaverlag, pp. 89–131.

Becker, G. S. 1978. *The Economic Approach to Human Behavior.* Chicago: University of Chicago Press.

Beckert, J. 2007. 'The Great Transformation of Embeddedness: Karl Polanyi and the New Economic Sociology', MPIfG Discussion Paper 07/1. Cologne: Max Planck Institute for the Study of Societies.

Bell, Daniel. [1973] 1976. *The Coming of Post-industrial Society.* New York: Beacon Press.

––––––. [1952] 1996. *Marxian Socialism in the United States.* Ithaca, NY: Cornell University Press.

Berndt, C. and M. Boeckler. 2012. 'Geographies of marketization', in T. J. Barnes, J. Peck and E. Sheppard (eds), *The Wiley-Blackwell Companion to Economic Geography.* Oxford: Wiley-Blackwell, pp. 199–212.

Berthoud, G. 1990. 'Toward a comparative approach: the contribution of Karl Polanyi', in K. Polanyi Levitt (ed.), 1990a.

Beveridge, W. 1942. *Social Insurance and Allied Services.* United Kingdom: His Majesty's Stationery Office.

––––––. 1944. *Full Employment in a Free Society.* United Kingdom: Allen & Unwin.

Block, Fred. 1977. *The Origins of the International Economic Disorder: A Study of United States International Monetary Policy from World War II to the Present.* Berkeley, CA: University of California Press.

––––––. 2001. 'Introduction', in Karl Polanyi [1944] 2001, pp. xviii–xxxviii.

––––––. 2003. 'Karl Polanyi and the writing of *The Great Transformation*', *Theory and Society*, 32:3, 275–306.

––––––. 2008. 'Swimming against the current: the rise of a hidden developmental state in the United States', *Politics & Society*, 36:2, 169–206.

––––––. 2012. 'Varieties of what? Should we still be using the concept of capitalism?', in J. Go (ed.), *Political Power and Social Theory*, 23. Bingley, Yorks: Emerald, pp. 269–291.

––––––. 2013. 'Relational work and the law: recapturing the legal realist critique of market fundamentalism', *Journal of Law and Society*, 40:1, 27–48.

––––––. 2014. 'Democratizing finance'. *Politics and Society*, 42:1, 3–28.

––––––. 2015. 'A Neo-Polanyian theory of economic crises', *American Journal of Economics and Sociology*, 74:2, 361–378.

––––––. 2018a. 'Karl Polanyi and human freedom', in Michael Brie and Claus Thomasberger (eds), 2018, pp. 168–184.

––––––. 2018b. *Capitalism: The Future of an Illusion.* Berkeley, CA: University of California Press.

Block, F. and M. R. Somers. 1984. 'Beyond the economistic fallacy: the holistic social science of Karl Polanyi', in T. Skocpol (ed.), *Vision and Method in Historical Sociology.* Cambridge: Cambridge University Press, pp. 47–84.

––––––. 2003. 'Karl Polanyi and the writing of *The Great Transformation*', *Theory and Society*, 32, 275–306.

_____. 2014. *The Power of Market Fundamentalism: Karl's Polanyi's Critique*. Cambridge, MA: Harvard University Press.

_____. 2017a. 'Karl Polanyi in an age of uncertainty', *Contemporary Sociology*, 46:4, 379–392.

_____. 2017b. 'Reply to Dale', *Contemporary Sociology*, 46:6, 734–735.

Board of Governors of the Federal Reserve. 2019. 'Federal Reserve banks', www.federal-reserve.gov/aboutthefed/federal-reserve-system.htm. Accessed 1 January 2020.

Bockman, J. 2013. *Markets in the Name of Socialism: The Left-Wing Origins of Neoliberalism*. Stanford, CA: Stanford University Press.

Bockman, J., A. Fischer and D. Woodruff. 2016. 'Preface "Socialism and the Embedded Economy" to "Socialist Accounting" by Karl Polanyi', *Theory and Society*, 45:5, 385–427.

Bolton, Matt and Frederick Harry Pitts. *Corbynism: A Critical Approach*. Bingley, Yorks: Emerald.

Bordo, M. and A. Schwartz. 2001. 'From the Exchange Stabilization Fund to the International Monetary Fund', *NBER Working Paper*, 8100, January.

Boyer, Robert and J. R. Hollingsworth. 1997. 'From national embeddedness to spatial and institutional nestedness', in J. R. Hollingsworth and R. Boyer (eds), *Contemporary Capitalism: The Embeddedness of Institutions*. Cambridge: Cambridge University Press, pp. 433–484.

Braudel, F. 1979. *The Wheels of Commerce: Civilization and Capitalism, 15th–18th Century, Vol. II*. Trans. S. Reynolds. New York: Harper & Row.

Brie, Michael. 2017. 'For an alliance of Liberal Socialists and Libertarian Commonist: Nancy Fraser and Karl Polanyi – a possible dialogue', in M. Brie (ed.), *Karl Polanyi in Dialogue: A Socialist Thinker for Our Times*. Montreal: Black Rose Books, pp. 7–64.

Brie, Michael and Claus Thomasberger (eds). 2018. *Karl Polanyi's Vision of a Socialist Transformation*. Montreal: Black Rose Books.

Buchanan, James M. and Gordon Tullock. 1962. *The Calculus of Consent: Logical Foundations of Constitutional Democracy*. Ann Arbor, MI: University of Michigan Press.

Bukharin, Nicolai. [1914] 1972. *The Economic Theory of the Leisure Class*. New York: Monthly Review Press.

Burawoy, M. 2003. 'For a sociological Marxism: the complementary convergence of Antonio Gramsci and Karl Polanyi', *Politics and Society*, 31:2, 193–261.

Burgin, Angus. 2015. *The Great Persuasion: Reinventing Free Markets since the Depression*. Cambridge, MA: Harvard University Press.

Cangiani, Michele. 1994. 'Prelude to *The Great Transformation*: Karl Polanyi's articles for *Der Oesterreichische Volkswirt*', in K. McRobbie (ed.), *Humanity, Society and Commitment: On Karl Polanyi*. Montréal: Black Rose Books, pp. 7–24.

_____. 2002. 'L'inattualita di Polanyi', *Contemporanea*, 5, 751–757.

_____. 2003. 'Machtpolitik, systemkonfrontation und friedliche Koexistenz: die Bedeutung der Demokratie: Karl Polanyi's Analysen der internationalen Beziehungen', in M. Cangiani and C. Thomasberger (eds), *Chronik der großen Transformation 2*. Marburg: Metropolis-Verlag, pp. 11–43.

_____. 2010. 'From Menger to Polanyi: the Institutional Way', in Harand Hagemann, Tamotsu Nishizawa and Yukihiro Ideda (eds), *Austrian Economics in Transition: From Carl Menger to Freidrich Hayek*. Basingstoke: Macmillan, pp. 138–153.

_____. 2011. 'Karl Polanyi's institutional theory: market society and its "disembedded" economy', *Journal of Economic Issues*, 45:1, 177–198.

Cangiani, Michele and Claus Thomasberger. 2002. 'Marketgesellschaft und Demokratie: die

Perspective der menschlichen Freiheit. Karl Polanyi's Arbeiten von 1920 bis 1945', in Karl Polanyi 2002, pp. 11–45.

_____. 2003. 'Machtpolitik, systemkonfrontation und friedliche Koexistenz: die Bedeutung der Demokratie: Karl Polanyis Analysen der internationalen Beziehungen', in M. Cangiani and C. Thomasberger (eds), *Chronik der großen Transformation 2*. Marburg: Metropolis-Verlag, pp. 11–43.

Cangiani, Michele, Kari Polanyi Levitt and Claus Thomasberger. 2005. 'Die Polarität: Menschliche Freiheit – marktwirtschaftliche Institutionen: Zu den grundlagen von Karl Polanyis Denken', in M. Cangiani, K. Polanyi Levitt, and C. Thomasberger (eds), *Chronik der großen Transformation 3*. Marburg: Metropolis-Verlag, pp. 15–64.

Catanzariti, Mariavittoria. 2014. 'Postface', in Karl Polanyi, 2014a, pp. 221–241.

Chandrasekhar, C. P. 2018. '"Wageless growth" not "jobless growth"' the new conundrum', *Frontline Print*, December.

Chancier, P., F. Joannès, P. Rouillard and A. Tenu (eds). 2005. *Autour de Polanyi: vocabulaires, théories et modalities des échanges*. Paris: De Boccard: Colloques de la Maison René-Ginouvès.

Chang, H. 2002. *Kicking Away the Ladder: Development Strategy in Historical Perspective*. London: Anthem.

Chang, H. and I. Grabel. 2014. *Reclaiming Development: An Alternative Economic Policy Manual*. London: Zed Books.

Charpin, Dominique. 2003. *Hammurabi of Babylon*. London and New York: I. B. Tauris & Co. Ltd..

Clark, G. L. 1998. 'Stylized facts and close dialogue: methodology in economic geography', *Annals of the Association of American Geographers*, 88:1, 73–87.

Clarke, Simon. 1991. *Marx, Marginalism and Modern Sociology: From Adam Smith to Max Weber*. 2nd ed. Basingstoke: Macmillan Academic and Professional.

Cohen, Benjamin J. 2008. *International Political Economy: An Intellectual History*. Princeton, NJ: Princeton University Press.

Cole, G. D. H. 1920. *Guild Socialism Re-stated*. London: L. Parsons.

Colletti, Lucio. 1974. 'Bernstein and the Marxism of the Second International', in *From Rousseau to Lenin*. London: New Left Books.

Coser, L. A. 1984. *Refugee Scholars in America: Their Impact and Their Experiences*. New Haven, CT: Yale University Press.

Crain, C. 2018. 'Is capitalism a threat to democracy?', *The New Yorker*, 14 May. Review of Robert Kuttner's *Can Democracy Survive Global Capitalism?*.

Crouch, Colin. 2011. *The Strange Non-death of Neoliberalism*. Oxford: Polity.

Dale, Gareth. 2008. 'Karl Polanyi's The Great Transformation: perverse effects, protectionism and Gemeinschaft', *Economy and Society*, 37:4, 495–524.

_____. 2010a. *Karl Polanyi: The Limits of the Market*. Cambridge: Polity.

_____. 2010b. 'Social democracy, embeddedness and decommodification: on the conceptual innovations and intellectual affiliations of Karl Polanyi', *New Political Economy*, 15:3, 369–393.

_____. 2011. 'Lineages of embeddedness: on the antecedents and successors of a Polanyian concept', *American Journal of Economics and Sociology*, 70:2, 306–339.

_____. 2012. 'Double movements and pendular forces: Polanyian perspectives on the neoliberal age', *Current Sociology*, 60:3, 3–27.

_____. 2013. 'The boundaries of cosmopolitanism: Karl Polanyi and the "Magyar–Jewish mongrel"', *Environment and Planning A*, 45:7, 1643–1649.

_____. 2016a. *Karl Polanyi: A Life on the Left*. New York: Columbia University Press.

_____. 2016b. *Reconstructing Karl Polanyi*. London: Pluto.

_____. 2016c. 'Introduction', in Karl Polanyi, 2016, pp. 1–37.

_____. 2017. 'Reply to Block and Somers', *Contemporary Sociology*, 46:6, 733–734.

_____. 2018. 'Karl Polanyi and the paradoxes of freedom', in M. Brie and C. Thomasberger (eds), 2018, pp. 126–139.

Dalós, György. 1990. 'The fidelity of equals: Ilona Duczynska and Karl Polanyi', in K. Polanyi Levitt, 1990a, pp. 38–42.

Dalton, G. 1965. 'Primitive, archaic, and modern economies: Karl Polanyi's contribution to economic anthropology and comparative economy', in J. Helm, P. Bohannan and M. Sahlins (eds), *Essays in Economic Anthropology*. Seattle, WA: American Ethnological Society and University of Washington, pp. 1–24.

_____. 1990. 'Writings that clarify theoretical disputes over Karl Polanyi's work', *Journal of Economic Issues*, 24:1, 249–261.

De Cecco, Marcello. 1984. *The International Gold Standard: Money and Empire*. 2nd ed. London: Pinter.

Delong, J. Bradford. 2016. 'Which thinkers will define our future?', 28 June, www.pro ject-syndicate.org/commentary/thinkers-who-define-future-by-j--bradford-delong-2016-06?barrier=accesspaylog. Accessed 29 December 2019.

Demandt, A. *Der Fall Roms: Die Auflösung des römischen Reiches im Urteil der Nachwelt*. Munich: C. H. Beck, 1984.

Derber, Milton 1975. 'The New Deal and Labor', in John Braeman, Robert H. Brenmer and David Brody (eds), *The New Deal, Vol. 1*. Columbus, OH: Ohio State University Press.

Desai, Radhika. 1994. 'Second-hand dealers in ideas: think-tanks and Thatcherite hegemony', *New Left Review*, no. I/203, 27–64.

_____. 2006. 'Neoliberalism and cultural nationalism', in Dieter Plehwe, Bernhard Walpen and Gisela Nuenhoeffer (eds), *Neo-liberal Hegemony: A Global Critique*. New York: Routledge, pp. 222–235.

_____. 2009a. 'The inadvertence of Benedict Anderson: engaging imagined communities', *Asia-Pacific Journal*, 11 (16 March), 1–22.

_____. 2009b. 'Keynes redux: from world money to international money at last?', in Wayne Anthony and Julie Guard (eds), *Bailouts and Bankruptcies*. Halifax: Fernwood Books.

_____. 2009c. *Developmental and Cultural Nationalisms*. London: Routledge.

_____. 2010. 'Consumption demand in Marx and in the current crisis', *Research in Political Economy*, 26, 101–141.

_____. 2012. 'Marx, List, and the materiality of nations.' *Rethinking Marxism*, 24:1, 47–67.

_____. 2013. *Geopolitical Economy: After US Hegemony, Globalization and Empire*. London: Pluto.

_____. 2016. 'The value of history and the history of value', in Turan Subasat (ed.), *The Great Meltdown of 2008: Systemic, Conjunctural or Policy-Created?* Cheltenham and Northampton, MA: Edward Elgar Publishing.

_____. 2018a. 'John Maynard Pangloss: *Indian Currency and Finance* in imperial context', in Sheila Dow, Jesper Jespersen and Geoff Tily (eds), *The General Theory and Keynes for the Twenty First Century*. Cheltenham: Edward Elgar, pp. 116–131.

_____. 2018b. 'Political economy', in Imre Szeman, Andrew Pendakis and Jeff Diamanti (eds), *The Bloomsbury Companion to Marx*. London: Bloomsbury, pp. 199–218.

_____. 2018c. 'With or without Trump: the crisis of multilateralism', keynote address at the Rosa Luxemburg Stiftung, Brussels, Strategic Workshop on 'The Global Economy and International Politics beyond Neo-liberalism', 22–23 November.

_____. 2019. 'Remastering the soundtrack of a clash of titans: Polanyi's *The Great Transformation* and Hayek's *The Road to Serfdom*', in Kirrily Freeman and John Munro (eds), *Reading the Postwar Future: Textual Turning Points from 1944*. London: Bloomsbury, pp. 17–42.

Devitt, M. 2018. 'CDC data show U.S. life expectancy continues to decline: suicides, drug overdose deaths named as key contributors', *American Academy of Family Physicians*, https://tinyurl.com/yyh4zhyv. Accessed 20 November 2019.

Dewey, C. 1978. 'The end of the imperialism of free trade: the eclipse of the Lancashire Lobby and the concession of fiscal autonomy to India', in C. Dewey and A. G. Hopkins (eds), *The Imperial Impact: Studies in the Economic History of Africa and India*. London: University of London, pp. 35–67.

Dicey, A. V. 1905. *Law and Opinion in England*. Oxford: Oxford University Press.

Dillard, D. 1948. 'The Keynesian revolution and economic development', *Journal of Economic History*, 8:2, 171–177.

Dobb, Maurice. 1973. *Theories of Value and Distribution since Adam Smith*. Cambridge: Cambridge University Press.

Dorgan, B. 1999. 'Financial services', speech in Capitol Hill, November, viewed in CSPAN2 at http://billmoyers.com/content/a-senators-prophetic-words-then-and-now/. Accessed 25 September 2012.

Dowling, J. H. 1979. 'The goodfellows vs. the Dalton gang: the assumptions of economic anthropology', *Journal of Anthropological Research*, 35:3, 292–308.

Duczynska Polanyi, I. 2006. 'I first met Karl Polanyi in 1920 …', in K. McRobbie and K. Polanyi Levitt (eds), *Karl Polanyi in Vienna: The Contemporary Significance of The Great Transformation*. Montréal: Black Rose Books, pp. 302–315.

Dunn, E. 2007. 'Of pufferfish and ethnography: plumbing new depths in economic geography', in A. Tickell, E. Sheppard, J. Peck and T. J. Barnes (eds), *Politics and Practice in Economic Geography*. London: Sage, pp. 82–93.

Economist, The. 2018. 'The great transformation', *The Economist*, 17 May.

Eichengreen, B. 2008. *Globalizing Capital: A History of the International Monetary System*. Princeton, NJ: Princeton University Press.

Eisenhower, D. 1961. 'Military-industrial complex farewell speech', Public Papers of the Presidents, Dwight D. Eisenhower, 1960–61: containing the public messages, speeches, and statements of the president, 1 January 1960, to 20 January 1961, pp. 1035–1040, https://quod.lib.umich.edu/p/ppotpus/4728424.1960.001/1087?rgn=full+text;view=image. Accessed 23 September 2012.

Elliot, Larry. 2012. 'Davos 2012: soul searching at the World Economic Forum', *The Guardian*, 25 January.

Elwell, C. K. 2011. 'Brief history of the Gold Standard in the United States', Congressional Research Service, 7-5700, R41887, www.fas.org/sgp/crs/misc/R41887.pdf. Accessed 24 September 2012.

Engels, F. [1876] 1983. 'Socialism: utopian and scientific', in Karl Marx and Fredriech Engels, *Collected Works, Vol. 24*. New York: International Publishers, pp. 281–325.

Escobar, P. 2018. 'Back in the (great) game: the revenge of Eurasian land powers', *Consortium News*, 29 August.

Esping-Andersen, Gøsta. 1990. *The Three Worlds of Welfare Capitalism*. Princeton, NJ: Princeton University Press.

Bibliography

Fay, Bernard. 1933. *Roosevelt and his America*. Boston, MA: Little, Brown and Company.

Ferguson, C.H. (2010), *The Inside Job*, documentary film. https://vimeo.com/330323183.

Ferrater Mora, José. 1964. *Diccionario de Filosofía*. 5th ed. Buenos Aires: Editorial Sudamericana.

Financial Crisis Inquiry Commission ('Angelides Commission'). 2010. *Official Transcript of Commission Hearing*, Wednesday, April 7, 2010, Washington DC, p. 93, lines 21–24, http://fcic-static.law.stanford.edu/cdn_media/fcic-testimony/2010-0407-Transcript.pdf. Accessed 14 December 2019.

Financial Crisis Inquiry Commission. 2011. *The Financial Crisis Inquiry Report: Final Report of the National Commission on the Causes of the Financial and Economic Crisis in the United States*, www.govinfo.gov/content/pkg/GPO-FCIC/pdf/GPO-FCIC.pdf. Accessed 2 April 2013.

Finley, Moses. 1985. *The Ancient Economy*. 2nd ed. Berkeley, CA: University of California Press.

Foroohar, Rana. 2016. *Makers and Takers: The Rise of Finance and the Fall of American Business*. New York: Crown Business.

Fraser, Nancy. 2012. 'Can society be commodities all the way down? Polanyian reflections on capitalist crisis', FMSHWP-2012–18, Fondation Maison des sciences de l'homme, Paris.

_____. 2013. 'A triple movement? Parsing the politics of crisis after Polanyi', *New Left Review*, 81, 119–132.

Frenkel, R. and M. Rappetti. 2011. 'Fragilidad externa o desindustrialización: ¿Cuál es la principal amenaza para América Latina en la próxima década?', *Cuadernos de la CEPAL, serie Macroeconomía para el desarrollo*. 116, Naciones Unidas, Comisión Económica para America Latina, Santiago de Chile.

Fried, Barbara H. 1998. *The Progressive Assault on Laissez Faire: Robert Hale and the First Law and Economics Movement*. Cambridge, MA: Harvard University Press.

Friedman, M. 1982. *Capitalism and Freedom*. Chicago: University of Chicago Press.

Fröbel, F., J. Heinrichs, O. Kreye and P. Burgess. 1980. *The New International Division of Labour: Structural Unemployment in Industrialised Countries and Industrialisation in Developing Countries*. Cambridge: Cambridge University Press.

Furtado, C. 1978. 'Accumulation and creativity', *CEPAL Review*, 6, 19–26.

Fusfeld, D. J. 1994. 'Karl Polanyi's lectures on General Economic History: a student remembers', in K. McRobbie (ed.), *Humanity, Society and Commitment: On Karl Polanyi*. Montréal: Black Rose Books, pp. 1–6.

Galbraith, J. K. 2014. *The End of Normal: The Great Crisis and the Future of Growth*. New York: Simon and Schuster.

_____. 2019. 'Inevitable war?', in *The Crisis of Globalisation*. London: Social Europe, pp. 30–33.

Gallagher, John and Ronald Robinson. 1953. 'The imperialism of free trade', *Economic History Review*, 6:1, 1–15.

Garber, P. 1991. 'The collapse of the Bretton Woods fixed exchange rate system', in M. Bordo and B. Eichengreen (eds), *A Retrospective on the Bretton Woods System: Lessons for International Monetary Reform*. Chicago: University of Chicago Press.

Garfinkle, Steven J. 2004a. 'Shepherds, merchants, and credit: some observations on lending practices in Ur III Mesopotamia', *Journal of the Economic and Social History of the Orient*, 47, 1–30.

_____. 2004b. 'Public versus private in the Ancient Near East', in Daniel C. Snell (ed.), *A Companion to the Ancient Near East*. Malden, MA: Blackwell, pp. 384–396.

Bibliography

_____. 2012. *Entrepreneurs and Enterprise in Early Mesopotamia: A Study of Three Archives from the Third Dynasty of Ur (2112–2004 BC)*. Bethesda, MD: CDL Press.

Gemici, K. 2008. 'Karl Polanyi and the antinomies of embeddedness', *Socio-Economic Review*, 6:1, 5–33.

Gerschenkron, Alexander. 1962. *Economic Backwardness in Historical Perspective: A Book of Essays*. Cambridge, MA: Harvard University Press.

Gertler, M. S. 2003. 'A cultural economic geography of production', in K. Anderson, M. Domosh, S. Pile and N. Thrift (eds), *Handbook of Cultural Geography*. London: Sage, pp. 131–146.

_____. 2010. 'Rules of the game: the place of institutions in regional economic change', *Regional Studies*, 44:1, 1–15.

Gibson-Graham, J. K. 2008. 'Diverse economies: performative practices for "other worlds"', *Progress in Human Geography*, 32:5, 613–632.

Gills, B. 2008. 'The swinging of the pendulum: the global crisis and beyond', *Globalizations*, 5:4, 513–522.

Goldfrank, W. L. (2000). 'Paradigm regained? The rules of Wallerstein's world-system method', *Journal of World Systems Research*, 11:2, 150–195.

Gordon, David, Richard Edwards and Michael Reich. 1982. *Segmented Work: Divided Workers*. Cambridge: Cambridge University Press.

Grabher, G. 2006. 'Trading routes, bypasses, and risky intersections: mapping the travels of "networks" between economic sociology and economic geography', *Progress in Human Geography*, 30:2, 163–189.

Graeber, David. 2011. *Debt: The First 5,000 Years*. New York: Melville House.

Gramsci, A. 1917. 'The revolution against "capital"', *Avanti!* (Milan), 24 November.

Granovetter, M. 1985. 'Economic action and social structure: the problem of embeddedness', *American Journal of Sociology*, 91:3, 481–510.

Greenspan, A. 1996. 'The challenge of central banking in a democratic society', remarks by Chairman Alan Greenspan at the Annual Dinner and Francis Boyer Lecture of the American Enterprise Institute for Public Policy Research, Washington, D. C. 5 December.

Gudeman, S. 2001. *The Anthropology of Economy: Community, Market, and Culture*. Oxford: Wiley-Blackwell.

Haass, R. N. 2008. 'The age of nonpolarity: what will follow U.S. dominance', *Foreign Affairs*, May/June, 44–56.

Haberly, D. and D. Wójcik. 2017. 'Earth Incorporated: centralization and variegation in the global company network', *Economic Geography*, 93:3, 241–266.

Habermas, J. [1981] 1987. *Theory of Communicative Action*. Boston: Beacon Press.

Hacker, Jacob. 2011. 'The institutional foundations of middle-class democracy', Policy Network, http://connection.ebscohost.com/c/articles/83851145/institutional-foundations-middle-class-democracy. Accessed 1 January 2020.

Hale, Robert L. 1923. 'Coercion and distribution in a supposedly non-coercive state', *Political Science Quarterly*, 38:3, 470–494.

Halevy, E. [1901] 1949. *The Growth of Philosophical Radicalism (La formation du Radicalisme Philosophique)*. London: Faber.

Halperin, R. H. 1984. 'Polanyi, Marx, and the institutional paradigm in economic anthropology', in B. L. Isaac (ed.), *Research in Economic Anthropology*, Volume 6. Greenwich, CT: JAI Press, pp. 245–272.

_____. 1988. *Economies Across Cultures: Towards a Comparative Science of the Economy*. Basingstoke: Macmillan.

_____. 1994. *Cultural Economies Past and Present*. Austin, TX: University of Texas Press.

Hann, C. and K. Hart. 2011. *Economic Anthropology: History, Ethnography, Culture*. Cambridge: Cambridge University Press.

Harvey, D. 2004. 'El nuevo imperialismo: acumulación por desposesión', in *Socialist Register*. Buenos Aires: CLASCO, , pp. 99129.

Harvey, M. 2010. 'Introduction: putting markets in their place', in M. Harvey (ed.), *Markets, Rules and Institutions of Exchange*. Manchester: Manchester University Press, pp. 1–31.

Hayek, F. A. 1937. 'Economics and knowledge', *Economica*, New Series, 4:13, 33–54.

_____. [1939] 1980. 'The economic conditions of interstate federalism', in *Individual and Economic Order*. Chicago: University of Chicago Press, pp. 255–272.

_____. [1944] 2001. *The Road to Serfdom*. London and New York: Routledge.

_____. 1945. 'The use of knowledge in society', *American Economic Review*, XXXV:4, 519–530.

_____. 1960. *The Constitution of Liberty*. Chicago: University of Chicago Press.

_____. [1960] 2009. *The Constitution of Liberty*. London and New York: Routledge.

_____. 1994. *The Road to Serfdom*. Chicago: University of Chicago Press.

Hayter, T. 1971. *Aid as Imperialism*. London: Penguin Books.

Heichelheim, Fritz. 1958. *An Ancient Economic History, from the Palaeolithic Age to the Migrations of the Germanic, Slavic and Arabic Nations, I*. Rev. ed. Leiden: A. W. Sijthoff.

_____. 1960. 'Review of Polanyi, Arensberg and Pearson, Trade and Market in the Early Empires', *Journal of the Economic and Social History of the Orient*, 3, 108–110.

Helleiner, Eric. 2005. 'Globalization and haute finance – déja vu', in Kenneth McRobbie and Kari Polanyi Levitt (eds), *Karl Polanyi in Vienna: The Contemporary Significance of the Great Transformation*. Montreal: Black Rose Books, pp. 12–31.

Helleiner, Eric and Andreas Pickel. 2005. *Economic Nationalism in a Globalizing World*. Ithaca, NY: Cornell University Press.

Hess, M. 2004. '"Spatial" relationships? Towards a reconceptualization of embeddedness', *Progress in Human Geography*, 28:2, 165–186.

Hetzel, Robert L. 1991. 'Too big to fail: origins, consequences, and outlook', *FRB Richmond Economic Review*, 77:6, 3–15.

Hirschman, A. 1991. *The Rhetoric of Reaction*. Cambridge, MA: Harvard University Press.

Hobsbawm, Eric. 1964. 'Introduction', in Karl Marx, *Pre-capitalist Economic Formations*. London: Lawrence and Wishart, pp. 9–66.

_____. 1968. *Industry and Empire: An Economic History of Britain Since 1750*. London: Weidenfeld & Nicolson.

_____. 1994. *Age of Extremes: The Short Twentieth Century, 1914–1991*. London: Michael Joseph.

Hudson, Michael. [1972] 2003. *Super Imperialism: The Origin and Fundamentals of U.S. World Dominance*. 2nd ed. London: Pluto Press.

_____. [1977] 2005. *Global Fracture: The New International Economic Order*. London: Pluto Press.

_____. 1992. 'Did the Phoenicians introduce the idea of interest to Greece and Italy – and if so, when?', in Gunter Kopcke (ed.), *Greece Between East and West: 10th–8th Centuries BC*. Mainz, Rhine: Verlag Philipp von Zabern, pp. 128–143.

_____. 2000. 'Karl Bücher's role in the evolution of economic anthropology', in Jürgen Backhaus (ed.), *Karl Bücher: Theory, History, Anthropology, Non-market Economies*. Marburg: Metropolis Verlag, pp. 301–336.

_____. 2002. 'Reconstructing the origins of interest-bearing debt and the logic of clean slates', in Michael Hudson and Marc Van De Mieroop (eds), *Debt and Economic Renewal in the Ancient Near East*. Bethesda, MD: CDL Press, pp. 7–58._____. 2003. 'The cartalist/monetarist debate in historical perspective', in Edward Nell and Stephanie Bell (eds), *The State, The Market and The Euro*. Cheltenham: Edward Elgar, pp. 39–76.

_____. 2004a. 'The development of money-of-account in Sumer's temples', in Michael Hudson and Cornelia Wunsch (eds), 2004, pp. 303–329.

_____. 2004b. 'The archaeology of money in light of Mesopotamian records', in L. Randall Wray (ed.), *Credit and State Theories of Money: The Contributions of A. Mitchell Innes*. Cheltenham: Edward Elgar.

_____. 2005/6. 'Reviewed works: *Autour de Polanyi: Vocabulaires, théories et modalités des échanges, Nanterre* by Ph. Clancier, F. Joannès, P. Rouillard, A. Tenu; *The Ancient Economy: Evidence and Models* by J. G. Manning, Ian Morris', *Archiv für Orientforschung*, 51, pp. 405–411.

_____. 2010. *Trade, Development and Foreign Debt*. 2nd ed. Dresden: ISLET.

_____. 2015. *Killing the Host*. Dresden: Islet

_____. 2018. '*... and forgive them their debts': Lending, Forclosure and Redemption, From Bronze Age Finance to the Jubilee Year*. Dresden: ISLET.

Hudson, Michael and Baruch A. Levine. 1996. *Privatization in the Ancient Near East and Classical World*. Peabody Museum Bulletin, vol. 5; The International Scholars Conference on Ancient Near Eastern Economies, vol. 1. Cambridge, MA: Peabody Museum of Archaeology and Ethnology.

_____. 1999. *Urbanization and Land Ownership in the Ancient Near East*. Ethnology, Peabody Museum Bulletin, 7. Cambridge, MA: Peabody Museum of Archaeology.

Hudson, Michael and Marc Van de Mieroop. 2002. *Debt and Economic Renewal in the Ancient Near East*. Bethesda, MD: CDL Press.

Hudson, Michael and Cornelia Wunsch. 2004. *Creating Economic Order: Record-Keeping, Standardization and the Development of Accounting in the Ancient Near East*. Bethesda, MD: CDL Press.

Hughes, J. P. and L. J. Mester. 1993. 'A quality and risk-adjusted cost function for banks: evidence on the "too-big-to-fail" doctrine', *Journal of Productivity Analysis*, 4, 293–315.

Humphreys, S. C. 1969. 'History, economics, and anthropology: the work of Karl Polanyi', *History and Theory*, 8:2, 165–212.

IMF. 1977. *The Monetary Approach to the Balance of Payments: A Collection of Research Papers by Members of the Staff of the International Monetary Fund*. Washington, D.C.: International Monetary Fund.

_____. 2018. *Capitalizing on Good Times*. Washington, D.C.: International Monetary Fund.

Immerwahr, Daniel. 2009. 'Polanyi in the United States: Peter Drucker, Karl Polanyi and the mid-century critique of economic society', *Journal of the History of Ideas*, 70:3, 445–466.

Isaac, B. L. 2005. 'Karl Polanyi', in J. G. Carrier (ed.), *A Handbook of Economic Anthropology*. Cheltenham: Edward Elgar, pp. 1–25.

Jahn, H. 2015. *Das Wunder des Roten Wien. Bd. 1 und 2*. Vienna: Phoibos.

Janicki, H. and E. S. Prescott. 2006. 'Changes in the size distribution of US banks; 1960–2005', *Federal Reserve Bank of Richmond Economic Quarterly* 92:4, 291–316.

Jenkins, A. 1977. '"Substantivism" as a theory of economic forms', in B. Hindess (ed.), *Sociological Theories of the Economy*. London: Macmillan, pp. 66–91.

Johnson, H. G. 1977. 'The monetary approach to balance of payments theory and policy: explanation and policy implications', *Economica*, 44:175, 217–229.

Johnson, S. 2009. 'The quiet coup', *The Atlantic*, May.

Bibliography

Johnson, S. and J. Kwak. 2010. *13 Bankers: The Wall Street Takeover and the Next Financial Meltdown*. New York: Random House.

Kaldor, N. 1945. 'The German war economy', *Review of Economic Studies*, 13:1, 33–52.

Kalecki, M. 1943. 'Political aspects of full employment', *Political Quarterly*, 14:4, 322–331. Based on a lecture given to the Marshall Society in Cambridge in 1942.

Kaplan, D. 1968. 'The formal–substantive controversy in economic anthropology: reflections on its wider implications', *Southwestern Journal of Anthropology*, 24:3, 228–251.

Keynes, J. M. 1913. *Indian Currency and Finance*, London: Macmillan.

_____. 1925. *The Economic Consequences of Mr. Churchill*. London: L. and V. Woolf at the Hogarth Press.

_____. 1933. 'National self sufficiency', *Yale Review*, 22:4 (June), 755–769.

_____. 1936. *The General Theory of Employment, Interest and Money* (in *The Collected Writings of J. M. Keynes VII*). London: Macmillan for the Royal Economic Society.

_____. [1936] 1967. *General Theory of Employment, Interest and Money*. London: Macmillan.

_____. 1940. *How to Pay for the War: A Radical Plan for the Chancellor of the Exchequer*. New York: Macmillan.

_____. 1980. *The Collected Writings of John Maynard Keynes Vol. XXV: Activities 1940–1944*. London: Macmillan and Cambridge University Press.

Kindleberger, C. P. 1974. '"The Great Transformation" by Karl Polanyi', *Daedalus* 103:1, 45–52.

Kitani, N. 2006. 'The Lancashire–Bombay talks and the Indo-Japanese trade negotiations with regard to Indian export of raw cotton: reconsideration of imperial preference in India in the first half of the 1930s' (in Japanese), *Shakai Keizai Shigaku*, 71:6, 657–679.

Knafo, Samuel. 2013. *The Making of Modern Finance: Liberal Governance and The Gold Standard*. London: Routledge.

Knapp, George. [1905] 1924. *The State Theory of Money*. London: Royal Economic Society and Macmillan. Translated by H. M. Lucas.

Kotz, David M., Terrence McDonough and Michael Reich (eds). 1994. *Social Structures of Accumulation*. Cambridge: Cambridge University Press.

Krippner, G. R. 2001. 'The elusive market: embeddedness and the paradigm of economic sociology', *Theory and Society*, 30:6, 775–810.

Krippner G., M. Granovetter, F. Block, N. Biggart, T. Beamish, Y. Hsing, G. Hart, G. Arrighi, M. Mendell, J. Hall, M. Burawoy, S. Vogel and S. O'Riain. 2004. 'Polanyi symposium: a conversation on embeddedness', *Socio-Economic Review*, 2:1, 109–135.

Kuprianov, Anatoli. 1985. 'The Monetary Control Act and the role of the Federal Reserve in the interbank clearing market', *Federal Reserve Bank of Richmond Economic Review*, July–August, 23–35.

Kuttner, R. 2017. 'The man from Red Vienna', *New York Review of Books*, 21 December. Review of Gareth Dale's *Karl Polanyi: A Life on the Left*.

_____. 2018. *Can Democracy Survive Global Capitalism?* New York: Norton.

Lacher, Hannes. 1999a. 'Embedded liberalism, disembedded markets: reconceptualizing the *Pax Americana*', *New Political Economy*, 4:3, 343–360.

_____. 1999b. 'The politics of the market: re-reading Karl Polanyi', *Global Society*, 13:3, 313–326.

_____. 2007a. 'The slight transformation: contesting the legacy of Karl Polanyi', in Ayse Bugra and Kaan Agartan (eds), *Reading Karl Polanyi for the Twenty-first Century: Market Economy as a Political Project*. Houndmills: Palgrave, pp. 343–360.

_____. 2007b. 'The slight transformation: contesting the legacy of Karl Polanyi', in Ayse Bugra and Kaan Agartan (eds), *Reading Karl Polanyi for the Twenty-first Century*. New York: Palgrave Macmillan, pp. 49–65.

_____. 2019. 'Karl Polanyi, the "always-embedded market economy", and the re-writing of *The Great Transformation*', *Theory and Society*, 48:5, 671–707.

Lamberg-Karlovsky, C. C. 2009. 'Structure, agency and commerce in the Ancient Near East', Harvard Library, https://dash.harvard.edu/bitstream/handle/1/34708493/ Structure%2cAgency%20CommerceFIN%232C%20copy.pdf?sequence=1. Accessed 1 October 2019.

Lapavitsas, C. 2009. 'Financialised capitalism: crisis and financial expropriation', *Historical Materialism*, 17, 114–148.

Larsen, Mogens Trolle. 2015. *Ancient Kanesh: A Merchant Colony in Bronze Age Anatolia*. Cambridge: Cambridge University Press.

Lazonick, W. 2014. 'Taking stock: why executive pay results in an unstable and inequitable economy', *Roosevelt Institute White Paper*, June.

Leontief, W. 1983. 'National perspective: the definition of problems and opportunities', in *Long-Term Impact of Technology on Employment and Unemployment: A National Academy of Engineering Symposium*. Washington, D.C.: National Academy Press, pp. 3–8.

Levy, Frank and Thomas Kochan. 2012. 'Addressing the problem of stagnant wages', *Comparative Economic Studies*, 54:4, 739–764.

Lewis, John, Karl Polanyi and Donald Kitchin. 1935. *Christianity and Social Revolution*. London: Gollacz.

Linden, Marcel van der. 2012. 'Gerschenkron's secret: a research note', *Critique: Journal of Socialist Theory*, 40:4, 553–562.

Lindsey, Brink. 2001. 'The decline and fall of the first global economy', *Reason*, 33:7, 42–52.

Lippmann, W. 1937. *The Good Society*. Boston: Little, Brown & Co.

Lipset, Seymour M. 1985. *Consensus and Conflict: Essays in Political Sociology*. London: Transaction.

Löfving, S. 2005. 'Introduction: peopled economies', in S. Löfving (ed.), *Peopled Economies: Conversations with Stephen Gudeman*. Uppsala: Interface, pp. 1–28.

MacLean, Nancy. 2017. *Democracy in Chains*. New York: Viking.

Maddison Project Database, version 2018. Bolt, Jutta, Robert Inklaar, Herman de Jong and Jan Luiten van Zanden. 2018. 'Rebasing "Maddison": new income comparisons and the shape of long-run economic development', *Maddison Project Working Paper 10*.

Malthus T. R. [1798] 1998. *An Essay on the Principle of Population*. London: J. Johnson.

Mamun, A., M. K. Hassan and N. Maroney. 2005. 'The wealth and risk effects of the Gramm–Leach–Bliley Act (GLBA) on the US banking industry', *Journal of Business Finance & Accounting*, 32:1 & 2, 351–388.

Mann, Michael. 1993. *The Sources of Social Power, Vol. 2*. New York: Cambridge University Press.

Marquand, David. 1997. *The New Reckoning: Capitalism, States and Citizens*. Oxford: Polity.

Marwick, Arthur. 1964. 'Middle opinion in the thirties: planning progress and political "agreement"', *English Historical Review*, LXXIX, 79.

Marx, Karl. [1858] 1973. *Grundrisse*. London: Penguin.

_____. [1867] 1977. *Capital*, Vol. I. London: Penguin.

_____. [1867] 1996. 'Capital: a critique of political economy. vol. I'. *Collected Works, Vol. 35*. New York: International Publishers.

_____. [1884] 1978. *Capital*, Vol. II. London: Penguin.

_____. [1894] 1981. *Capital*, Vol. III. London: Penguin.

_____. 1973. 'The Eighteenth Brumaire of Louis Bonaparte', in *Surveys from Exile: Political Writings, Volume II*. Harmondsworth: Penguin.

Marx, Karl and Fredrick Engels. [1848] 1967. *The Communist Manifesto*. Trans. Samuel Moore with an introduction by A. J. P. Taylor. London: Penguin.

Mason, P. 2009. *Meltdown: The End of the Age of Greed*. London and New York: Verso.

Massey, D. 1995. *Spatial Divisions of Labour*. 2nd ed. Basingstoke: Macmillan.

Mendell, M. and D. Salée (eds). 1991. *The Legacy of Karl Polanyi*. New York: St. Martin's Press.

Menger, Carl. [1871] 1892. 'On the origin of money', translated in *Economic Journal*, 2, 239–255.

Mills, C. Wright. [1951] 2002. *White Collar: The American Middle Classes*. Oxford: Oxford University Press.

Mirowski, Philip. 2018. 'Polanyi vs. Hayek?', *Globalizations*. DOI: 10.1080/14747 731.2018.1498174.

Mirowski, P. and D. Plehwe (eds). 2009. *The Road from Mont Pelerin: The Making of the Neoliberal Thought Collective*. Cambridge, MA: Harvard University Press.

Mises, L. von. 1920a. 'Die Wirtschaftsrechnung im sozialistischen Gemeinwesen', *Archiv für Sozialwissenschaft und Sozialpolitik*, 47, 86–121.

_____. 1920b. 'Die Abschaffung des Geldes in Russland', *Neue Freie Presse*, 17 November, 1920, www.mises.de/public_home/article/97/9. Accessed 19 January 2019.

_____. [1920] 1935. 'Economic calculation in the socialist commonwealth', in F. A. Hayek (ed.), *Collectivist Economic Planning*. London: Routledge and Kegan Paul Ltd., pp. 87–130.

_____. [1922] 2010. *Socialism: An Economic and Sociological Analysis*. New Haven, CT: Yale University Press.

_____. [1922] 1951. *Socialism: An Economic and Sociological Analysis*. Trans. J. Kahane. New Haven, CT: Yale University Press.

Moyer, R. and R. Lamy. 1992. '"Too big to fail": rationale, consequences, and alternatives', *Business Economics*, 27:3, 19–24.

Muellerleile, C. 2013. 'Turning financial markets inside out: Polanyi, performativity and disembeddedness', *Environment and Planning A*, 45:7, 1625–1642.

Murphy, J. T. 2008. 'Economic geographies of the Global South: missed opportunities and promising intersections with development studies', *Geography Compass*, 2:3, 851–873.

Myrdal, G. [1930] 1965. *The Political Element in the Development of Economic Theory*. London: Routledge and Kegan Paul Ltd.

_____. 1956. *An International Economy: Problems and Prospects*. London: Routledge and Kegan Paul Ltd.

_____. 1957. *Economic Theory and the Underdeveloped Regions*. London: Duckworth.

_____. 1958. *Value in Economic Theory*. London: Routledge and Kegan Paul Ltd.

Nakayama, C. 2018. 'Polanyi's concept of peace in a complex society', in Michael Brie and Claus Thomasberger (eds), 2018, pp. 185–197.

Neurath, O. 1919. *Durch die Kriegswirtschaft zur Naturalwirtschaft*. Munich: G.D.W. Callwey.

Nölke, A. 2011. 'Transnational economic order and national economic institutions: comparative capitalism meets international political economy', *MPIfG Working Paper*, 11:3, Max Planck Institut Für Gesellschaftsforschung, April.

Bibliography

North, D. C. 1977. 'Markets and other allocation systems in history: the challenge of Karl Polanyi', *Journal of European Economic History*, 6:3, 703–716.

Ohlin, B. 1929. 'Transfer difficulties, real and imagined', *Economic Journal* (June): 'A rejoinder,' pp. 403f., 'Transfer difficulties, real and imagined', pp. 172f. and 'Keynes's reply', p. 180.

Oppenheim, Leo. 1949. 'The golden garments of the gods', *Journal of Near Eastern Studies*, 8, 172–193.

_____. 1957. 'A bird's-eye view of Mesopotamian economic history', in K. Polanyi, C. M. Arensberg and H. W. Pearson (eds), *Trade and Market in the Early Empires*. Glencoe, IL: Free Press and Falcon's Wing Press, pp. 27–37.

——. 1964. *Ancient Mesopotamia: Portrait of a Dead Civilization*. Chicago: University of Chicago Press.

Palma, J. G. 2009. 'The revenge of the market on the rentiers: why neo-liberal reports of the end of history turned out to be premature', *Cambridge Journal of Economics*, 33:4, 829–869.

Pålsson Syll, L. 2005. 'The pitfalls of postmodern economics: remarks on a provocative project', in S. Löfving (ed.), *Peopled Economies: Conversations with Stephen Gudeman*. Uppsala: Interface, pp. 83–114.

Peck, J. 2005. 'Economic sociologies in space', *Economic Geography*, 81:2, 129–175.

_____. 2012. 'Economic geography: island life', *Dialogues in Human Geography*, 2:2, 113–133.

_____. 2013a. 'Disembedding Polanyi: exploring Polanyian economic geographies', *Environment and Planning A*, 45:7, 1536–1544.

_____. 2013b. 'For Polanyian economic geographies', *Environment and Planning A*, 45:7, 1545–1568.

_____. 2015. 'Polanyian pathways', *Economic Geography*, 92:2, 226–233.

_____. 2016. 'Macroeconomic geographies', *Area Development and Policy*, 1:3, 305–322.

_____. 2017a. 'Uneven regional development', in D. Richardson, N. Castree, M. F. Goodchild, A. Kobayashi, W. Liu and R. A. Marston (eds), *The Wiley-AAG International Encyclopedia of Geography*. Oxford: Wiley-Blackwell, pp. 7270–7282.

_____. 2017b. 'Transatlantic city, part 1: conjunctural urbanism', *Urban Studies*, 54:1, 4–30.

Peck, J. and N. Theodore. 2007. 'Variegated capitalism', *Progress in Human Geography*, 31:6, 731–772.

Peck, J. and A. Tickell. 2002. 'Neoliberalizing space', *Antipode*, 34:3, 380–404.

Peck, J. and J. Zhang. 2013. 'A variety of capitalism ... with Chinese characteristics?', *Journal of Economic Geography*, 13:3, 357–396.

Pettifor, Ann. 2017. 'Introduction' to Karl Polanyi, *The Present Age of Transformation: Five Lectures by Karl Polanyi, Bennington College 1940*. London: Prime Economics.

Piketty, Thomas. 2014. *Capital in the Twenty-first Century*. Cambridge, MA: Harvard University Press.

Piraino, Thomas A. Jr. 2007. 'Reconciling the Harvard and Chicago Schools: a new antitrust approach for the 21st century', *Indiana Law Journal*, 82:2, Article 4, 345–409.

Polak, J. 1991. 'The changing nature of IMF conditionality', *Working Paper 41: Research Programme on: Financial Policies for the Global Dissemination of Economic Growth*. Paris: OECD.

_____. 2001. 'The two monetary approaches to the balance of payments: Keynesian and Johnsonian', *IMF Working Paper*, wp/01/100, Washington D.C.

Polanyi, Karl. [1910] 2016. 'The crisis of our ideologies', in Karl Polanyi, 2016, pp. 83–85.

_____. [1911] 2016. 'Credo and credulity', in Karl Polanyi, 2016, pp. 49–51.

_____. [1913] 2016a. 'Radical bourgeois politics', in Karl Polanyi, 2016, pp. 169–170.

_____. [1913] 2016b. 'Speech on the meaning of conviction', in Karl Polanyi, 2016, pp. 55–59.

_____. [1918] 2016a. 'The calling of our generation', in Karl Polanyi, 2016, pp. 64–73.

_____. [1918] 2016b. 'The test of socialism', in Karl Polanyi, 2016, pp. 86–91.

_____. [1919] 2016. 'Civil war', in Karl Polanyi, 2016, pp. 95–98.

_____. [1919] 2018. 'Ideologies in crisis', in Michael Brie and Claus Thomasberger (eds), 2018, pp. 264–267.

_____. [1921] 2016. 'Believing and unbelieving politics', in Karl Polanyi, 2016, pp. 99–107.

_____. [1922] 2016a. 'Guild socialism', in Karl Polanyi, 2016, pp. 118–119.

_____. [1922] 2016b. 'Socialist accounting', *Theory and Society*, 45:5, 398–427.

_____. [1922] 2016c. 'Socialist accounting (Sozialistische Rechnungslegung)', *Theory and Society*, 45:5, 385–427. Translated by A. Fischer, D. Woodruff and J. Bockman.

_____. [1925] 2000. 'Letter to a friend', in K. McRobbie and K. Polanyi Levitt (eds), *Karl Polanyi in Vienna: The Contemporary Significance of the Great Transformation*. Montréal: Black Rose Books, pp. 316–318.

_____. [1925] 2018. 'New reflections concerning our theory and practice', in Polanyi, 2018a, pp. 41–50.

_____. [1927] 2018. 'On freedom', in Michael Brie and Claus Thomasberger (eds), 2018, pp. 289–319.

_____. [1932] 2002. 'Wirtschaft und Demokratie', in Karl Polanyi, 2002, pp. 149–154.

_____. [1932] 2018. 'Economy and democracy', in Karl Polanyi, 2018a, pp. 61–65.

_____. [1934] 2002a. 'Lohntarif-Bill für Lancashire', in Karl Polanyi, 2002, pp. 228–229.

_____. [1934] 2002b. 'Lancashire im Fegefeuer', in Polanyi, 2002, pp. 230–235.

_____. [1934] 2002c. 'Lancashire als Menschenheitsfrage', in Karl Polanyi, 2002, pp. 236–248.

_____. [1934] 2018a. 'Fascism and Marxian terminology', in Karl Polanyi, 2018a, pp. 125–134.

_____. [1934] 2018b. 'The essence of fascism', in Karl Polanyi, 2018a, pp. 81–107.

_____. [1937] 2018a. 'Christianity and economic life', in Karl Polanyi, 2018a, pp. 154–164.

_____. [1937] 2018b. 'Community and society: the Christian criticism of our social order', in Karl Polanyi, 2018a, pp. 145–153.

_____. [1940] 2014. 'The present age of transformation. Lecture 2: the trend toward an integrated society', in Karl Polanyi, 2014a, pp. 214–219.

_____. [1940] 2017. *The Present Age of Transformation: Five Lectures by Karl Polanyi, Bennington College 1940*. London: Prime Economics.

_____. 1940a. 'The present age of transformation. Lecture 3: the breakdown of the international system'. Bennington College, https://crossettlibrary.dspacedirect.org/handle/11209/8516. Accessed 19 December 2019.

_____. 1940b. 'The present age of transformation. Lecture 4: is America an exception?' Bennington College, https://crossettlibrary.dspacedirect.org/handle/11209/8517. Accessed 19 December 2019.

_____. 1941. Rockefeller Archive 310-3693, 'book plan, origins of the cataclysm'.

_____. [1943] 1991. 'Letter to Oskar Jaszi', 1 March 1943. Reproduced in Marguerite Mendell and Daniel Salee (eds), 1991, pp. 231–248.

_____. [1943] 2017. 'The common man's masterplan', in M. Brie (ed.), *Karl Polanyi in Dialogue: A Socialist Thinker for Our Times*. Montreal: Black Rose Books, pp. 79–94.

_____. 1944. *The Great Transformation: The Political and Economic Origins of Our Time.* New York: Farrar & Rinehart.

_____. [1944] 1957. *The Great Transformation: The Political and Economic Origins of Our Time.* New York: Beacon Press.

_____. 1944 [2001]. *The Great Transformation: The Political and Economic Origins of Our Time.* 2nd ed. Boston: Beacon Paperback.

_____. 1945. 'Universal capitalism or regional planning?', *London Quarterly of World Affairs*, 10:3, 86–91.

_____. [1945] 2018. 'Universal capitalism or regional planning?', in Karl Polanyi, 2018a, pp. 231–240.

_____. 1947. 'Our obsolete market mentality: civilization must find a new thought pattern', *Commentary*, 3:, 109–117.

_____. [1947] 2018a. 'British Labour and American New Dealers', in Karl Polanyi, 2018a, pp. 226–230.

_____. [1947] 2018b. 'Our obsolete market mentality', in Karl Polanyi, 2018a, pp. 198–211.

_____. [1950] 2016. 'Letter to Oscar Jaszi, Pickering, Canada, 27 October 1950', in Karl Polanyi, 2016, pp. 227–230.

_____. [1953] 2018. 'Jean-Jacques Rousseau, or is a free society possible?', in Karl Polanyi, 2018a, pp. 167–176.

_____. [1954] 2017. 'Hamlet', in M. Brie (ed.), *Karl Polanyi in Dialogue: A Socialist Thinker for Our Times.* Montreal: Black Rose Books, pp. 95–108.

_____.1957a. 'The economy as instituted process', in K. Polanyi, C. M. Arensberg and H. W. Pearson (eds), 1957, pp. 243–69.

_____. 1957b. 'The economy as instituted process', in K. Polanyi, C. M. Arensberg and H. W. Pearson (eds), *Trade and Market in the Early Empires*, Chicago: A Gateway Edition, pp. 243–270.

_____. [1957] 2018. 'Freedom in a complex society', in Michael Brie and Claus Thomasberger (eds), 2018, pp. 320–324.

_____. 1959. 'Anthropology and economic theory', in M. F. Fried (ed.), *Readings in Anthropology*, Volume 2. New York: Crowell, pp. 161–184.

_____. 1960. 'On the comparative treatment of economic institutions in antiquity, with illustrations from Athens, Mycenae, and Alalakh', in C. H. Kraeling and R. M. Adams (eds), *City Invincible.* Chicago: University of Chicago Press, pp. 329–350.

_____. 1962. 'Karl Bücher', *International Encyclopedia of the Social Sciences*, II, 164.

_____. 1968. *Primitive, Archaic and Modern Economies: Essays of Karl Polanyi.* Edited by George Dalton. New York: Anchor Books.

_____. 1971. *The Great Transformation: The Political and Economic Origins of Our Time.* Boston, MA: Beacon Press.

_____. 1977. *The Livelihood of Man.* Edited by H. Pearson. New York: Academic Press.

_____. 2002. *Chronik der großen Transformation: Artikel und Aufsätze (1920–1945). Bd. 1: Wirtschaftliche Transformation, Gegenbewegungen und der Kampf um die Demokratie.* Edited by Michele Cangiani and Claus Thomasberger. Marburg: Metropolis.

_____. 2003. *Chronik der großen Transformation: Artikel und Aufsätze (1920–1945). Bd.2: Die internationale Politik zwischen den beiden Weltkriegen.* Edited by Michele Cangiani and Claus Thomasberger. Marburg: Metropolis.

_____. 2005a. *Chronik der großen Transformation: Artikel und Aufsätze (1920–1945). Bd. 3: Menschliche Freiheit, politische Demokratie und die Auseinandersetzung zwischen*

Sozialismus und Faschismus. Edited by Michele Cangiani and Claus Thomasberger. Marburg: Metropolis.

_____. 2005b. 'Zur Sozialisierungsfrage', in Karl Polanyi 2005a, pp. 126–136.

_____. 2005c. 'Die geistigen Voraussetzungen des Faschismus', in Karl Polanyi, 2005a, pp. 216–221.

_____. 2005d (1925–30). 'Zur Sozialisierungsfrage (On the Question of Socialization)', in Karl Polanyi, 2005a, pp. 126–136.

_____. 2014a. *For a New West 1919–1958.* Edited by Giorgio Resta and Mariavittoria Catanzariti. Cambridge: Polity Press.

_____. 2014b. 'How to make use of the social sciences', in Karl Polanyi, 2014a, pp. 109–118.

_____. 2014c. 'On political theory', in Karl Polanyi, 2014a, pp. 119–124.

_____. 2016. *The Hungarian Writings.* Edited by G. Gareth Dale. Manchester: Manchester University Press.

_____. 2018a. *Economy and Society: Selected Writings.* Edited by Michele Cangiani and Claus Thomasberger. Cambridge: Polity.

_____. 2018b. 'Science and morality (1920–22)', in Michael Brie and Claus Thomasberger (eds), 2018, pp. 268–286.

_____. 2018c. 'Being and thinking', in Michael Brie and Claus Thomasberger (eds), 2018, pp. 287–292.

_____. 2018d. 'Mechanism of the world economic crisis', in Karl Polanyi, 2018a, pp. 66–80.

_____. 2018e. 'The functionalist theory of society and the problem of socialist economy accounting (a rejoinder to Professor L. von Mises and Dr. Felix Weil)', in Karl Polanyi, 2018a, pp. 51–60.

Polanyi, K., C. M. Arensberg and H. W. Pearson (eds). 1957. *Trade and Market in the Early Empires.* New York: Free Press.

Polanyi Levitt, Kari (ed.). 1990a. *The Life and Work of Karl Polanyi: A Celebration.* Montreal: Black Rose Books.

_____. 1990b. 'The origins and significance of *The Great Transformation*', in Kari Polanyi Levitt (ed.), 1990a, pp. 111–124.

_____. 2006a. 'Keynes and Polanyi: the 1920s and the 1990s', *Review of International Political Economy,* 13:1, 152–177.

_____. 2006b. 'Tracing Polanyi's institutional political economy to its Central European source,' in K. Polanyi Levitt and K. McRobbie (eds), *Karl Polanyi in Vienna: The Contemporary Significance of The Great Transformation.* 2nd ed. Montreal: Black Rose Books, pp. 378–391.

_____. 2012. 'The power of ideas: Keynes, Hayek, and Polanyi', *International Journal of Political Economy,* 41:4, 5–15.

_____. 2013a. *From the Great Transformation to the Great Financialization: On Karl Polanyi and Other Essays.* London: Zed Books.

_____. 2013b. *From the Great Transformation to the Great Financialization: On Karl Polanyi and other Essays.* Blackpoint: Fernwood Publishing.

_____. 2018. 'Freedom of action and freedom of thought', in Karl Polanyi, 2018a, pp. 18–50.

Pollard, J., C. McEwan, N. Laurie and A. Stenning. 2009. 'Economic geography under post-colonial scrutiny', *Transactions of the Institute of British Geographers,* 34:4, 137–142.

Popper, K. [1963] 2006. *Conjectures and Refutations.* London and New York: Routledge and Kegan Paul Ltd.

Posen, A. S. 1995. 'Declarations are not enough: financial sector sources of central bank independence', in B. Bernanke and J. Rotemberg (eds) *NBER Macroeconomics Annual 1995*, 10 (1996). Cambridge, MA: MIT Press, pp. 253–274.

Prince, C. E. and S. Taylor. 1981. 'Government and the American economy: three stages of historical change: 1790–1941', in R. Weible, O. Ford and P. Marion (eds), *Essays from the Lowell Conference on Industrial History*. Lowell, MA: Lowell Conference, pp. 114–127.

Radcliffe, S. A. 2005. 'Development and geography: towards a postcolonial development geography?', *Progress in Human Geography*, 29:3, 291–298.

Rahman, K. Sabeel. 2014. 'Domination, democracy, and constitutional political economy in the new gilded age: towards a fourth wave of legal realism?', *Texas Law Review*, 94, 1329–1359.

_____. 2016. *Democracy against Domination*. New York: Oxford University Press.

Rankin, K. N. 2013. 'Polanyian pedagogies in planning and economic geography', *Environment and Planning A*, 45:7, 1650–1655.

Ravallion, M., D. Jolliffe and J. Margitic. 2018. 'Alongside rising top incomes, the level of living of America's poorest has fallen', *Vox CEPR Policy Portal*, https://voxeu.org/arti cle/alongside-rising-top-incomes-level-living-america-s-poorest-has-fallen. Accessed 14 December 2019.

Real World Economics Review. 2016. '2016: top 10 economics books of the last 100 years', 75, (27 June), 159–160.

Reich, Robert B. 2015. *Saving Capitalism: For the Many, Not the Few*. New York: Knopf.

Reinhart, Carmen M. and Kenneth S. Rogoff. 2010. 'Growth in a time of debt', *American Economic Review* 100:2, 573–578. https://doi.org/10.1257/aer.100.2.573.

Renger, Johannes. 1972. 'Flucht als soziales Problem in der altbabylonischen Gesellschaft', in Dietz O. Edzard (ed.), *Gesellschaftsklassen im Alten Zweistromland und in den angren- zenden Gebieten*. Munich: Verlag der Bayerischen Akademie der Wissenschaften, pp. 167–182.

_____. 1979. 'Interaction of temple, palace, and "private enterprise" in the Old Babylonian economy', in Eduard Lipinski (ed.), *State and Temple Economy in the Ancient Near East*. Leuven: Department Orientalistiek, pp. 249–256.

_____. 1984. 'Patterns of non-institutional trade and non-commercial exchange in Ancient Mesopotamia at the beginning of the second millennium BC', in Alphonse Archi (ed.), *Circulation of Goods in Non-palatial Context in the Ancient Near East*. Rome: Incunabula Graeca 82, pp. 31–115.

_____. 1994. 'On economic structures in Ancient Mesopotamia', *Orientalia*, 18, 157–208.

Resta, G. 2014. 'Introduction', in Karl Polanyi, 2014a, pp. 1–25.

Ricardo, D. [1817] 1984. *On the Principles of Political Economy and Taxation*. London/ Melbourne: Everyman's Library.

Robbins, L. 1932. *An Essay on the Nature and Significance of Economic Science*. London: Macmillan.

_____. [1937] 1972. *Economic Planning and International Order*. New York: Arno Press.

Roberts, S. M. 2012. 'Worlds apart? Economic geography and questions of "development"', in T. J. Barnes, J. Peck and E. Sheppard (eds), *The Wiley- Blackwell Companion to Economic Geography*. Oxford: Wiley-Blackwell, pp. 552–566.

Rockefeller Foundation Records. 1942. Anne Bezanson to Joseph H. Willits, 9 April Box 310, Folder 3694, projects, RG 1.1 (FA386), Series 200: United States, Subseries 200.

Rodrik, Dani. 1998. 'The global fix', *New Republic*, 2 November.

_____. 2007. 'The inescapable trilemma of the world economy', *Dani Rodrik's weblog*, https://rodrik.typepad.com/dani_rodriks_weblog/2007/06/the-inescapable.html. Accessed 14 December 2019.

_____. 2017. 'The trouble with globalization', *The Milken Institute Review*, 20 October, www.milkenreview.org/articles/the-trouble-with-globalization. Accessed 14 December 2019.

_____. 2018. 'What's been stopping the left?', *Project Syndicate*, 20 April. www.project-syndicate.org/commentary/left-timidity-after-neoliberal-failure-by-dani-rodrik-2018-04. Accessed 14 December 2019.

Rogan, Tim. 2017. *The Moral Economists: R H Tawney, Karl Polanyi and E P Thompson and the Critique of Capitalism*. Princeton, NJ: Princeton University Press.

Rostow, W.W. 1960. *The Stages of Economic Growth: A Non-Communist Manifesto*. Cambridge: Cambridge University Press.

Roubini, N. 2014. 'Make no mistake: the machines are coming', *Business Insider*, 14. December. www.businessinsider.com/rise-of-the-machines-us-economy-roubini-2014-12. Accessed 14 December 2019.

Rousseau, J.-J. [1762] 1994. 'The social contract', in *Discourse on Political Economy and the Social Contract*. Oxford: Oxford University Press, pp. 43–175.

Rueff, Jacques. 1929. 'Mr. Keynes' views on the transfer problem', *Economic Journal*, 39:155, 388–399.

_____. 1967. *Balance of Payments: Proposals for the Resolution of the Most Pressing World Economic Problem of Our Time*. New York: Macmillan.

Ruggie, John Gerard. 1982. 'International regimes, transactions, and change: embedded liberalism in the postwar economic order', *International Organization*, 36:2, 379–415.

Rupert, Mark. 1995. *Producing Hegemony*. Cambridge: Cambridge University Press.

Salsano, A. 1990. '*The Great Transformation* in the oeuvre of Karl Polanyi', in Kari Polanyi Levitt (ed.), *The Life and Work of Karl Polanyi*. Montreal: Black Rose Books, pp. 139–144.

Sardoni, C. 1997. 'Keynes and Marx', in G. C. Harcourt and P. Riach (eds), *A 'Second Edition' of The General Theory*. London: Routledge.

Sauvé, P. and K. Steinfatt. 2001. *Financial Services and the WTO: What Next?* Washington, D.C.: Brookings Institution.

Scheiber, Harry N. 1966. *The Condition of American Federalism: An Historian's View*. Washington, D.C.: US Government Printing Office.

Schlesinger, A. M. 1989. *Cycles of American History*. London: Pelican.

Schumpeter, Joseph, A. 1942. *Capitalism, Socialism, and Democracy*. New York: Harper & Row.

Schwartz, Herman. 2009. *Subprime Nation*. Ithaca, NY: Cornell University Press.

Silver, B. and G. Arrighi. 2003. 'Polanyi's "double-movement": The Bell Époques of British and US hegemony compared', *Politics and Society*, 31:2, 325–355.

Silver, Morris. 1983. *Prophets and Markets: The Political Economy of Ancient Israel*. Boston, MA and The Hague: Kluwer-Nijhoff.

_____. 1995. 'Prophets and markets revisited', in K. D. Irani and Morris Silver (eds), *Social Justice in the Ancient World*. Westport, CT: Greenwood Publishing Group, pp. 179–198.

Slobodian, Quinn. 2018. *Globalists: The End of Empire and the Birth of Neoliberalism*. Cambridge, MA: Harvard University Press.

Smith, N. [1984] 2008. *Uneven Development: Nature, Capital and the Production of Space*. 3rd ed. Athens and London: University of Georgia Press.

Sombart, Werner. [1906] 1976. *Why Is There No Socialism in the United States?* White Plains, NY: M.E. Sharpe.

Bibliography

Somers, Margaret R. 1997. 'Deconstructing and reconstructing class formation theory: narrativity, relational analysis, and social theory', in John R. Hall (ed.), *Reworking Class*. Ithaca, NY: Cornell University Press, pp. 73–106.

_____. 2008. *Genealogies of Citizenship: Markets, Statelessness, and the Right to Have Rights*. Cambridge: Cambridge University Press.

_____. 2012. 'Zombie entanglements: how corporate power stalks among us', *Socio-Economic Review*, 10:3, 617–623.

_____.2017. 'How Grandpa became a Welfare Queen: social insurance, the economisation of citizenship, and a new political economy of moral worth', in Jürgen Mackert and Bryan S. Turner (eds), *The Transformation of Citizenship: Political Economy* (Vol. 1). New York: Routledge, pp. 76–98.

_____.2018. 'Utopianism and the reality of society: decoding Polanyi's socialism, freedom, and the alchemy of misrecognition', in Michael Brie and Claus Thomasberger (eds), 2018, pp. 91–109.

Spero, J. 1999. *The Failure of the Franklin National Bank: Challenge to the International Banking System*. New York: Beard Books.

Steinkeller, P. and M. Hudson. 2015. *Labor in the Ancient World*. Dresden: ISLET.

Stern, G. H. and R. J. Feldman. 2004. *Too Big to Fail: The Hazards of Bank Bailouts*. Washington, D.C.: Brookings Institution Press.

Stiglitz, Joseph. 2010. *The Stiglitz Report: Reforming the International Monetary and Financial Systems in the Wake of the Global Crisis*. New York: New Press.

_____. 2016. *Rewriting the Rules of the American Economy*. New York: Norton.

Storm, S. 2018. 'Financialization and economic development: a debate on the social efficiency of modern finance', *Development and Change*, 49:2 (January), 302–329.

Streeck, Wolfgang. 2009. 'Institutions in history. bringing capitalism back', *MPIfG Discussion Paper*, Max-Planck-Institut für Gesellschaftsforschung, www.mpifg.de/pu/mpifg_dp/dp09-8.pdf. Accessed 1 December 2019.

_____. 2011. 'Taking capitalism seriously: towards an institutionalist approach to contemporary political economy', *Socio-Economic Review*, 9:1, 137–167.

_____. 2014a. *Buying Time: The Delayed Crisis of Democratic Capitalism*. New York: Verso.

_____. 2014b. 'How will capitalism end?', *New Left Review*, 87, 35–64.

_____. 2017. 'The return of the repressed', *New Left Review*, 104, 5–18.

_____. 2019. 'Fighting the state', *Development and Change*, 50:3, 836–847.

Szelenyi, I. 1991. 'Karl Polanyi and the theory of a socialist mixed economy', in M. Mendell and D. Salee (eds), 1991, pp. 231–248.

Thomasberger, C. 2009. '"Planung für den Markt" versus "Planung für die Freiheit". Zu den stillschweigenden Voraussetzungen des Neoliberalismus', in W. O. Ötsch and C. Thomasberger (eds), *Der neoliberale Markt-Diskurs: Ursprünge, Geschichte, Wirkungen*. Marburg: Metropolis, pp. 63–96.

_____. 2012/13. 'The belief in economic determinism, neoliberalism, and the significance of Polanyi's contribution in the twenty-first century', *International Journal of Political Economy*, 41:4 (Winter), 16–33.

_____. 2015. 'Europe at a crossroads: failed ideas, fictional facts, and fatal consequences', *Forum for Social Economics*, 44:2, 179–200.

_____. 2018. 'Freedom, responsibility and the recognition of the reality of complex society', in Michael Brie and Claus Thomasberger (eds), 2018, pp. 52–66.

Tilly, C. 1985. 'War making and state making as organized crime', in P. B. Evans,

D. Rueschenmeyer and T. Skocpol (eds) *Bringing the State Back In*. Cambridge: Cambridge University Press, pp. 169–191.

Tönnies, Ferdinand. [1887] 1957a. *Community and Society*. New York: Harper and Row.

_____. [1887] 1957b. *Community and Society*. East Lansing, MI: Michigan State University Press.

_____. [1887] 2001. *Community and Civil Society*. Cambridge: Cambridge University Press.

Triffin, R. 1986. 'Correcting the world monetary scandal', *Challenge*, 28:6, 4–14. Originally presented at the US Congressional Summit on Exchange Rates and the Dollar in November 1985.

Ugarteche, O. 2014. *La Gran Mutacion*, México: Instituto de Investigaciones Económicas UNAM, http://ru.iiec.unam.mx/2447/1/LAGRANMUTACION6ago13Cortado.pdf. Accessed 19 December 2019.

_____. 2018. *La Arquitectura Financiera Internacional: una Genealogia 1850-2015*, AKAL-IIEC UNAM, Mexico DF.

United Way 2018. 'ALICE: a new lens for financial hardship'.www.unitedforalice.org/national-comparison. Accessed 19 December 2019.

Vilar, Pierre. 1976. *A History of Gold and Money*. London: Verso.

Von Bertalanffy, L. 1968. *General Systems Theory: Foundations, Development, Applications*. New York: George Braziller.

Wallerstein, I. 2004. *World-Systems Analysis: An Introduction*. Durham, NC: Duke University Press.

Werner, M. 2015. *Global Displacements: The Making of Uneven Development in the Caribbean*. Oxford: Wiley.

Wieser, F. [1914] 1927. *Social Economy*. New York: Adelphi Company.

Wiles, Richard. 1987. 'The development of mercantilist economic thought', in S. T. Lowry (ed.), *Pre-Classical Economic Thought*. Dordrecht and Lancaster: Kluwer Publishers.

Wittfogel, Karl. 1957. *Oriental Despotism: A Comparative Study of Total Power*. New Haven, CT: Yale University Press.

Wittgenstein, W. [1953] 2009. *Philosophical Investigations*. Chichester and Malden, MA: Wiley-Blackwell.

Woodward, Bob. 2001. *Maestro: Greenspan's Fed and the American Boom*. New York: Simon and Schuster.

World Bank Statistical Database. 2018. 'Trade (% of GDP)', World Bank, https://data.worldbank.org/indicator/NE.TRD.GNFS.ZS. Accessed 14 December 2019.

World Wildlife Fund. 2018. *Living Planet Report - 2018: Aiming Higher*, M. Grooten and R. E. A. Almond (eds), Gland, Switzerland: Word Wildlife Fund.

Wurm, C. 1993. *Business, Politics and International Relations: Steel, Cotton and International Cartels in British Politics, 1924-1939*. Trans. P. Salmon. Cambridge: Cambridge University Press.

Yamashita, N. 2011. 'Shihonshugi kara Shijo Shakai e (From capitalism to market society)' (in Japanese), excursus for the Japanese translation of *Adam Smith in Beijing*. Tokyo: Sakuhin-sha, pp. 589–621.

Yeung, H. W. and G. Lin. 2003. 'Theorizing economic geographies of Asia', *Economic Geography*, 79:2, 107–128.

Yoffee, Norman. 1977. *The Economic Role of the Crown in the Old Babylonian Period*. Malibu, CA: Undena Publications.

Zeisel, H. (1968), 'Karl Polanyi', in David L. Sills (ed.), *International Encyclopedia of the Social Sciences*, vol. 12, New York: Macmillan, pp. 172–174.

Bibliography

Zhang, J. 2013. 'Marketization beyond neoliberalization: a neo-Polanyian perspective on China's transition to a market economy', *Environment and Planning A*, 45:7, 1605–1624.

Zhang, J. and J. Peck. 2016. 'Variegated capitalism, Chinese-style: regional models, multi-scalar constructions', *Regional Studies*, 50:1, 52–78.

Zhou, Chen. 2010. 'Are banks too big to fail? Measuring systemic importance of financial institutions', *International Journal of Central Banking*, 23:4, 205–250.

Zweig, P. 1995. *Wriston: Walter Wriston, Citibank, and the Rise and Fall of American Financial Supremacy.* New York: Crown Publishers.

Index

Index